OSHO

Beyond Enlightenment

Publisher : **Diamond Pocket Books (P) Ltd.**
X-30, Okhla Industrial Area, Phase-II
New Delhi - 110020
Phone : 011-40712200
E-mail : sales@dpb.in
Website : www.diamondbook.in
Printed by :

The material in this book is a transcript of a series of original OSHO Talks, Beyond Enlightenment given to a live audience. All of Osho's talks have been published in full as books, and are also available as original audio recordings. Audio recordings and the complete text archive can be found via the online OSHO Library at www.osho.com/library
Printed in India by G.S. Enterprises

Contents

Preface

The moment the mind is put aside and you see eye to eye with reality, it is so beautiful, indescribably beautiful. And in those moments certainly you will not feel that you even *want* to be enlightened. If this reality can go on and on forever, then what more can enlightenment give you?

And you are right, because this is the beginning of enlightenment. You have got just a glimpse, and even the glimpse makes you drop the desire for enlightenment – and dropping the desire makes enlightenment easily possible. It simply happens. One day suddenly you wake up in the morning and you are not the same person, and with your change the whole existence has changed. And then it is not a question of doing something to keep it; it remains with you.

In fact, even if you want to drop it, you cannot drop it. You cannot go back; you can only go forward. And one day, that day also comes in your life when enlightenment becomes so natural to you – just like breathing, just like the heartbeat, just like the blood running through your veins – that you don't even feel it. And the blood is going really fast, round and round from feet to head, but we don't feel it; we are born with it, we are accustomed to it.

When enlightenment becomes just a natural phenomenon, then the last mystery opens its door: one goes even beyond enlightenment. Going beyond enlightenment means one becomes just ordinary, part of this vast universe – without any claim, without any superiority, without any ego. One simply dissolves in the ocean of reality, just like a dewdrop in the morning sun slipping from the lotus leaf into the ocean. That is the last... Then there is nothing else left to happen; you have become the ocean.

Enlightenment still keeps something of you – very fragile, but there is still some idea of "I." And because of enlightenment, not knowingly, you are superior and you feel superior. That's why the last step, when even that smallest part of "I" also dissolves, now you are neither superior nor inferior. You are not; existence is. Buddha calls it nirvana. He has chosen the best word for it.

Osho

The Path of the Mystic

1 Beyond Enlightenment Is Only Beyondness

Osho,
What is beyond enlightenment?

Beyond enlightenment is only beyondness. Enlightenment is the last host. Beyond it, all boundaries disappear, all experiences disappear. Experience comes to its utmost in enlightenment; it is the very peak of all that is beautiful, of all that is immortal, of all that is blissful – but it is an experience. Beyond enlightenment there is no experience at all, because the experiencer has disappeared. Enlightenment is not only the peak of experience; it is also the finest definition of your being. Beyond it there is only nothingness; you will not come again to a point which has to be transcended.

Experience, the experiencer, enlightenment – all have been left behind. You are part of the tremendous nothingness that is infinite. This is the nothingness out of which the whole existence comes, the womb; and this is the nothingness in which all existence disappears.

Science has something parallel – there is bound to be something parallel. The spiritual experience is of the interior world, and science is the exploration of the exterior. But both are wings of the same existence: the inwardness and the outwardness. They always have similar points.

Scientists have come to a strange conclusion in this century: that a few stars suddenly disappear – and stars are not small things; they are not so small as they look to you. They look small because they are so far away, millions of light years away, but they are huge. Our sun is a star, but of a mediocre size, medium size. In comparison to the earth it is vast, but in comparison to other stars it is a small, medium-sized star. There are stars which are a thousand times bigger than the sun.

And in this century, for the first time we have had the instruments of observation and we have been very much puzzled: suddenly a star disappears, not even leaving behind a trace of where it has gone. Such a huge phenomenon, and not even footprints – in what direction has it gone? It has just moved simply into nothingness. This was happening continually.

It took almost twenty years to figure out this new phenomenon: that in existence there are black holes. You cannot see them, but they have tremendous gravitation. Even the biggest star, if it comes within their radius of magnetism, will be pulled in. And once it is pulled into a black hole, it disappears. It is the ultimate death. We can only see the effect; we cannot see the black hole, we only see that one star is disappearing.

After the black hole was almost an established theory, scientists started thinking that there must be something like a white hole – there has to be. If it is possible that in a certain gravitation, magnetic force, a big star simply disappears out of existence... We have been aware that every day many stars are born. From where are they coming? – nobody has asked it before.

In fact, birth we always take for granted; nobody asks from where the babies are coming. Death we never accept, because we are so much afraid of it. There is not a single philosophy in the whole history of man which thinks about where babies come from, but there are philosophies and philosophies thinking about what death is, where people go on disappearing to, what happens after death.

In my whole life I have come across millions of people, and not a single person has asked what happens before birth – and thousands have asked what happens after death. I have always been thinking: why is birth taken without any question? Why is death not taken in the same way?

We were aware for centuries, almost three centuries, that stars are being born every day – big stars, huge stars – and nobody raised the question: "From where are these stars coming?" But when we came to know about the black holes and we saw the stars disappearing, then the second question became almost an absolute necessity. If black holes can take stars into nothingness, then there must be something like white holes where stars come out of nothingness.

I am reminded...

Mulla Nasruddin applied for a post on a ship. He was interviewed. The captain and the high officials of the ship were sitting in a room. Mulla entered. The captain asked, "If the seas are in a turmoil, winds are strong, waves are huge and mountainous, what are you going to do to save the ship? It is tossed from here to there..."

Mulla Nasruddin said, "It is not much of a problem. I will just drop a huge anchor to keep the ship stable against the winds, against the waves. It is not much of a problem."

The captain again said, "Suppose another mountainous wave comes and the ship is going to be drowned; what are you going to do?"

He said, "Nothing – another *huge* anchor."

The captain looked at him and asked a third time, "Suppose it is a great typhoon and it is impossible to save the ship. What are you going to do?"

He said, "Nothing, the same, a huge anchor."

The captain said, "From where are you getting these huge anchors?"

He said, "From the same place. The same place from where you are getting these great, mountainous waves, strong winds. You go on getting them, I will go on getting bigger and bigger anchors."

If there are holes in existence where things simply disappear into non-existence, then there must be holes from where things appear from nothingness – just a little imagination is needed. Scientists have not worked on it yet.

My suggestion is that a black hole is like a door: from one side it is a black door, a black hole – things go into it and disappear into nothingness. And from the other side of the tunnel – it is the same door, just from the other side – it is a white hole; things are born again, renewed. It is the same womb.

Beyond enlightenment you enter into nothingness. Experience disappears, the experiencer disappears. Just pure nothingness remains, utter silence. Perhaps this is the destiny of every human being, sooner or later to be achieved.

We don't know yet whether there is a white hole or not – there must be. Just as you enter beyond enlightenment into nothingness, there must be a possibility of coming out of nothingness back into form, back into existence – renewed, refreshed, luminous – on a totally different plane. Because nothing is destroyed, things can only go into a dormant state; things can only go into deep sleep. Then in the morning they wake up again. This is how existence goes on.

In the West, this idea has never happened in the two thousand years' history of philosophy. They only think of this creation: "Who created this?" And they get into trouble because whatever the answer is, it is going to create more questions.

In the East we have a conception of circles of existence and non-existence, just like day and night. Creation is followed by de-creation; everything goes into nothingness, just as day is followed by night and everything goes into darkness. And the period is going to be the same: as long as the creation is, so is the resting period going to be; and again there will be a creation of a higher order.

And this will go on from eternity to eternity – creation, de-creation, creation, again de-creation – but each time the morning is more beautiful. Each dawn is more colorful, more alive; the birds are singing better, the flowers are bigger, with more fragrance. And the East has the tremendous courage of accepting the idea that this will go on forever and forever. There has never been any beginning, and there will be no end.

After enlightenment, you have to disappear. The world is left behind, the body is left behind, the mind is left behind; just your consciousness, as individuality, is still there.

To go beyond enlightenment is to go beyond individuality and to become universal. This way, each individual will go on moving into nothingness. And one day, the whole existence moves into nothingness and a great peace, a great night, a deep, dark womb, a great waiting for the dawn. And it has been happening always, and each time you are always born on a higher level of consciousness.

Enlightenment is the goal of human beings. But those who are enlightened cannot remain static; they will have to move, they will have to change. And now they have only one thing to lose – themselves.

They have enjoyed everything. They have enjoyed the purity of individuality; now they have to enjoy the disappearing of individuality. They have seen the beauty of individuality; now they have to see the disappearance and its beauty, and the silence that follows, that abysmal serenity that follows.

Osho,

The other night when you talked about the ego and how, with awareness, one can see that it does not exist, I realized that I never put much emphasis on awareness. For me, being with you always meant loving you as much as I can, longing for you and trying to be as close to you as possible.

Osho, can you please show the way for a female German lover to become more aware?

Love is enough unto itself.

If your love is not the ordinary, biological instinctive love, if it is not part of your ego, if it is not a power trip to dominate someone; if your love is just a pure joy, rejoicing in the being of the other for no reason at all, a sheer joy, awareness will follow this pure love just like a shadow. You need not worry about awareness.

There are only two ways: either you become aware, then love follows as a shadow; or you become so loving that awareness comes on its own accord. They are two sides of the same coin. You need not bother about the other side, just keep one side; the other side cannot escape. The other side is bound to come.

And the path of love is easier, rosier, innocent, simple. The path of awareness is a little arduous.

Those who cannot love, for them I suggest the path of awareness. There are people who cannot love – their hearts have become stones. Their upbringing, their culture, their society has killed the very capacity to love – because this whole world is not run by love, it is run by cunningness. To succeed in this world you don't need love, you need a hard heart and a sharp mind. In fact, you don't need the heart at all.

I have heard about one great politician who was in the hospital and who had some great complications with his heart. So they put him on a plastic heart and took out his real heart, because it was going to take hours to clean it. And certainly a politician's heart... Even if you can clean it in hours, it is too soon. The surgeons were working in the other room – it was a disgusting job – and the politician was lying down.

A man came into the room and shook the politician; he opened his eyes and the man said, "What are you doing here? You have been chosen the prime minister of the country."

He jumped out of the bed. The doctors looked from the other room, "What is happening?" The politician was going out. They said, "Wait! Your heart...we are cleaning it."

The politician said, "Now, at least for five years I won't need it. You can clean it as much as you want. Take your time. What does a prime minister need a heart for? But keep it safe in case something goes wrong; then I will come back. But if things go well, I may perhaps never need it."

In this world the heart is not needed. The people of the heart are crushed, exploited, oppressed. This world is run by the cunning, by the clever, by the heartless and the cruel. So the whole of society is managed in such a way that every child starts losing his heart, and his energy starts moving directly towards the head. The heart is ignored.

I have heard an ancient parable from Tibet, that in the beginning of time the heart used to be exactly in the middle part of the body. But because of continuously being pushed aside, out of the way, it is now no longer in the middle of the body. The poor fellow waits by the side of the road: "If some day you need, I am here" – but it gets no nourishment, no encouragement. It gets all kinds of condemnation.

If you do something and you say, "I did it because I felt like doing it," everybody is going to laugh: "*Felt*? Have you lost your head? Give your reason, logic. Feeling is no logic." Even if you fall in love, you have to find reasons why you have fallen in love: because the woman's nose is very beautiful, her eyes have such depth, her body is so proportionate. These are not the reasons. You have never calculated all these reasons on your calculator and then found that this woman seems to be worthy of falling in love with: fall in love with this woman – exactly the right length of nose, the right kind of hair, the right color, the right proportion of the body. What more do you want?

But this is not the way that anybody ever falls in love. You fall in love first; then just to satisfy the idiots around you that you are not a fool, that you have calculated everything and only then you have taken the step... It is a reasonable, rational, logical step. Nobody hears the heart.

And the mind is so chattering, so continuously chattering – yakkety-yak, yakkety-yak – that even if the heart sometimes says something, it never reaches to you. It *cannot* reach. The bazaar in your head is buzzing so much that it is impossible, absolutely impossible for the heart. Slowly, slowly, the heart stops saying anything. Not heard again and again, ignored again and again, it falls silent.

The head runs the show in the society; otherwise, we would have lived in a totally different world: more loving, less hate, less war, no possibility of nuclear weapons. The heart will never give support for any destructive methods to be evolved. The heart will never be in the service of death. It is life – it throbs for life, it beats for life.

Because of the whole conditioning of society, the method of awareness has to be chosen, because awareness appears to be very logical, rational. But if you can love, then there is no need to go on a long, arduous route unnecessarily. Love is the most shortcut way, the most natural – so easy that it is possible even for a small child. It needs no training. You are born with the quality of it, if it is not corrupted by others.

But love should be pure. It should not be impure.

You will be surprised to know that the English word *love* comes from a very ugly root in Sanskrit. It comes from *lobh*. *Lobh* means greed. And as far as ordinary love is concerned, it is a kind of greed. That's why there are people who love money, there are people who love houses, there are people who love this, who love that. Even if they love a woman or a man, it is simply their greed; they want to possess everything beautiful.

It is a power trip. Hence, you will find lovers continually fighting, fighting about such trivia that they both feel ashamed: "About what things we go on fighting." In their silent moments when they are alone, they feel, "Do I become possessed by some evil spirit? – such trivia, so meaningless." But it is not a question of trivia; it is a question of who has power, who is more dominant, whose voice is heard. Love cannot exist in such circumstances.

I have heard a story:

In the life of one of the great emperors of India, Akbar, there is a small story. He was very much interested in all kinds of talented people, and from all over India he had collected nine people, the most talented geniuses, who were known as the "nine jewels of Akbar's court."

One day, just gossiping with his vice-councilors, he said, "Last night I was discussing with my wife. She is very insistent that every husband is henpecked. I tried hard, but she says, 'I know many families, but I have never found any husband who is not henpecked.' What do you think?" he asked the councilors.

One of the councilors, Birbal, said, "Perhaps she is right, because you could not prove it. You yourself are a henpecked husband;

otherwise, you could have given her a good beating, then and there proving that: 'Look, here is a husband!'"

He said, "That I cannot do, because I have to live with her. It is easy to advise somebody else to beat his wife. Can you beat your wife?"

Birbal said, "No, I cannot. I simply accept that I am a henpecked husband, and your wife is right."

But Akbar said, "It has to be found... In the capital there must be at least one husband who is not henpecked. There is no rule in the world which has no exception, and this is not a rule at all."

So he said to Birbal, "You take my two beautiful Arabian horses" – one was black, one was white – "and go around the capital. And if you can find a man who is not henpecked, you can give him the choice: whichever horse he wants is a present from me." They were valuable. In those days horses were very valuable, and those were the most beautiful horses.

Birbal said, "It is useless, but if you say, I will go."

He went, and everybody was found to be henpecked. It was very ordinary: he would just call the person and call his wife, and ask, "Are you henpecked or not?"

The man would look at the wife and say, "You should have asked when I was alone. This is not right. You will create unnecessary trouble. Just for a horse I am not going to destroy my life. Take your horses, I don't want any."

But one man was sitting in front of his house and two persons were massaging him. He was a wrestler, a champion wrestler, a very strong man. Birbal thought, "Perhaps this man... He can kill anybody without any weapons. If he gets hold of your neck, you are finished!" Birbal said, "Can I ask you a question?"

He said, "Question? What question?"

Birbal said, "Are you henpecked?"

That man said, "First, let us greet each other, a handshake." And he crushed Birbal's hand and said, "Unless you start crying and tears start coming from your eyes, I will not leave your hand; your hand is finished. You dared to ask me such a question?"

And Birbal was dying – the man was almost a man of steel – and tears started coming, and he said, "Just leave me. You are not henpecked. I have just come to a wrong place. But where is your wife?"

He said, "Look, she is there, cooking my breakfast." A very small woman was cooking his breakfast.

The woman was so small and the man was so big that Birbal said, "There is a possibility that perhaps this man is not henpecked. He could kill this woman."

So he said, "Now there is no need to go further into investigation. You can choose either horse from these two, black and white, a reward from the king for the one who is not henpecked.

And at that time that small woman said, "Don't choose the black! Otherwise I will make your life hell."

The man said, "No, no, I will choose the white. Just keep quiet."

Birbal said, "You don't get either, neither white nor black. It is all finished, you lost the game. You *are* a henpecked husband."

There is a continuous fight for domination. Love cannot blossom in such an atmosphere. The man is fighting in the world for all kinds of ambitions. The woman is fighting the man because she is afraid – he is out of the house the whole day. Who knows? He may be having affairs with other women. She is jealous, suspicious; she wants to be sure that this man remains controlled. So, in the house he is fighting with the wife, in the outside he is fighting with the world. Where do you think the flower of love can blossom?

The flower of love can blossom only when there is no ego, when there is no effort to dominate, when one is humble, when one is trying not to be somebody but is ready to be nobody. Naturally, in the ordinary world it cannot happen, but with a master it is a possibility. The love for the master is not biological. Biology has nothing to do with masters and disciples. The love for the master has nothing to do with domination.

The flower can blossom because love is pure, without ego. You are simply rejoicing in the presence, in the fulfillment of the master, in the contentment of the master. You are rejoicing as if it is your contentment, it is your fulfillment. In the radiance of the master you are feeling it is your radiance. You are *part* of the master; you have become so harmonious with him that his heart and your heart are no longer two.

Awareness will come on its own accord, and love is the most beautiful way, the most innocent way: a path full of flowers, a path that passes through beautiful lakes, rivers, groves, greenery. The path of awareness is the path that passes through a desert. It is only for those who cannot manage to get back into their hearts.

If you can easily be heartful, forget all about awareness; it will come on its own accord. Each step of love will bring its own awareness. This love will not be falling in love; I call it rising in love.

Osho,

There are always two parts in me related to you. One part of me has the drive to work, run around, organize, jump up and down, fight, talk to the press and politicians, and just shout from the rooftops. The other part, which has become so much stronger over the last years, just wants to sit at your side and absorb everything: you, your silence and your words.

Was it that I had to be so active just to be able to sit silently now?

Osho, please can you say something about your outer and your inner work.

There is no split in you. If a part fights in the outer world for my message to be spread to all nooks and corners, and the other part simply wants to sit close to me, drinking my silence, my presence, my peace, rejoicing in my blissfulness, being ecstatic just without doing anything... Ordinarily it may seem that these two parts are against each other. They are not. The more you shout from the housetops, the more you will be able to sit silently, close to me; and the more you can sit silently, close to me, the more you will have something to share with the world, something to fight for.

Man is both the inner and the outer, and it has been a fallacy, a very ancient fallacy, to condemn one in favor of the other. In the East, people renounce the outer in favor of the inner. They escape from the world into the caves in the Himalayas so that they can devote their whole life and their whole time and their whole energy to the inner journey. But they don't understand the dialectics of life. In the West, just the opposite has been done. They have renounced the inner so that they can put their whole energy into the outer world and the conquest of the outer world.

Both have been wrong, and both have been right. Both have been wrong because both remained halves; one part grew bigger and bigger, and the other part remained retarded. You can see it: in the East there is so much poverty, so much disease, so much sickness, so much death. Still, there is a certain contentment. With all this, there seems to be no revolutionary approach that we should change the whole world. We cannot go on living in this poverty, and we have lived in this poverty for centuries, in slavery for centuries. And we have accepted everything – poverty, slavery, disease, death – without any resistance, because these are outer things. Our whole effort has been inner.

In the West they have destroyed poverty, they have destroyed much disease, they have made man's life longer. They have made man's body more beautiful, they have made man's existence more comfortable, but the man himself, for whom all these comforts, all these conquests of science and technology have been done, is missing. They have completely forgotten for whom it was done. The inside is hollow. Everything is there, all around, and in the middle there is a retarded consciousness, almost non-existential.

So both have succeeded in what they were doing, and both have failed – because they have chosen only half of man's life. My attitude is that of accepting man in his totality, in his wholeness. And it has to be understood that once you accept the totality of man, you have to understand the law of dialectics.

For example, the whole day you work hard, in the fields, in the garden – you perspire. In the night you will have a beautiful sleep. Don't think that because you have been working so hard the whole day, how can you sleep in the night? – it is so against your whole day's work. It is not against. The whole day's hard work has prepared you to relax; in the night you will be in deep relaxation.

Beggars sleep the best. Emperors cannot sleep because the emperor has forgotten the dialectics of life. You need two legs to walk, you need two hands, you need two hemispheres in your brain.

It has now become an accepted psychological truth that you can do hard mathematical work – because it is done by one part of the mind – and then you can do the same hard work on your musical instrument, and because it is done by another part of the mind, it is not continuous labor. In fact, when you are working hard on mathematics, the musical part of your mind is resting; and when you are working hard on the musical part, your mathematical mind is resting.

In the universities, in the colleges all over the world, we change the class period every forty minutes because it has been found that after each forty minutes, the part that you have been working with gets tired. Just change the subject; that part goes into rest.

Sitting with me, fill your cup with as much juice as possible. Feel silence to its uttermost depth, so that you can shout from the housetops. And there is no contradiction: your shouting from the housetops is simply part of a dialectic process. Your silence and your shouting are just like two hands, your two legs, your day and night, your work and rest period. Don't divide them as antagonistic to each other – that's how the whole world has suffered.

The East has created great geniuses, but we are still living in the bullock cart age because our geniuses simply meditated. Their meditation never came into action. If they had meditated for a few hours and used their silence and peace and meditativeness for scientific research, this country would have been the richest in the world – outer and inner, both.

The same is true about the West: they created great geniuses, but they were all involved with things, objects. They forgot themselves completely. Once in a while a genius remembered, but it was too late. Albert Einstein, at the time of death, said his last words – and remember, the last words are the most important a person ever speaks in his life, because they are a conclusion, the essential experience. His last words were, "If there is another life, I would like to be a plumber. I don't want to be a physicist. I want to be something very simple – a plumber."

A tired brain, a burned brain...and what was his achievement? – Hiroshima and Nagasaki. This man was capable of becoming a Gautam Buddha. If he had looked inwards, he had such insight that perhaps he would have gone deeper than any Gautam Buddha, because he looked towards the stars and went further than any astronomer has ever done. It is the same power; it is only a question of direction.

But why get fixed? Why not keep yourself available to both dimensions? What is the need of getting fixed? – "I can only see outwardly, I cannot see inwardly," or vice-versa. One should only learn how to see deeply, and then use that insight in both dimensions. Then one can give better science and better technology to the world and can become better human beings, a better humanity, at the same time. And remember, only in a better human being's hands is a better technology right; otherwise, it is dangerous.

The East is dying with poverty. The West is dying with power. Strange, they have created so much power that they can only kill. They don't know anything about life because they have never looked in. The East knows everything about life, but without food you cannot meditate. When you are hungry and you close your eyes, you can see only chapatis just floating all around.

It has happened in the life of a poet, Heinrich Heine. He was lost in a jungle for three days, hungry, tired, could not sleep out of fear: wild animals were staying in the tops of the trees in the night. And for three days continuously he did not come across a single human being to ask whether he was moving right or wrong, where he was going or if he was moving in a circle. Three days continuously...and then came the full moon night. Hungry, tired, hanging onto a tree, he looked at the full moon. He was a great poet, and he was surprised, he could not believe it. He himself had written about the moon, he had read about the moon. So much is written about the moon – so much poetry, so much painting, so much art is around the moon. But Heinrich Heine had a revelation: before, he used to see his beloved's face in the moon; today he saw only a chapati floating in the sky. He tried hard, but the beloved's face did not appear.

It is perfectly good to be dialectical. And always remember to see the opposites as complementaries. Use all the opposites as complementaries and your life will be fuller, your life will be whole.

To me, this is the only holy life: a whole life is the only holy life.

Osho,

Today I observed a tightrope walker and how he trained a young girl partner to walk on the rope. He was sometimes hitting her, sometimes persuading her, but it seemed to me that she was mainly encouraged to try it again and again because she felt his trust in her potential to be able to walk the rope alone.

Can you please say something about the master's trust in the disciple?

The very fact that the master accepts a disciple shows his trust in the potential of the disciple. Otherwise, he would not have been accepted.

Every man has the potential, but the right time, the right place, the right experience, make all the difference. Otherwise, every human being is capable of being enlightened, will be enlightened, but when, at what time – whether in this life or in another life – depends on many things: how much is your experience of being frustrated in the world, how much you are in misery.

Are you still hoping that tomorrow things will be better, or have you lost all hope? Is your despair ultimate, or only momentary? Have you come to the master because today you have fought with your wife, but after fifteen minutes things will be different – anger will be gone?

I used to live on a university campus. The first day, I entered into my bungalow. I was alone, and the attached bungalow was occupied by a Bengali professor. And the walls were so thin that even if you plugged your ears, you would still be able to hear what was going on on the other side of the wall.

Because the husband and wife were fighting so badly, I thought that there was going to be some blood. I could not sleep. It was one o'clock in the night and they were fighting and fighting and fighting. And I could not understand what they were saying either, but things must have been serious because finally the professor said, "I am going to commit suicide" – he said that in English.

I said, "This is something good; at least I can understand this much." So I came out of my house to prevent him: "Just wait. In the middle of the night, where will you go to commit suicide? In the morning it will be better." But by the time I was out he was gone – fast.

I asked his wife – who had not come out even to say good-bye – I said, "What am I supposed to do? Should I go to the police station? Somebody has to be informed by phone? What has to be done?"

She said, "Nothing has to be done. Do you see his umbrella is here? Without his umbrella he cannot go anywhere. He will be coming soon – the moment he remembers the umbrella. In anger, he has forgotten the umbrella. A Bengali without an umbrella?"

I said, "But suicide is such a serious matter, and an umbrella is not needed at all."

She said, "Just wait. Sit here. I will make coffee for you because you have been... I know that you must have heard all this."

And within fifteen minutes he was back.

And I said, "What happened?"

He said, "What happened? I forgot my umbrella! And now it must be at least two o'clock in the morning."

I said, "That's the right thing to do. In the morning, take your umbrella and go out, find the right place." But who goes in the morning?

In the morning I reminded him, "You are still here. The sun has risen. You should go now and search for the right place."

He said, "I was thinking to go, but when I opened the umbrella it was not repaired because the rains have not come."

I said, "I see you with that umbrella every day, going to the university."

He said, "That is just habitual. Because there are no rains, nothing, so there is no question of opening it; one just carries it. Now I tried and opened it – it is not repaired. And I have been telling my wife that my umbrella should be kept repaired in case some emergency arises. Now I wanted to commit suicide and the umbrella is not ready."

I thought, "This is really great of you, and every person who intends to commit suicide should learn something from you."

One day, it must have been afternoon, three o'clock or some time, I again heard that he was going to commit suicide. But this time I was not so much excited, because I thought that this is the usual business. Still, I came out to say good-bye.

He looked at me with a very strange face. He said, "What do you mean by good-bye?"

I said, "You are going to commit suicide, and I don't think that we will be meeting again, so I am saying good-bye. But what are you carrying?" He was carrying a tiffin.

I said, "Where are you taking the tiffin?"

He said, "You know these Indian railway trains – sometimes they are ten hours late, twelve hours late. And I cannot tolerate hunger at all, so I will lie down by the line and wait for the train. If it comes, good; otherwise, I am taking my supper with me."

I said, "You are a clever and intelligent person – anybody looking at you would think you are going on some picnic."

And when he had gone, his wife came. She said, "Has he gone?"

I said, "He has gone."

She said, "He will be coming soon. This idiot," she said, "whenever he wants to go for a picnic... But he is such a miser that he will not even take me with him, so he says that he is going to commit suicide. He must be eating just near the railway station; you can go and see right now."

The railway station was not very far away, so I went and I saw him. He was enjoying all Bengali sweets and things.

I said, "Chatterji, the train is standing on the platform. Leave your tiffin, run! Just lie down ahead of the train!"

He said, "It is too late. First I have to finish everything that I brought, and today I have missed. And the train comes to this station only once in twenty-four hours" – because it was not a big station, it was a small station, and the train used to stop only once for the university because the university was outside the city. So he said,

"Today it is finished."

But I said, "You first said, 'I am going to wait.' And this is not suppertime; it is only three o'clock."

He said, "When you have such sweets in your hand, you cannot wait. And I am just coming back home with you."

There are people who would like to become sannyasins, who would like to become disciples. It may be just an emotional, sentimental, temporal thing, and within two minutes it has come and it is gone. They had the potential, but it was not the right time.

Even if they take sannyas, even if they become disciples – because no master is so unkind as to say no to somebody who wants to become a disciple – they are going to betray. They are going to leave sooner or later because it was not something very deep, coming from their very heart. It was something very superficial, something so superficial that if they had waited for a few minutes more, they would have changed their minds. It was a mind thing, and mind is never stable, it is continuously changing.

You cannot stay with one thought in the mind even for a few seconds. Sometimes, try: just one thought, and try to stay with it; you will be surprised that in not more than thirty seconds you have forgotten about it and your mind has moved somewhere else. And then suddenly you remember that you were trying to stay with one thought, and you could remain for only thirty seconds.

Gurdjieff used to give this experiment to everyone who came to become a disciple. He would give the person his own pocket watch and tell him, "Keep it in front of you, watch the second hand and choose any word – your name. Keep just that name in your mind, and tell me for how long you can keep it – fifteen seconds, thirty seconds, at the most, forty seconds, not even one whole minute."

Mind is in a flux. So those who want to become disciples because of some mind thing are not going to stay. There is no need to say no to them, they will be going themselves.

But the master knows perfectly well when somebody comes with an urge from the heart, with an urge that he can stake his whole life for and he will not turn back. Only these few people attain to fulfillment.

Everybody has the potential, but everybody is not ripe at this moment – perhaps at some other time, in some other life, with some other master. But one day is going to come in everybody's life that is a turning point, a 180 degree turn, and then disciplehood is a beautiful growth.

Then the whole energy is moving in one direction with one intention, with no diversions. Then the distance from the goal is less. The more intense is your urge, the smaller is the distance. If your intention is total, then there is no distance at all; then you need not come to the goal, the goal comes to you.

2 Innocence Is a Light unto Itself

Osho,
I have questions, but they are never complete, and I don't know how to ask.

No question is ever complete, because the completion of a question will mean it has its answer in itself. A question by its very nature is incomplete. It is a desire, a longing, an inquiry, because something needs to be completed. It is part of human consciousness that it demands completion. Leave anything incomplete and it becomes an obsession; complete it and you are free of it. Completion brings freedom.

Hence, it is not only *your* questions that are incomplete. You are more alert so that you have seen the incompleteness of each question.

Secondly, you don't know what to ask. Nobody knows. All of our questions are out of our ignorance, out of our unconscious, out of our dark soul. Nobody knows exactly what his question is, what is essential to be asked – because the moment you know what your question is, you will immediately find the answer within yourself.

To be absolutely confident about the question means the answer is not very far away. It is very close, because confidence comes from the answer, not from the question.

But still, man has to ask. Although all questions are incomplete and you do not know what to ask, still man has to ask, because man cannot remain silent. It is possible not to ask – that does not mean you don't have questions, that simply means you are not bringing them out. Perhaps you are afraid to be exposed, because each question will indicate your ignorance.

There are millions of people who never ask, for the simple reason that to be silent at least appears to be wise. To ask the question is to show your wounds, is to show all the dark spots in your being. It needs courage.

Secondly, there are questions which are not out of your ignorance but out of your borrowed knowledge – which are the worst questions possible.

A question that comes out of ignorance is innocent, has purity. It is unpolluted, uncorrupted; it shows your courage, your trust.

But there are questions which come out of your borrowed knowledge. You have heard much, you have read much, you have been informed by the parents, teachers, priests, politicians, all kinds of demagogues, all kinds of pretenders to knowledge – and you have been collecting their whole garbage.

Purna has sent me a beautiful present: a very artistic, beautiful wastepaper basket with a note: "Osho, if you feel my questions are just garbage, throw them in this wastepaper basket. You need not answer them."

Questions coming out of knowledge are garbage.

You don't know anything about God, the universe; you don't know anything about the soul, reincarnation, future lives, past lives. All that you know is simply hearsay. People have been chattering around you and you are collecting all kinds of information that seems to be important to you. Why does it seem important? It seems important because it covers your ignorance. It helps you to feel as if you know. But remember, it is a very big "as if." You do not know, it is only "as if."

All holy scriptures, all books on philosophy, theology, should be categorized into one category: as if. They are talking about every possible impossible thing they know nothing of, but they are articulate, imaginative intellectuals who can create systems out of nothing.

That's why no philosopher agrees with any other philosopher. And every philosopher thinks that he has found the whole system that explains everything in the world. And all other philosophers laugh at him; they find thousands of loopholes in his system. But as far as they themselves are concerned, they commit the same mistake: they claim that their system is complete and now there is no question of further inquiry.

And the strangest thing is that these are the people who are very insightful in seeing the loopholes of others, but they cannot see the loopholes of their own system. Perhaps they don't want to see. Loopholes are there, everybody else can see them; it is impossible that they themselves do not see them. They ignore them, hoping that nobody sees them.

Every philosophy has failed. Every religion has failed.

And you are carrying the ruins of all the philosophies and all the religions in your mind, and out of those ruins, questions arise. Those questions are meaningless; you should not ask them. They really show your stupidity.

But questions arising out of your ignorance – just like a child asking – those questions are incomplete, not very great questions, but tremendously important.

One day a small child was walking with D.H. Lawrence in a garden, and was continuously asking questions of all kinds. And D.H. Lawrence was one of the most sincere men of this century, condemned by governments, by priests because of his sincerity, because he would say only the truth, because he was not ready to be diplomatic, a hypocrite, because he would not compromise. Even before this small child he showed such authentic sincerity, which even your great saints have not shown.

The child asked, "Why are the trees green?" – a very simple question, but very profound. All the trees are green – why? What is the matter with the trees? When there are so many colors, when the whole rainbow of colors is available: some tree can be yellow, some tree can be red, some tree can be blue. Why have all the trees chosen to be green?

In D.H. Lawrence's place, any parent, any teacher, any priest, anybody – x, y, z – would have told some lie: that God made them green because green is very soothing to the eyes. But this would have been deceptive, a lie, because D.H. Lawrence does not know anything about God, does not know why the trees are green.

In fact, no scientist who has been working with trees knows, although he can show that it is because of a certain element, chlorophyll, that trees are green. But that is not the answer for the child. He will simply ask, "Why have they chosen chlorophyll – *all* the trees?" It is not a satisfactory answer.

D.H. Lawrence closed his eyes, waited for a moment in silence...what to say to this child? He did not want to be a deceiving person to an innocent child – although the question is ordinary, any answer would do. But the question has come from innocence; hence it is very profound.

And D.H. Lawrence opened his eyes, looked at the trees and said to the child, "The trees are green because they are green."

The child said, "Right. I was also thinking that."

But D.H. Lawrence remembered it in his memoirs: "To me it was a great experience – the love and the trust the child showed towards me because of sheer sincerity. My answer was not an answer; according to logicians, it was a tautology. 'The trees are green because they are green' – is this an answer?"

In fact, D.H. Lawrence is accepting that: "My child, I am as much ignorant as you are. Just because there is a difference of age does not mean that I know and you do not know." The difference of age is not the difference between ignorance and knowledge.

The trees being green is part of the mystery of the whole existence.

Things are what they are. A woman is a woman, a man is a man. A rose is a rose; call it by any name, it still remains the rose.

That morning, in that small incident, something tremendously beautiful is hidden.

Ask questions – not out of knowledge, because all that knowledge is borrowed, unfounded, pure rubbish. But ask out of your ignorance. Remember, the ignorance is yours – be proud of it. The knowledge is not yours. How can you be proud of it?

And the question is not to cover the ignorance. The question is to bring some light, so that the ignorance, the darkness, disappears.

I cannot give you any better answer than D.H. Lawrence, but I can give you something else which Lawrence has no insight about. I can give you a space, a silence in which you can realize the mystery on your own.

You ask the question, whatever the question is. Just remember, don't ask out of knowledge; ask out of your own authentic ignorance.

And my answers are not answers, in fact. My answers are killers – they simply kill the question, they take away the question, they don't give you any answer to hold on to.

And that is the difference between a teacher and a master: the teacher gives you answers so that you can hold those answers and remain ignorant – on the surface beautifully decorated, libraries full of answers, but underneath, below the surface, an abysmal ignorance.

The master simply kills your questions. He does not give you an answer, he takes away the question.

If all your questions can be taken away – listen carefully to what I am saying – if all your questions can be taken away, your ignorance is bound to disappear, and what remains is innocence.

And innocence is a light unto itself.

In that innocence you don't know any question, any answer, because the whole realm of questions and answers is left behind. It has become irrelevant, you have transcended it. You are pure of questions and pure of answers.

This state is enlightenment. And if you are courageous enough, you even can go beyond it. This will give you all the beautiful experiences described by the mystics down the ages: your heart will dance with ecstasy, your whole being will become a beautiful sunrise...thousands of lotuses blossoming in you.

If you want, you can make your home here. In the past, people have stopped here, because where can you find a better place? Gautam Buddha has called this place the "Lotus Paradise."

But if you are a born seeker... I will suggest: have a little rest, enjoy all the beauties of enlightenment but don't make it a full-stop. Go beyond, because life, its journey, is unending and much more is going to happen which is absolutely indescribable.

The experience of enlightenment is also beyond description, but it has been described by all who have experienced it. They all say it is beyond description and still they describe it: that it is full of light, that it is full of joy, that it is the ultimate in blissfulness. If this is not description then what is description?

I am saying it for the first time: for thousands of years the people who have become enlightened have been saying that it cannot be described, and at the same time have been describing it, have been their whole lives singing it. But beyond enlightenment you certainly enter into a world which *is* indescribable.

Because in enlightenment you still are; otherwise who is feeling the blissfulness, who is seeing the light? Kabir says, "...as if thousands of suns have risen." Who is seeing it? Enlightenment is the ultimate experience – but still it is experience, and the experiencer is there.

Going beyond it, there is no experiencer. You dissolve.

First you were trying to dissolve your problems; now *you* dissolve – because existentially you are the problem. Your separation from existence is the only question which has to be solved. You lose your boundaries, you are no more. Who is there to experience?

You need tremendous courage to drop the ego to achieve enlightenment. You will need a million times more courage to drop yourself to attain the beyond – and the beyond is the real.

Osho,

I am familiar with the master-disciple relationship after years of being around you.

Could you please comment on the disciple-disciple relationship?

There is no such thing. Disciples in the past have created organizations. That was their relationship, that "we are Christians," that "we are Mohammedans," that "we belong to one religion, to one faith and because we belong to one faith, we are brothers and sisters. We will live for the faith and we will die for the faith."

All organizations have arisen out of the relationships between disciples. In fact, two disciples are not connected with each other at all. Each disciple is connected with the master in his individual capacity. A master can be connected with millions of disciples, but the connection is personal, not organizational.

Disciples don't have any relationship. Yes, they have a certain friendliness, a certain lovingness. I am avoiding the word *relationship* because that is binding. I am not even calling it "friendship" but "friendliness" – because they are all fellow travelers walking on the same path, in love with the same master, but they are related to each other through the master. They are not related to each other directly.

This has been the most unfortunate thing in the past: that disciples became organized, related amongst themselves, and they were all ignorant. And ignorant people can only create more nuisance in the world than anything else. All the religions have done exactly that.

My people are related to me individually. And because they are on the same path, certainly they become acquainted with each other. A friendliness arises, a loving atmosphere, but I don't want to call it any kind of relationship.

We have suffered too much because of disciples getting directly related to each other, creating religions, sects, cults, and then fighting. They cannot do anything else. At least with me, remember it, you are not related to each other in any way at all. Just a liquid friendliness, not a solid friendship, is enough – and far more beautiful, and without any possibility of harming humanity in the future.

Osho,

Since I have been here, I have been torn apart between wanting to ask you a question – wanting to expose myself – and trying everything to avoid that. It feels as if I have been stuck in this position for years.

Osho, what is this fear?

There is only one basic fear. All other small fears are byproducts of the one main fear that every human being carries with himself: the fear is of losing yourself. It may be in death, it may be in love, but the fear is the same: you are afraid of losing yourself.

And the strangest thing is that only those people are afraid of losing themselves who don't have themselves. Those who have themselves are not afraid. So it is really a question of exposure You don't have anything to lose; you just believe that you have something to lose.

I was traveling with Mulla Nasruddin and the ticket checker came. I showed him my ticket, and Mulla started searching for his ticket. He opened one of his suitcases, then another suitcase, and went through all his pockets – coat, pants, shirt – but I saw that he was avoiding one pocket.

Watching him, even the ticket checker said, "Don't be worried. You are a well-known person. You can't travel without a ticket; it must be somewhere. You have so much luggage." He said, "I will be coming back in the second round. By that time you may have found it."

He went away, and Mulla was still perspiring and searching for the ticket.

I said, "Mulla, I can see only one thing – that you are looking into everything but you are not looking into one pocket."

He said, "Just don't raise that question, because I am already in such trouble."

But I said, "What has that pocket to do with trouble?"

He said, "It has everything to do with it. That is the only place I am hoping that the ticket may be, and I don't want to lose that hope. First let me look in everything else. That is my *last* resort; I also know that I am avoiding it. The ticket checker was looking at that pocket, you are also looking at that pocket. It is not that I am not aware. With full consciousness I am avoiding it, because if it is not there then the ticket is nowhere."

The fear of coming close is the fear of exposure.

Who knows? – as you come close to the master, in his presence, in his light you may find that you don't exist. And that will be almost a death...bigger than death. So people keep at a certain distance.

Watching wild animals in the jungles, in the mountains, scientists have come to discover a certain idea: that they have a territorial imperative, that each animal has his own territory. If you don't enter his territory, he will not bother you, but if you enter his territory you are in danger, he can attack you. In fact, he feels the danger: you are in his territory, coming too close, and who knows if you are a friend or a foe?

And they have a very strange way of creating the demarcation line of their territory. You see dogs pissing – they are creating their territory. Each dog has his own territory; he creates it not by visible walls and fences but by the smell. Other dogs immediately smell it: this territory belongs to some dog – be careful.

And even lions do the same; they will go pissing around a large territory. And their urine has a very strong smell; no animal is so insensitive that he will not sense it. And once he senses the smell, he will avoid that place – that is a prohibited area.

Scientists studying the whole thing came to a conclusion: why are these animals so interested in keeping a certain space of their own and do not allow anybody else to enter? They found that it is because of fear. The other animal can mean death. It is better to warn him, and before he attacks the best way to defend yourself is to attack. So if anybody enters your territory, you attack him before he attacks you, and whoever attacks first has more chances to be victorious.

In zoos, where man has kept animals in small spaces... Psychologists have been shocked to learn that in the wild, animals never go mad, never commit suicide, never become homosexuals, never attack their own species. But in a zoo they start doing strange things: they become homosexuals, they start attacking their own species. Otherwise, except man, no animal attacks his own species. It is a prerogative of humanity: only a man kills another man. No lion kills another lion.

But in a zoo it happens that they lose all their natural instinctive intelligence; they start going crazy, mad. And strangely enough, they even start committing suicide, and the reason is that their territory has been taken away and they are living in constant fear. So many animals so close – they cannot sleep, they cannot relax, the other animal may attack. They have lost their freedom, they have lost their sleep, they have lost their sanity. And to live in such conditions, a point comes when it is better to commit suicide rather than live in such torture. You don't see the torture because you don't know that they are suffering from a special cause: they need space.

And as humanity has grown in population, murders have grown, crimes have grown, homosexuality has grown, lesbianism has grown. People are committing suicide like anything. War seems to be the only thing we are preparing for; it seems war is the only thing we are born for.

Perhaps it is the territorial imperative. Perhaps man has lost his feeling of space.

Just see what territorial imperative is possible in a local train. Look at what territorial imperative is possible on the road. Still, if you watch carefully, even in a local train people are standing in such a way that nobody touches them, still making their last effort to keep a certain distance. It may be just inches, but just a little distance will give them breathing space.

Psychologically, man is afraid to come close to anybody whose presence can become an exposure, whose eyes can be so penetrative like x-rays, who can see you through and through. And you are afraid that perhaps nothing will be found – there is nobody, the house is empty.

The same is true about questions: you are afraid to ask authentic questions coming out of your ignorance because you will be allowing yourself to be exposed as an ignorant person. Everybody is pretending to be knowledgeable.

In my village there was a certain man...a little loose in the head, so I was very much interested in him. I am always interested in people who are a little loose; they are special people.

His name was Sunderlal, but I used to call him Doctor Sunderlal. At first he could not believe it: why am I calling him doctor? He asked me, "You said *doctor*?"

I said, "You are 'doctor.' In this village, nobody is more knowledgeable than you are."

He said, "That's true."

I said, "In this village, you are a DLitt, a doctor."

He said, "Are you joking?"

I said, "Why should I joke? A fact is a fact. If you want, I can bring a few people as witnesses."

He said, "No, no, there is no need. I trust in you, if you are saying it then it must be so."

The next day I saw that he had hung a board on his house: Doctor Sunderlal, DLitt.

The whole town was agog: "Suddenly this crazy man... Which university has given him a DLitt ?"

I reached his home and I said, "You have done the right thing. It is not a question of any university – what rights do they have to give you a DLitt? – it is your declaration."

He said, "That's right. Because my father was saying, 'You idiot, you are writing Doctor Sunderlal, DLitt – the police will come! You will be caught in some trouble; don't listen to that man.'"

I said, "There is no question; it is your declaration that 'In this village I am the most knowledgeable person.' If anybody has any doubts...open challenge!"

He said, "Should it be written underneath the board?"

I said, "It should be written underneath the board."

So a certain board was made on which he wrote, "This is a declaration that in this village I am the most knowledgeable person. And if somebody has any doubts, that means an open challenge for a discussion."

Now, who wanted to discuss with that fellow? He was so crazy; nobody turned up. And he was sitting in a chair just by the side of the board waiting for somebody to come.

I inquired two or three times, "Has anybody turned up?"

He said, "Nobody People come, they read and they go again. Even my father said that there seems to be something in it, because nobody is making any objection. Even the police inspector came, read the whole thing and went away: 'If it is a declaration...'"

Just a few years ago the man died, and he died as "Doctor Sunderlal, DLitt." In the newspapers it was printed, "Doctor Sunderlal, DLitt has died." And nobody ever asked or bothered, because nobody was ready to accept the challenge. Everybody was afraid, because to discuss with that crazy fellow...he could say anything. He could raise questions that you could not answer; he could criticize anything.

And they all knew that I was supporting him. I had told him, "Don't be worried. If somebody accepts the challenge, I will be there by your side to help you."

He said, "I am not worried. I have defeated my wife, my cousin, my brother. I have completely defeated my family, and I know that in this village they are the average people, so I have defeated the village. Should I try to make the territory a little bigger?"

I said, "No, you should keep the territory just as the village. It is enough that you have the DLitt; you have declared it. Now, there is no need to make the territory bigger, because that may create trouble. In this village you are the only one whose head is loose. In other villages there may be somebody who has the same kind of loose head – unnecessary trouble will arise. Just remain silent."

And people started calling him "Doctor Sunderlal." And by and by, people forgot all about...he was accepted as Doctor Sunderlal, DLitt. That almost became his name.

Your knowledge...whether you have declared it or not, deep down you believe that you know so much. And all that you know is not yours. Coming closer to a person in whose light your knowledge will start melting, disappearing, evaporating, leaving you naked in your ignorance, you are afraid even to ask a question.

I have seen people, thousands of people in my life, asking me questions and saying, "This is a question from one of my friends."

And when I used to see people personally, I would tell them, "The best way will be that you send your friend. And he can say the same thing: 'This is a question from one of my friends.'"

Someone would say, "What do you mean?"

I would tell him, "You have understood... This is your question. But you don't even have guts to say 'This is my question.' Knowledge, which you claim as yours, is all from others. And the question – which you are saying is some friend's question – is yours." I said, "Bring your friend. Tomorrow, come with your friend. I would like to see the friend, because the question is very important."

He said, "The question is important?"

I said, "It is a very important question, and I would like to see the person."

He said, "Forgive me, really it is my question."

People are afraid to expose themselves. But to be with a master, one of the basic rules is that you will drop your fears and you will stand naked in your ignorance, because from that ignorance your innocence can be achieved.

From your knowledge, no route goes to innocence. Only from your ignorance is there a pathway to innocence.

Hence I repeat again: a vast knowledge which is borrowed is of no meaning. But a small ignorance that is yours is a treasure, because from that ignorance opens the door to your innocence.

And it is innocence that becomes the light, becomes the incense and the fragrance.

Osho,

Once you told me that the spring had come, but my anxiety is that I have lost everything, that the garbage has taken over completely, and that I cannot keep myself open to you as a disciple unless I am continually in your presence.

Can you say something about the seed of spiritual growth which you plant in us and whether it can die?

The seed is immortal, it cannot die. But it can remain dormant, it can remain dormant for lives.

If the right soil is not provided, if the right water is not provided, if the right exposure to the sunlight is not provided, it will remain dormant, a potentiality, a waiting – but it cannot die. You may die many times, but the seed, once planted in you, will go on following your consciousness wherever you are.

Unless you give it your attention, nourishment, your care, your love, it cannot become a living sprout. Small, fresh green leaves cannot come out of it. Only your love and your consciousness can create the miracle. And the day will not be far away when there will be flowers.

There are people here who have been carrying seeds from other masters. I do not need to sow new seeds in them; all that I need is to help their dormant seeds to open up. You are not here for the first time. You have been here always – perhaps with Zarathustra, perhaps with Pythagoras, perhaps with Heraclitus, perhaps with Gautam Buddha.

It is very rare that a person comes to me who needs a new seed – because you are all ancient people. It is almost impossible not to have come in contact with one of the magicians of the soul; those people are magnets. So in some life, somewhere, you may have met al-Hillaj Mansoor, Jalaluddin Rumi, Kabir or Nanak.

Very rarely do I find a person who is not already pregnant – but the seed has remained the seed, you have not been a gardener to it. Somebody, with great compassion, must have sown the seed, but you have not been kind enough to yourself.

The seed never dies.

And Pankaja, you understand perfectly well that your mind is full of garbage. This very understanding is enough to get rid of it. But it seems the problem is that this garbage is paying you; in some way it is fulfilling your ego.

Pankaja is a novelist, is well known as a novelist. I have worked with many kinds of celebrities; they are the most third-rate people to work with for the simple reason that their celebrity has become part of their ego. They cannot drop the ego, because if they drop the ego the celebrity disappears. And the celebrity, the famousness, their name, has become so important to them; it has become their identity in the world. Whereas millions of people are without any identity, they have an identity. For them, to drop the ego is very difficult – and understandably; it is arduous.

A person who is not a celebrity has a small ego. In fact, to have it or not to have it does not make much difference; he is already nobody. He can drop it, and by dropping it he can gain the whole beautiful existence and all its benediction. By becoming nobody, he can open the doors to the universe and its blessings.

But all the celebrities that have come to me from different fields, have all proved to be failures. They take the most time, but they have a problem because their ego is involved with their name and fame. Even if they understand that it is garbage, the garbage is paying them so much that they want to cling to it a little more – perhaps tomorrow or the day after tomorrow they will drop it. They have understood the point, but just to drop it right now seems too much.

I am reminded of a very great thinker, Voltaire. He was famous in his country, and it was a convention in the country that if you could get a small piece of cloth from a famous man like Voltaire, you could make a beautiful locket out of it. It was a great security, safety against dangers, disease, sickness, death.

When Voltaire used to go out of his house, he would come home almost naked, because crowds would follow him, tearing his clothes – and not only his clothes, he would get scratched on the body. He had to ask for police protection if he wanted to go to the railway station or to go to some other place. Without police protection it was impossible, because to reach the railway station naked, scratched all over, blood all over, would not look right – although he deeply enjoyed it, because he was the only man in the whole country who was so much respected. This was a respect given by people.

But in the world, everything goes on changing. The name and the fame is just a soap bubble. It may become very big – the bigger it becomes, the more dangerous, because it is going to burst soon.

And the day came when Voltaire was forgotten; somebody else had become the celebrity. Now there was no need for police protection. People even forgot that he was alive. In his notebooks he has written, "I enjoyed those days. But at that time I used to think that it would be better not to be known at all, just to be a nobody, to live silently, because life had become a nightmare. But when I became nobody, then I started feeling great despair that I had lost my respect, my name, my fame."

And he does not say in his notes that this was what he wanted: to be nobody. He had become nobody now, but it was not a joy, it was a defeat.

He wrote, "I'm dying a defeated man." And the day he died, only four persons carried his body to the graveyard. Of the four persons, one was his dog and three were his neighbors – and those three *had* to carry the body because otherwise it would start rotting and the neighborhood would become a hell to live in. Somehow he had to be thrown into a grave. So in fact the only person who lovingly followed was the dog. And this was the man who was followed by thousands of people wherever he went.

Your garbage is paying you. You can choose it; there is no problem. But choose consciously, that you choose garbage because it is paying you. Consciously chosen, it won't last long. Don't fight with it; fighting will not help.

Or if you are courageous enough, see a simple point: even if you write hundreds of novels and inside you remain just a wound which is hurting twenty-four hours a day, your whole life is wasted in misery just to fulfill a non-existential ego. Tomorrow you will die, and the day after tomorrow nobody will remember you. How many novelists have there been in this world? And who cares about them today? And they must all have suffered in the same way, because what they were doing was garbage.

You may be a big garbage truck. It does not matter – big or small – if you can have a little courage and throw away all this garbage and clean yourself, perhaps something beautiful may come out of you which may be helpful to humanity, which may be remembered for centuries, not only remembered, but may have a certain transforming effect on people.

But the garbage that you are writing is just journalistic. Nobody bothers tomorrow about today's newspaper.

I used to live in a place where a retired man, who was a little eccentric... Retired people become eccentric, having nothing to do. And nobody wants to become useless – it hurts. Nobody wants to be just a burden.

And in the family, nobody cares about an old man. In fact, they want to get rid of these people because they are unnecessarily a nuisance. Young people have their own life, their own enjoyment, their own entertainment, and these old fellows are continually interrupting, condemning, making them feel guilty or constantly irritable. And they have nothing to do; twenty-four hours a day they are sitting there. Naturally, they need some work; they become great critics about everything.

He used to come to me. I was in the university – for just one or two hours I was teaching in the university and then I was back. He used to come to me, and I loved to listen to him. He was very happy with me, because he said "You are the only man who has patience to listen; otherwise, nobody bothers. I am saying such significant things and nobody cares." But how long could *I* tolerate him?

So I used to give him the newspapers and magazines, so he would read them and would get into them and leave me alone. Sometimes it would happen that I would give him an old newspaper just by mistake. He would start reading it – so deeply engrossed – and then I would look at the date. I would think, "My God, I have given him an old newspaper." And I would tell him, "This is an old newspaper. I will give you the new, the fresh."

He said, "It doesn't matter – almost ninety percent of it is the same news. Just for ten percent, who cares? To me, it is all the same. When you are not in the house, I come and ask the gardener. He does not allow me into your study, but he brings newspapers and I sit in the garden. And sometimes he brings one-year-old newspapers. But I say it does not matter; the same things go on happening, so I read. Even your gardener says to me, 'My God, this is one year old. You wait, my master will be coming soon; then I will bring the fresh newspapers.' And I say, 'Don't be worried, I just enjoy reading.' And it is the same: somebody has been killed, somebody has been murdered, somebody has committed suicide, somebody has been assassinated, somewhere some government is changed. It does not matter to me who rules in Brazil – what does it matter?"

My gardener told me, "That old fellow is a philosopher."

I said, "How have you discovered that he is a philosopher?"

He said, "He has a very philosophical attitude; he reads a year-old newspaper and he reads it with such concentration. And when I ask, he says, 'What does it matter? Time passes on. Just one year ago this was new, and what is new today will be old one year afterwards. And as far as I am concerned, it is only a question of passing time, so what I am reading does not matter.'"

I would like you first to be clean, innocent, silent. And then if out of that silence something is born, that will be a contribution to the universe. Otherwise, out of the garbage you can go on writing novels, and they will sell, because people need something to read and throw away. But they don't know that somebody has put his life...wasted his life in writing these novels. Somebody has missed his buddhahood.

It is up to you to choose. It cannot be forced upon anybody. I can just give you a hint – that it is *time*. And you are mature enough: you have written your novels, and you know all that is garbage.

It shows, because people love to read anything. Railway bookstalls need garbage, airport bookstalls need garbage; everywhere garbage is needed because people need garbage. But why should you waste your life?

And you have the possibility to give birth to something really significant – but a breakthrough is needed. You need a discontinuity. Forget what you have been doing, forget the name and the fame and anything that it brings to you.

Just be a nobody, enjoy being nobody. And I tell you that in being nobody there is freedom.

And then one day you will find that the seed within you has started growing. And then if something out of your own experience comes to be written by you, it will be significant for you, it will be significant for others. Anything that can really make life a little more beautiful, a little more musical, a little more poetic, is going to help you too. It is possible only because of your growth.

You can collect all kinds of information – read ten novels, and the eleventh is born – that is one way that is being followed by all writers, poets, painters. But they are third-rate, and they will be forgotten.

Something meaningful only comes from your very innermost being.

But before that, you have to throw all the rubbish off; otherwise, the rubbish is so much and the seed is so small, it is lost in the rubbish. I hope that you will be able to do what I am saying; otherwise, I would not have said it.

3 No Other Path but Life

Osho,
How come everything is going so well?

The question is not a laughing matter. It touches something of tremendous value in human misery, in human anguish, in human reality. It creates laughter because it looks absurd to ask why things are going so well.

We have become accustomed to things never going so well. We are well acquainted with the misery, the pain, the darkness, the meaninglessness, the whole tragedy of human existence. It has gone to our very bones, blood and marrow; we accept it as if it is our nature.

If things are going wrong, it seems natural.

If things are not going wrong, then something must be wrong – how come things are going so well? We have forgotten the language of well-being, we have forgotten the taste of blissfulness.

We have forgotten our own nature. The natural thing is that things *should* go well; for their going well, no reason is needed.

You are healthy – you don't go to the doctor to ask him, "What is the matter with me? I am healthy." You go to the doctor when you are *not* healthy, when you are sick.

When people are young, they don't ask, "What is the meaning of life?" Their youth, their overflowing energy, is enough meaning, is enough significance. They are still capable of love. They are still capable of a dance, a song, a celebration. Death has not overshadowed their lives yet.

The moment a person starts asking, "What is the meaning of life?" it means he has become old – it does not matter at what age. His question emphatically shows that he has lost touch with life, lost touch with love, lost touch with vitality, and wherever he looks it is all emptiness. The question has become significant to him. Why is he living? In fact, he has died; his life is posthumous.

The moment a person asks, "What is the meaning of life?" it is the question of a dead man – who still breathes, whose heart still beats, but it is all like a robot. All poetry, all rainbows have disappeared...no sunrises at all. It seems the night is eternal. It seems that he must have dreamt about the days when he had seen the light; they were not real.

Old age, when death is just standing close to you, creates the question, "What is the meaning of life?" But when you are alive, when death is far away beyond the horizon of your vision, who cares about the meaning of life? You *live* it, you *have* it, you *sing* it, you *dance* it. It is in every breath, it is in every beat of your heart.

One thing has to be understood clearly: that the people who have asked so-called great questions about the meaning of life, about the meaning of the very existence, about the meaning of love, about the meaning of beauty, are thought to be great philosophers but they have one foot in the grave. Just before slipping into their graves, they are raising all these questions.

One of the great aestheticians, a great philosopher of aesthetics, Croce, devoted his whole life to a single question: what is beauty? In this century he stands alone as a high peak, incomparable to anybody else. His dedication to the question of beauty is total. He wrote about it, he talked about it, he taught about it, he dreamt about it; his whole life was woven around the question: what is beauty?

I have gone through his writings, and on each step I have felt that this man must have been blind – only a blind person can ask, "What is beauty?" And for almost one century, nobody has raised the question of whether Croce was blind or not. I say he was definitely blind. He may have had eyes, just as you have, but he had no perception, no sensitivity. He was asking the question what is beauty? And went on inquiring about it – and the whole existence is full of beauty.

Even the smallest blade of grass is beautiful. All around there are flowers and stars, birds and trees and rivers and mountains, and beautiful human beings. Why could a man of the intelligence of Croce not see a simple thing – that beauty has to be felt, not thought about? You have to see it; you have to experience it. You are capable of creating it, but it is such a mystery that it is beyond explanation. You cannot confine it in a definition.

But his whole lifelong effort shows only one thing: the poor man never experienced even a single moment of beauty; otherwise, his whole questioning would have changed. Instead he would have devoted his life to creating beauty, to experiencing beauty, to rejoicing with the stars and with the moon and with the flowers and with the birds. But he wasted his whole life.

And to what conclusion did he come in the end? – that beauty is indefinable. This could have been told to him by anybody in the very beginning. There was no need to waste a beautiful life, a precious gift of existence.

And one cannot be certain that it will be given to you again; you cannot even be certain why it has been given to you this time. Do you deserve it? Have you earned it? Does existence owe it to you? It seems to be a sheer gift, a gift of an abundant existence, not bothering about whether you deserve it or not. Not asking for your qualifications, not inquiring about your character, your morality, making no demands on you, just giving it without any conditions attached to it. Giving it not as a business, but without any expectations from you in return, giving it and allowing you total freedom to do whatever you want to do with it.

Everything should go beautifully, easily, with wellbeing. It is natural. If something is not going well that means something is sick, something is ill.

But all the great moralists of the world, all the theologians, all the prophets and messengers of God have really messed you up.

They have made such demands on you. They have taken away all your freedom. They have asked you to do impossible things, and naturally you have failed in doing them. It has left wounds in you – wounds of failure, inferiority, wounds of unworthiness – and you are living with all those wounds. Naturally, everything goes wrong.

It is not nature; it is your great benefactors: the people who have been promising you "We are the saviors." In fact, they are the people who have created a sick humanity, a diseased human mind, a psychology that is not sane.

Demanding anything unnatural is bound to create guilt. If you do not do it, you feel guilty that you are not really a human being; that you are behaving like subhuman beings, animals, that you are a sinner, that you are doing things against the prophets and the messengers who represent God. And if you try to follow them, you get into a trap. If you follow them you have to go against nature, and nature is all that you are.

You cannot go against yourself, so on each step there is failure. On each step you become more and more schizophrenic: a small part becomes the priest, condemning your whole nature. Whatever you do is wrong.

Life becomes a nightmare. And that's how man has lived for thousands of years: a life which could have been a beautiful experience, has been turned into an unbearable torture, a nightmare. Even if you want to wake up you cannot. The nightmare is heavy and long – it is not only yours, it is coming from your forefathers; generation after generation has cultivated it. It has roots as ancient as man; you cannot fight with it. You are torn apart. You cannot fight with your nature, you cannot fight with your sick heritage.

And I say that on the whole earth every man is living under the burden of a sick heritage. It does not matter whether he is Christian or Hindu or Mohammedan – these are different names for the same sickness.

If you follow your nature, you condemn yourself. The whole society condemns you. The whole world is against you, and you are also against yourself.

But you have to live your nature.

Friedrich Nietzsche has a beautiful insight. He says that all the religions of the world have been against sex, but they have not been successful in destroying sex; otherwise, from where do these people go on coming? This whole population explosion... If your priests had succeeded, churches would be empty. But there are seven hundred million Catholics – certainly the Catholic priests have failed utterly.

Nietzsche is right. The religions have not succeeded in destroying sex. But they have succeeded in one thing: they have made sex poison, poisonous. It is no more a joy, it is no more a thing of beauty; it is no more sacred. They have been able to create great guilt out of it. And what is right about sex is right about all your natural instincts, but everything has been poisoned.

So when things are not going right, you are perfectly at ease. When things are going right, you start feeling uneasy: "What is the matter?"

If there are wars, it is perfectly right. If there are riots between Hindus and Mohammedans, if Mohammedans and Jews are killing each other, it is perfectly right. But if suddenly Jews and Mohammedans start dancing and singing and rejoicing together, the whole world will be shocked: "What is going on? Have these people gone mad?"

We are suffering a wrong heritage, and unless we get ourselves free from the past we cannot live peacefully. The people who are gathered here with me and the people around the earth who are with me have dropped the past. They are no longer Hindus, no longer Christians, no longer Buddhists; they are simply human beings. And they are trying to live their nature fully, authentically, without any guilt and without any feeling of sin.

Things are going beautifully well. They are living in freedom.

The past is our slavery, and if the past is too much, then it is going to create our future. We are crushed between past and future, and the future is nothing but a reproduction of the past. And a small moment of present is almost powerless against two eternities pressing it from both sides.

Once you are free of the past a tremendous realization happens: you are free of the future also. And your being free of the future means that now you are free to *make* your future. It will not be made by the past; it will be made by your nature, by your intelligence, by your meditation, by your silence, by your love.

Around my sannyasins things are bound to go easy, because there is no sin, no guilt, no imposed morality. I corrupt people so much that they become innocent.

People are living innocently. They don't have any moral codes, any ten commandments, any holy Bibles. They have only their own insight and freedom to create their future, to live according to their nature without any fear: there is no hell, and there is no God to decide whether you are right or wrong.

If you are right, your life will be a life of joy; if you are wrong, your life will be a life of misery. There is no need for any God. Each act is intrinsically decisive.

So you can feel your way: if you are moving rightly, your life will go on growing more and more flowers, will go on growing bigger and bigger wings. Your reach towards the stars will become easier. And if you are doing something wrong, your very nature will say it is wrong because you will be suffering the consequences of your wrong acts *here* and *now*. You will not have to wait for the last judgment day.

What a stupid kind of hypothesis, "the last judgment day" – one day everybody will be awakened from his grave. Just visualize what will happen: all skeletons, and there is going to be such a crowd. At the place where you are sitting there are at least ten skeletons underneath you. When all the skeletons stand up there is not going to be elbow room, and there is going to be such shrieking, shouting, moaning. Even for poor God, it is going to be very difficult to recognize who is who – because there will only be skeletons.

Then to judge who is going to heaven and who is going to hell... And do you think in just one day? Each person has millions of acts, good and bad, which have to be balanced, and there is only one God – and not a very intelligent one either.

George Bernard Shaw used to say, "Just the very crowd makes me feel that it will be difficult to make judgments. Moreover, half of the crowd will be women –who will make it almost impossible!"

Perhaps that's why the last judgment day has not happened and is not going to happen. Because Jesus used to say to his disciples, "Soon, in your life, you will see the last judgment day happen" – in his disciples' lifetime. That means, at the most, seventy years.

Two thousand years have passed, and as the days go by the skeletons go on growing. I think God has changed his mind. Judgment is not possible any longer.

As far as I am concerned each act brings its own judgment, and that is more scientific. Why go on collecting acts for a certain day and then deciding? And why decide from outside, when there is a possibility to decide from inside? Each act has its intrinsic consequence.

You can figure it out; if your life is miserable then you are doing something wrong, and if your life is a merry-go-round then you are doing everything that should be done perfectly. So it is up to you whether you make your life a merry-go-round or a sorry-go-round. There is nobody to decide it, you are the act and you are the judge. And this seems to be more scientific, simple.

If everything is going well, be happy. And remember why things are going well so they can continue to go better and better, because wellness also has depth. Just find out what it is that is making your life blissful, peaceful, silent, happy – simple arithmetic – and your life can become a holy life.

According to me, if you are living joyously, you are a holy man. Only one thing you have to do: die to the past so that you can be reborn in a fresh present and a free future.

Osho,

Is there another way without death and insecurity?

There is no death in the first place. Death is an illusion. It is always somebody else who dies; *you* never die. It means death has always been seen from the outside, it is the outsider's view. Those who have seen their inner world are unanimous in saying that there is no death.

You don't know what constitutes your consciousness; it is not constituted of breathing, it is not constituted of heartbeats, it is not constituted of blood circulation. So when the doctor says that a man is dead, it is an outsider's conclusion; all that he is saying is, "This man is no longer breathing, his pulse has stopped, his heart is not beating." Are these three things equivalent to death? They are not!

Consciousness is not your body, nor your mind, nor your heart. So when a person dies, he dies for you, not for himself. For himself he simply changes the house, perhaps moves into a better apartment. But because the old apartment is left, and you are searching for him in the old apartment and you don't find him there, you think the poor guy is dead. All that you should say is, "The poor guy escaped. Now, we don't know where he has gone."

In fact, medical science is going beyond its limits when it says that some person is dead. Medical science has no right yet, because it has no definition yet of what constitutes death. It can simply say, "This man is no longer breathing. His heart has stopped. His pulse is no longer functioning." To conclude that he is dead is going beyond what you are seeing. But because science does not have any idea of consciousness, the death of the body becomes the death of the being.

Those who have known the being say it is not necessary that you should die and then you know; you can just go inside. That's what I call meditation. Just go inside and find out what is your center, and at your center there is no breathing, there is no heartbeat, there is no thought, no mind, no heart, no body, and still you are.

Once a person has experienced himself – that he is not the body, not the mind, not the heart, but pure awareness – he knows there is no death for him, because he does not depend on the body. Awareness has no dependence on blood circulation. It does not depend on whether the heart beats or not, it does not depend on whether the mind functions or not. It is a totally different world; it is not constituted of any material thing, it is immaterial.

So the first thing to understand is that there is no death – it has never been found. And if there is no death, what insecurity can there be? For an immortal life there can be no insecurity. Your immortality is not dependent on your bank balance; the beggar is as immortal as the emperor.

As far as people's consciousnesses are concerned, that is the only world where true communism exists: they all have equal qualities, and they don't have anything that can be lost or taken away. They don't have anything that can be destroyed, burned.

There is no insecurity. All insecurity is a shadow of death.

If you look deeply, then every insecure feeling is rooted in the fear of death. But I am saying to you that there is no death; hence there cannot be any insecurity. You are immortal beings, *amritasya putrah*.

That's what the seers in the ancient East have said: You are the sons of immortality. And they were not misers like Jesus Christ: that "I am the only begotten son of God." A strange idea, even to say it one should feel ashamed. "I am the only begotten son of God." What about others? Are they all bastards? Jesus is condemning the whole world. He is the son of God, and whose sons and daughters are all these people? And it is strange, why should God stop by giving birth to only one child? Is he spent with just one child? Or was he a believer of birth control?

I have been asking the pope and Mother Teresa, "Your God must be a believer of birth control, must be using things which you are prohibiting to people, condoms and all; otherwise, how is it possible? Once he created a son, then at least one daughter – that's a natural tendency."

And in the whole eternity having no fun. The psychologists say that poor people create more children for the simple reason that they don't have any other fun. To go to the cinema you need money, to go to the circus you need money, to go to Chowpatty Beach you need money. Wherever there is fun, you need money. So just go to bed – that is the only fun without money, nobody asks for money.

What is God doing? He can neither go to Chowpatty nor can he go to a circus, nor to a cinema hall. Sitting eternally bored. Just created one son. It has many implications: perhaps he was so frustrated with this one son that he became a celibate – "I am not going to create any more idiots."

Jesus was teaching on the earth for just three years. His age was only thirty-three, and he was crucified – a great savior who could not save himself. God must have felt tremendously let down: "Be finished! No more sons, no more daughters."

But the reality is that there is a certain element of egoism in being the only one, with no competitors. Krishna may be the incarnation of God but he is not the son – just a photocopy. Mohammed may be a messenger – just a postman. But Jesus is special; he is the only begotten son of God. There is a certain egoism in it.

The ancient seers were not so egoistic. They called the whole humanity – past, present, future – *amritasya putrah*: You are all sons of immortality. They were not putting themselves higher than you, they were not pretending to be holier than you. They were making every human being, as far as consciousness is concerned, absolutely equal, eternal.

There is no insecurity. There is no need for any other path – and anyway, there is no other path. Life is the path, which passes through the illusory gate of death.

You can pass the gate consciously. If you are meditative enough, then you can go through death knowing perfectly that you are changing the house; you can enter another womb knowing perfectly that you are entering the new apartment – and it is always better, because life is always evolving. And if you can die consciously, then certainly your new life will be on a very high level from the very beginning.

And I don't see any insecurity. You come into the world without anything, so one thing is certain: nothing belongs to you.

You come absolutely naked, but with illusions. That's why every child is born with closed hands, fists – believing that he is bringing treasures – and those fists are just empty. And everybody dies with open hands. Try to die with fists; nobody has been successful up to now. Or try to be born with open hands; nobody has been successful in that either.

The child is born with fists, with illusions that he is bringing treasures into the world, but there is nothing in the fist. Nothing belongs to you, so what insecurity? Nothing can be stolen, nothing can be taken away from you.

Everything that you are using belongs to the world. And one day, you have to leave everything here. You will not be able to take anything with you.

I have heard about a rich man in a village who was such a miser that he had never given anything to any beggar. The whole community of beggars knew about it, so whenever they saw some beggar standing before his house they knew: "This man seems to be new, from some other village. Tell him, 'You won't get anything from there.'"

The man's wife was dying, but he wouldn't call the doctor. He only had one friend, because to have many friends means unnecessary insecurity – somebody may ask for money, somebody may ask for something. He had only one friend, and that one was also such a miser that there was no problem between them. They both understood each other's psychology – no conflict, no asking, no question of creating any embarrassment.

The friend said, "But this is the time that the doctor should be called – your wife is dying."

The man said, "It is all in the hands of God. What can a doctor do? If she is going to die, she is going to die. You will unnecessarily put me in trouble: paying the fee to the doctor for the medicine, this and that. I am a religious man, and if she is not going to die she will recover without any doctor. The real doctor is God, nobody else. And I believe in God because he never asks for a fee or anything."

The wife died.

His friend said, "Look, just for a little money you didn't call a doctor."

He said, "Little money? Money is money; it is never a question of a little. And death comes to everybody."

The friend was a little angry. He said, "This is too much. I am also a miser, but if my wife is dying at least I will call a compounder, a pharmacist – but I will call somebody. But you are really hard. What are you going to do with all this money?"

He said, "I am going to take it with me."

The friend said, "Nobody has ever heard of it."

He said, "But nobody has ever tried." That too was true. He said,

"Just see. I have my own plan – I will take everything with me."

The friend said, "Just tell me your secret, because some day I will have to die also, and you are such a friend."

He said, "Friendship is one thing, but this secret I cannot tell. And the secret is such that you cannot use it when you are dying – it has to be done before, because you have to carry all your money and all your gold and diamonds and everything to the river."

He said, "What do you mean?"

He said, "Yes, and go into a small boat in the middle of the river and jump with all your money and be drowned – so you have taken it. Try! Nobody has tried. If you don't succeed there is no harm, because everybody goes without it. If you succeed, then you will be the pioneer, the first one who reaches paradise with his whole bag of money. And all those saints will be looking with wide-open eyes: 'This man has done something!'"

But the friend said, "That means you have to die."

He said, "Naturally, and you have to be in good health. When you are dying, it will then be very difficult to carry that heavy load. I am going to do it soon, because my wife is gone, now nobody is there."

But even if you jump into the ocean with all your money, the money will remain in the ocean, your body will remain in the ocean.

You will have to go alone, alone just as consciousness. Nothing belongs to you, because you bring nothing here and you can take nothing from here.

Life is the only way. Death is the only illusion to be understood.

If you can live fully, totally, understanding death as an illusion – not because I am saying it, but by your own experience in deep meditation – then live life fully, as totally as possible, without any fear. There is no insecurity, because even death is illusory.

Only the living being in you is real.

Clean it, sharpen it, make it fully aware so that not even a small part of it is drowned in darkness, so that you are luminous all over, you become aflame. This is the only way; there is no other alternative. And there is no need.

Osho,

To be open and to be witnessing are two different things. Is it so, or is this a duality created by my mind?

Mind always creates duality; otherwise, to be open or to be witnessing are not two things. If you are open, you will be witnessing. Without being a witness, you cannot be open; or if you are a witness, you will be open – because being a witness and yet remaining closed is impossible. So those are only two words.

You can either start with witnessing – then opening will come on its own accord; or you can start by opening your heart – all windows, all doors – then witnessing will be found, coming on its own. But if you are simply thinking, without doing anything, then they look separate.

Mind cannot think without duality. Duality is the way of thinking.

In silence, all dualities disappear. Oneness is the experience of silence.

For example, day and night are very clear dualities, but they are not two. There are animals that see in the night. Their eyes are more sensitive, capable of seeing in darkness. For them, there is no darkness. Those animals cannot open their eyes in the day because their eyes are so delicate that the sun hurts. So while it is day for you, for those animals it is night; the eyes are closed, all is darkness. When it is night for you, it is day for them. The whole day they sleep, the whole night they are awake.

And if you ask a scientist and a logician, you will see the difference. If you ask the logician, "What is day?" he will say, "That which is not night." And what is not night? It is a circular game. If you ask, "What is night?" the logician is going to say, "That which is not day."

You need day to define night, you need night to define day. Strange duality, strange opposition... If there is no day, can you think of night? If there is no night, can you think of day? It is impossible.

Ask the scientist, who is closer to reality than the logician. For the scientist darkness is less light, light is less darkness. Now it is one phenomenon, just like a thermometer. Somebody has a temperature of 110 degrees, just ready to move out of the house.

Somebody has a temperature of 98 degrees, the normal temperature for human beings, but somebody falls below 96 degrees, again ready for a move. Your existence is not very big, just between 96 and 110 degrees. Sixteen degrees below is death, above is death; just a small slit in between, a small window of life.

If we could have a thermometer for light and darkness, the situation would be the same, just as it is between heat and cold – the same thermometer will do for both. The cold is less hot and the hot is less cold, but it is one phenomenon; there is no duality. It is the same with darkness and light.

And the same is true about all oppositions that mind creates. Openness, witnessing... If you think intellectually, they look very different. They seem to be unrelated, how can they be one? But in experience they are one.

Osho,

I have been your disciple for two and a half years now, and all the time I have longed to be in your presence. Now I have met you for the first time, and everything has changed. I want to run away from you. I am totally confused.

Please comment.

It is almost normal. You fall in love with me; just hearing my words, it appeals to your intellect. Your reason feels satisfied, and then a desire arises to be, at least for some time, with me.

And then a great shock...because I am not a man of words. Although I have spoken more words than anybody else in the whole world, but still I say I am not a man of words. My words are just like nets thrown to catch fish.

My message is wordless.

When you come close to me, then you see the point: that I am not a reasonable, rational, logical person; that you have come to an irrational mystic. You had come with a certain rational conviction, and here you find that reason has to be abandoned. You have to take a jump into the unknown, for which I cannot provide any logic, any evidence, except my own presence.

Anybody who has come here, caught by my words, will feel like escaping. Because he had come for a different reason, and here he finds a totally different situation – not only different, but diametrically opposite.

I am not a teacher. I am not a philosopher. I am not interested in creating systems and hypotheses.

My interest is in destroying you as you are, so that you can be reborn in your existential potential. I am here to destroy your personality, to give birth to your individuality.

It is a natural reaction, it happens to everybody. But you cannot escape either. At the most, you may go up to Dadar Station and come back again. You can try, and exactly from Dadar you will come back; that is the radius.

Once you are caught up with me, you cannot escape.

But I will not prevent you; trying to escape will be helpful. If you try to escape and then you have to come back, the next time the desire will arise but it will not have any effect on you. You will simply drop it, because it does not work. Now you have to go the whole way, whatever it means. It may mean the death of the ego, of the personality; then you have to take the risk.

If you had not come to me you would have continued to enjoy my words, because it was just borrowed knowledge for you. And here I want you to drop all borrowed knowledge, including that which you have gathered from me.

I want you to become a knower, a seer.

Certainly, you have to pass through fire. But the fire only looks like fire from afar. The closer you come, the cooler you will find it. And the moment you pass through the fire you will be surprised that fire can also be so cool, so refreshing.

There is a story in Moses' life that Jews have not been able to explain in four thousand years.

On Mount Sinai, Moses encountered a strange phenomenon that he thought was God. Certainly, it was very mysterious: a bush was afire but it was not burning; it was as green as any bush. Its flowers were as juicy and young as any flowers, and yet there was fire in the bush. Naturally attracted, curious, he wanted to look from close quarters at what was happening. He had never thought that fire could be there; flames were rising above the bush – and the bush was green!

He came close, and just as he was coming very close a voice shouted, "Leave your shoes behind, Moses! You are entering into holy land, into a sacred place." Trembling, he left his shoes. He could not see anybody, but it was certainly a miraculous experience. He thought it was God's voice.

My own explanation of the story is that everybody who goes through a transformation comes to the same bush, which is afire, but the fire is cool. It is nourishing the bush, not destroying it. It only looks like fire; it is cool flames of life. For life, Moses' word is *God* – that's the only difference. That is a difference of language, nothing much.

You have come here; you have seen the flames. And the first idea will be "Escape as quickly as possible; otherwise you will be burned."

Don't be worried. If I am not burned, if all these people here are not burned, you also are not going to be burned.

The fire is cool; it transforms.

It takes away your mask and helps you to discover your original face. But still, freedom is available to you up to Dadar Station.

Osho,

I heard you talking about the Sri Lankan mystic asking his followers to stand up if they wanted to go the shortcut towards enlightenment.

I want you to know that I'm waiting for the chance to stand up as soon as I hear you asking – knowing that my legs will most likely be trembling, my body perspiring, and my heart beating like mad.

It is necessary that I should repeat the story first:

A mystic in Sri Lanka is dying. He has thousands of followers; they have all gathered. Just before closing his eyes he says, "If anybody wants to come with me, I can take him with me – and this is the *most* shortcut way. You will not have to do anything. I don't have much time. Anybody wanting to go the most shortcut way... Otherwise, it takes so many lives to achieve enlightenment. I can take you with me from the back door. Just stand up!"

There was absolute silence, pin-drop silence. People looked at each other thinking, "This man has been listening to him for forty years, perhaps he may be ready." But he was looking at somebody else, because he had so many problems still to solve: "Business is not good."

Everybody has problems: somebody has a girl to marry, somebody has a boy who is a troublemaker; somebody has a case in the court and this is not the time to become enlightened, first the court case has to be finished, and so on, so forth.

But one man raised one hand. He said, "I cannot stand up because I am not ready to go yet, but I cannot resist the temptation to know where the back door is, because if sometime I am ready, I can follow the shortcut. Right now, I am not ready – let it be completely clear to you that I am not coming with you – but just tell us where the back door is."

The old man said, "The back door is such that you can enter only with your master, not alone. It is a very narrow gate; only one can enter at a time. If you are ready to dissolve yourself in the being of the master, then there is no problem – one or one thousand, they will all enter through the door as one being. Alone, you will not be able to find it."

Now, Deva Prem wants me to ask him some day to come along from the back door. And he thinks he is ready and he will stand up – although even thinking, he perspires and his legs tremble and his heart beats faster.

My feeling is, Deva Prem, you are the man who had raised his hand.

And one day I will ask, and I know that this time also you will only raise your hand, or perhaps you may not even raise your hand. Because I am a different type of man. That old man was very compassionate.

I would have taken even this man – at least he had raised his hand. That is enough – what is the need of making him stand up? Just raising the hand is enough.

So when I ask, remember I will ask you to simply raise the hand.

This time be alert, and get prepared – because with trembling legs and perspiring it will be difficult to enter that back door.

That back door needs people who can disappear into nothingness, dancing, singing, celebrating.

So learn to sing, learn to dance, learn to celebrate. Any day, I can ask.

And I hate perspiration. I am very allergic –you will have to stop perspiring.

And trembling... That gate won't allow you in; it will immediately see that there are two persons. You have to be absolutely still, and one with me – no trembling.

And this time I will not ask you to stand up. The last time, it was my fault.

4 In the End There Is No Word

Osho,
Sitting before you, feeling your words flowing towards me from your great heart, I found my own heart bursting open and receiving the sun and moon of your being. Soon a great peace fell over me, followed by a never-known calmness so that I feel that I am resting in the arms of existence itself.

I bow down before you in gratefulness to kiss the earth that gave you life. I lift my arms to the stars and sing hallelujah, hallelujah, hallelujah. Osho, because of you I am alive to realize the beauty, the joy, the purity of love that is the very expanse of existence. These words seem unable to express the truest feelings that arise from the depth of my being. But I bow down before you now, and again and again and again to dance, to sing, to shout: thank you, Osho, thank you, thank you, thank you. Hallelujah! Hallelujah! Hallelujah!

There is much more yet to happen. What has happened to you is immense. What will happen to you will be greater, but remember one thing: it is *never* enough.

Existence is such an abundance – we cannot exhaust it. It is inexhaustible in its beauty, in its blissfulness, in its benediction.

You are feeling difficulty in expressing what is happening to you.

And this is only the beginning – just think of the difficulties of those who have gone far ahead of you. There comes a moment when even to say that this cannot be said is not possible – because to say that this cannot be said is still saying something about it. It is still defining it in a very negative way.

There comes a moment when only silence, utter silence, remains your expression.

That is your thankfulness, that is your gratitude, that is your hallelujah – a dance which is invisible, a song which is not heard, a beauty which cannot be painted, described. And only when we have come to the point where words are to be left behind does what I call religiousness begin. I do not say renounce the world, but I certainly say move towards the moment when you will have to renounce the word.

The Bible says, "In the beginning was the word." Nobody knows about the beginning. Nobody can know about the beginning, because nobody can be a witness about the beginning. If somebody had been witnessing the beginning then it would not have been the beginning, because somebody was already there.

The Bible may be right, may be wrong, about the beginning, but I say unto you: In the end there is no word. And that has been witnessed by thousands of mystics in thousands of years past.

And the moment you come to realize that words are slipping out of your hands, that the boundary line of language is crossed...a tremendous innocence, a new childhood. For the first time you can understand that which cannot be spoken. You can understand the message of the wind blowing through the pine trees, you can understand the poetry of the sound of running water.

To be freed from language is to be freed from all human limitations. Language is the greatest imprisonment.

I am happy that you are feeling great difficulty in expressing something that you are experiencing. Slowly, it will become more and more clear that there is no word, no language; no concept to explain it, to express it. Just silence is the only answer to all your questions, the only meeting with existence without any barrier, any wall.

As the language disappears, the mind is no longer of any use. For the first time you contact existence directly, without the mediation of the mind – and that experience is enlightenment. And nobody is far away from it; it is within everybody's reach.

But people are searching for their happiness where it does not exist. They are looking for living waters in deserts. And when frustration comes, failure comes, despair comes, they are angry with life, not angry with themselves.

What can life do? It is available, but somehow you manage to search in the wrong direction. Perhaps you are afraid, deep down, that life may be too much, love may be too much, existence may drown you.

And in a way, your fear is right: the closer you come to reality, the less you will be. The moment you encounter reality face to face, you will not be at all.

I have said many times that nobody has seen God – neither Moses nor Jesus nor Krishna. And naturally, people have misunderstood me. Whenever I have said that nobody has seen God, I was not saying there is no God; I was simply saying the moment you come close enough to God to see, you are no more. Who is going to see God? As long as you are – to see, to feel, to say, to question, to inquire – God is not.

And God is another name of reality. It is not a person, it is only a quality, a fragrance, a sweetness, a music.

One day will come when you will be in the state of hallelujah but you will not be able to say the word, because the word will fall short of the experience.

Osho,

In these five years of relationship with you, I have never felt things going as fast as now! When I finish writing a letter or a question to you, I immediately keep it, feeling it to be ridiculous.

Sometimes I accept the challenge and deliver it, and then I feel as if I have an idiotic face: worry, repentance, shyness...I feel that it is not worth coming to you being "dressed up" with intelligence, humbleness, meditativeness, or whatsoever I could dress in to show to you. In spite of all my efforts, I still have the feeling of dressing up, of using a kind of mask.

Please tell me, master, how to be totally sincere to you and "undressed"?

The problem is not only of one person; everybody is dressed up. Everybody is showing his best side to the world. The heart may be full of tears, but people are smiling.

This is how we have been brought up by a hypocritical society. We are children of a hypocritical society. Rather than teaching every child to be just himself – sincere, honest, naked – we are helping every child to be exactly the opposite.

Just two days ago, one of my old friends came to see me. He has a son who is thought by everybody to be crazy, insane – except by me. So the first thing I inquired about was his son, and he said, "Leave that subject. It makes me so sad, because now he is eighteen years old and he still goes naked all over the town. He is such a shame to the family."

I said, "In what way is he hurting anybody? He is not violent. He simply enjoys being naked."

They force clothes on him, and he throws them away on the street and goes towards the market. And they are running after him – "Please, at least take the underwear."

And he says, "No underwear. The breeze is so cool."

And the boy is very intelligent. Of course, he is in a crowd which cannot accept him. He never lies; he is always utterly honest. Whatever he does, he does with totality. He has never gone to school because he asks those who have gone what they have gained. His father is a post-graduate; he asks him, "What have you gained? Just a certificate." He says, "I want to live my life. I don't want to be dictated to by anybody, wrong or right. I simply want to be myself."

He is a hard worker. He will be working in the garden, and you can see how hard he works, but he works at only what he feels like working at. He plays beautiful flute, but the whole town thinks that he is mad.

And I have tried my best to find where his madness is. I have not been able to find his madness anywhere. He is just not willing to be part of the mob psychology. The crowd cannot accept that he is sane, because if he is sane, then what about the whole crowd?

Even his parents, my friend his father, cannot accept him. He said, "Except for you, nobody accepts that he is sane."

I said, "You are his father, you love him. Have you seen any madness in him?"

He said, "What more do you want? You want more madness? – going naked in the streets. And he is now eighteen years old, and he will approach a woman and he will say 'You are so beautiful. Can I kiss you?'"

Naturally, the society cannot accept such a person – although he is absolutely honest. And he has honored the woman, he has praised her beauty, he has asked her permission. Otherwise he is very strong – living naked, doing hard work, never going to school; he is really strong – he could have kissed any woman without any permission.

But a crowd gathers, and the woman starts shouting that he is being nasty to her, misbehaving with her.

Many times when I was there, I had to go inside the crowd and tell them, "You are making unnecessary fuss. The boy is alone, that's true, but he is not insane. He is a minority of one, and you are the majority of many – but just because you are many, do you think you are right?"

Nobody has been ever able to point out to me that something is wrong with him. And he is being dragged to this doctor and to that doctor.

And he says, "What is wrong with me? I am not sick. The doctor cannot make any difference to me."

The truth is, the doctor is sick. The doctor is not honest.

The boy is very intelligent in seeing things. He has a strange clarity. He says, "I have been watching this doctor" – because the doctor lives just in front of his house; his dispensary is there – "and seeing that poor people get well quickly, and rich people linger on for months. And I am sitting there outside and enjoying the whole scene – what kind of society is this? The poor man gets well because the doctor wants to get rid of him; you cannot get much money out of him. Instead the poor man starts asking, 'Give me some money; I will return later on for the medicine. You are suggesting fruits and milk, but you will have to give me some money.'

"But the rich man, once he falls sick, is kept sick; he is sent to this expert for x-rays, to that expert for something else. It seems to be almost a conspiracy of experts exploiting the rich sick man."

I asked him how the boy was doing. He said, "Because of him, I feel so ashamed to go out of the house. And I always wanted you to help me, but you think he is right and we are wrong. You want me also to go naked? – so I cannot raise the question, 'What should be done with him?'"

I said, "He needs nothing to be done, he is no harm to anybody. Give him work; he is always ready to work, he enjoys working. But he is not ready to have a mask. He is not ready to be continuously an actor, dressed up."

But the whole society that we have created is almost a drama. Here, everybody is repeating dialogues from books, from films, from stories. Nobody is opening his own heart.

I can understand your problem. You are afraid to ask authentic questions because they will expose you.

People ask questions which make them feel very knowledgeable. They want to ask questions not to get the answer, but just to show their knowledge. Whenever you ask a knowledgeable question, you don't feel guilty, you feel great.

But I am a crazy person. I never answer those questions which come out of your knowledge. I simply throw them away.

I only answer questions which open up your wounds, because once your wounds are open there is a possibility of healing. Once you expose yourself, you are on the way to transformation.

Once you are sincere in asking a question, you will listen to the answer because it is your need, it is your food. Your question was your thirst, and the answer can quench it.

So, always remember, this is not a philosophical association, not a theosophical society where everybody is trying to prove that he knows more than you know. This is a place of transformation, of going through a revolution. And unless you show your real face, it is impossible to make any changes in your life, any transformations in your consciousness.

At the most, I can paint your mask, but I cannot change your real face by painting the mask. The mask has to be put aside. Hence, love and trust are needed – that you can be utterly nude, without any fear.

You are not going to be condemned here. You will be accepted as you are, and we will begin from that acceptance to reach for a higher stage, for growth. But that growth is not a condemnation of your present state. That growth is based on your present state of being; it has to be accepted.

But the religions of the world have really poisoned people's minds. Nobody is ready to open up and show who he is, because for centuries things have been condemned, you have to hide them. Nobody wants to be condemned. And there are things which have been praised, so you have to show them – whether you have them or not does not matter.

It is very human and very natural; you want to be loved and to be accepted.

And the society has made the rules of the game, that these are the things to be condemned, so if you have those things hide them, repress them so deeply that even you become unaware of them. And if you don't have those things which society praises, honors, then pretend, and pretend so cleverly that it seems almost real.

Sometimes it is possible that the pretender may look more real than the real person, because the real person never goes through rehearsals. The pretender practices, disciplines himself.

I have always liked a beautiful incident in the life of Charlie Chaplin. It was his birthday, perhaps the fiftieth birthday, and all his fans and friends wanted to celebrate it in a special way. And they found a special way: all over England, in every place, there were competitions, and people were invited to play the part of Charlie Chaplin. And in those competitions there were selections, and then there were other competitions from district to district. Then the semi-finals were in London and there was a final decision about who would get the first prize.

Just to give his friends a great surprise, Charlie Chaplin himself entered into the competition from a nearby district. He came to the semi-finals, but rather than surprising his friends he was surprised himself: he got second prize. Somebody played his act better than him; he had never thought about the possibility. But it happened because the other person was practicing it, rehearsing it, and Charlie Chaplin simply appeared as he was. There was no need for him to rehearse – he *was* Charlie Chaplin. But getting the second prize...

And when people came to know that he had got the second prize, he was so ashamed of himself. He said, "I have been such an idiot to enter into it in the first place. I entered because I thought that I was going to be the first, without question."

So you have the possibility of pretenders posing qualities, values, characters, which are not real. Inside they are just the opposite kind of people. Criminals become saints – it is easy; you just have to practice certain values, certain disciplines which are expected from a saint. Who cares that you are carrying a thousand and one criminal tendencies within you? People only see your face; nobody dives deep into you.

So the whole society has become a very strange phenomenon, almost weird, and everybody is suffering. The person who is pretending to be a saint cannot enjoy it because his whole being is against it, his whole nature is against it. He is continuously fighting a battle with himself, and there is no greater misery than to be continuously in a fight with yourself. So those who are honored, respected citizens – you will never see them joyful, cheerful, rejoicing. They are always sad, and to hide the fact of sadness they call it seriousness: that they take life very seriously.

And the other part of humanity, which has decided to go with its natural feelings, is condemned; they become criminals. In the eyes of the religions they are sinners; they will fill the space in hell reserved for them. In life nobody will respect them, and after life also. Even their God is not capable of accepting his own creation.

If anybody is responsible, God is responsible. Only one person is responsible for all the sinners. There is no need to send everybody into hell – just throw God into hell and that will do, because he is the sole cause.

And these hypocrites, these phony people who are showing something but are not what they are showing, can they also cheat existence? Can they also cheat God? Here they are respectable, but will they also be in paradise after life, enjoying all the pleasures? We have put such tremendous pressure on poor human beings to destroy their integrity, to create a split in them.

My approach is totally different.

First, I want you to accept yourself as you are. That's how existence wanted you to be. You have not created yourself; naturally the whole responsibility goes to existence. And there must be a need for a person like you; otherwise, you would not exist. Existence needs you as you are.

The first principle of an authentic religious man is to accept himself as he is, without any judgment – and only from there does your authentic pilgrimage begin.

Ask me questions without any fear, because I have never condemned anybody. My whole love and respect is for the person who accepts himself totally, as he is. He has courage. He has courage to face the whole pressure of the society which is bent upon splitting him into divisions – into good and bad, into saint and sinner. He is really a brave, courageous being who stands against the whole history of man, of morality, and declares to the skies his reality, whatever it is.

And at least with the master, the disciple has to be absolutely clean and clear so the master can start working with your reality, not with your phoniness – because everything done with your phoniness is a sheer wastage.

Only the real you is capable of growing, of coming to a flowering.

Osho,

I always want a total change in my life because I feel so discontented, so limited, so frustrated.

When I heard you saying, "Come closer," it touched my heart deeply. I saw that I am always managing my life reasonably and out of my mind, that I live a life full of lies and go on postponing being really alive.

I decided to stay here with you longer than I intended to, in spite of all reasons and problems that may come. But I don't feel at ease, and I don't know if it is not again something coming from my mind. Will you please say something about the miracle of transformation and how to live more out of the heart?

The first thing to remember is, never ask for the impossible. Begin slowly, bit by bit, step by step.

Just by walking step by step, you can cover ten thousand miles easily. But if you start thinking from the very beginning that "I want to cross ten thousand miles," your legs may start wavering, your heart may start feeling tremendously afraid.

Your mind will say, "You are asking too much; it is unreasonable." You are a small human being. Ten thousand miles...just walking one step each time – because nobody can walk two steps at one time. Ten thousand miles looks too big. Make small goals.

You are asking for total change. You don't see the impossibility of it at this point. At some other point it will not be impossible, but at this point it will be impossible to ask for a total change, because there will be so many implications in it.

Why not go a little slowly? Why not take one part of your being and clean it? Put your total energy into cleaning one part of your being, then move to the second part. And of course, finally you will be able to have a total change.

But mind is very cunning: whatever it wants to avoid, from the very beginning it creates such a situation – it asks for the impossible. So you remain where you are, more frustrated, more in despair because the total change is not happening. The mind has given you a goal and deceived you. Total change certainly *is* the goal, but don't try to have it in a single step. Go in a more human way, changing small parts.

I used to live with a man for many years. He was a rich man, and he loved me very much. I had a bungalow in the university but he wouldn't allow me to live there. He had a beautiful mansion in the city. He said, "If you want, you can have the whole mansion. I will move to another house." He had many houses.

I said, "No, there is no need. What will I do? I need only one room. You can live and take care of the whole mansion and the garden and my room, because I am a lazy man. This big mansion...who is going to clean it?"

In my university days I used to keep my bed just near the door and all my books around my bed, so I didn't have to enter into the room, because there was such thick dust gathering. For two years I had never entered – why unnecessarily disturb settled things? So from the door I would directly jump into my bed, and all my books were around my bed so I could find them. This was a perfect arrangement: neither did the dust disturb me nor did I disturb the dust.

So I told him, "I don't need the whole mansion. Just one room is enough for me."

So he lived with me. He was very rich but very miserly. Perhaps the word *miserly* is not enough to describe it. He used to go for a walk in the morning with me, and anything he would find by the side of the road here and there, he would grab it.

I said, "What will you do with it? – just a handle of a bicycle; somebody had thrown it away.

He said, "You don't know. Just come with me, I will show you."

So I went into his house, in his part of the mansion, and he showed me. And I was really amazed! He said, "All these parts of the cycle I have found on the street. Just a few things are missing...and I hope I have enough life left; I have not yet found a chain. Two wheels are there, the seat is there, today I have found the handlebars. Mud guards are not necessary, just a chain. And I am not asking for too much. What do you think I go walking with you for?"

I said, "I never thought that you were going in search of a chain."

He said, "A chain, or anything..."

His house was full of strange things...just one shoe. I said, "Where is the other?"

He said, "Some day I will find it, because the other one must be somewhere."

And he himself was so clever that he would go to the temple

and he would put one shoe in one corner, the other shoe in another corner so nobody could steal them – because who will steal one shoe? And in a crowd of shoes who is going to search for the other? Where is the other? – because a thief is in a hurry.

He said, "I am perhaps the only person who, when he is worshipping never looks back. Otherwise, everybody is looking back: what is happening to the shoes? Their worship is false! Are they bowing down to God or to their shoes? I am the only person who does not look back at all. I have figured it out that this way nobody can and nobody has ever been able... And I go every day to the temple because I am looking for the other shoe. This shoe...the other must be somewhere."

And there were many things that he had found; people had thrown them and he would collect them. But when I saw his bicycle, I was really amazed that he had managed, *almost* managed; just a chain was missing. That could even be purchased. But he was such a miser, he was not going to purchase it; he was waiting.

He said, "Just as you say...trust! I trust that the chain will be found one day."

Jabalpur had the largest number of cycles in India. So he said, "This is the place where it is impossible to miss a chain. I will find it." And one day he found it.

In the middle of the night he woke me. I said, "What is the matter? Has something gone wrong?"

He said, "No, I have found the chain."

"In the middle of the night? Where have you been?"

He said, "I was just not feeling sleepy, so I thought why not have a look for the chain around the park? And it is a miracle – I found it. Perhaps that's why I was not feeling sleepy. Now I can sleep with ease. One tension was always there on my mind, that death might come before the chain comes."

And I saw him within three days sitting on the bicycle without mud guards, without any carrier, going to his shop. I said, "I have been telling people to trust – but it seems that trust works! You have proved me right."

And he said, "One more thing is good about this: there are no brakes on it. And it makes so much noise that you can hear it from almost half a mile away. So when I am coming home my wife knows that I am coming, so she starts preparing things for me. By the time I reach the house everything is ready; no need for wasting time in waiting. And nobody else can sit on my bicycle."

I said, "Why?"

He said, "Its seat is such – it hurts so much. So there is no question of its ever being stolen. I leave it anywhere, and I go and do my work and I always find it in its place. People have tried – I have come to know that people have tried to steal it – but they come back and put it in its place, because it is unnecessary trouble. First, it makes so much noise that everybody will know who has stolen it. Secondly, it hurts so much, and thirdly, it has no brakes, so any time, any accident..."

I said, "But how do *you* manage?"

He said, "There is no problem. Just in front of my shop there is a big mango tree. I just go there; it needs a tree to stop."

And in the mansion where I was living with him there were very big trees, ancient trees all around, so there was no question, no need. He said, "There is no need – I go to my shop, there is a tree; I go to my home, there is a tree. Unless you have a very ancient tree, you cannot have my bicycle."

Just go slowly, part by part, and trust. Total change will also happen, but don't ask too much from the very beginning. Always be alert that mind is cunning and gives you impossible goals, so you go on running after them.

Nothing is impossible if you go slowly, if you make many stopovers and you are not in a hurry. Whether the total change happens or not is not important. Even small changes in life are precious, because the total change will be simply the accumulated effect of all the small changes. Total change is not one whole; it is simply the effect of all the small changes, the accumulated revolution that happens in you.

So always remain human.

The past of man has been concentrated on giving you goals which are impossible. That is just to make you humiliated, because you cannot fulfill them – you feel too tiny, too small, too fragile, with so many weaknesses.

I don't want you to think about impossible things. I want you to go very slowly, changing small parts of your life – which is not difficult. One day, you will suddenly find that total change has happened.

Osho,

I used to be so scared of being hit or exposed. Since I have been here with you and melting into you, I'm longing for it with an unknown impatience. I long to get the obstacles out of the way, to be over and done with 'this one' so that I can move on the journey to the next rock on my path. Fear seems to be just a quite unimportant, old habit.

I am experiencing you as a boundless invitation. No barriers are there which I can use to rationalize a lack of courage. I feel thankful about the lack of organization around you; there is no more fear that getting a hit from you may be used by people who are in power to feed their own judgments, to put me down or to make me feel guilty.

Osho,

I am so tired of me and me and me.

Is this a healthy or unhealthy impatience?

It is the case with most of the sannyasins: if they get a hit they feel bad about it, their ego feels hurt. Rather than understanding the hit, they become resentful, angry.

If they are not hit, then they start feeling that I am not taking care of them, that I am not paying attention to them, that while others are being hit, they are being left out. They feel as if they are not important enough.

This is how the human mind creates misery out of every situation. If you get the hit, you are hurt; if you don't get the hit, you are hurt all the same.

But as far as I am concerned, I am not interested in hitting you or hurting you or ignoring anybody. To me, all are equally important.

The same longing has brought them to me, the same thirst has brought them to me.

It will be very kind of you all to leave it to me that whenever a hit is necessary you will get it – because a hit is medicinal, it is a kind of surgery. But don't feel that because surgery is not being done on you, you are being ignored. If somebody else is hospitalized and nobody is taking care of you... No, whenever you need to be hospitalized you will be hospitalized, each according to his need.

Whenever a hit is necessary to help your growth, you will not miss it. And whenever it is not necessary, then unnecessarily hitting you will only make your skull thick. Then when the time comes to hit you, you will have already been so disciplined in getting hits...

In my high school days, I was almost always late because I was interested in so many things on the way. I always started from home to reach the school at the right time, but I never reached because so much was going on along the way – some magician was doing his tricks, and it was irresistible. Just to leave that magician and go to study – some stupid teacher talking about geography...

So I was punished continually, but soon my teachers realized that it was useless to punish me. Their first punishment was to tell me to go around the high school building seven times. I would ask, "If I go eleven times will it do?"

They would say, "Are you mad? This is a punishment."

I said, "I know this is a punishment, but I have missed my morning exercise. So if I make it my morning exercise, you are not losing anything. Your punishment is covered, my morning exercise is complete; nobody is losing anything, both are gaining."

So they stopped that, because this wouldn't do. They would tell me to stand outside the class. I said, "That's good, because I love the open air. The class is dark and dirty, and outside it is so beautiful. And in fact, sitting inside I am always looking outside. Who cares what you are teaching? The birds are singing, the trees are blossoming – it is so beautiful outside."

The headmaster would come on his round, and every day he would find me standing outside. And he would say, "What is the matter?"

I said, "Nothing is the matter. I love to stand outside; it is healthier, hygienic. And you can see how beautiful it is."

But he said, "I will see your teacher. How is it that he allows you to stand outside?"

I said, "I don't know, but he tells me himself, every day, 'Stand outside.' So now I don't even ask him. It has become a routine, so I simply come and stand here."

He asked the teacher. The teacher said, "It must have been thirty days ago! I told him only once to stand outside – since then he has not entered the class. I was thinking it was a punishment, and he is enjoying it. Not only that, he is spreading the rumor among the students that it is hygienic, it is healthy. And they are asking me, 'Sir, can we also stand outside?' Then what am I to do here? Then I will also go and stand outside."

It is a question of how you take things. So first, don't be worried. If you are not getting a hit, perhaps you don't need it, or perhaps it is not the right time. Or if you are getting the hit then don't feel hurt, because I am not hitting *you*, I am always hitting your ego – something that is your disease, something that has to be dropped.

But leave it to me. I will not follow your expectations that because you want a hit – the *biggest* hit, so you can show everybody, "Look, I have got the biggest hit"... Then the ego has used the hit. Rather than destroying the ego, the ego has taken the hit as nourishment.

So leave it completely to me. It is none of your business. Whenever I feel that you need a hit, you will get it – and you will get it in the right quantity that you need. Don't brag about it, and don't feel sorry for it; just try to understand it.

This is a school of understanding.

Osho,

Twenty-five years to get to you, three years to hang around you, four years to run away from you in a roller-coaster relationship. Four years to stagger back towards you, eleven years to get a question through to you – and you give the answer to this German fellow, Gunakar, and want to send me back to hell and some difficult woman. And in twenty-eight years' time, maybe you have escaped when I crawl back to ask you, "What's next?"

Osho, do you want to kill me or something?

Gunateet, you are right. The question was yours – at least written by you – but Gunakar needed the answer more. So there has not been any misunderstanding.

He was also surprised, because he had not asked the question. But it was his question. And he could not believe how somebody else had written exactly the question that he was going to ask. And it was not time for you, for that question. Perhaps you got the vibration of the German Gunakar, and wrote down the question; it was not *your* question.

And I can understand your difficulty: it took eleven years for you to ask the question and now you are worried that I am sending you back to your old life and the hard woman. About that you are wrong. Once you get a woman, it is always hard. If you miss a woman, it is just ice cream. Once you get a woman, suddenly she is steel hard.

But without women there would have been no enlightenment in this world. Just think – a world without women. Then you cannot find any Gautam Buddha, because there is nobody to run away from. If there is no woman, there is no problem. Women are the real incentive. They say that behind every great man there is a woman; it may be true, it may not be true. But behind every *enlightened* man there are *many* women – one won't do.

Enlightenment is a little difficult subject. When many women go on making a football of you, then at last you become enlightened. You will say, "Enough! Stop the game, I am going home."

Women are a blessing in the world. Without them, there is nothing. So just be thankful to your hard woman; perhaps you are here because of her.

And you are saying that next time you come it will be in twenty-eight years, and you will ask, "What next?"

I am reminded of two stories...

Mulla Nasruddin was on Chowpatty Beach with his wife, and suddenly he said, "Would you like *bhelpuri* once more?"

The wife said, "Once more? But we have not had any *bhelpuri*."

He said, "Beloved, it seems you are losing your memory. Just fifty years ago when we got married and we had come here for the first time, we had *bhelpuri*. That's why I am saying, 'Would you like it once more?'"

Going back to your life, to your wife, to your work...but you will not be the same man. You will be taking something of me with you. I may not have answered you, but you have felt me. Answers and questions are superficial. You have tasted my love, my presence. So if by chance, after twenty-eight years, we meet again I will ask, "Do you want it once more?"

Most probably, you will not need to ask me again because the seed is sown. You know exactly what has to be done: you have to slip your energies from the mind towards the heart. Those energies falling towards the heart are just like rain falling, and the seed will start sprouting.

Perhaps after twenty-eight years, if existence allows it, it will not be you who asks what is next. I will ask you what is next. You will have come to flowering. You will have come just to show your gratitude.

It is good that you are not German. The German soil is a little hard. It has its negative points and its positive points, its pros and cons. It is hard, it is very difficult for the seed to settle in it – but once a seed settles in it, then it is very hard not to grow.

Your question was a mind question, and Gunakar needed it. You don't need it. You have a soft heart. And the seed is already in your heart, and you know it is growing.

It is almost like a pregnant woman: when the child starts growing she knows that the child is growing. An experienced mother of two or three children even knows whether the child is a boy or a girl – because the boy starts kicking, and the girl remains very centered, calm and quiet. Boys are, after all, boys. From the very beginning, they are trouble.

An experienced mother can say after the third or fourth month whether the child will be a boy or a girl, because the boy is doing all kinds of gymnastics, and the girl is simply sitting silently, waiting for her own chance. Later on, she will do the gymnastics and the boy will sit and read the newspaper. Everybody has his own chance.

The second story I was going to tell you is about a very rich American, a billionaire. He becomes fed up with money, fed up with all kinds of luxuries, fed up with all pleasures. And naturally he starts searching – is there something more, or is this all? Because if this is all then there is no point anymore for him to live; he has had enough of it. It is a question of life and death.

And he moves, and goes from one master to another: some Tibetan lamas, some Sufi mystic, some Zen master. And then he comes to India and meets many saints. They all say, "There is one very wise old man in the Himalayas; only he can help you."

So he travels to the Himalayas, then by foot carries his luggage. He has never carried luggage in his life. He has never walked uphill in the mountains. It is too cold, but somehow he manages. Tired, he falls at the feet of the old man, who looks very ancient, and he says, "I have found you after all! I want to know what is the meaning of life?"

The old man said, "First things first. Have you got a Havana cigar?"

The man said, "What kind of question...Havana cigar? Yes, I have got one. In fact, I am a chain smoker, and I have been keeping one in case you make me enlightened. Before enlightenment, the last Havana cigar... I would like just a few minutes more to enjoy it, and then make me enlightened and do whatsoever you want. After enlightenment, I was thinking Havana cigars would not be allowed, because I have not seen Buddha smoking, or..."

He said, "Forget all about those old fellows. Bring the Havana cigar." And the old man started smoking.

The tired American watched, and said, "But what about my question?"

He said, "The time is not right. You go back. Come again after a few years."

The man said, "This is strange. Any message?"

He said, "When you come, bring as many Havana cigars as you can because once you are enlightened we will both be smoking. On this hill there is nothing else to do. Just go fast and come back – but bring them. I am sending you especially for Havana cigars. Enlightenment is a very simple thing, but to get Havana cigars in the Himalayas is very difficult."

Don't be worried – I am not a smoker! You need not bring any Havana cigars, just come. Don't wait for twenty-eight years. Whenever you feel the flower has opened its petals in you, come back.

I would just like to see you luminous, radiant, ecstatic. And I say it is possible because you have a heart, Gunateet, that is ripe to grow any moment. No hard woman can prevent it; she can only help it.

So just go back, and whenever the spring comes and the flower is there, come back so I can see that the flower has lived to its potentiality and you have become fragrant.

And meanwhile, you can smoke as many Havana cigars as you want.

5 Questions: Exposing Your Way from Ignorance to Innocence

Osho,
The first time I met you, I said no to your question as to whether I had a question, and in all these eight years I have never asked any.
Now my mind seems to be exploding with questions, out of which it is hard to choose any satisfying to a German perfectionist; yet I feel almost in panic – I don't want to miss that chance.
Osho, why is there that constant fear of missing the train?

There are people who really do not have questions. They have a quest, but not questions. They have a thirst, a deep hunger for being and more being, but no desire for gathering and accumulating knowledge. Hence they don't have any questions.

They are the best kind of disciples.

There are other people who do not ask questions, but that does not mean that they don't have questions. They do not ask because asking a question goes against their ego. And if the ego is German, then the problem becomes more difficult.

It is not coincidental that Germany has produced great philosophers, philosophers who are ready to give answers to every question. But Germany has not produced sincere inquirers, seekers, who are thirsty for the answer. It has not created disciples; it creates only masters, and these masters are only great intellectuals, not mystics.

Germany has contributed much as far as knowledge is concerned – Hegel, Kant, Feuerbach, Karl Marx – but it has not contributed a single mystic. In the whole of history, not a single Kabir, not a single Nanak, not a single Farid – very strange, but it is not coincidental.

The German ego is ready to give the answer, whether it knows or not; but it is very reluctant to ask the question, whether it has the question or not. The same is your situation. For eight years you have been repressing, perhaps unconsciously, and there is a limit to everything. You can repress only so much, and then a point comes when you are sitting on a volcano. Now your mind is exploding with questions. From where have they come? For eight years they were not there, and suddenly out of nowhere they are almost creating in you a state of insanity – so many questions that you cannot even find which one is worthy to be asked.

You will have to look backwards. Those eight years that you kept them repressed are your responsibility. If you had allowed them to come, in those eight years you might have been completely cleansed of all questions; you might have become a tabula rasa, an innocent child.

But because to ask is to show one's ignorance, you went on repressing. And there is always a hope: somebody else here may ask it, so why expose yourself?

But remember, each person's question has a personality of its own. Even though the words may be the same, the language exactly the same, the phrasing of the question not a bit different, but because the questioner is different, it makes such a difference that it is almost unbridgeable. Each person has grown in a different way, has lived a different life, has passed through different ups and downs. You cannot find another person who has gone through the same experiences. Hence, the question may appear to be the same, but it cannot be the same.

So never wait, thinking that somebody is bound to ask the question and save you the trouble of exposing yourself as ignorant, so you can remain silent, looking wise. Just not asking the question does not mean that you know. It only means that you are not courageous enough, it only means that you are afraid to show your darker side. But unless you show your disease, unless you say something about it, the physician cannot do anything.

I had a professor friend. He was a great scholar of ancient Sanskrit. Not only was he a scholar of ancient Sanskrit, his mind was also very old and rotten.

He was feeling sick, and as I was coming out of my classroom he told me, "I am feeling very weak and very sick. I don't know what the problem is, but you have to give me a lift and take me to the nearby doctor." So I took him to a friend who was one of the best doctors near the university campus.

Now, in ancient Indian medicine the patient does not say anything to the physician; that is thought to be insulting. The physician takes the wrist of the patient, checks his pulse; that's all. And he decides what the disease is and he decides what the medicine is going to be. And the Indian medicine, Ayurveda, has been very proud about it.

So this ancient Sanskrit scholar would not say to the doctor what the problem was. He said, "You are a doctor, you have studied in England, you have got the best education; you have to find out what my disease is."

The doctor said, "This is strange. I am not a doctor of animals; I am a doctor of human beings. Of course as far as animals are concerned they cannot say what the problem is, so the vet has to find out, to figure out what the donkey is suffering from

And sometimes things go very wrong. I remember one case. One of my neighbors in my village had a donkey, a very good donkey.

And suddenly there was some epidemic among donkeys and many donkeys in the town died. The veterinary hospital and its doctors were at a loss what to do because the donkeys could not say what was happening. And they were unable to find out. The disease seemed to be something very new.

My friend was very much afraid for his donkey. He said, "Before anything happens, I want to take all precautions."

So we both took his donkey – because I used to sit on his donkey; he was the best in the town – to the doctor. And the doctor said, "He is not sick at all."

We said, "We know and he knows too, because he was not willing to come this way; we have brought him forcibly. But we want to take precautions. Other donkeys are dying, and this is such a beautiful fellow. So if you can just help; as a precaution give him some medicine so that he is not affected by the epidemic."

He gave us some solution, and also a small bamboo pipe, and he told the man whose donkey it was, "You have to put this medicine in your mouth."

The man said, "What are you saying – a donkey's medicine? Why should I put it in *my* mouth?"

The vet said, "This is the way it has to be given to the donkey, because the donkey will create a thousand and one troubles. Put the other end of the pipe in the donkey's mouth and blow the medicine into his mouth."

He said, "Strange way..."

But the vet said, "You don't know how to deal with animals."

But an accident happened. When he was about to give the medicine, the donkey did such a great job. He blew such a forceful breath from his mouth that the man drank all the medicine! And he said, "Now what is going to happen? This was a freak accident, and this idiot...at the right time, just as I was going to give the medicine; he managed to force it into my body. Now let us go back to the doctor. It may have some bad effects on me – it was a precaution for the donkey, not a precaution for me."

I said, "Now I cannot go, you can go."

This Sanskrit scholar wanted to be told by the doctor what was wrong just by having his pulse checked.

The doctor said, "I know that in Ayurveda, this has been the ancient method, but at that time there were no other instruments. At that time people were not so intelligent and aware and sensitive to their own bodies, feelings. They were coming almost from the world of animals. When Ayurveda was born, human beings were just emerging out of the animal kingdom; that's why feeling the pulse was the only way."

But the scholar was not satisfied. He said, "The reality is that you are not so proficient in the subtle vibrations of the pulse rate. You are not ready to acknowledge your ignorance."

I said to him, "You have not come here to discuss whether Ayurveda is a better medical system than modern medicine. You have come here for your own sickness. Don't waste my time, and don't waste the time of the doctor – he is not ignorant. No modern medical practitioner is going to tell you your disease; man has come of age you have to tell him."

You can sit here silently for eight years without asking a question, just hiding yourself behind silence – which is not true silence, because inside the questions are boiling. But the German mind is not ready to accept easily that it is ignorant.

It is good that you are now ready – because your mind is exploring its questions – that you are not afraid you will be understood as ignorant. Nobody is going to understand you as ignorant. Ignorance is our natural state, there is nothing wrong with it. Just as everybody is naked behind clothes – however thick your clothes are, however many layers of clothes you have, your nakedness is still there. There is nothing in it to be ashamed of.

Naked we are born; ignorant we are born.

And it will be helpful to recognize the fact of ignorance sooner, so that you will not die ignorant. Ignorant we are born, but if we can die innocent, life has been a successful journey. And the only way to be innocent is to get rid of all your questions.

Don't hide anything, because whatever you are hiding will come up sooner or later, will surface. It is better to bring it out yourself into the open, into the light.

And the function of a master is not to give you an answer, but to destroy your question. Nobody can give you the answer. The answer will arise in you, will grow in you. It will be your growth, your enlightenment. It cannot be given from outside.

But questions can be destroyed. So it is good that you have started, even though you have wasted eight years unnecessarily. And that's why your mind is continuously worried and scared of only one thing: am I going to miss the train this time? Eight years you have been missing, every day, every moment. But there are a few people who are very expert in missing trains.

I have heard that three persons, all professors of a university, are standing on a platform. The train is getting ready to leave – two have come to see one off – and they are involved in deep discussion.

Suddenly, the conductor shows the flag and the train starts, and they are so absorbed that they don't notice. They notice only when the train has almost left the platform. So they all three run to catch it – two succeed, and one fails. And the one who fails starts laughing.

A crowd gathers; they say, "What is the matter?"

But he is laughing so much, a belly laughter, that he cannot contain himself.

He says, "Just wait a minute... I have missed the train."

They say, "But missing a train does not mean that you have to laugh."

He said, "You don't know the whole story – just wait: the two who have caught the train came to see me off! But in a hurry..."

There are people who are always missing. Missing becomes the habit for their whole life.

Each moment – you have to be alert not to miss it. But you are not there, you are somewhere else. Naturally you go on missing. You will think of this moment when it has gone. You will say, "My God, I missed that opportunity."

Henry Ford was asked by a journalist, "What is the secret of your success?" – because he was a poor man, born poor, and became the richest man in the world.

Ford said, "My secret is simple, it is an open secret, I never miss an opportunity."

But the journalist said, "It still remains a mystery. Nobody wants to miss an opportunity, but people go on missing. So tell me just in a little detail how you manage – because people become aware of an opportunity only when it has gone, but by that time it is too late."

Henry Ford said, "The way not to miss an opportunity is just to keep jumping. So whenever it comes, it doesn't matter, you will jump and ride on it. Don't stand and wait; otherwise you will get engaged in other thoughts and other things.

"I keep on jumping. Let the opportunity come whenever it comes – I am not going to miss it."

In a London museum there is a beautiful painting titled *Opportunity*. A very strange painting... When for the first time, a century ago, it was acquired by the museum, the painter himself was alive and he was present there for the opening ceremony. The museum had asked him to be there to explain it to people – because it is a beautiful painting but a little difficult, a little strange.

There is the face of a man, but you have never come across such a face: all the hairs are growing not on the head but on the forehead, and the head is clean-shaven. And the title is *Opportunity*.

"What kind of man...? Where have you found this man?"

He said, "This is the opportunity. When it comes you cannot see it, because the face is covered with hair. When it is just passing by, you cannot see it because the face is covered and by the time you recognize it and say, 'Jesus!' your hand slips because the head is clean-shaven. It has gone. And no moment comes back; once gone, it is gone forever."

You are afraid of missing the train. Whether you are afraid or not, everybody is missing the train. It is good that you are afraid, because that may help you to understand why you are missing.

You are not in the moment. You are either in the past or in the future – both are non-existent. Neither can you do anything with the past, nor can you do anything with the future. All that you can do is with the present, and the present is such a small, split second that if you are engaged somewhere else, it simply slips by and you have missed the train.

Learn to be in the present. Withdraw your energy from the past. Don't waste your time in memories; what is gone is gone – say good-bye to it and close the chapter. What has not come yet has not come yet; don't unnecessarily waste your time and energy in imagination, because no imagination is ever fulfilled. It is because of this that the proverb exists in every language: "Man proposes, and God disposes" – because you imagine a certain thing in the future, and it is never so.

Withdrawing yourself from past and future, you will become a tremendously intense energy, focused in the present, concentrated in the present like an arrow. No train could manage to leave the platform without you. Each moment being aware, alert, watchful, in the herenow, is the way not to miss the train. Every experience needs your presence here – this moment. And this is a simple secret, but it opens the doors of existence, of all the mysteries, of all that is worth knowing, worth tasting, worth feeling, worth being.

Osho,

It is such a joy seeking out a question – it comes word by word and surprises me as it appears on the paper.

Being here with you has been more moment-to-moment and less plan-filled than any other time in my life.

The question is: where do these questions come from? How does seeking them out empty our minds and cleanse our beings?

I love you beyond my understanding. Thank you again and again.

We are born not knowing anything. Questions don't come from outside. As you grow, as you face different situations, as you move into different moments, encountering different circumstances, your ignorance goes on and on becoming questions.

These are the right questions. And if you insist on asking only the right questions, which come out of your ignorance in encountering existence, you will be able to get rid of them without any difficulty.

The problem arises because you have many questions which

are not right questions, which have not arisen out of your ignorance but which have arisen out of your borrowed knowledge. You read something in a book and a question arises; if you had not read the book, the question would have never arisen, you may have lived from eternity to eternity.

For example, I have been around the world, but except for followers of Jainism – who are not many, only three and a half million, and confined only to India – nobody can ask a question that a Jaina can ask. Only a Jaina can ask it, because his scriptures give him the question. The question is not a right question; otherwise, it would arise in every human being if it *was* a natural question.

For example, you may never have wondered what *nigodh* is. Only a Jaina will ask what *nigodh* is. And for Jainism it is a very important question; it is as important as God is to other religions – in fact, it is a replacement for God, because Jainism does not believe in God. Then the question arises: from where does this universe come?

Jainism has a simple, scientific answer to it: the universe does not come from anywhere; it is always here. But because the population goes on growing one problem gets them into trouble: where do these people come from if nobody is creating them?

In Mahavira's time, there were only two million people in India – just in India. Now there are seven hundred million people in India. Where are these people coming from? Where have they been hiding all this time? Who is managing the whole circus – when they should come and not come, why they should come at a particular time and not come at a particular time?

Jainism has to invent a hypothesis. The hypothesis is called *nigodh*; *nigodh* is a dormant state of human souls. Just as you go to sleep and in the morning you wake up, so there are millions of souls who are sleeping for eternity; from those dormant souls a few wake up and start moving into existence. But all such hypotheses are as dubitable as God.

I have asked Jaina monks how many souls are dormant – because there will be one day when *nigodh* is empty, all souls will have awakened. Then the population will remain static, there will be no need for any birth control. Whatever you do, you cannot produce a child. But they don't have any answer. They say, "We don't know. The scriptures say an infinite number of souls."

I said, "This is just befooling people. Who has counted them? Who has the right to say that they are infinite? This can be said only when they have been counted. If they have been counted, they are not infinite. Do you see the simple logic? If you say they have been counted, then they may be many but they cannot be infinite. And if you say they have not been counted, you cannot say they are infinite."

But nobody in the whole world is ever going to ask, "What is *nigodh*?" This is a false question; it is a bookish question. Now, Jainas never ask about God. All over the world, every other religion will ask about God, because they have been told about God from their very childhood. And naturally, curiosity arises: what is God, how does he look?

Strangely enough, different religions have different ideas of God, and nobody bothers that God cannot have so many appearances unless he has many masks. He shows one face to the Christians, another face to the Jews, another face to the Hindus, but why should he take such trouble? And none of these fellows who are talking about God have seen him. But centuries have passed, and people are discussing and inquiring and questioning, and all questions concerned with such things are absolutely futile.

"How many hands does God have?" Now, is this a question that really means anything to you? – whether he has two hands or four hands or one thousand hands. What does it matter to you? But there are people who believe that God has one thousand hands, because to take care of this big world, two hands are not enough. But who says to that one thousand hands will be enough? The world is still big. If two hands are too few, one thousand hands are also too few. And just think of a god who has one thousand hands!

I think two hands can do things in a better way than a person who has one thousand hands. He is bound to get confused. And to carry one thousand hands... The weight of one thousand hands will be too much.

There was one very famous Hindu monk, Swami Shivananda, who became world famous. Seeing him, I dropped the idea of one thousand hands – because he was not able even to carry his two hands. His hands became so fat that he was not able to raise them. Two persons used to raise his hands, then he would be able to move; otherwise those hands were so much of a weight. And nobody even thinks – because he was a medical doctor before he became a mahatma – first, medically he is living a wrong life; otherwise how have these hands become so heavy? Secondly, he is thought to be a great yogi – according to Yoga he is living a wrong life; otherwise how have these hands gone out of proportion? And still he is worshipped as a great saint.

When I saw him, I said to him, "One thing is settled in my mind, that God cannot have one thousand hands. Seeing you...you need two persons to carry you from one place to another place. If you had one thousand hands, it would really be a great trouble." Perhaps trucks would have been needed. "Bring all your transport, Swami Shivananda is going to the bathroom," otherwise how would he go? One hand in one truck...at least one thousand trucks would be needed. And for the transport company it would be a problem: how to manage one thousand trucks around him? There would be a parking problem.

But just hypotheses...and there are thousands of things which have kept human beings engaged in creating questions. And there are always so-called wise people who are ready to answer them. They are the enemies of humanity. Rather than saying that your question is wrong because it has no relevance to your growth, it has no relevance to your own spirituality, that whether God exists or not does not matter, or how many heads he has...

The Hindu god has three heads. No other god in the world has three heads – naturally he is superior. He can look in three dimensions; a three-dimensional god, in all dimensions he is looking. Other gods are one-dimensional.

You cannot cheat a Hindu god, but a Mohammedan god or a Christian god – you can hit him from behind, he cannot see. You cannot hit the Hindu god. Three heads, one thousand hands... If you got caught in his hands, it would take eternity to get out of the jungle.

All useless, fictitious, meaningless things are in the air, and they have been there for centuries. They create many questions in you. So you have to remember one very basic thing: that any question that is not concerned with your individual growth has no meaning, no substance for you. Only then can you sort out those few questions which can be of help.

And then ask them, and expose yourself. Then don't wait a single moment and don't hesitate, don't feel embarrassed. It is your right to ask the question. It is nature demanding that you ask the question, because once the question is solved – or better, *dissolved* – you will feel light; your heaviness will be gone.

The day you don't have any question will be a day of great celebration, because you will be as light as you can conceive. And then existence becomes just a pure dance – no more questions. Existence becomes a trust – no more questions. There are no more tensions in the mind – life becomes a let-go, a tremendous relaxation. You become part of the trees and the mountains and the ocean and the rivers and the stars. You are no longer separate; your questions keep you separate.

Your unquestionable trust in existence allows you to merge into it.

Osho,

Govind Siddharth's enlightenment showed me that I am not connected with enlightenment at all. I cannot imagine how I would feel being enlightened. I realized how far away it is for me, and that I am not really seeking it.

Concerning myself, I have mostly forgotten about the state called enlightenment. I see that I am only longing for it when I am in a state of pain, and feel lost, and don't know any more what to do. But in moments of happiness and fulfillment, enlightenment does not exist at all.

Would you please comment on this?

Lokita, enlightenment is absolutely un-Germanic. I have gone through all the great philosophers of Germany; nobody has any idea of enlightenment.

So you need not be worried. It simply shows you are a pure Nordic German, stuck with another German, Niskriya. One German is enough of a hindrance towards enlightenment, and two Germans together – it is impossible. You both will tug at each other's legs and will not allow anybody to become enlightened!

And the idea of enlightenment has arisen because of Govind Siddharth's enlightenment. It is not your longing or your search. This is what I have been calling *borrowed*. If it is not nature that is desiring something in you, a longing coming out of your very soul, out of your very roots, then don't waste time on it.

That's why when you are in pain, in misery, in anguish, you think of enlightenment and when you are happy and contented and enjoying yourself, you never think about it. In fact, if you are contented, happy and feeling pleasure, and I offer you enlightenment you will refuse it. You will say, "Osho, when I am in pain I will come myself. Don't disturb my happiness at this moment. It is so difficult to be happy with Niskriya, and now you have come with enlightenment..." Remember: anything that comes out of pain and anguish and anxiety is at most an effort to escape from all these painful experiences.

Hearing again and again that enlightenment is blissful, you think that rather than suffering pain it is better to be enlightened. But when you are contented and feeling happy, joyful, no fight with Niskriya...because I know perfectly well that two Germans in one room must be fighting twenty-three hours a day at least. For one hour, naturally, they need rest and contentment. At that time if somebody comes and says, "Come on and this is enlightenment," you will say, "No, not at this time; I have hardly got one hour of peace and you have come to disturb that peace also."

You have to understand one thing: that enlightenment is not an escape from pain but an understanding of pain, an understanding of your anguish, an understanding of your misery – not a cover-up, not a substitute, but a deep insight: "Why am I miserable, why is there so much anxiety, why is there so much anguish, what are the causes in me that are creating it?" And to see those causes clearly is to be free from them. Just an insight into your misery brings a freedom from misery. And what remains is enlightenment.

Enlightenment is not something that comes to you. It is when pain and misery and anguish and anxiety have been understood perfectly well, and they have evaporated because now they have no cause to exist in you... That state is enlightenment. It will bring you, for the first time, real contentment, real blissfulness, authentic ecstasy. And only then can you compare.

What you used to call contentment before was not contentment. What you used to call happiness before was not happiness. But right now you don't have anything to compare it with. Once enlightenment gives you a taste of the real, you will see that all your pleasures, all your happinesses were simply the stuff dreams are made of; they were not real. And what has come now, has come forever.

That is the definition of the real: a contentment that comes and never leaves you again is real contentment. A contentment that comes and goes again is not contentment; it is simply a gap between two miseries. It is like we call a gap between two wars peace time – it is not a peaceful time, it is simply preparation for another war. If the war is a positive war, the time between two wars is a negative war, a cold war. It goes on underground; you are getting ready for a hot war. Anything that comes and goes is a dream. Let that be the definition. Anything that comes and never goes is reality.

Don't be bothered about the word *enlightenment*. What you call it does not matter; you can call it illumination, you can call it blissfulness, you can call it self-realization, you can call it actualization of all your potentials – whatever you want to call it. But remember one quality: that it knows only a beginning; it knows no end. Anything that comes and goes, beware – that is simply illusory, it is only a gap, because one gets tired.

Niskriya also gets tired, and when one is tired one thinks, "Just be loving, be peaceful." So for an hour or two hours there is love, but it does not last long; just a small thing, anything, and the quarrel begins. And every other day you are ready to separate. Just look in one week how many times you decide to separate.

You don't know I have been keeping you together. Niskriya is a very obedient follower. I tell him, "Niskriya, just let things be as they are. One woman is absolutely needed for your enlightenment; just remain..." And the same is true for you: he is needed for your enlightenment.

Separately – because there will be no fight, no anxiety, no pain – you may start thinking that life is perfectly peaceful, what is the need of enlightenment? But it will not be peace; it will be the peace of the graveyard.

I want the peace of the garden, not of the graveyard. The birds should be singing, because their songs deepen the peace. The flowers should be blossoming because their colors, their fragrance make the peace alive: the foliage, the greenery, everything is overflowing with life.

In a graveyard there is also silence and there is peace, because everybody is dead. They are waiting for the last judgment day; then they will come out of their graves and you will see such a quarrel as you have never seen, not imagined. Because lying in their graveyards, they are repressing everything, and when they come out...just skeletons hitting each other!

You will see the scene, the last judgment day. Nobody will bother who is hitting whom, just hitting will be such a joy. So much has been repressed – because somebody has been in the grave for thousands of years. Just think of yourself in a grave for thousands of years – how much anger you must be gathering! It will explode in just one day, in twenty-four hours. More time is not given; perhaps God is afraid to give more time. Because if you give more time, that quarrel will never end, it will continue. So finish it in twenty-four hours.

And in twenty-four hours in that crowd you cannot find your enemy or where your wife is, where your neighbor is. So don't waste time – whoever you meet, hit him hard! Somebody must be hitting your wife, so you hit somebody else's wife; it does not matter, the question is of hitting.

There is a peace in the graveyard. If people live separately... And that's what religions have thought: renounce the world and go into the caves, and there will be peace. It will be the peace of the graveyard, your cave will be your grave, because there is nobody to provoke you, nobody to insult you. Just being alone, what can you do except be silent? But that is not the peace that passeth understanding, that is a deadness, a suicide.

Try to understand your misery. Live it, go to the very depth of it, find out the cause, why it is there. Let understanding be your meditation. And try to understand your contentment also, your happiness also; and you will see their superficiality. Once you know that your happiness is superficial and your anguish is very deep – and it is in your hands – you can change your whole style of consciousness. Your contentment can become your whole being; not even a small space is left for discontentment.

Your love becomes your very life. And it remains. Time passes, but what you have achieved goes on deepening. More and more flowers, more and more songs are born out of it.

That's what we call enlightenment. The word is Eastern, but the experience has nothing to do with East or West.

Osho,

I have a story to tell:

It happened in the early second half of the month of June, 1985, when I was living in Rajneeshpuram.

One morning, soon after I woke, I took a pee in the bathroom, and felt a tidal wave of relaxation descending on me as it sometimes happens in the last stage of your meditation techniques. The relaxation was all over me, and my eyelids closed gently and instantly. I couldn't move or stop this tidal wave feeling.

As my eyes closed, you appeared in all your beauty. Your physical presence was so real and intoxicating – as one sees and feels you in a darshan, sitting in the first row. But in a moment you started disappearing, beginning from all sides of your body, and a deep blackness started taking your place. Soon all that was left was a deep, deep blackness of a kind I have never seen before. It gave a feeling of terror, and lasted for a couple of minutes.

As I came out of this experience I was stunned, dazed, almost drained. I was full of a deep inner pain; I was very shaky and upset, as the meaning that somehow had revealed itself to me was in the impact of the experience. It meant physical death to your body, or at least a death-like calamity.

I tried to force myself to be normal, but couldn't talk to people. When my friend noticed I was disturbed, and asked me the reason, I told her of the incident. I continued to feel that something grave was peeping over the horizon.

In the late afternoon when I was working, suddenly out of nowhere a deep tidal wave of relaxation overpowered me again. My eyes closed and a bright purple color appeared all over in front of me, amidst which you appeared again in your fullest glory, beaming. Beautiful flowers were popping open all around you like bubbles – it was psychedelic! I felt now fully assured that no real harm was going to come to your body. Whatever calamities that came would pass away, and a more-glorious-than-ever phase for you and your people would follow.

In the later months a great calamity did come to your body in the form of your illegal arrest by the power-blinded US government – which was a physical threat to your life. Now, in the light of the first part of my story turning into a reality, it is quite natural for me to feel that the second part of the story has already started turning into a reality, slowly, slowly.

Osho, would you like to comment?

You have related your story with absolutely the right interpretation. It needs no comment. This is a good sign. Slowly, slowly, to other sannyasins also, the same is going to happen. They will come to feel an experience, and they will also be able to interpret it correctly. I can only say you are blessed that your mind has not interfered, has not misled you, and your heart has been in complete control seeing the experience and interpreting it.

Osho,

A glimpse of your eyes, a flash of total love – it happens in a second but stays forever.

Osho, how could this happen?

It is a simple phenomenon. A moment of love is a moment of eternity. The depth of it is so great that time cannot erase it.

Although the happening was in a single moment, it is like a woman becoming pregnant: the happening is in a single moment, but it gives birth to a child who may live seventy, eighty years, who may give birth to many more children. It may become a tree: many branches, and each branch bifurcating into new branches.

I am reminded... If you go to Bodhgaya, where Gautam Buddha became enlightened, the tree under which he was sitting is still there, although it is not the same tree but the continuity of the same tree, a child of the same tree.

When Ashoka was the emperor of India, he sent his daughter Sanghamitra, who had become a sannyasin, to Sri Lanka with a branch of the original tree. Sri Lanka was converted by Sanghamitra to the ideology of Gautam Buddha, and the branch was planted there and became a big tree.

Here in India, after Gautam Buddha, a strange tragedy happened: Buddhism disappeared and Hindus burned the tree under which Gautam Buddha had become enlightened. It was only when India became independent just forty years ago that a branch from Sri Lanka was brought back. Now you see a beautiful tree again flourishing in Bodhgaya – although it is not the same tree, but it is the same tree.

A moment of deep love goes so deep in your being that time cannot erase it. It goes on and on giving birth to itself within you.

Hence I say that a moment of love is a moment of eternity.

Osho,

Most of humanity lives to eat and sleep, work, accumulate power and money, or to propagate itself.

Osho, what do you live for?

I will tell you a real historical fact...

In Greece, there was a great philosopher, Xeno. He lived a long life – in those days it was really very long, because the average life in those days was not more than twenty-five years. Xeno lived ninety years.

And he is a strange philosopher, unique in a sense, because his teaching is that life is meaningless; so meaningless that any man of intelligence will commit suicide, that is the only intelligent act you can do. So many of his disciples committed suicide, went on committing suicide. Ninety years long, thousands of disciples – and he was a very convincing man. What he was saying was so accurate, because ordinary life is certainly so meaningless. Unless you know how to change it into a divine phenomenon, it is meaningless.

And he was a great logician; he argued and convinced people, and people committed suicide, young people committed suicide.

When he was dying, somebody asked, "Xeno, one thing has always disturbed us. Because of your philosophy, thousands of people have committed suicide. Why have you gone on living?"

He said, "It was just to teach people to commit suicide; otherwise who will do my job? I *had* to live."

People are living absolutely meaningless lives. I also teach them a kind of suicide – not exactly the same as Xeno. I teach them a suicide in which they are reborn in a more luminous life, of a greater glory, of a divine ecstasy. I have to live because it would be absolutely unkind, knowing the path of transformation and not telling it to the people who need it.

6 Truth Knows No Fifty-Fifty

Osho,
I am requesting your guidance on my answer to something I heard you say to me – which you never actually said.

During my sannyas darshan you spoke to me at length about what happened to Buddha's teachings after Buddha left his body. I heard you say that Buddha's disciples compromised Buddha's teaching. They created safe religions, and thus compromised. You told me, "Do not compromise."

While you were speaking these words to me, I heard another communication. The request that I silently heard spoken was, "Do not let it happen to me."

Since that day I have continually looked for what I might be able to do to fulfill this request. Much to my wonder, I know what to do, I know how to fulfill the unspoken request – but I want your guidance.

Will you please give me your specific guidance?

What happened to Gautam Buddha and his teachings is almost the rule, not the exception. The moment the master leaves his body the disciples start compromising with the surrounding world to survive, to continue to exist. And truth is something that cannot be compromised.

Just Gautam Buddha's teachings...five hundred years afterwards, there was not a single Buddhist in the whole of India. The greatest man who has ever walked on the earth, and the most refined teaching and the clearest perception of truth simply disappeared like a dream.

One wonders – it has not happened to Christianity, it has not happened to Mohammedanism, it has not happened to Jainism. So the complexity of the phenomenon has to be understood. The people who had followed Gautam Buddha refused to compromise. That was the cause of the disappearance of Buddhism from India. The Buddhists were either killed, burned alive or forcibly converted into Hinduism, or the fortunate ones escaped to the neighboring countries.

In a way, it was a blessing in disguise because the Buddhists who escaped India spread all over Asia and converted the whole continent to the teachings of Gautam Buddha. But the problem was, they had learned something that a disciple should never learn: they had learned in India that if you insist on truth, crucifixion is the result. If you want to survive, you have to compromise with all kinds of lies which are prevalent.

What they did not do in India they did in China, they did in Japan, they did in Korea, and they did in Ceylon. All over Asia they compromised with the local population, its superstitions, its ancient ideologies founded on untruths, just created out of fear. But because they compromised with them, they survived. And it was not only that they survived, they became very respectable. Buddhism became the religion of the whole of Asia *except* India.

It is a very strange phenomenon, because Buddha was born here; all his great disciples were born here. Hundreds of people became enlightened under his guidance. The consciousness of this country reached its highest point in the presence of Gautam Buddha. And yet the moment Buddha had gone, the tremendous experience disappeared, evaporated – because the people who remained behind were still not ready to betray their master. They were ready to die, but not to betray; they were not going to compromise.

And Hinduism took revenge with great vengeance, because in

the presence of Gautam Buddha, Hinduism did not have the guts to encounter this man. Efforts were made. Hindu pundits, scholars went to argue, but they were mere parrots. In the presence of Gautam Buddha, their borrowed knowledge proved completely inadequate for human growth. The very presence of Gautam Buddha was enough to convince them that this man had experienced something that they had not experienced. What they were saying was simply a repetition of old scriptures. What he was saying was a valid individual experience: his own. And when the experience is your own, it has an authority.

Hinduism had to wait for Buddha's death. In his presence, it was impossible to argue in favor of superstitions. They had to wait five hundred years because after Buddha, his immediate disciples – Sariputta, Moggalayan, Mahakashyap, Ananda, and hundreds of others, were filled with the same light, with the same silence. They created more living enlightened people. This continued for five hundred years.

Slowly, slowly, it died out. Instead of the enlightened man, slowly, slowly the scholar, the pundit became more important. That was the time when Hinduism came with vengeance – and certainly Hinduism is a far older religion. It had great scholars. The Buddhist scholars were amateurs, they could not withstand Hindu scholarship; they were defeated very easily, because now, it was *not* their own experience.

These were the people who have written Buddhist scriptures. You will be surprised to know that every Buddhist scripture begins with the words *I have heard*. These people had not seen, these people had not experienced. These people had simply heard from others about the innermost reality, but it was only hearsay.

Hindus were more proficient scholars, almost ten thousand years old, very refined logicians, rationalists. The poor Buddhist scholars could not manage to prove anything. They were defeated so utterly that they had to move back into the Hindu fold. The Buddhist monks who had escaped from India learned a lesson: if you don't have your own experience, then it is better to compromise to survive. They had burned their fingers in arguing for somebody else's experience.

They dropped argument. They started talking of the synthesis of all religions; they started spreading the idea that all religions are right. Nobody is wrong, the question of discussion does not arise. And they were the first in the world to bring this idea that all religions are right. Naturally all religions respected these people – they were not quarrelsome. Up to now every religion had been quarrelsome, arguing, proving that "We have got the truth; we are right and you are wrong."

And these were the first people who were saying, "Everybody is right. There are millions of paths, but the goal is one. There is no need for any argument. We may be moving on different paths, but we are moving towards the same goal."

The same has happened with Jainism in India, which was a contemporary religion to Buddha. Jainas are still in existence in India. It is also a strange fact that Mahavira, their greatest teacher, and Buddha were contemporaries. In the presence of Gautam Buddha, Mahavira could not make any impact on the country. Yes, he had a small following, but Buddha loomed so large, he was such a huge tree that for three hundred years British scholars, historians, philosophers, thought that Mahavira was not separate from Gautam Buddha, that Mahavira was another name of Gautam Buddha. Because it is a title, just as *buddha* is a title.

Buddha means the awakened one; *Mahavira* means one who has conquered. And they both had the same title of Jaina – *Jaina* also means one who has conquered. Because the same title belonged to both, it was thought that Mahavira was not somebody separate. It was just recently that scholars started feeling that this was not right, that these were two different people.

Buddha created so much impact, he overshadowed everybody – but within five hundred years he disappeared. Mahavira's followers are still in existence because they compromised with the Hindus. They were not burned; they were not killed. They compromised so much that you cannot find much difference. And they had to compromise because they are dependent on the Hindus for everything. They are not a whole culture. If they need shoes –

they cannot make shoes and certainly they need shoes – they will have to depend on the Hindus. They need their toilets to be cleaned; they cannot do that, they have to depend on Hindus.

It is a strange phenomenon that Jainism and Buddhism both arose as a revolt against Hinduism. Mahavira is very strongly against Hinduism, but Jainas compromised on every point – because from where are you going to get your clothes? The weavers are either Hindu or Mohammedan. Who is going to make your houses? Who is going to cultivate food for you? – because Jainas cannot even cultivate. It is against their religion, because plants have life, and if you cultivate you will have to cut plants and you will be doing violence.

So all the violence has to be done by Hindus; then naturally you have to be dependent on them, and you cannot argue, and you cannot insist that you have the truth. You have to say that everybody has the truth; just the languages are different, paths are different, ways are different, but the basic experience is the same. Jainism survived. The same is true about Mohammedanism, Christianity – they have all compromised with the existing people.

Just a few months ago, the present pope visited India. The Indian Christians are the low caste Hindus, converted to Christianity because of poverty. There is no other reason for their conversion – they are poor, uneducated, and Christianity promises them...

But the pope was faced with great difficulties because the Hindus who have become converted cannot simply drop their habits of thousands of years. In the church they bring incense before Jesus Christ. And it was reported to him by the bishops and the cardinals: "What should be done? We try to prevent them but they don't listen. They bring flowers, they bring incense...not only that, in the church they repeat the mantra *omkar*." And the pope agreed that they should be allowed; otherwise, they will desert. And this is something so deep in them: they cannot think that om, the sound of om, can be anything other than the most spiritual thing. They are Christians, and om has nothing to do with Christianity – but basically they are Hindus. And the pope's concession is a compromise, it is cunning.

Tomorrow these people will start painting Jesus Christ in the color red, and you will have to accept it because without the red color no stone can become God. It has never happened in India. When for the first time the British government made roads and milestones, they had no idea what they were doing. They painted the milestones red, because red shows from far away, it stands out against the greenery, is clearer. So they painted them red, and they were surprised that every milestone was being worshipped! The villagers came with flowers, incense...every milestone had become the monkey god Hanuman.

Their engineers tried to explain that "These are not gods, these are milestones."

The people said, "You don't know. We have been doing this for thousands of years. Any stone painted red becomes divine." They were very happy – not happy because of the roads, they were happy because of the milestones.

Christianity has been compromising from the very beginning in every country. That has been its way of survival. You will be surprised to know that Indian Christianity is older than the Vatican. Indian Christianity is the oldest in the world, because one of Jesus' closest disciples, Thomas, came to India. It was difficult to convert Indians to any other religion. They have seen so much, they have heard so much about religion, they have so many beliefs.

Thomas was at a loss in the beginning, but finally he managed to compromise. He started dressing like a Hindu. If you see pictures of Thomas, you will be surprised that he shaved his head just like a Hindu *shankaracharya*. And he started using the thread that Hindus use, and he also used the wooden sandals that Hindu monks were using to avoid leather. And he would wear just a small *dhoti* with no shirt on top, just like the old brahmins. He learned Sanskrit. And seeing him, that he was just like a Brahmin – so whatever he was saying must be right – many people started following. They were the first Christians.

But this is more businesslike; it is salesmanship. It is not real conversion; it is tricky, it is exploiting innocent people. In every country Christianity has compromised with the local population. Whatever its religion was, Christianity has compromised with it, taken its principles, its behavior. It is because of this compromising attitude that Christianity has become the biggest religion in the world – almost half of the world is Christian.

Truth cannot be so cheap. And truth cannot be so appealing to such a big mob. The crowd psychology is that whatever it believes should be accepted as true; then there is a possibility of fifty-fifty: "You believe something from us, we will take something from you." But truth knows no fifty-fifty. It has to be a hundred percent pure; otherwise it is worse than a lie.

So when I said to you, "Don't compromise" I was saying many things in that.

First, to compromise means that convenience and survival are more important to you than truth. Secondly, it means that truth is not a revolution but a business, that it is not a transformation of your being but a social conformity. Thirdly, it means that you will never find yourself on the path. Once you have learned to compromise, you have started going astray.

Not to compromise is one of the basic, essential principles to follow if you want to find truth in its purity and full glory. And when I said this to you, certainly you rightly heard something more which was not said: "Please don't do it to me."

My whole effort is to make you individuals, courageous enough even to stand against the whole world. If you feel that you are right and you are experiencing the truth in your innermost core, then the whole world may be against you – it does not matter. Then even crucifixion is nothing but a seal of validity. A man who can go to his crucifixion laughing has proved beyond doubt that he knows something more than the mortal body.

Jesus seems to be wayward. At the crucifixion, on the cross, he was not joyous, he was not smiling, laughing. On the contrary, he was complaining. He was shouting at God, "Have you forsaken me?" Because his expectation was not crucifixion; his expectation was crowning. He is the only begotten son of God, how can God allow him to be crucified? A miracle is bound to happen. But the miracle did not happen, because miracles don't come from outside. The miracle would have happened if he had smiled and laughed because he knew that "You can only crucify a dead body, you cannot crucify my consciousness."

It happened in the case of al-Hillaj Mansoor. He was laughing – and his crucifixion was crueler than Jesus' because Mohammedans are more violent, more fanatic than any Jew. They cut him piece by piece, it was not a single stroke. First they cut his legs, then they cut his hands, then they made him blind, then they made him deaf. They killed him piece by piece and still he was smiling, to the very last.

And somebody asked, "Before they cut your tongue, we want to know – why are you smiling?"

He said, "I am smiling because they are punishing somebody else. The body that they are punishing is not me."

This is the miracle. It does not depend on God, it does not depend on anybody else. It depends on your experience. Al-Hillaj proves himself to be far closer to truth, just by his simple action. He is not grumbling, he is not saying to God that "This is not right that they are behaving in this primitive way with me and you are simply silent." He is not talking about God at all. He is simply enjoying the whole thing and laughing at the stupidity of people: "You are punishing somebody else. And I have always been telling you that you cannot punish me, you cannot even touch me. Punishment is not the question at all."

When you heard, although I did not say it to you, "Don't do it to me" you heard rightly. I was just going to say it, but seeing that you heard it, I did not say it. All these years it has haunted you that you heard it and I have not said it: was it your imagination or was I really saying something without saying it?

No, it was not your imagination. I was saying it without saying it. I say many things to you without saying them. I simply create the atmosphere by saying many other things in which you can hear the unsaid. This is because there are a few things which can only be whispered, not shouted. And there are a few things that cannot even be whispered but only indicated indirectly. Only then are they beautiful.

Osho,

Recently it has started happening that as I begin to open my eyes first thing in the morning I can see a vision, like a scene from a movie – and that scene happens days after in reality, just like a repetition.

Before I arrived here in Mumbai, I had a vision of the Golden Manor Hotel – the setting, the garden, the people – and when I arrived here, it was exactly the same as my vision. I wrote you a letter about this earlier, but did not have the courage to deliver it. Now it has been happening often, and I don't know if it is good or bad.

Also, when you were in Uruguay and I was in Brazil, I had the sudden compulsion to go to my room, to sit on the floor and close my eyes. I did so, and like a flash, I saw you sitting at a table, laughing joyously. I could only see the back of another man who seemed a little bit serious or sad. Then you saw me and invited me in, and the man turned his face to see me. He was beautiful, very beautiful The scene was so full of light! I'm sure he was not Jesus – the beard was different and the eyes were deeper and more direct. Hours later, the radio gave the news that Krishnamurti had died hours before.

Osho, from that day on, I was totally sure that you live on two levels simultaneously, and I don't know on which level you are for most of the time during your daily life.

You answered Turiya that you don't come into our dreams.

But isn't it true that you are so close to the disciple that we are one with you all the time, not only in our dreams?

One very fundamental thing has to be understood: a dream and a vision look alike, but they are two totally different phenomena. A dream is a mind projection. It has no validity of its own. It is only a thought in picture form.

Small children cannot think in thoughts, but they can understand pictures; hence, in their books you will see big pictures, beautiful colors, and very little writing. Slowly, slowly, as the child grows up, the pictures go on becoming smaller and the writing in his books increases. Finally, when he is in the university, pictures disappear and only writing remains. You may not have inquired why this is so...

If you give a child in kindergarten school a book which has no pictures, he will not be interested at all because he has not yet learned to think in words. But he can dream more perfectly than you can dream; he dreams so perfectly that once in a while you will find a child waking up in the morning and crying, "Just now I had my bicycle. Where has it gone?" He was dreaming of riding on his bicycle, and as he opens his eyes he is in his bed and the bicycle has gone. And his dream is so clear that it is very difficult for him to make a distinction between the real bicycle and a dream bicycle; they look almost alike.

We are grown up, but our unconscious never grows, it remains a child. So in sleep, when your conscious mind – which has learned language, concepts, words – is fast asleep, your unconscious starts dreaming. It is a child, so every thought form has to be translated by the unconscious mind into a picture form.

This is one of the great discoveries of Sigmund Freud: listening to your dreams. And he does the opposite process, translates your dream back from picture form into language, into concepts, into words. It needs a tremendous expertise. Still, nobody can be certain about it. If you go to Sigmund Freud, each dream will end up as something sexual, because it is his idea, that all sex is repressed.

It is true that much sexuality is repressed, but there are many other things also which are repressed; it is not only sex. But it is a problem with inventors and pioneers particularly; they become so obsessed with their findings that they don't take note of other possibilities. Freud's own disciple, Adler, went away from him just because Adler said that sex can be a part of repression, but that is not all. His own idea was that ambition, will to power, is far more important, and that a major part of your dreams concerns the will to power.

For example, you dream that you have become a bird and you are flying. To Sigmund Freud it will symbolize only that you want the same sexual freedom as the birds and the animals, nothing else. But to Adler it will mean that flying upwards means you are ambitious, you want to become the prime minister. But this is all guesswork.

Another disciple, Carl Gustav Jung, also went away from Freud because he was more interested in ancient mythologies and he thought that our dreams are part of our previous lives. So if you are a bird flying, he will interpret it that in some of your past lives you have been a bird.

Now what to do with these people, and how to decide? The language of pictures cannot be precise. It is almost like a painting: many people can see it and can decide its meaning in different ways. Just as the child has a picture language, your unconscious has a picture language.

I am not interested in interpreting your dreams because it is such a rubbish job. You can go on interpreting for years and years, and the dreams will not come to an end – every day, six hours every night you have to dream. And you have inexhaustible sources of dreaming. And it is very quick – the dream time is not the same as your ordinary time. Just reading your newspaper, you may fall asleep for a minute and you may see a dream which spreads for years. When you wake up you look at your watch and only one minute has passed. You say, "My God, in one minute I saw a dream which was spread for a whole year, or even for years."

Dream time is totally different. Up to now there has been no way to invent dream wristwatches, and perhaps there never will be a possibility, because there are lazy people and there are speedy people; some people are running fast, some people are simply sitting still. In dreams also, the same differences exist: lazy people dream in a lazy way, speedy people dream in a speedy way; your dream reflects you. So I don't think there is any possibility of making a watch which can function for everybody. It is not possible, because everybody's dream speed is different.

A vision also appears to be just like a dream, but it is not a dream. A vision is an objective phenomenon; it is not projected by your mind. You are seeing something; you are not projecting. With a certain clarity, your mind is capable of seeing things.

For example, I was traveling with one of my friends. He is a poet. We were in an air-conditioned bus, and it must have been nearabout ten o'clock in the night, and he suddenly heard, *Munna, Munna*. Nobody else heard. I was sitting by his side, and he asked me, "Have you heard? Somebody is calling 'Munna, Munna.'"

I said, "I have not heard anything. You must be dreaming."

He said, "No, I am awake. I was smoking, I was not dreaming. And only my father calls me Munna. Nobody else calls me Munna, that is my childhood name. My mother, who used to call me Munna, has died. My father is the only person alive who calls me Munna, nobody else even knows. And the voice was exactly like my father's."

I said, "Let us reach the destination and we can phone your house from there, to see what is the matter."

We reached Nagpur nearabout twelve o'clock, and we phoned and we found that the father had died at exactly ten o'clock. Perhaps at the time of death he remembered his only son, and remembered the name that he always used.

Now, this is not a dream. He had not seen anything, but he had heard; it is objective. And the father was almost sixty miles away, and a dying man cannot shout to reach sixty miles. And if he had shouted that loudly, then everybody in the bus would have heard it. But only his son heard it. Even I was not aware that his father called him Munna.

This is a vision...not visual, this is audio vision – not video, Niskriya! I may not come into your dreams – and if I come it is your projection, I am not responsible for it. If I do anything, I am not responsible for it. But I can come into a vision, and then the whole responsibility is mine.

The difference is very delicate. The dream always happens when you are asleep. The vision always happens when you are not asleep.

This is the first distinction: you are fully awake. And the vision always appears to be coming from outside, reaching to you. And sooner or later, you will find its validity, its reality.

You will never find the reality of dream. It is simply garbage, it is really the unwinding of the mind. The whole day the mind has to work, and it gets wound up, and needs unwinding to be fresh for tomorrow. So it is unwinding. Inconsistent things go on coming: you had been talking to somebody, you wanted to say something but you did not say it. Now it is hanging, it needs to be released – in the dream it will be released.

The dream is a great help, a cleaning. It is not against you, it keeps you sane; otherwise, everybody will go insane. For six hours your mind goes on cleaning itself of every impression that has remained incomplete in the mind – throws it off, prepares itself for tomorrow's work. But dreaming has no other significance.

Vision is a reality. The dream is of the mind. And the vision has a connection with the heart. These things you will have to feel, because the differences are very, very fine. Whenever you feel something coming as a vision to you, be in a meditative mood, silent. Allow it to happen, be receptive, don't interfere, don't interpret. Just first let it be complete so that you can see it from the very beginning to the very end. Most probably there will be no need of interpretation. Just seeing it in its completion will be enough; you will have the understanding. And then, soon some events will follow which will validate your vision.

Your dreams will never be validated by existence. So whatever you have seen was a vision – you were awake. And if you are silent, you can see things happening thousands of miles away. Space makes no difference. And you can see things which do not happen on the material level but happen on the level of consciousness. That's what you are mentioning: two levels.

Yes, it is true. I have to work on two levels: one is the level where you live, where you are, and one is the level where I am and I want you also to be. From the top of a hill I have to come into the valley where you are; otherwise you won't listen, you won't believe the sunlit top. I have to take your hand in my hand and persuade you – and on the way, tell stories which are not true! But they keep you engaged, and you don't create any trouble while walking; you go on, engaged with the story. And when you have reached the hilltop, you will know why I was telling long stories, and you will feel grateful that I told those stories; otherwise you would not have been able to travel that long, that far uphill.

It is something to be remembered: all the masters of the world have been telling stories, parables – why? The truth can be said simply, there is no need to give you so many stories. But the night is long, and you have to be kept awake; without stories you are going to fall asleep. Till the morning comes there is an absolute necessity to keep you engaged, and the stories the masters have been telling are the most intriguing things possible.

The truth cannot be said, but you can be led to the point from where you can see it. Now, the question is how to lead you to the point from where you can see it.

There is a story in Sarmad's life. He was teaching his students, his disciples, and suddenly he said, "Come on out of the class, something is happening." So they all came out.

A man was dragging a bull, but the bull was very powerful. The man was also powerful, but a bull is a bull! So although the man was dragging the bull...the man was being dragged.

Sarmad showed his disciples, "Look, this is the situation."

They said, "What do you mean?"

He said, "This is the situation between me and you, but I am not so stupid as this man."

And he said, "Listen! Are you taking the bull for the first time?"

The man said, "I am a new servant, and I come from the city and I don't know what to do – because I drag him one foot and he drags me four feet. It has been going on for hours, and I don't think that it is going to end."

Sarmad said, "Drop it. You don't understand the ways of the village, and particularly the language of bulls."

And he took a little grass, green and beautiful, and just walked ahead of the bull, without even touching the bull – and the bull followed him. And Sarmad started walking faster, and the bull walked faster.

The man said, "This is great! He is not even dragging him, the bull is going on its own."

And Sarmad said, "Take this grass. Don't let him eat; otherwise, you will be in trouble. If he creates trouble, start running – he will run with you, but you will reach home."

And he said to his disciples, "This is what I have been doing with you. All the parables, all the stories are nothing but green grass."

Visions should not be made an object of thinking. You should just wait, and life will provide you the right validity. Then accept it with gratitude.

Whatever you have seen was a vision, and it has been validated by life itself. Now there is no need to think about it. If you start thinking, you will create a mess. And if you don't think, you will allow more visions to happen to you.

And a man of visions starts moving from the lower plane, from the valley, to the higher plane, towards the top, without much effort.

It is a good indication that you are ready.

Osho,

The longer I am your disciple, the less I know and understand.

A magic pull brought me to Mumbai, and sitting in your presence has been like coming home again – glimpses of two hearts beating together, moments of love and wonder, days of joy and playfulness.

Being back in Holland there is only this big longing left inside my heart: to sit at your feet again and again and again.

Beloved Master, my mind is losing control, and my heart starts singing. What is happening?

The mind is a habit. Even if there are moments when the heart is singing and the whole being is full of joy, the mind cannot leave its old habits. It will certainly ask what is happening. Can't you allow things to happen without asking why, what?

Do you understand why we ask such questions? The mind asks these questions because it wants to control your lifestyle, it wants to know everything that is going on. Nothing should happen which is beyond it; everything should be in its control. The mind is a great controller. And if everything remains in its control, it will be a tragedy because nothing great can happen to you. Everything that is great, magnificent, is beyond mind.

And mind can never get the answer why, what, how. You have to learn one thing: that it is not necessary to satisfy the mind about every experience. Experiences of the heart, experiences of the being, experiences of the transcendental should not be made a point of inquiry. You should not ask why, you should enjoy them. You should not ask what is happening, because if you insist on these questions the happening will stop. These questions are not your friends. Let the mind ask questions only when something is going wrong. You are sick, you have a headache, your stomach has cramps – let the mind ask; that is the right realm for the mind.

But your heart is dancing – what has the mind to do with it? Just tell the mind, "Keep quiet, this is not your world. Look at your affairs. You should not go on poking your nose everywhere." The heart is a higher reality. The being is still higher, and there are realities higher than the being. Mind cannot ask questions about them, and no answer is possible. You will have to learn some new ways, and you will have to drop some old habits.

So just make it a simple point,: if there is something wrong, you are miserable, misery is perfectly the right terrain where mind is needed. Without mind, you cannot create misery; it is the world of mind – *then* ask why. But it is strange: nobody comes to ask, "Why am I miserable?" But when the heart is dancing, people ask, "Why? What is happening?"

The reason is because your heart has not danced for centuries, so the experience is so new that you get scared. You start feeling perhaps you are a little bit crazy, getting old, senile. What is happening? – because the experience is new. But remember, the mind's area of concern is only with anything going wrong. The mind has the right to ask and to find the right cause and to put things right.

But celebration, rejoicing, ecstasy – mind has nothing to do with them. Just tell the mind, "Rest, everything is going fine, you need not worry." If you can teach the mind to ask the right questions and not to interfere in realms which are beyond it, you will have disciplined yourself for more and more, greater and higher experiences.

Osho,

It seems that my problems are getting more and more since I have become your sannyasin. Is that your work?

It is my work.

My work is to make you more and more aware, and when you become more aware you become aware of more problems. Those problems were there before. I don't create your problems, it is just that you were unconscious, you were not taking any note. Those problems were there.

It is just like a house which is in darkness, and many spiders are weaving their nests and scorpions are living and snakes are enjoying, and suddenly you bring light there. The light does not create the spiders or the scorpions or the snakes, but it makes you aware of them. And it is good to be aware, because then the house can be cleaned, then you can avoid the snakes.

You have many problems which you are not seeing – which in fact, you do not want to see. You go on postponing. You are so afraid of seeing those problems because then you will have to solve them. But by postponing they are not solved; it is not so easy. Problems are not letters written to George Bernard Shaw.

George Bernard Shaw used to collect letters; he would not open them. He would open them on the first of every month, so for thirty days he would collect thousands of letters from all over the world. His date was fixed: on the first of every month he would open them. And he would go on throwing them, because most of them had already been answered. It was rarely that some letter was left that had not answered itself.

Somebody asked him, "This is a strange way..."

He said, "It is not strange, it is the simplest way. When somebody does not get an answer for two weeks, three weeks, he gets the answer that this man is not going to answer. He drops the hope."

"And most of those letters are useless anyway. I am not going to waste my whole month. I have given them just one day – and any really authentic letter that needs my attention, I answer. This way, I save my time, I save their time; otherwise they would have to read...and this is such a difficult world that they would not only read they would reply also...again you have to read it.

"It is better to finish it from the very beginning. It is a chain phenomenon; it can go on endlessly. And the more you allow it and then stop, the more it hurts. The first letter and it is finished – it does not hurt. The man just understands that this man is not the type who answers letters."

But problems are not letters, and life is not George Bernard Shaw. You cannot postpone. But people *are* postponing. They go on pushing them this way and that way, everywhere hiding them, thinking that some miracle...and things will settle down and problems will be solved. This is not going to happen. On the contrary, those problems will create their children. They will start finding boyfriends, girlfriends – two problems meeting together and a third problem is produced, and you will be in more difficulty.

It is better to go on facing each problem as it comes by.

It is not sannyas that has created your problems. Sannyas has simply given you a little more awareness. Your problems have always been there. Sannyas has given you the opportunity to solve them.

And one should enjoy solving one's problems. It sharpens your intelligence. Each problem is a challenge. Each problem makes you more intelligent. And the day you do not have any problems, your mind will come to its utmost clarity – because no dust, no problem. Your mind becomes a mirror, so pure that it reflects reality.

Yes, it is my work. But don't think that I am creating your problems. I am just giving you insight, awareness, silence, so that you can see your problems and solve them.

7 Zorba and Buddha: Their Split Is Your Social Disease

Osho,
When I came to Greece to see you, everything reflected more and more of the zorba.

Now, being here in India, everything around you is reflecting more of the buddha.

Osho, does this depend on being in Greece or India?

Human history has been a tragedy. And the reason for it being a tragedy is not very complex. You do not have to go very far to find it out; it is in everybody.

The whole past of man has created a split in man; there is a constant civil war in every human being. If you do not feel at ease, the reason is not personal. Your disease is social. The strategy that has been used is to divide you into two enemy camps: the zorba and the buddha, the materialist and the spiritualist.

You are not divided in reality. In reality you are a harmonious whole. But in your mind the conditioning is that you are not one whole, one piece; you have to fight against your body. If you want to be a spiritual being, the body has to be conquered, defeated, destroyed, tortured in every possible way. This has been the accepted ideology all over the world. In different cultures, different religions, the formulations may be different, but the basic rule is the same: divide man, create a conflict in him so one part starts feeling higher, becomes holy, starts condemning the other part as the sinner.

And the trouble is that you are one, there is no way to divide you. Every division is going to create misery in you, every division will mean that half of your being is fighting with the other half. And if you are fighting within yourself, how can you be at ease? The whole of humanity up to now has lived in a schizophrenic way. Everyone has been cut into pieces, fragments. Your religions, your philosophies, your ideologies have not been healing processes; they have been root causes of inner conflict and war. You have been wounding yourself. Your right hand wounds the left hand, your left hand wounds the right hand; both your hands become wounded.

The West finally chose to go with the zorba. There was no other way to remain sane – one part had to be completely destroyed, ignored, forgotten. The West denied the inner reality of man, his consciousness – there is no soul, man is only body, and eat, drink and be merry is the only religion. This was simply a way to find some peace of mind, to get out of the conflict, to come to a decision and a conclusion, because this is accepting that you are one: just matter, just body.

The East has chosen the other way, but the basic problem is the same. The East has chosen that you are the soul, and the body is an illusion. Matter does not exist, the world is made of the same stuff as dreams are made of, so don't be bothered about it. Renounce it, forget all about it; it is not worth taking note of.

On the surface it seems that East and West are doing different things, but essentially they are not doing different things. Essentially they are trying to find a rational way to be one, because to be two means a constant dis-ease, a conflict. It is better to drop the idea of the other.

The East says that the body is illusory, it is only an appearance, a shadow; it has no reality. The West says that consciousness is a byproduct – it does not exist in itself, it is an appearance. When the body dies nothing remains, the body is all, and the consciousness that you feel is just the combination of all the elements of the body.

For example, if you take all the parts of your car separately, or all the parts of your watch separately, do you think something like a soul will be released out of the watch? Who was running the watch? It was just because of the combination of the parts in a certain way that the watch was running, the car was running, that all machines are working; it is a byproduct. Put all the parts together again and the watch will start ticking. The soul has not gone anywhere, there has been no soul in the first place.

As far as I am concerned, I see that the fundamental reason is to somehow choose one and decide that the other is illusory, so that you can be at peace, so that there is no need to fight, torture, and be in constant fear of being defeated. Why have the East and the West chosen differently? That also has to be understood.

The Eastern mind, in search of a unitary being, tried to find out: what exactly is this inner consciousness that the Eastern mystics, saints and sages have been talking about, and calling the body illusory? To us the body seems to be real, and consciousness is just a word. But because all the saints in the East were insisting that this word *consciousness* is your reality, the East has tried to find out what this reality is before deciding in favor of the body. The natural tendency will be to decide in favor of the body, because the body is there, already appearing real – consciousness you have to search for, you have to go into an inner pilgrimage.

The East, because of people like Gautam Buddha and Mahavira, could not deny that these people were sincere. Their sincerity was so clear, their presence was so impressive, their words were so authoritative – it was impossible to deny. No argument was enough, because these people were their own argument, their own validity. And they were so peaceful and so joyful, so relaxed, so fearless. They had everything that every human being desires – and in a way they had nothing. Certainly they had found a source within themselves, a treasure. And you cannot just deny it without giving enough time to the search. Unless you find that there is no consciousness, you cannot deny it. We had people so fragrant... We could not see their roses, but the fragrance was so much that the

East tried to look inside, and found that the soul is far more real. The body is just an appearance.

And just by the way, it will be significant to remind you that modern science has come to the conclusion that matter is illusory, that matter does not exist; it only appears. They have come to the conclusion from a very different route. By searching deeply, they have found that, as they reach deeper into matter, it is less and less substantial. And at a point after the atom, there is no matter at all: there are only electrons, which are particles of electricity – which is not matter but energy. Just a hundred years ago, Nietzsche declared, "God is dead," not knowing at all that within a hundred years the whole of science would agree that perhaps God may be *alive*, but matter is *dead*.

The East has moved inwards and found that the body, matter, is relatively non-substantial. The ultimate reality belongs to consciousness. In the West, development happened in a different way. And there are reasons why it happened in that way.

The East is ancient. At least ten thousand years of constant, consistent search for the inner reality of man – and all the genius of the East has been devoted to it. When the Upanishads were being written in the East, nearabout five thousand years ago, the West did not exist as a human society at all. In India we have Mohenjo Daro, Harrapur: cities that existed seven thousand years ago, with such refined development – they have streets as wide as those in Mumbai. They have bedrooms with attached bathrooms.

And you will be surprised at why I am saying this: because just a hundred years ago in America, there was a court case against bathrooms, which went up to the Supreme Court. The first man who made a bathroom attached to his bedroom... Christianity was against it because this is dirty – making your bathroom attached to your bedroom. This is un-Christian; cleanliness is next to godliness – and here is the bathroom next to the bedroom! Just a hundred years ago...and the Supreme Court had to decide that there is nothing unclean in it, and if somebody wants to have a bathroom attached to his bedroom it is nobody else's business to interfere, and it has nothing to do with your religion. But the church was fighting.

In Harapur, seven thousand years ago, they had bathrooms

attached to their bedrooms, they had bathtubs, and they had a very special arrangement for circulation of water in the city. Hot and cold water in your bathroom is not a new thing; it was available in Harapur, in Mohenjo Daro. They had swimming pools. It must have been a very highly cultured society.

At the time of Gautam Buddha, just twenty-five centuries ago, even then the West was not very evolved. And you can see it. We did not crucify Gautam Buddha, and the West crucified Jesus Christ five hundred years after Gautam Buddha.

And what Jesus was saying was nothing compared to Gautam Buddha. Gautam Buddha was saying that there is no God; still, nobody thought of crucifying him. Jesus Christ was not saying anything against Judaism; on the contrary, he was simply saying that he was their lost prophet. And he was repeating everything written in the Old Testament – he was not saying anything that was contradicting the old religion. And Gautam Buddha was contradicting everything in Hinduism: he said that the Vedas are idiotic, he said that there is no God, he said that all priests are the most cunning people in the world. And priests in India, the brahmins, are the highest caste. But nobody thought of crucifying him.

People challenged him for discussions, people discussed, and because they could not defeat him in argument... They could not defeat him. When they came in front of him, they were sincere enough to realize and recognize that he knew better, that their knowledge was only bookish, and his knowledge was authentic experience.

Western development is childish compared to Eastern development. It begins in Greece. But even a man like Socrates, who was neither denying God nor affirming God, who was simply saying, "I have not experienced, hence I cannot be untruthful. I cannot say whether God exists or not. And I would like everybody to be sincere about it. Unless you encounter, don't say yes, don't say no; remain agnostic, keep your conclusions suspended." A very reasonable man, but he was poisoned. He has not denied your tradition, he has not denied your past, he has not denied anything – he simply argued for a more rational approach, a more logical approach. It is not a crime.

And this is the reward that he gets: he is poisoned, society decides that he is a dangerous man. Those people who could have changed Western society towards inner reality are being crucified or poisoned. Naturally, the talented people became afraid even of talking about inner things, mysteries. They started talking only about objective things, matter, because matter cannot be denied. And there is no problem with going into a deep search into matter.

The crucifixion of Jesus and the death of Socrates closed the door for Western genius to move inwards. Anybody who had any intelligence became aware that it is simply inviting your death; it is better to use your talents and genius in such a way that the society cannot condemn it. So the whole genius of Western humanity became a servant for creating more comforts for the body, more technology, more machines, more knowledge about matter – and everybody was happy. Even in these matters, if there was something that went against religion, immediately the church was there to stop it.

For example, when Galileo wrote that the sun does not go around the earth as it appears to, but that in actuality the earth goes around the sun, as it does not appear to, he was called by the pope to his court and told – and he was old, seventy-five years old, sick and almost on his deathbed – "You have to change your book because it goes against the Bible. In the Bible the statement is that the sun goes around the earth, and we are not ready to listen to any argument. Simply change it; otherwise death will be your punishment."

Such an idiotic church, which is not even ready to listen to any argument, which only knows to dictate: "Do it or be ready to die." Galileo must have had a great sense of humor. He said, "There is no need for you to take so much trouble to kill me. I am going to die anyway. As far as the book is concerned, I will change it, but I want you to remember that by my changing the book, neither is the earth going to change nor is the sun going to change. The earth will still go around the sun, because they don't read my book and they don't care what I write." So he canceled the statement in his book. And in the footnote he wrote, "I am canceling the statement, knowing perfectly well that it makes no difference. The reality remains the same."

When Copernicus found that the earth is not flat, as it is said in the Bible, but round, he was immediately in trouble. Now, these matters have nothing to do with religion. What has religion to do with whether the earth is round or flat? It can have any geometrical shape – religion does not have anything to do with it.

But Christianity, Mohammedanism, are very primitive religions. They don't have the cultured, sophisticated attitude of Hinduism, Jainism, Buddhism, Taoism. They don't know how to argue, they only know how to fight. Their only argument is the sword: at the point of the sword, it is to be decided who is right.

It is the church – you will be surprised to know – that has prevented the West from going in the direction of inwardness. It forced Western humanity to go towards matter. The inner was the church's absolute monopoly, and it decided everything about it. There was no need to search, there was no need to discover, there was no need to meditate. You were only supposed to believe in God. But if did something as far as matter is concerned, there would be no problem as long as it did not come in conflict with the Bible.

Copernicus said to the pope, "It is just a small thing, and I have every proof that the earth is round. It is my lifelong work, and it does not affect your religiousness."

The pope said, "You don't understand. The question is not whether it affects our religiousness or not; the question is that the Bible is God's book, the holy book. If one statement in the Bible is proved wrong, that has great implications: first, that God can be wrong. We cannot accept that."

They cannot even accept that the pope can be wrong, what to say about God? The pope is a faraway representative. Jesus represents God, and the pope represents Jesus – not directly, but through hundreds of popes who have died before him. He is connected through them to Jesus, and Jesus has a direct telephone line to God.

Just one statement against the Bible, if it is proved valid, makes God fallible. And it cannot be accepted – that's one thing.

Secondly, if one statement is proved wrong, what is the guarantee about other statements? It creates suspicion. It destroys the very foundation of belief and faith. "So we cannot accept anything in the Bible as wrong, but you can do everything that does not go against the Bible." Naturally only matter is left. You can do research in physics, in chemistry, in biology, in zoology, in geology. You can do all these things; you are free to do so.

The church has been like the Great China Wall, preventing people from going inwards. It looks strange, but it is a fact: the Christian church has proved to be the greatest enemy of religion on the earth. Other religions have also proved to be enemies, but not that great. Genius was left to work only with matter. In the East, the genius had first preference for the inner journey. Only second-class, mediocre people would work for the outer, material things; real intelligence would always move into meditativeness.

Slowly, slowly, the distance became bigger. The West became materialist – and the whole responsibility goes to the Christian church – and the Eastern humanity became more and more spiritualist. The division, the split that was created in each man, became a split on a wider scale: as East and West.

One great poet has written, "East is East and West is West, and never the twain shall meet." And this man, Lord Kipling, was very much interested in the East. He lived in India for years; he was in the government service. But seeing the difference: the whole Eastern consciousness moves inwards and the Western consciousness moves outwards – how could they meet?

My whole work is just to prove Lord Kipling wrong. I would like to say – neither West is West nor East is East, and the twain have already met.

What do you mean by *east*? In Mumbai, Calcutta is east; in Calcutta, Mumbai is west. This is nonsense; these words are relative words. You cannot say that a certain place is east and a certain place is west; they are all relative. For the people of Calcutta, Tokyo is east – and that's what the Japanese think. They call their land "the land of sunrise" and they call their king "the only begotten son of the sun god." The sun god is the real god, and Hirohito, the king of Japan, is his only son.

In fact, in the Second World War when the Japanese were

defeated, they could not believe it. Thousands of soldiers committed suicide just out of shame – "How can it happen that God's son should be defeated? Now there is no point in living, everything has gone wrong." They believe that they are the real east.

Nobody is east and nobody is west. But the attitudes can be understood, and they are very prominent. And my whole approach is to bring a bridge into each individual, so that you are one whole. Don't be against your body; it is your home. Don't be against your consciousness, because without consciousness your house may be very decorated but it won't have any master, it will be empty. Together they create a beauty, a fuller life.

Symbolically, I have chosen Zorba for the body and Buddha for the soul.

Your question is that when I was in Greece I was talking more about Zorba, and here in India the atmosphere seems to be closer to Buddha. Your observation is true.

In Greece I was talking about Zorba. Still they deported me. If I had been talking about Buddha, you would not have seen me again! I was talking about Zorba because that is the foundation. But I was making it clear that Zorba alone is only the foundation of the house, it is not the house itself.

In India I am talking about Buddha, but I have not forgotten Zorba. Each statement that I make – whether it is about Zorba or about Buddha – implies the other automatically, because to me they are inseparable. It is only a question of emphasis. To make the Greek mind understand, I emphasized Zorba.

The ambassador to America in Sri Lanka wrote me a letter saying, "Your followers around the world are making restaurants, discos, and calling them *Zorba the Buddha*. It is very insulting to Buddha. And if you do such a thing in a country like Sri Lanka, there can be violence. I advise you to drop this name."

I told my secretary to write to him "In the first place, nobody has a monopoly on Zorba or on Buddha. Secondly, we are not concerned with Gautam the Buddha; *buddha* is not a personal name, it is a quality. It means the awakened one. Anyone who is awakened can be called the buddha. Gautam Buddha is only one of the millions of buddhas who have happened and who will happen. And you cannot prevent Zorba from becoming a buddha. In fact, you should help me to make zorbas into buddhas, because that is the only real revolution – that a materialist, a zorba, who knows nothing of higher consciousness, becomes a buddha." He never replied.

Zorba has his own beauty. And the island in Greece where I was staying is the place where Kazantzakis, the novelist who created the novel *Zorba the Greek*... Zorba is a fictitious name; he is not a historical person. But the island where I was staying was the island where Kazantzakis was born.

And Kazantzakis is one of the best novelists of this century, and he suffered tremendously at the hands of the church. Finally, when he wrote *Zorba the Greek,* he was expelled from the church. By writing *Zorba* he was forced: "Withdraw your book *Zorba*; otherwise you will be expelled." Because he did not withdraw the book, he was expelled from Christianity and condemned to hell.

Zorba is really Kazantzakis' own individuality, which Christianity had repressed, which he could not live, which he wanted to live. He expressed that whole unlived part of his life in the name of Zorba. Zorba is a beautiful man – no fear of hell, no greed for heaven, living moment to moment, enjoying small things: food, drink, women. After the day's work, he would take his musical instrument and dance on the beach for hours.

And the other part of Kazantzakis, which he lived in *Zorba the Greek* – Zorba is the servant – the other part is the master who employed Zorba as his servant. He is always sad and sitting in his office, doing his files, never laughing, never enjoying himself, never going out and always feeling deep down jealous of Zorba because he earns a little, not much, but he lives like an emperor, not thinking of tomorrow, of what will happen. He eats well, he drinks well, he sings well, he dances well. And his master, who is very rich, is just sitting there sad, tense, in anguish, in misery, suffering.

One day Zorba says to his master – which is Kazantzakis himself – "Master, there is only one thing wrong with you: you think too much. Come with me." It was a full-moon night.

Kazantzakis objected: "No, no! What are you doing?"

But Zorba pulled him out to the beach and started dancing, playing his instrument. And he told Kazantzakis, "Try. Jump! If you cannot dance, do *something*." And with Zorba's energy and his vibe, Kazantzakis also started dancing. For the first time in his life he felt that he was alive. Zorba is the unlived part of every so-called religious person.

And when *Zorba* was published why was the church so much against it? It was just a novel; there was nothing for the church to be worried about. But it was so clear that it was about the unlived Christian in every Christian; this book could be a dangerous book. And it *is* a dangerous book.

But Zorba is tremendously beautiful. Kazantzakis sends him to purchase some things from the city, and he forgets all. He drinks and goes to the prostitutes and enjoys, and once in a while he remembers that it seems many days have passed but still, the money is with him. Unless all the money is finished, how can he return? The master will be very angry, but nothing can be done about it – it is *his* problem. And after three weeks he comes back, and he had gone only for three days, and he does not bring anything that he was sent for. And he comes with all the stories: "What a great journey it was, you should have been there. I met such beautiful *bubalinas*...and such good wine."

And the master said, "But what about the things? For three weeks I have been sitting here boiling."

He said, "When there are so many beautiful things available, who bothers about such small things? You can cut my salary every week, by and by, slowly, and take your money back. I am sorry I could not come earlier. And you should be happy that I have come – because the money was finished I had to come. But next time when I go, I will bring all the things."

He said, "You will never go again. I will send somebody else."

Zorba's whole life is a life of simple, physical enjoyment, but without any anxiety, without any guilt, without any botheration about sin and virtue and...

I would like this man Zorba to be alive in everybody, because it is your natural inheritance. But you should not stop at Zorba. Zorba is only the beginning. Sooner or later, if you allow your zorba full expression, you are bound to find something better, higher, greater. It will not come out of thinking; it will come out of your experiences, because those small experiences will become boring.

Buddha himself had come to be a buddha because he had lived the life of a zorba. That thing has not been noticed by the East: that for twenty-nine years Buddha lived as no Zorba could ever live. Zorba was so poor in comparison.

Gautam Buddha's father had arranged for all the beautiful girls to be picked from the whole kingdom for Buddha's enjoyment. He made three beautiful palaces in three different places for different seasons. He had beautiful gardens and lakes. Buddha's whole life was just luxury, pure luxury. But he got bored.

One of the most significant experiences that he comes across was when one night beautiful girls were dancing He was drinking, they were drinking, and then everybody fell asleep drunk. In the middle of the night he woke up and looked around, and he was shocked, and that shock was one of the turning points in his life. Some girl was snoring – she was a beautiful girl, but her mouth was open and snoring she looked so ugly; the saliva was coming out. Somebody's nose was flowing. He said, "My God, this is what beauty is!" He was finished. Those girls were dispersed the next morning. "I don't want any girls in my palaces. Enough is enough."

In fact, it was too much. In twenty-nine years he lived almost the equivalent of four or five lives of an ordinary man. With all that luxury, he soon found himself tired and bored, and a question became very prominent in his mind: "Is this all? Then what am I going to live tomorrow for? Life must mean something more; otherwise, it is meaningless." It was out of the zorba that the search for the buddha, started. Not everybody becomes a buddha; and the basic reason is that the zorba remains unlived.

Do you see my argument? My argument is: live Zorba fully, and you will naturally enter into the life of a buddha.

Kazantzakis has written *Zorba the Greek*. He's dead. If he had been allowed to live longer... He was sick, he was very tense; he remained very miserable because he was always afraid of sin. And then when he was expelled from the Christian church – that means condemned to hell; only Christians can go to paradise – it was such a shock that he could not survive. He was really killed by the Christian church expelling him.

If he were alive, I would have told him: "Your book is half. You need to write another book, *Zorba the Buddha*. Then it will be a complete phenomenon. But you can write the other book only if you live your zorba. You have not even lived zorba; how can you live the buddha?"

Enjoy your body; enjoy your physical existence. There is no sin in it. Hidden behind it is your spiritual growing, is your spiritual blissfulness. When you are tired of physical pleasures, only then will you ask, "Is there something more?" And this question cannot be only intellectual, it has to be existential. "Is there something more?" And when the question is existential, you will find within yourself something more.

There is something much more. Zorba is only the beginning. Once the buddha, the awakened soul, takes possession of you, then you will know that pleasure was not even a shadow. There is so much bliss. This bliss is not against pleasure. In fact, it is pleasure, which has brought you to bliss. There is no fight between Zorba and Buddha. Zorba is the arrow – if you follow it rightly, you will reach the Buddha.

Certainly in Greece there is an atmosphere different from that in India. The Greek personality has remained materialistic. In India, the basic, essential atmosphere is that of the awakened soul. Whether you go on sleeping, it doesn't matter, but the atmosphere around you is that of the sunrise. The birds are singing, the f owers are blossoming, and from everywhere the indication is for you to wake up.

I will go to Greece again because I have been enjoying al these deportations. And next time I have to talk about Buddha – because I have talked only about Zorba, and I never leave anything incomplete. And already, the minister of interior in Greece has invited me: "We will make arrangements, you come."

I said, "I will come but, at least for three weeks, don't deport me" – because no country seems to be able to have me for more than three weeks. A few countries are so stupid that they cannot even have me for thirty-six hours.

England proved to be the worst. They would not allow me six hours to sleep at the airport – not even entering England, but just the airport lounge. They wouldn't allow me to sleep there for six hours.

I said, "What reasons have you got?"

And the airport officer said, "We have no reasons. This is the file, the information from the prime minister is that this man is dangerous and should not be allowed in."

But I said, "I am not entering England, and from the lounge there is no way to enter into England. And you have checked me well – I am not carrying any bombs or anything. And sleeping six hours in the airport, what danger can I cause? Just think..."

He said, "Don't put me in trouble, because tomorrow it is going to be in parliament and then I will be answerable – 'Why did you allow him?'"

So I had to go to jail for six hours. They said, "The only place we can allow you to remain is in jail."

And the next day in parliament the question was there, and I am always surprised that the question is asked and the same answer is given, that the man is very dangerous. But nobody in the parliament has the intelligence to ask, "What danger could he have been just sleeping in the lounge at the airport? He may be dangerous, but what danger could he have been?" Nobody in the parliament asked.

So I have informed the minister in Greece that I will go. I have to go. I was really thinking to stay longer, and I had fifteen more days on the visa to stay, but the archbishop of Greece threatened the government that if they didn't deport me immediately then they were going to burn down the house where I was staying – burn me alive and all the people who were staying with me, – dynamite the house. And the government was threatened, and they thought, "Some problem may arise, it is better to send this man away immediately."

I was asleep when I was arrested. You don't arrest people when they are asleep. And they had no reason, because I had not gone out of the house for fifteen days. I said, "You have to show some reason why you are deporting me."

They said, "We don't have any reason, just orders from above." And all the orders were based on the threat of the archbishop. It is the same archbishop who expelled Kazantzakis.

And these people are living almost out of date, out of time. They are not contemporaries. Because the day they deported me from the island, the people of the island, who had no idea about me, just rumors... But seeing the threat of the archbishop they all felt ashamed. And they asked me, "What can we do? We are poor people."

I said, "All of you go to the airport to show the archbishop how many people are with him and how many people are with me – although I have been here for only fifteen days and they have been here for two thousand years." And there were only six old women with the archbishop in the church, and three thousand people, the whole island, at the airport.

Still they don't understand that they are no longer needed, that their time is finished. And they talk about loving your enemy and loving your neighbor, and God is love – and they threaten a man, who has not done anything, that they will burn him alive, with all his friends. At least twenty-five people were staying in that big mansion.

This shows that somehow the Western mind has not grown towards inwardness, towards love, towards non-violence. Their whole approach is materialistic. Two thousand years after Jesus was crucified, and this man is threatening me – Jesus Christ's representative in Greece is threatening me – that he will burn me alive. Does he represent Jesus Christ or was he also one of the rabbis who crucified Jesus Christ?

The mind of the priest in the west has been a hindrance to Western growth towards meditation. But a strange time of revolution has come – at least for the new generation, because the new generation is not with these old priests and these old churches. And the new generation in the West is looking towards the East. That's a great hope.

That is Zorba searching for Gautam Buddha.

Osho,

Thoughts of death have been a frequent visitor during my discipleship. How can a disciple die in a master's presence, especially when the master is physically distant?

Osho, is Mahakashyap the only answer?

The question is not whether or not you are in the presence of the master, but whether or not you are filled with love and trust for the master. Physical closeness means nothing. Only spiritual closeness is significant. Your love, your trust is enough. You can be on the moon and the master will be by your side – really, the master will be inside you – because as your love deepens, something of the master, his energies, start melting and merging with you. The fear of physical distance is the fear of lack of love and trust.

Mahakashyap alone is not the answer. Everybody has to be an answer unto himself. Mahakashyap remained with Buddha, and after Buddha's death he died; he could not survive separately. But that is Mahakashyapa's uniqueness. It is not the only answer.

I will tell you a few other stories around Buddha so you can understand:

Ananda lived with Buddha for forty-two years. Nobody else lived so long with Buddha, nobody was allowed to live so long with him. But there was a problem. Ananda was Buddha's cousin-brother, and older than him, and the Eastern tradition... Before taking initiation – Ananda was the elder brother – he said to Gautam Buddha, "Siddharth" – Siddharth was his family name – "Listen, after initiation, whatever you say I will have to do. I will be your disciple; you will be my master. Right now I am your elder brother, you are my younger brother; whatever I say you have to do. Three things you have to remember – don't forget them when I become a disciple." It is a beautiful story.

Buddha said, "What are the three things?"

Ananda said, "First, I will always live with you; you cannot send me anywhere else to spread the message. Second, if I want anybody to meet you – even in the middle of the night – you cannot say no; that is my personal privilege. And thirdly, I will sleep in the same room where you sleep. Even in sleep, you cannot make me stay in a different place." Buddha promised, and these three conditions were followed for forty-two years. But Ananda did not become enlightened. You can understand his pain and his anguish – people who had come long after him became enlightened, and he remained in his ignorance just the same as before. The day Buddha died he said, "What will happen to me? I could not become enlightened even though I was with you for forty-two years, day in, day out, twenty-four hours a day. Without you, I don't see any hope."

Buddha said, "You don't understand the dynamics of life. Perhaps you will become enlightened only when I am gone; *I* am the barrier. You take me for granted. "The day you asked those three conditions, I thought that those conditions were going to be a barrier for you. You cannot forget that you are my elder brother, even now. You cannot forget that you have a certain privilege over others. You cannot forget that I have agreed on three conditions only for you, for nobody else. Perhaps my death will help."

Buddha died. And after twenty-four hours, there was a great meeting of all the enlightened disciples to write down whatever Buddha had said in those forty-two years. But the problem was that nobody had been with him continuously for forty-two years except Ananda – but *he* could not be allowed in the meeting because he was not enlightened. An ignorant man, unenlightened – you cannot rely on what he is saying, whether he heard it or imagined it, whether he has forgotten something, whether he has put his own interpretation on it. It was difficult.

And the scene was really tragic. The conference was inside a hall and Ananda was sitting outside on the steps crying. Because he had lived with Buddha for forty-two years, he knew more than anybody else. He remembered each single moment, but he was unenlightened. Crying, sitting there outside the hall, something transpired. He had not cried his whole life. With those tears, his ego disappeared; he became like a child. They opened the door to see whether Ananda was still sitting outside – because they had told him, "Sit outside. If we need some confirmation from you, we will ask you, but you cannot enter the conference."

They saw a transformed being. The old Ananda, the old egoist had gone. An innocent being with tears of joy...and they all could see the light surrounding him.

They invited him, "Come in. Now there is no need for us to be worried. But it is strange. You could not become enlightened for forty-two years, and just after twenty-four hours you have attained that state" – and this situation had been continually emphasized by Gautam Buddha.

Ananda said, "It was my fault. His death became the death of my ego too."

All the scriptures that are in existence were related by Ananda. There were other enlightened disciples who did not die with Gautam Buddha. It was asked – when Mahakashyap died, it became a very significant question, it was asked of other enlightened disciples – "If Mahakashyap has died, how are you living?"

One of the disciples, Moggalayan, said, "I have to live now for my master's message. *I* am not living anymore – I died with him; now he is living in me. That was one way, the way of Mahakashyap – to dissolve into Gautam Buddha. This is another way. I have also dissolved, but dying is not going to help anybody. And there are so many blind people in the world who need eyes, there are so many people in darkness who need light. I will live. I will live as long as it is possible; I will live for Buddha."

So it is not a question of one person being decisive. Each person has to be unique in his own way. Somebody dies for the master, somebody lives for the master, and you cannot say who is greater – perhaps no comparison is right. Both are themselves.

Just remember one thing: your love. Then wherever you are, space and the distance in space do not matter. And at a certain depth, even time does not matter.

And when both time and space are immaterial, then you have really touched the feet of the master. Then whatsoever transpires in you – to live for the message or to die, whatever comes naturally and spontaneously – let it happen.

8 Indifference to the Mind Is Meditation

Osho,
I often wanted to ask you some questions, but after waiting for a while, I always found my questions answered by you. And at the same time I found out that all those questions were just silly questions, coming from my mind without any connection to my heart. My heart only wants to cry, and my mind only wants to know, despite any answer.

Could you please comment on how to deal with a continuous questioning mind that is not interested in any answer anyway? Or am I just a Greek donkey?

The disciple who can wait will find all his questions answered at the right moment. But waiting is a great quality; it is deep patience, it is great trust. The mind cannot wait, it is always in a hurry. It knows nothing about patience; hence it goes on piling questions upon questions without getting the answer.

It is something very delicate to understand: that it is not the answer that is significant but the right timing, your readiness to receive it; otherwise it will just go above your head. The impatient mind is too occupied in questioning. It forgets that questioning in itself is a meaningless activity – the real thing is the answer, but for the answer you need a certain silence, peace, openness, receptivity. The mind is incapable of these qualities; hence, for thousands of years the mind has been asking and asking but it finds no answer.

In the world of the mind there are only questions. And in the world of the heart there is only the answer, because the heart knows how not to ask, how to wait – let the spring come by itself; wait like a thirsty earth, the rainclouds will come, they have always been coming. There is no need to distrust, because there is not even a single exception where trust has failed, where waiting is not fulfilled, where patience is not immensely rewarded.

The functioning of the heart and the mind are totally different, not only different but diametrically opposite. The mind creates philosophies, theologies, ideologies – they are all questions that don't have any answer. The heart simply waits. At the right moment, the answer blossoms by itself.

The heart has no question, yet it receives the answer. The mind has a thousand and one questions, yet it never receives any answer because it does not know how to receive.

Your mind is full of questions; yet you have been observing that, by and by, they are being answered. This should create in you a new insight, a new trust. A new dimension is opening: that you have just to wait, alert and awake, and if it is needed the answer will come to you.

You are also seeing that most of the questions that the mind is filled with are silly. They are – not most of them, all of them are – silly for the simple reason that mind does not go through the discipline of asking receptively. It is more concerned with questions. Even while the answer is being given, it has moved on to another question. Perhaps, listening to the answer, it has created ten more questions out of the answer itself.

Questions arise out of the mind just like leaves grow on trees. And slowly, slowly, they become more and more silly, because it is very difficult to find many significant questions, and the mind is not satisfied with a small quantity of questions. It is greedy. It wants to ask everything; it wants to know everything without being ready to understand anything.

There are few significant questions – and there is only one really fundamental question – but that small quantity does not satisfy the greed of the mind. You will be amazed to know that the English word *greed* comes from a very strange word in Sanskrit – and if you want to see those people from where this word has come, Mumbai has most of them. In Sanskrit the vulture is called *giddha*, and from *giddha* comes greed. And Mumbai has the greatest number of vultures in the whole world, because Mumbai has the greatest number of Parsis.

There is a certain relationship between Parsis and vultures. Parsis have a very strange way of disposing of their dead. They don't burn them like Hindus, Buddhists, Jainas; they don't bury them like Christians, Mohammedans and Jews. They have a unique way of their own, and they have a certain rationale for it. In their cemetery – and Mumbai has the biggest, because Mumbai has the biggest population of Parsis – they have a big well. There are steel rods on top of the well. The dead body is put on those steel rods, and between the steel rods there are gaps. All around, there are big, ancient trees and thousands of vultures sit there, waiting for some poor Parsi to die. The vultures need food every day; Parsis supply the food. The dead body of the Parsi is put on those rods on top of the well, and the vultures eat whatever is edible. And whatever is not edible – bones, et cetera – goes on falling through the gaps between the rods into the well.

On the surface it looks very strange: "What are you doing?" – but the Parsis have their rationale. In this world everybody has some reasonable grounds for every superstition. They say, "Because we have been eating everything, now it is our duty to be eaten." A beautiful logic – you have been eating for your whole life. If you are a meat-eater you have been eating animals. If you are a vegetarian, then you have been eating vegetables; they too are life. For your whole life you have been eating, and it is natural to be part of the same circle by being eaten.

According to the Parsis, this is the most natural thing. And I think people who believe in nature will support their idea – because to burn a body is to destroy food, is to unnecessarily kill a few vultures, or keep them hungry.

In a Hindu village, vultures don't exist – what will they do there? At the most, once in a while a cow dies, or a buffalo, and they can eat that. Now there is a widespread movement amongst intellectuals around the earth that we should not break natural cycles anywhere. For our whole lives we have been eating – now it is time that we should be eaten. And anyway you are dead; why unnecessarily destroy good food for the vultures?

Just go there in Mumbai, you will see a beautiful scene – you will not see it anywhere else in the whole world – so many vultures sitting together just waiting for poor Parsis to die, praying to God, "Finish someone today." And God seems to listen to the vultures; some Parsi is bound to come.

The English word *greed* comes from the same root as *giddha*, the vulture. The vulture is one of the ugliest birds you can conceive of. And greed is certainly one of the ugliest things in man that you can think of. But the mind is a vulture. It is never satisfied with anything. You go on giving to it; it goes on taking and goes on asking for more. It never feels grateful; it is always complaining that it is not enough. Nothing is enough to the mind. Question after question – meaningful, meaningless, relevant, irrelevant – and not even a small space for any answer to enter into your mind. It is so crowded with questions.

The heart knows no questions. And this is one of the mysteries of life: that the mind questions the whole life long and never receives any answer, and the heart never asks but receives the answer. But there is one thing to be remembered: the mind is noisy, there is maddening noise. The heart may be receiving the answer, but because of the noise of the mind you may not come to feel that the answer has been received, that you are carrying it with you, that you are pregnant with it.

Not only does the mind disturb your peace, your silence; it disturbs it to such an extent that the heart, which is capable of listening to silence, waiting, receptive, is denied all connection with your being. The mind monopolizes your being; it simply puts the heart aside. And because the heart is silent, and a gentleman, it does not quarrel; it simply goes down the street, waits by the side of the road.

Mind wants to occupy the whole space. The disciple has to understand this whole situation – that the dictatorship of the mind has to be destroyed, that the mind is only a servant, not a master. The master is the heart, because all that is beautiful grows in the heart; all that is valuable comes out of the heart: your love, your compassion, your meditation. Anything that is valuable grows in the garden of the heart.

Mind is a desert, nothing grows there – only sand and sand and barren land. It has never given any fruit, any flower. You have to understand it: mind should not be supported as much as you have been supporting it up to now. Mind has to be put in its right place.

The throne belongs to the heart. And this is the revolution through which the disciple becomes a devotee: when the heart becomes the master, and the mind becomes a servant. This has to be remembered: that as a servant, the mind is perfect. As a master, it is the worst master possible; as a servant, it is the best.

And the heart – wherever it is, either on the throne or on the street – is your only hope, the only possibility for you to be bridged with your being, to be bridged with existence. It is the only possibility for songs to arise in you, stars to descend in you, for your life to become a rejoicing, a dance.

You are asking me how to stop this mind, its constant questioning, its silly crowd of questions. That is where everybody takes the wrong step. If you try to stop it, you will never be able to stop it. Ignore it. Be indifferent to it. Let it chatter. Be aloof, unconcerned – as if it does not matter whether it chatters or not, whether there are questions or not. Only this aloofness, this ignoring – Buddha has given it the right name, *upeksha* – this indifference slowly, slowly makes the miracle happen.

What you want to achieve by fighting is not possible, because when you fight with someone you are giving energy to the enemy. You are giving attention, and attention is food; you are getting entangled with the mind, and mind enjoys a good fight. It has never happened that anybody has been able to stop the mind by fighting with it. That is the most important thing to understand: don't take any step towards fighting. Just ignore, just be aloof, just let the mind do whatever it wants to do. When the mind feels unwelcome, when the mind sees that you are no longer interested in it, that it is pointless to go on shouting – you are not even hearing it, you are not even curious about what is going on in the mind – it stops.

It happened...and I have remembered it because the boy is here today. He is my sister's son.

He was very young, six years old. We had gone to see the chief minister of Madhya Pradesh and the boy's father was driving. The father had gone to make inquiries, to say that I had come, and ask whether the chief minister was in the house or not.

At that very moment – the boy must have been feeling sleepy in the jeep; we had come a long distance – he fell asleep and hit his head on the dashboard in front of him. He looked at me. I didn't pay any attention; I looked outside the jeep. He was going to cry and create trouble – he looked again and again I looked outside.

Then his father came out. I went in for a half-hour meeting. Then we went home. It was almost two hours later, as we arrived home, that he started crying. As soon as he saw his mother he immediately started crying. I said, "What happened?"

He said, "I hit my head on the jeep."

I said, "That happened two hours ago!"

He said, "I know, but there was no point in crying because twice I looked at you and you looked outside the window. What is the point in crying with such a man? You did not even ask what had happened...you had seen that I had hit my head. Now my mother is here; now I can cry."

Even that small child could understand that when there is indifference, it is pointless to make any fuss; it is as if there was nobody in the jeep.

When you are indifferent, the mind starts feeling as if there is nobody – what is the point of all the questions? Because you are interested, curious, you get involved; you are giving juice to the mind.

Indifference to the mind is meditation.

And all those questions will disappear, because they are absolutely meaningless. And when the chattering of the mind has disappeared, there is a silence, a peace, so that you can hear the still, small voice of your heart. Only the heart knows the answer – it already knows it.

And if you are with a master, the heart simply says yes to the master, because the heart knows the answer already. Perhaps the master is putting it in a better way, more articulate, but the heart is in complete agreement. And that agreement dissolves all distances between the master and the disciple. Then silence is not only silence, it is also communion. Then things are not said but heard; then things are not said but shown.

And when the heart is totally willing, life is such a simple, uncomplicated phenomenon that you cannot conceive of anything more simple. It is the mind which creates complications, goes on creating complications and questions. Mind's whole expertise is to create complications. If you want to live a simple, a beautiful, a silent, a joyful, a blissful life, let the mind be ignored and let the heart be restored to its status as master. This is the whole work of a religious seeker; nothing more is needed.

Osho,

I have never been good at remembering my dreams. They seem to be there only in times of emotional crisis. Once or twice a year I have a 'big' dream which is more like a vision – and that's it.

During the last years it has become worse, and now it's down to zero. Considering dreams as important for my work as a therapist, I have tried hard with all kinds of methods but had no success.

Recently I made peace with it. As lots of flashes and intuitions come up in the daytime, or before I'm falling asleep, I thought this might be fine too. After yesterday's discourse where you said that to unburden the subconscious is the way to the superconscious, I started worrying and wondering again. Am I so repressive? What am I scared of that makes me incapable of remembering my dreams?

The process of dreaming and the process of remembering the dream are two things. Very few people remember dreams; that does not mean that they don't have dreams.

Everybody has dreams – but remembering a dream is a totally different thing. Even the people who remember dreams remember only the last dreams, the dreams of the early morning when you are just waking up, because the mechanism of memory is part of the conscious mind. Dreams happen in the unconscious; the unconscious doesn't have any memory mechanism. Only the conscious mind has the memory mechanism. So if a dream is happening in the unconscious mind but very close to the conscious mind, then it is remembered faintly, vaguely.

In the morning when you are waking up you are coming closer to the conscious mind, from the unconscious back to the conscious mind. The last dream, the tail end, will be remembered, because it will be very close to when you wake up. So even people who remember, remember only the last dreams. They have been dreaming for almost six hours through the whole night; if they sleep for eight hours, they dream for six hours. You can catch hold of just a faint reflection of the last dream, but if you don't catch hold of it for a few seconds, it will have gone. As you become more awake, you are farther away from the unconscious. So to different people, different things will be happening. There are people who wake up very slowly; they don't wake up quickly, in a jump. The people who wake up quickly, in a jump, will have a different kind of memory from the people who wake up very slowly. They will have another kind of memory.

It also depends on what kind of dreams you are having. Because you are a therapist – and not only a therapist, but *my* therapist – your repression cannot be superficial. Because my whole teaching is: Don't repress; live out every instinct, every feeling, every emotion. If you are living out your emotions, your feelings, then you will not have superficial dreams; your dreams will be very deep. They will be less in the unconscious and more in the collective unconscious – so deep that you will not be able to remember them. Unless a special effort is made, they cannot be remembered. And the only effort that is possible is hypnosis.

If you are hypnotized and led by your hypnotist deep into your unconscious and asked, "What is happening there? What kind of dream is going on?" only then will you be able to express it to him. When you wake up, you will not be able to remember what you have said either. It will take a long training between you and the hypnotist. After each hypnosis he has to suggest to you that you will remember it when you wake up. He has to emphasize it every time so much that it becomes a deep-rooted impression. Then you may be able to remember your dreams. But there is no need. Unless you are especially working on dreams, for some specific purpose, there is no need.

I am emphasizing that you should ignore the mind. Now the unconscious, collective unconscious, cosmic unconscious... These are all parts of the mind, and you are trying to remember them. Just the conscious mind is enough to torture you – why do you need to remember the unconscious mind?

In the East we have been aware that the conscious mind is not the only mind. Below it, there is the unconscious mind; then below that is the collective unconscious mind, then below that is the cosmic unconscious mind. Above it, there is the superconscious mind; above that there is the collective superconscious mind, above that there is the cosmic superconscious mind. And when I say *mind* I mean this whole range; they are one entity, one rainbow.

Ignore them all. There is no need to remember. Many people are in madhouses because by some accident their collective unconscious has broken up and released its memories. Now their conscious mind is not capable of holding those memories, the weight is too much; that's what is driving them mad.

For example, in your collective unconscious mind, the woman who is your wife now may have been your mother in your past life. If this memory comes to your mind then you are going to be in trouble. Then how are you going to behave with your wife – as your mother or as your wife? Just being your wife was enough; just being your mother was enough too; now she is both. And you will be crushed, because you cannot have a sexual relationship with a woman who is your mother...the whole inhibition of thousands of years. And how will you manage your wife? Because she has no remembrance she is going to say, "You are crazy, just forget all about it." But you cannot forget about it.

Nature has a beautiful arrangement: with each death, a thick layer of forgetfulness comes over your memories. You are carrying all the memories of all your lives. But a small human being finds it so difficult to live with a small conscious mind of one life – if so many lives burst upon him he is bound to be insane. It is a natural protection.

It happened...

I was in Jabalpur and a girl was brought to me. She must have been, at that time, nine years of age. She remembered her past life completely – so realistically that it was not a memory for her, it was a continuity. It was just some accidental error in nature that there was no barrier between the past life and this life.

There is a place just eighty miles away from Jabalpur, Katni. She was born in Katni and she remembered that she had her family in Jabalpur. She remembered the names, she remembered her husband, she remembered her sons, the house – she remembered everything. One of my friends brought them to me.

I said, "This is strange, because the people she is remembering are living just three or four blocks away from my house." They had a petrol pump, so I used to go for petrol at their petrol pump every day. But I said, "Wait, wait in my house and I will call them – the Pathak brothers – I will call them and we will see whether this girl remembers them or not."

So they came with their servants and a few neighbors. There were twelve, thirteen people in the crowd, so that they could see whether she could find out... She immediately jumped, and said, "Brother, have you recognized me or not?" She caught hold of both brothers, among thirteen people, and she inquired about the mother and the children...and father had died, and she was crying. It was not a memory, it was a continuity. They took her to their home and then it was a problem: the girl was torn apart about whether to go to this family's house in Jabalpur and live there, or to go back to Katni to the new family where she had been born.

Of course, in this family she had lived for seventy years, so the pull was more towards the past-life family. And in the new family she had been born only nine years before; there was no pull – but that was her family, her real family. This other family was only a memory, but to her it was such a heart-rending problem. And both the families were disturbed about what to do: if she remained in Jabalpur, she would remember the other family continuously, worry about what was happening to them and feel, "I want to go there." If she was there, she would be thinking that she wanted to be in Jabalpur.

Finally I suggested that the only way – it was a freak case, there was nothing spiritual in it – was that she needed a deep hypnosis for a few days, so the barrier could be created. She had to be hypnotized to forget the old and the past. Unless she could forget the past, her whole life was going to be a misery. Both families were ready to accept that something had to be done. She was hypnotized continually for at least ten days, to forget. It took ten sessions to create a small barrier so that the old life's memories didn't float into the new life.

I have been inquiring about her. She is now perfectly okay – married, has children, has forgotten completely. Even when those people come to see her, she does not recognize them. But her barrier is very thin and artificial. Any accident, and the barrier could be broken, or any hypnotist could break it very easily within ten sessions; or some great shock, and the barrier could be broken.

There is no need for you to remember. It is perfectly good. We have to get free from the mind. The East has known all the layers of the mind, but the East has emphasized a totally different aspect than the West: ignore it – you are the pure consciousness behind all these layers.

Western psychology is just childish, just born at the end of the last century. It is not even a hundred years old. They have taken up the desire to enter into dreams and to find out, to dig deeper into what is there in the mind. There is nothing. You will find more and more memories, more and more dreams, and you will destroy the person because you will make him vulnerable to an unnecessary burden which has to be erased. One has to go beyond mind, not within the mind. And you don't have any memory as far as the state of beyond mind is concerned.

Just drop the idea of the mind. Don't meddle with it; it is getting into unnecessary trouble and a nightmare. You have to surpass the mind, you have to transcend the mind. Your whole effort should be one-pointed, and that is how to be a no-mind: no dreams, no memories, no experiences. Then you are at the very center of your being. Only then do you taste something of immortality. Only then, for the first time, do you know what intelligence is.

Osho,

Only just now I discovered that a master-disciple relationship is really a two-way affair, in which the disciple needs to respond openly to the master in order for the master to be able to do his work.

I myself, on the contrary, have always watched passively, kept a distance and drawn my own conclusions.

Please comment.

The master never does anything – and if you remain aloof, nothing will ever happen to you. Your receptivity and openness are not needed for the master to do something; your openness and receptivity are needed so that the very presence of the master can provoke something to happen in you – and these are two different things. Doing something is a very positive effort, and just allowing your presence for something to happen in you is a totally different thing. There is no positive effort. The effort is on the side of the disciple.

So what you have discovered you have discovered wrongly: it is not a two-way affair, not a two-way road; it is a one-way street. It is up to you to be open, ready, available.

The presence of the master is there, just like the light – you open your eyes and the light is there. The light does not travel to your eyes in particular. You can keep your eyes closed and the light will not knock on your eyelids: "Please open your eyes." You can keep your eyes closed; the light is very democratic, it will not interfere. But if you open your eyes you will see the light; not only the light, but in the light you will see many other things too: the flowers, the people, the whole world. Still, you cannot say that light has been doing something to you. Something is transpiring in you. It will not transpire without the light, so certainly the presence of the light is needed – but just the presence is needed, not the action.

Action is needed on your part, not just presence, because you can be present here and closed – nothing will evolve out of it. The disciple has to do everything.

And this is the beauty of the whole phenomenon. Otherwise, you will become a puppet in the hands of the master. Then he will do things that he wants to do; then he will make you the way he wants to make you – the ideal, the mold. He will destroy your individuality; he will destroy your freedom. No master worth the name can do that. The master can give his whole being to you, can make it available – but only as a presence, not as an action.

The doing is on the part of the disciple. You have to be receptive, you have to be silent, you have to be meditative, you have to trust *everything*, because it is your life and you should be responsible for it. You are not a painting that the master painter can change in whatever way he wants.

I have heard that in a small school, a beautiful painting was shown that had been made by the drawing teacher of the school. He was showing the students the art and the craft of painting. And he said, "It is such a delicate phenomenon. Look at the painting."

And they said, "Yes, we can see a man with a sad face."

The painter went to the painting and just gave one or two touches with his brush and the whole painting changed – the face was smiling. And because the face was smiling, the whole complex of trees and flowers and stars now had a different effect. Everybody was impressed; the teachers were impressed. Parents had come; they were very much impressed. Just one small boy was not interested.

The painter asked, "Are you not interested?"

He said, "I am interested. But this is not something great; my mother does it every day."

He said, "What do you mean? Is she a painter?"

He said, "She is not a painter. But I go home smiling, and with one slap the whole world changes into tears and tears and crying. And if you want me to show you, I can show you here, because I have also become an expert. Every day it is happening."

He simply went and hit a small girl sitting there, and the girl started crying. And she had been smiling and enjoying, but suddenly the hit, and tears came to her eyes and she started crying. And because of her crying and this boy's craftsmanship, the whole crowd fell silent.

And even the drawing teacher said, "This is right. I was thinking that I had some great art. Your mother knows better. Without brush, without color, just a hit and everything changes; the whole world changes."

The master can change you, but that change is very costly. He can do many things, but you are becoming more and more of a slave. You had come to be liberated, and it is going the wrong way. No authentic master has ever done anything. He has made himself available in many ways. He has taught you how to be available, how to be open, how to be receptive – and then whatever your potential is, it will start growing. In the blissful showering of the presence of the master your potential will grow, but it will grow according to its own intrinsic qualities. Nothing is imposed from outside.

So please note it down: your observation is not right, it is not two-way traffic. From the master's side there is no traffic at all. You have to do something. Certainly the master is present and available, his love is available. In his shadow, in his loving radiation, you will start growing. But he will not touch you; he will let you be whatever you can be. Whatsoever is your destiny, you should not be carried away from it.

He is just a silent help: without touching you, he transforms you. That is the miracle of the master.

Osho,

Sitting in your presence, meditation is really at its best. If asked why, I would say that it is because your blissful presence is contagious and somehow motivates me to be as total as possible.

Osho, would you please explain again how it is possible to be in such a nice meditation when not being in your presence?

My presence has to be only a lesson. Once you have learned the art of opening, the art of being silent, it does not matter whether I am present or not. If you have really learned it, it will happen anywhere. It may be a little difficult in the beginning, but soon you will get the knack of it.

It is almost like swimming. The teacher who teaches swimming just gives you courage and trust, and is there so that nothing goes wrong. Just in three or four days' time, one hour each day, you start swimming. And the moment you start swimming you are surprised – why didn't you start it from the very beginning? There is nothing to it. It's just that in the beginning you were not moving your arms artfully; it was haphazard. In just three or four days you have learned to move your arms more smoothly, more harmoniously; now the teacher is not needed. Now you can go anywhere, for any distance, because the depth of the bottom does not matter; you are swimming on the surface. The depth can be one thousand feet, ten thousand feet, five miles deep; it does not matter, because you are always swimming on the surface.

And once you have learned... It has not been heard of in the whole history of humanity that anybody who has learned swimming has forgotten it. You may not swim for fifty years, and when again somebody pushes you into the swimming pool, you start swimming. You cannot say, "For fifty years I have not practiced." It is not a question of practice at all. It is a knack: once you have known it, you have known it; there is no way not to know it anymore.

Meditation is also a knack.

You have not to become attached to the presence of the master, because that will be learning something wrong. You have to learn how you are opening. Forget about the master; that is his business: to be present or not to be present. Your business is to see how you are opening, what happens in your opening, and then try on your own, when you are alone to see whether it can happen or not. It is bound to happen. Maybe in the beginning you will feel that it is a little difficult; a certain attachment grows unconsciously. But you cannot say that the teacher has to follow you everywhere, wherever you go swimming. That will not do. Then each swimmer will need one teacher; it will be too much. Each meditator will need one master with him; it will be too costly, and there is no need at all. You just have to see what is happening in you, and let the same happen when the master is not present.

Or, you can visualize. He will be present somewhere, a few miles away. Here, it is a few feet away. It is only a question of visualizing – just visualize that your master is a few feet away. Space makes no difference, but you have to learn what happens in you, so that you can repeat it in the absence of the master. Otherwise, one can become attached to things which were there to help you – but now they will hinder you. The presence of the master was to help you; now it has become a hindrance, because the master is not there, so you cannot meditate.

Remember, no attachment should grow, no clinging should grow. They are all against your independence, your freedom, your individuality. And whatever is happening here can happen anywhere; it just needs a little understanding of how it happens here. Just try. Even if you fail a few times, don't be worried. It is a knack which will come to you. And once it happens without any support from outside – even the smallest support, such as the presence of the master – you will feel a great joy, because a great freedom has happened. Now there are no barriers for you. Wherever you are you can be in meditation, you can be in silence, you can be peaceful. Now you can carry your paradise within you. And unless that happens, a disciple has not matured.

9 The Master Is a Mirror

Osho,
What is it that reduces me to a hysterical, incoherent child in your presence or even at the thought of being in your presence?

Is it something inherent in the master-disciple relationship, or my psychological immaturity, or both?

Humanity is not yet mature. We have the faces of human beings, but our minds are lagging far behind.

In the ordinary world, it is easy to manage your mask, your pretension, your hypocrisy. But when you come to a master... The very urge to come to a master shows a tremendous desire in you to know your original face, to know yourself. The face that you are now carrying is not your original face; it is not you. I am saying you are not *you*, and you know it.

The master is only a mirror. You cannot deceive the mirror, it simply reflects your reality.

There is an ancient parable of a very ugly woman who was very antagonistic towards mirrors because she thought, just as you all think, that it was the mirror that created the ugliness in her – because when the mirror was not there, she was no longer ugly. She was so madly against mirrors that whenever she would see a mirror, she would immediately break it. The parable is significant. That's what we are all doing in our lives in many ways. Whatsoever reflects our reality we want to escape from, because it is not gratifying.

Here in my presence, or even when you think of me, if you feel yourself as immature, a retarded child, don't try to explain it away in any way. This is the truth. And this is not only your truth; this is the truth of the whole of humanity. You are just fortunate that you have become aware of it. You have come across a mirror.

Breaking the mirror is not going to help. Poisoning Socrates has not helped the Greeks – he was a mirror. Crucifying Jesus has not helped the Jews – he was a mirror. Killing al-Hillaj Mansoor has not helped the Mohammedans – he was a mirror. On the contrary, people have remained retarded, childish, because there is no one to show them where they are, who they are. They are in a crowd of similar kinds of retarded children.

After the First World War, for the first time in Germany they tried to figure out the average mental age of a soldier. Thousands of soldiers went through the process, through many experiments, and the result was shocking and shattering to the whole of human pride. The result was that the average mental age of the soldiers was only fourteen years. And the average age of those who are not soldiers cannot be much more. A man may be seventy years old – his body has aged, but his mind has remained at the age of fourteen. And once in a while you can see it in yourself; you can see it in others in certain situations.

Every woman knows moments when she starts throwing tantrums; the tantrums cannot be coming out of maturity. Every man knows that whenever he feels nervous, he starts smoking. Now, smoking cannot help in any way, but it diverts your mind from nervousness. Only nervous people smoke. And you can watch: some days you smoke more; some days you smoke less. The days you smoke more are the days when you are very tense, worried, very much in anguish. The world is too much. You are feeling so nervous that you want to divert your mind to something, something uncomplicated, something not involving anybody else – because that could bring more complications. The cigarette is very innocent and very soothing, because it has a chemical like the one in tea and coffee, which gives a certain soothing effect of the moment.

And more specifically, smoking has a resemblance to a deep-rooted remembrance of drinking milk at your mother's breast. The breast has almost the same warmth, the milk is warm just as the smoke from your cigarette or cigar is warm. The cigarette or cigar have the same feel on your lips as the nipples of your mother, and the smoke is flowing inside you just like the milk through the nipple. You have fallen back into childhood: those golden days when there were no anxieties, no problems, no worries. So whenever you feel nervous, you start looking for your cigarette. When you are not nervous – when you are feeling happy and blissful and joyous – you completely forget all about cigarettes. All smokers are retarded people, so the retarded people are in the majority in the world.

And there are other substitutes. You may not be smoking and you may think, "I'm not retarded because I use chewing gum." And it is worse than cigarettes – chewing gum! You are not only retarded, you are stupid, engaged in an activity which is absolutely useless, uncreative, unnecessarily tiring your mouth and your teeth. But it proves Charles Darwin was right. Although scientists have tried in many ways to disprove the theory of evolution proposed by Charles Darwin, the theory has such psychological significance that even if it is proved wrong, its significance cannot be destroyed.

Just watch a monkey. He cannot sit in one posture, he cannot sit on one branch. The whole day he is continually chewing this or that, eating this or that.. From the time he wakes up in the morning till he goes back to sleep, he is chewing something. Perhaps man is not yet completely free from his animal heritage – although he walks on two legs, that does not make much difference. As far as I know, monkeys don't think that you have evolved, developed, gone forward further than them. They laugh at the very idea. They think you have fallen from the trees. And they have substantial reasoning behind it. You are no longer as strong as a monkey; you cannot live in trees, you cannot go on jumping from one tree to another tree for miles. You have lost the beauty of the body that the monkey has. Just because you started walking on two legs...

Monkeys think, "Poor fellows...those few monkeys can't make it living in the trees" – because it is a very challenging life, risky, full of danger – "those cowards have got down onto the earth and started walking on two legs. Not only that, to hide their cowardice, they are proposing a theory of evolution!" No monkey agrees with the theory of evolution.

If in my presence you feel in yourself a childishness, a mind which has not become mature. This awareness has to be welcomed. Once you become aware that you are retarded somewhere, that something is blocking your consciousness, then those blocks can be removed. In fact, to be aware that there are some blocks – the very awareness removes them. There are things which one has just to be aware of. The very awareness brings the transformation; it is not that after being aware you have to do something to make the change. Seeing your mind as childish, you can also see that you are not the mind – otherwise, who is seeing the mind as childish? There is something beyond the mind: the watcher on the hills. You are only looking at the mind. You have completely forgotten who is looking at it.

Watch the mind, but don't forget the watcher – because your reality is centered in the watcher, not in the mind. And the watcher is always a fully grown-up, mature, centered consciousness. It needs no growth. And once you become aware that the mind is only an instrument in the hands of your witnessing soul, then there is no problem; the mind can be used in the right way. Now the master is awake, and the servant can be ordered to do whatever is needed. Ordinarily the master is asleep. We have forgotten the watcher, and the servant has become the master. And the servant is a servant – it is certainly not very intelligent.

You have to be reminded of a basic fact: intelligence belongs to the watching consciousness; memory belongs to the mind. Memory is one thing; memory is not intelligence. But the whole of humanity has been deceived for centuries and told indirectly that the memory is intelligence. Your schools, your colleges, your universities are not trying to find your intelligence; they are trying to find out who is capable of memorizing more.

And now we know perfectly well that memory is a mechanical thing. A computer can have memory, but a computer cannot have intelligence. And a computer can have a better memory than you have. The day is not far off when people will be carrying small computers in their pockets rather than unnecessarily going through years of studying history and geography and chemistry and physics. All that can be contained in a small computer which you can carry in your pocket, and whatever information you want, the computer can supply it immediately, and it is going to be absolutely correct.

Man's memory is not so reliable. It can forget; it can get mixed up, it can get blocked. Sometimes you say, "I remember it, it is just on the tip of my tongue." Strange, it is on the tip of your tongue, then why don't you speak?

But you say it is not coming, "It is on the tip of my tongue, I know that I know, and it is not very far; it is very close." But still some block, some very thin block – it may be just a curtain – is not allowing it to surface.

And the more you try, the more tense you become, the less is the possibility of remembering it. Finally, you forget all about it, you start doing something else – preparing a cup of tea or digging a hole in the garden – and suddenly it is there because you were relaxed, you had forgotten all about it, there was no tension. It surfaced. A tense mind becomes narrow. A relaxed mind becomes wide – many more memories can pass through it. A tense mind becomes so narrow that only very few memories can pass through it.

But for thousands of years a misunderstanding has continued, and it continues still, as if memory is intelligence. It is not. You will find people who have a great memory but no intelligence, and you can also find people who have great intelligence and no memory at all.

It is said about Thomas Alva Edison that perhaps he is the only man who is credited with at least one thousand inventions, but his memory was nil.

In the First World War he was standing in a queue to receive his ration card. Ration cards had come into existence for the first time. By and by the queue became smaller and smaller, and finally he came to the front and the clerk shouted, "Thomas Alva Edison!" – he looked here and there, because he had forgotten his name. Because it was long, long ago...when his father and mother were alive, they used to call him by name. Now he was so well known, such a great scientist, a great professor that nobody used his name, people called him 'Professor.' He himself had forgotten. Fortunately, one man in the queue behind him recognized that this fellow looked like Thomas Alva Edison, who was standing in front and looking here and there.

And the man said, "What is your name?"

Edison said, "My God, I will have to go home and ask my wife."

The man said, "As far as I know, you are Thomas Alva Edison."

Edison said, "It seems I have heard this name somewhere before. Perhaps I am. If nobody else claims it, then that card is mine."

He was such a great intelligence. You cannot find many more people of that intelligence. But, going for a lecture tour, before getting into the car, he said good-bye to his wife and kissed her and waved at her maidservant. And the wife said, "You are absolutely wrong; I am your maidservant and she is your wife!"

He said, "The whole day I am so engaged in experiments. I only come home at night. It is a long time since I have seen my wife in the sunlight, so please forgive me – whichever is my wife, I kiss her, and whichever is my maidservant, I wave to her. But let me go, because the train is standing at the platform."

Absolutely no memory! His wife used to keep notes of his thoughts because sometimes he would come to a thought, but it was incomplete. And before he forgot it, he would tell somebody, whoever was close by, "Please write it down and keep it for me. Whenever I need it, just remind me – because half is missing. It will come, but my fear is that when the other half comes, this half may be lost."

Somebody suggested, "You are behaving strangely. Why don't *you* keep a notebook?"

He said, "That is the trouble. I have been keeping notebooks, but then I go on forgetting where I have put them. Then the notebook becomes the problem. This is far better. At least somebody is responsible for the half thought and he will remind me: 'This is half your thought. If the other half has come to your mind, take this and relieve me of the burden.'"

In India – as in Arabia, China, Greece, Rome, in all old countries – all the old languages depend on memory, not on intelligence. You can become a great Sanskrit scholar without a bit of intelligence – no need for intelligence, just your memory has to be perfect. Just like a parrot; the parrot does not understand what he is saying, but he can say it absolutely correctly, with the right pronunciation. You can teach him whatever you want. All old languages depend on memory.

And the whole educational system of the world depends on memory. In examinations, they don't ask the student something that will show his intelligence, but something that will show his memory, how much he remembers from textbooks. This is one of the reasons for your retarded mind. You have used memory as if it were your intelligence – a tremendously grave misunderstanding. Because you know and remember and you can quote scriptures, you start thinking that you are grown up, you are mature, that you are knowledgeable, you are wise. This is the problem that you are feeling.

I am not a man of memory. And my effort here is to provoke a challenge in you so that you start moving towards your intelligence. It is of no use how much you remember. What is significant is how much you have experienced yourself.

And for experiencing the inner world, you need great intelligence – memory is of no help. Yes, if you want to be a scholar, a professor, a pundit, you can memorize scriptures and you can have a great pride that you know so much. And other people will also think that you know so much, and deep down your memory is nothing but ignorance.

In front of me, you cannot hide your ignorance. In every possible way, I try to bring your ignorance in front of you because the sooner you get hold of your ignorance, the sooner you can get rid of it. And to know is such a beautiful experience that in comparison, borrowed knowledge is just idiotic.

I have heard about the archbishop of Japan. He wanted to convert a Zen master to Christianity. Not knowing, not understanding anything of the inner world, he went to the master. He was received with great love and respect.

He opened the Bible that he carried with him and started reading the Sermon on the Mount. He wanted to impress upon the Zen master that: "We follow this man. What do you think about these words, about this man?"

He had read only two sentences and the Zen master said, "That will do. You are following a good man, but he was following other good men. Neither you know nor does he know. Just go home."

The archbishop was very shocked. He said, "You should at least let me finish the whole thing."

The Zen master said, "No nonsense here. If you know something, you say it. Close the book because we are not believers in books. You carry the very truth in your being, and yet you are searching in dead books. Go home and look within. If you have found something inside, then come back. If you think these lines that you have repeated to me are from Jesus Christ, you are wrong."

Jesus Christ was simply repeating the Old Testament. He was trying his whole life to convince people: "I am the last prophet of the Jews." He had never heard the word *Christian*, he had never heard the word *Christ*. He was born a Jew, he lived a Jew, he died a Jew. And his whole effort was to convince the Jews: "I am the awaited prophet, the savior which Moses has promised. I have come."

The Jews could have forgiven him. Jews are not bad people. And Jews are not violent people either. Nobody who is as intelligent as the Jews are can be violent. Forty percent of Nobel Prizes go to Jews – it is simply out of all proportion to their population. Almost half the Nobel Prizes go to Jews, and the other half to the rest of the world. Such intelligent people would not have crucified Jesus if he was saying something which was of his own experience. But he was saying things which were not his experience – all borrowed, and yet he was pretending that they were his. Jews could not forgive that, that dishonesty.

Otherwise, Jesus was not creating any trouble for anybody. He was a little bit of a nuisance. Just like the Witnesses of Jehovah or the Hare Krishna people; they are a little bit of a nuisance. If they catch hold of you they will not listen to you at all and they will go on giving you all kinds of wisdom, advice – and you are not interested;

you are going to some other work, you want to be left alone. But they are determined to save you. Whether you want to be saved or not does not matter – you have to be saved.

It happened that I was sitting near the Ganges in Allahabad, and it was just as the sun was setting. A man started shouting from the water, "Save me! Save me!"

I am not interested in saving anybody. So I looked all around... If somebody was interested in saving him, let him have the first chance. But there was nobody, so finally I had to jump. And with difficulty – he was a heavy, fat man,. The fattest men in India you will find in Allahabad and Varanasi – the brahmins, the Hindu priests, who do nothing except eat.

Somehow I pulled him out. And he started being angry: "Why did you pull me out?"

I said, "This is something! You were asking for help, you were shouting, 'Save me!'"

He said, "It was because I was becoming afraid of death. But in fact I was committing suicide."

I said, "I am sorry, I had no idea that you were committing suicide."

I pushed the man back! And he started shouting again, "Help!"

I said, "Now wait for somebody else to come. I will sit here and watch you commit suicide."

He said, "What kind of man are you? I am dying!"

I said, "Die! That is your business!"

But there are people who are bent upon saving you. The Zen master said to the archbishop, "Jesus was repeating old prophets. You are repeating Jesus. Repetition is not going to help anybody. You need your own experience – that is the only deliverance, the only liberation."

It is good you understand that your mind starts behaving like a child, immature. Remember also who is watching the child, the immature mind, and be with the watcher. Pull out all your attachments from the mind – because the mind is only a mechanism – and the mind will start functioning perfectly well. Once your watcher is alert, your intelligence starts growing for the first time.

Mind's work is memory, which the mind can do very well. But the mind has been burdened with intelligence, which is not its work, by the society,. It has crippled its memory. It has not made you more intelligent, it has simply made your memory erroneous, fallible.

Always remember: your eyes are for seeing, don't try to listen with the eyes. Your ears are for listening, don't try to see with the ears. Otherwise, you will get into an insane state. While your eyes are perfectly all right, your ears are perfectly all right, you are trying to do something with a mechanism that is not meant to do it. If your watcher is clear, then the body does its own functions, the mind does its own functions, the heart does its own functions. Nobody interferes in each others' work.

And life becomes a harmony, an orchestra.

Osho,

Why do I always feel so miserable? Have I ever really let you in? The moment I sit in front of you, all is gone. What is happening? Can't you take it all away?

The answer is in your question. You don't want to take responsibility for your own being; somebody else should do it. And that's the sole cause of misery. There is no way that anybody else can take away your misery. There is no way that anybody else can make you blissful. But if you become aware that you are responsible for whether you are miserable or blissful... Nobody else can do anything. Your misery is your doing; your bliss will also be your doing. But it is hard to accept: misery is *my* doing?

Everybody feels that others are responsible for his misery. The husband thinks the wife is responsible for his misery, the wife thinks the husband is responsible for her misery, the children think the parents are responsible for their misery, the parents think the children are responsible for their misery. It has become such a complexity. And whenever somebody else is responsible for your misery, you are not aware that by giving them responsibility you are losing your freedom.

Responsibility and freedom are two sides of the same coin.

And because you think others are responsible for your misery... That's why there are charlatans, so-called saviors, messengers of God, prophets who go on telling you, "You have not to do anything, just follow me. Believe in me and I will save you. I am your shepherd, you are my sheep."

Strange, that not a single person stood up against people like Jesus Christ and said, "This is utterly insulting to say that you are the shepherd and we are sheep, and you are the savior and we are just dependent on your compassion, that our whole religion is just to believe in you." But because we have been throwing the responsibility for our misery on others, we have accepted the corollary that bliss will also come from others. Naturally, if misery comes from others, then bliss has to come from others. But then what are *you* doing? You are neither responsible for misery nor are you responsible for bliss – then what is your function? What is your purpose – just to be a target for a few people to make you miserable and for others to help you and save you and make you blissful? Are you just a puppet?

All the strings are in the hands of others. You are not respectful of your humanity; you do not respect yourself. You don't have any love for your own being, for your own freedom. If you are respectful of your life, you will refuse all saviors. You will say to all the saviors, "Get lost! Just save yourself, that's enough. It is *our* life and we have to live it. If we do something wrong, we will suffer the misery; we will accept the consequences of our wrong action without any complaint."

Perhaps that is the way one learns – by falling, one gets up again; by going astray, one comes back again. You commit a mistake but each mistake makes you more intelligent; you will not commit the same mistake again. If you commit the same mistake again, that means you are not learning. You are not using your intelligence, you are behaving like a robot.

My whole effort is to give back to every human being the self-respect that belongs to him – which he has given to just anybody. And the whole stupidity starts because you are not ready to accept that *you* are responsible for your misery.

Just think, you cannot find a single misery for which you are not responsible. It may be jealousy, it may be anger, it may be greed – but something in *you* must be the reason that is creating the misery. And have you seen anybody in the world ever making anybody else blissful? That too depends on you, on your silence, your love, your peace, your trust. And the miracle happens – nobody does it.

In Tibet, there is a beautiful story about Marpa. It may not be factual, but it is tremendously significant. I don't care much about facts. My emphasis is on the significance and the truth, which is a totally different thing.

Marpa heard about a master. He was searching and he went to the master, he surrendered to the master, he trusted totally. And he asked the master, "What am I supposed to do now?"

The master said, "Once you have surrendered to me, you are not supposed to do anything. Just believe in me. My name is the only secret mantra for you. Whenever you are in difficulty, just remember my name and everything will be all right."

Marpa touched his feet. And he tried it immediately – he was such a simple man. He walked on the river. Other disciples who had been with the master for years could not believe it – he was walking on the water!

They reported to the master that: "That man, you have not understood him. He is no ordinary man, he is walking on water!"

The master said, "What?"

They all ran towards the river and Marpa was walking on the water, singing songs, dancing. When he came to the shore, the master asked, "What is the secret?"

He said, "What is the secret? It is the same secret that you have given to me: your name. I remembered you. I said, 'Master, allow me to walk on water' and it happened."

The master could not believe that his name... He himself could not walk on water. But perhaps...he had never tried. But it would be better to check a few more things before he tried. So he said to Marpa, "Can you jump from that hill?"

Marpa said, "Whatever you say." He went up on the hill and jumped, and they were all standing in the valley waiting – just *pieces* of Marpa will be there! Even if they can find pieces of him, that will be enough – the hill was very high.

But Marpa came down smiling, sitting in a lotus posture. He came just under a tree in the valley, and sat down. They all surrounded him. They looked at him – not even a scratch.

The master said, "This is something. You used my name?"

He said, "It was your name."

The master said, "This is enough, now I am going to try," and the first step in the water, he sank.

Marpa could not believe it when he sank. His disciples jumped in and somehow pulled him out. He was half dead. The water was taken out of his lungs...somehow he survived.

And Marpa said, "What is the matter?"

The master said, "You just forgive me. I am no master, I am just a pretender."

But Marpa said, "If you are a pretender, then how did your name work?"

The pretender said, "My name has not worked. It is your trust. It does not matter who you trust – it is the trust, the love, the totality of it. I don't trust myself. I don't trust anybody. I cheat everybody – how can I trust? And I am always afraid of being cheated by others, because I cheat others. Trust is impossible for me. You are an innocent man, you trusted me. It is because of your trust that the miracles have happened."

Whether the story is true or not does not matter. One thing is certain, that your misery is caused by your mistakes and your bliss is caused by your trust, by your love. Your bondage is your creation and your freedom is your declaration.

You are asking me, "Why am I miserable?" You are miserable because you have not accepted the responsibility for it. Just see what your misery is, find out the cause and you will find the cause within yourself. Remove the cause and the misery will disappear. But people don't want to remove the cause, they want to remove the misery. That is impossible, that is absolutely unscientific.

And then you ask me to save you, to help you. There is no need for you to become a beggar. My people are not to become beggars.

My people are not sheep; my people are emperors. Accept your responsibility for misery, and you will find that just hidden inside you are all the causes of bliss, freedom, joy, enlightenment, immortality. No savior is needed. And there has never been any savior; all saviors are pseudo. They have been worshipped because you always wanted somebody to save you. They have always appeared because they were always in demand, and wherever there is a demand, there is a supply.

Once you depend on others, you are losing your soul. You are forgetting that you have a consciousness as universal as anybody else's, that you have a consciousness as great as any Gautam Buddha's – you are just not aware of it, you have not looked for it. And you have not looked because you are looking to others – somebody else to save you, somebody else to help you. So you go on begging without recognizing that this whole kingdom is yours.

This has to be understood as one of the most basic principles of sannyas: a declaration of self-respect and freedom and responsibility.

Osho,

Would you please talk about the *sadhana* based on holding as much as possible to the "I" thought or the sense "I am" and on asking oneself the questions, "Who am I?" Or "From where does this I arise?" In what way does this approach to meditation differ from that of watching the gaps between one's in-breath and out-breath? Does it make any difference whether one witnesses the breath focusing on the heart center or on the lower belly center?

It is an ancient method of meditation, but full of dangers. Unless you are alert, the greater possibility is that you will be led astray by the method rather than to the right goal. The method is simple – concentrating yourself on the concept of I, closing your eyes and inquiring, "Who am I?"

The greatest problem is that when you ask, "Who am I," who is going to answer you? Most probably the answer will come from your tradition, from your scriptures, from your conditioning. You have heard that: "I am not the body, I am not the mind. I am the soul, I am the ultimate, *Brahma*, I am God." You have heard all these kinds of thoughts before.

You will ask a few times, "Who am I? Who am I?" And then you will say, "I am the ultimate, Brahma." And this is not a discovery; it is simply stupid. If you want to go into the method rightly, then the question has not to be verbally asked. "Who am I?" has not to be repeated verbally. Because as long as it remains a verbal question, you will supply a verbal answer from the head. You have to drop the verbal question. It has to remain just a vague idea, just like a thirst. Not "I am thirsty." Can you see the difference? When you are thirsty, you feel the thirst. And if you are in a desert, you feel the thirst in every fiber of your body. You don't say, "I am thirsty, I am thirsty." It is no longer a linguistic question; it is existential.

If "Who am I?" is an existential question, if you are not asking it in language but instead the feeling of the question is settling inside your center, then there is no need for any answer. Then it is none of the mind's business. The mind will not hear that which is non-verbal, and the mind will not answer that which is non-verbal.

All your scriptures are in the mind, all your knowledge is gathered there.

Now you are entering an innocent space. You will not get the answer. You will get the feel, you will get the taste, you will get the smell. As you go deeper, you will be filled more with the feeling of being, of immortality, blissfulness, silence – a tremendous benediction.

But there is no answer like, "I am this, I am that." All that is from the scriptures. This feeling is from you, and this feeling has a truth about it. It is a perfectly valid method.

One of the great masters of this century, Raman Maharshi, used only this method for his disciples: "Who am I?" But I have come across hundreds of his disciples and they are nowhere near the ultimate experience. And the reason is because they know the answer already.

I have asked them, "Do you know the answer?"

They said, "We know the answer."

I said, "If you know the answer, then why are you asking? And your asking cannot go on very long – do it two or three times and the answer comes. The answer was already there, before the question." So it is just a mind game. If you want to play it, you can play it. But if you really want to go into it as it was meant by Raman Maharshi, and by all the ancient seers, it is a non-verbal thirst. So if you can avoid the danger of falling into a verbal question, it is perfectly good, you can go ahead.

Not knowing oneself hurts, it is a wound. Not knowing oneself makes the whole of life meaningless. You may know everything, only you do not know yourself – and that would be the *first* thing to know.

You have also asked about witnessing, watching the breath and where one should watch. Anywhere – because the point is not *where* you are watching, the point is that you are *watching*. The emphasis is on watching, watchfulness. All those points are just excuses. You can watch the breath at the tip of the nose where the breath goes in, you can watch it while it is going in, you can watch it when it returns – you can watch it anywhere. You can watch thoughts moving inside. The whole point is not to get lost in what you are watching, as if that is important. That is not important. The important thing is that you are watchful, that you have not forgotten to watch, that you are watching...watching...watching.

And slowly, slowly, as the watcher becomes more and more solid, stable, unwavering, a transformation happens. The things that you were watching disappear. For the first time, the watcher itself becomes the watched, the observer itself becomes the observed. You have come home.

Osho,

I have not expected anything from you, yet you have tricked me and given me some beautiful things. Is there anything a sannyasin has to ask for, or does everything happen on its own?

Everything happens on its own, but a sannyasin has to be alert not to miss the train. The train comes on its own, but you have to be alert. All around you so much is happening; every twenty-four hours – awake, asleep – you have to be watchful of what is happening. And the more you are alert, the more you will be surprised. The same things are happening that were happening before, but the meaning has changed, the significance is different.

The roseflower is the same, but now it is radiant, surrounded by some new energy that you were not aware of before – a new beauty. It seems you used to see only the outer side of the rose; now you are able to see its inner world. You used to watch the palace from the outside; now you have entered into its innermost chambers. You have seen the moon hundreds of times, but when you see it silently, peacefully, meditatively, you become aware of a beauty that you were not aware of before, a beauty that is not ordinarily available, for which you need to grow some insight. And that insight grows in silence, in peace.

It happened – a very significant incident. One of the Indian poets, Rabindranath Tagore, translated one of his small books of poems, *Gitanjali: "Offering Of Songs."* He was awarded the Nobel Prize for that small book. In India it had been available for at least fifteen years. But unless a book meets the international standards of language and gains international appreciation, it is difficult for it to get a Nobel Prize.

Rabindranath himself was a little worried, because he translated it and to translate poetry is always a very difficult affair. To translate prose is simple; to translate poetry is immensely difficult, because prose is of the marketplace and poetry is something of the world of love, of the world of beauty, of the world of the moon and stars. It is a delicate affair. And every language has its own nuances, which are almost untranslatable. Although the poet himself translated his own poetry, he was doubtful about the translation. So he showed it to one of the Christian missionaries, a very famous man of those days, C.F. Andrews – a very literate, cultured, sophisticated man.

Andrews suggested four changes. He said, "Everything else is right, but in four places it is not grammatically correct."

So Rabindranath simply accepted his advice, and changed those four places. In London, his friend, the Irish poet Yeats, called a meeting of English poets to hear Rabindranath's translation. Everybody appreciated it. The beauty of it was something absolutely new to the Western world.

But Yeats, who was the most prominent poet of England in those days, said, "Everything else is right, but in four places it seems that somebody who is not a poet has made some changes."

Rabindranath could not believe it. He asked, "Where are those four places?"

Yeats pointed out the four places exactly.

Rabindranath asked, "What is wrong?"

Yeats said, "There is nothing wrong, they are grammatically correct. But poetically... Whoever suggested them is a man who knows his grammar but does not know poetry. He is a man of the mind but not a man of the heart. The flow is obstructed, as if a river had come across a rock."

Rabindranath told him, "I asked C.F. Andrews; these are *his* words. I will tell you the words that I put there before."

And when he put his words in, Yeats said, "They are perfectly right although grammatically wrong. But grammar is not important. When it is a question of poetry, grammar is not important. Change it back, use your own words."

I have always thought that there are ways of the mind and there are ways of the heart; they need not be supportive of each other. And if it happens that the mind is not in agreement with the heart, then the mind is wrong. Its agreement or disagreement does not matter. What matters is that your heart feels at ease, peaceful, silent, harmonious, at home.

We are trained for the mind, so our mind is very articulate. And nobody takes any care of the heart. In fact, it is pushed aside by everybody because it is of no use in the marketplace, it is no use in the world of ambitions, no use in politics, no use in business. But with me, the situation is just the opposite – the mind is of no use. The heart...

Everything happens, your heart just has to be ready to receive it. Everything comes, but if your heart is closed... The secret laws of life are such that the doors of your heart will not even be knocked on.

Existence knows how to wait; it can wait for eternity.

It all depends on you. Everything is ready to happen any moment. Just open all your doors, all your windows, so that existence can pour into you from every side. There is no other god than existence, and there is no other paradise than your very being. When existence pours into your being, paradise has entered into you – or you have entered into paradise, just different ways of saying the same thing.

But remember: nothing is expected of you. All the religions have been telling you for centuries that you have to do this; you have to do that. That you have to torture yourself, you have to renounce pleasures, you have to fight with your body, you have to renounce the world.

The Buddhist scriptures have thirty-three thousand principles that a sannyasin should follow. It is almost impossible to remember them – following them is out of the question. I don't have a single principle for you to follow; just a simple understanding that it is *your* life – enjoy it, allow it to sing a song in you, allow it to become a dance in you. You have nothing else to do but simply to be available. And flowers are going to shower on you.

10 I Answer Your Questions Just to Kill Them

Osho,
What is the difference between obeying the master and following his guidance?

The question is complex. In the first place, the master does not expect to be obeyed but to be understood. He does not give you guidelines either. In his presence, your loving heart finds them.

It means that those who order and expect that their orders should be followed, complied with, are not authentic masters. The master is not a commander. He does not issue things like "Ten Commandments." Certainly, he explains to you his experience, his realization, and then it is up to your intelligence to do whatever is right. It is not a direct order, it is an appeal to your intelligence.

An order never cares about your intelligence, an order never wants you to understand anything. The basic purpose of all ordering of people is to reduce them into robots. All over the world, in every army, they are turning millions of people into machines – of course, in such a way that you don't understand what is going on. Their methodology is very indirect. What does it mean that thousands of people every morning are marching, following orders – "Right turn, left turn, move forward, move backward" – for what is all this circus going on? And for years it goes on. It is in order to destroy your intelligence.

The strategy is that if for years continuously you go on following any kind of stupid thing, meaningless, every day in the morning, every day in the evening, and you are not supposed to ask why – you just have to do it, to do it as perfectly as possible – there is no need for you to understand why. And when a person goes through such a training for years, the natural effect is that he stops asking why. And why? – because the questioning attitude is the very base of all intelligence. The moment you stop asking why, you have stopped growing as far as intelligence is concerned.

It happened in the Second World War...

A retired army man, who had fought in the First World War, and was honored well; he was a brave man. And now almost twenty-five years had passed. He had a small farm and lived silently.

He was going from the farm to his house with a bucket full of eggs, and a few people in a restaurant, just jokingly, played a trick on the poor old army man. One of the men in the restaurant shouted, "Attention!" and the man dropped the bucket and stood in the position of attention.

It had been twenty-five years since he had gone through the training. But the training had gone into the bones, into the blood, into the marrow; it had become part of the unconscious. He completely forgot what he was doing – it happened almost autonomously, mechanically.

He was very angry. But those people said, "Your anger is not right, because we can call out any word we want. Who is telling you to follow it?"

He said, "It is too late for me to decide whether to follow it or not to follow it. My whole mind functions like a machine. Those twenty-five years simply disappeared. 'Attention' only means 'attention.' You destroyed my eggs. I am a poor man."

But this is being done all over the world. And not only today; from the very beginning armies have been trained not to use intelligence, but to follow orders. You have to understand one thing very clearly: that to follow an order and to understand a thing are two diametrically opposite things. If, by understanding, your intelligence feels satisfied and you do something out of that, you are not following an order from the outside; you are following your own intelligence.

And an authentic master is not your commander. He loves you, and he wants you to be more understanding, more intelligent, more capable of finding your way, more insightful, more intuitive. This cannot be done by orders.

I am reminded of another incident in the First World War. In Berlin, one German professor of logic was recruited into the army. There was a shortage of soldiers, and everybody who was physically able was asked to volunteer; otherwise they were forcing people to go into the army because all the societies, all the nations, all the cultures have taken it for granted that the individuals exist for them, not vice-versa. To me, just the opposite is the case: the society exists for the individual, the culture exists for the individual, the nation exists for the individual. Everything can be sacrificed, but the individual cannot be sacrificed for anything. Individuality is the very flowering of existence – nothing is higher than it. But no culture, no society, no civilization is ready to accept a simple truth.

The professor was forced. He said, "I am not a man who can fight. I can argue; I am a logician. If you need somebody to argue with the enemies, I am ready, but fighting is not my business. It is barbarous to fight."

But nobody listened, and finally he was brought to the parade grounds. The parade started, and the commander said, "Left turn." Everybody turned left, but the professor remained standing as he was.

The commander was a little worried: "What is the matter? Perhaps the man is deaf." So he shouted loudly, "Now turn to the left again!" All the people turned to the left again, but that man remained standing as if he had not heard anything.

Forward, backward...all the orders were given and everybody followed. That man remained just standing in his place.

He was a well-known professor; even the commander knew him. He could not be treated just like any other soldier; he had a certain respect. Finally, when the parade ended and everybody came back to the same line from where they had started, the commander went to the professor and asked, "Is there some problem with your ears? Can't you hear?"

He said, "I can hear."

"But then," the commander said, "why did you remain standing? Why did you not follow the orders?"

He said, "What is the point? When everybody finally has to come back to the same state, after all this movement going forward and backward, left and right, what have they gained?"

The commander said, "It is not a question of gaining, it is a training!"

But he said, "I don't need any training. This kind of stupid thing... You come to the same place after doing all kinds of stupid things, which I don't see any point in. Can you explain to me why I should turn left and not right?"

The commander said, "Strange, no soldier asks such questions."

The professor said, "I am not a soldier, I am a professor. I have been forced to be here, but you cannot force me to do things against my intelligence."

The commander went to the higher authorities and asked, "What to do with this man? He may spoil other people – because everybody is laughing at me, and everybody is saying, 'Professor, you did great!' I cannot tackle that man. He asks...each thing has to be explained: 'Unless I understand it, unless my intelligence supports it, I am not going to do it.'"

The commander in chief said, "I know the man. He is a great logician. His whole life's training is in questioning everything. I will take care of him, don't be worried."

He called the professor to his office and said, "I am sorry, but we cannot do anything. You have been recruited; the country needs soldiers. But I will give you some work which will not create any difficulty for you and will not create any difficulty for others. You come with me to the army mess."

He took the professor there, and showed him a big pile of green peas. He told the professor, "Do one thing, sit down here. You have to sort out the big peas on one side, the small peas on the other side. And after one hour I will come to see how things are progressing."

After one hour he came back. The professor was sitting there and the peas were also sitting there, in the same place. He said, "What is the matter? You have not even started."

He said, "For the first and for the last time, I want you all to understand that unless you explain to me why I should sort out the peas... My intelligence feels insulted by you. Am I an idiot, to sort the peas? What is the need? Moreover, there are other problems. Sitting here, I thought that perhaps there is some need, but there are questions which have to be decided: there are peas which are big and there are peas which are small, but there are peas of many other sizes. Where are they going to go? You have not given me any criterion."

A mystery school, a spiritual path, is not the path of a soldier. Here, orders are prohibited. Here, only intelligence is appealed to. The decision is always on your part.

It is only the phony masters who give you orders, because they cannot satisfy your intelligence. An authentic master is perfectly capable of satisfying your intelligence and then leaving it up to you. It is your life, and the final decision has to be made not by anyone else other than you. You have to take the responsibility on your own shoulders. So there are no orders as far as true masters are concerned.

You have also asked about guidelines. People have been told such nonsense for centuries – as if spirituality is a kind of geography, so that maps are given to you, guidelines are provided to you: follow the right guidelines and you will reach the goal.

Alas, things are not so cheap. There are no maps in existence, no solid guidelines either, because each individual is so unique that what may be a guideline for one may prove a distraction for another; what may be medicine to one may prove poison to another. Individuals are so different. And if a master cannot understand the difference of individuals, their unique qualities, talents, genius, then who is going to understand? No general guidelines can be provided. The master simply goes on dropping all kinds of hints. Remember my word *hints* – not guidelines. You have to choose whatever suits you, and you have to experiment to see whether it is workable for you or not. If it works, go deeper into it; if it does not work, don't feel guilty. You have not committed any sin; you have simply failed in an experiment.

With a master, life becomes a scientific experiment. It is no longer a question of heaven and hell, punishment and reward. It is a question of exploration. And each individual has to explore in his own way. There are no golden rules. This is the only golden rule there is. There is no superhighway with milestones telling you how far you are from the goal. In spiritual exploration, you have to walk and create your path by your walking; there is no ready-made path so that you have simply to walk on it.

And my feeling is that this is tremendously blissful and ecstatic. You are not like railway trains. Running on rails, you cannot run into the jungles, into the mountains, anywhere you like. The railway train is a prisoner. But a river is not a prisoner. It also travels long. It may have come thousands of miles from the Himalayas, and it finally reaches to the ocean – with no map, with no guidelines, with no guides, and nobody on the way to whom the river can inquire, "Which way am I to go now?" – because each step is a crossroad. But strangely enough, every river reaches to the ocean with great freedom, finding its own path.

The master can only give you certain hints about how to find your path. He can give you certain indications whether you have found it or not, can give you certain criteria to judge whether you are moving towards the goal or away from the goal. But he does not give you guidelines. In the very nature of things, it is not possible. The moment you have found a master, you have found the path.

And who is the master? – not one who fulfills your mind

expectations. A Christian mind has Christian expectations, a Hindu mind has Hindu expectations, a Buddhist mind has Buddhist expectations. A master is one who fulfills the longing of your heart. It has nothing to do with the mind. It is a love affair. You simply find that you are in love. You simply find that your heart feels at home, at ease, that your heart has found a treasure, feels a tremendous benediction. And as you come closer to the master – in your love, in your trust – your peace deepens; your silence becomes something not dead, the silence of a graveyard, but something singing and dancing, alive.

The more you are moving towards your life's fulfillment, the more your life becomes a rejoicing, a deep joy for no reason at all, a blissfulness so deep and so abundant that you can start sharing it with others. In fact, you have to share it with others because it is overflowing, you cannot contain it. For the first time, you are small and your bliss is infinite. These are the indications that you are moving towards home: your ecstasies go on growing deeper and higher.

And if you are moving away, you will become more miserable, more sad, more saintly, more Christian, more Hindu, more Jaina – all kinds of diseases. More knowledgeable, but more and more empty inside, a beggar living by a thin thread of hope that somewhere in the other life, somewhere in the other world, you will be rewarded for all your sadness, your long British faces. Saints don't laugh. They have fallen below humanity, because only human beings laugh. Buffaloes don't laugh, donkeys don't laugh – they all belong to the category of the saints and sages. Perhaps these fellows – donkeys and buffaloes – may have been great sages in their past lives and now they are getting their reward. Don't misbehave with them. Be respectful. One never knows... But as far as I am concerned, your sense of humor, your laughter will become deeper as you grow in consciousness. You will become more playful in life.

So there are neither orders nor guidelines but only vague hints: indications, and a constant effort to sharpen your intelligence so that you can find your way. And when you have found, you have the courage to burst into song, into dance, into rejoicing. That's the function of the master: to make you more intelligent and more courageous, more loving, more understanding. But there are no orders, no disciplines, no guidelines. Orders, disciplines, guidelines – these have been used by people who wanted to dominate you, by people who wanted to dictate their terms, to enforce their ideas on other people's lives. I call all such people great criminals. To impose your idea on somebody, to give some ideal, some mold, is violence, sheer violence. You are being destructive, and a master cannot do that. A master is always creative.

Osho,

I am having questions coming to me. I write them down and read them over. Meditating again, I often get the answer, and coincidentally, many times the same question is read out to you in the discourse or at the video that night. Even if it is from someone else, I feel that it is my question, and I feel as if I am being answered. Also, being here with you, my intuition is functioning more clearly than ever.

Beloved master, can you please comment?

It is a fallacy that any question is yours. It is just an old habit of possessiveness: the house is mine, the wife is mine, the child is mine, even the question is mine. All human beings are potentially capable of all the questions that any one of you can ask, because all questions come out of your insane mind and you are all equally insane. There are only a few things in which you are equal – insanity is one of them. Only once in a while somebody is more insane than others; then he is caught. And the whole function of psychologists, psychiatrists, psychotherapists is not to destroy insanity – they cannot; they don't have any understanding about what sanity is. All that they can do is that when somebody has gone a little ahead of the average insane humanity, they can pull him back: "Just be normal." *Just be normal* means just be normally insane; don't try to be abnormal. Abnormally insane people are thought to be mad. Normally insane people raise no questions, no problems, because they are the only kind of people there are, although they are full of the same problems as the mad people. But the difference is of quantity.

Just sit down in your room, close all the doors and lock them from inside and write down on your pad anything that goes on in your mind. Don't do any kind of editing work, simply go on writing whatever comes into your mind. And you will be surprised; after ten minutes, read it, and you will be shocked: is it written by you or by some insane person? What kind of nonsense, what rubbish goes on and on in your mind?

It is said that God made the world. There are many people who prove that there are so many mistakes in the world it cannot be made by God. A perfect God cannot make such an imperfect world. But on one point I have a soft spot for him: he has not made small windows in your head through which others can look inside at what is going on. Otherwise, it would have been such a perfect world – just little windows, so at least your friends can just have a look at what is going on. And they will be surprised that on the face nothing shows, and inside this man is carrying such garbage. And it goes on, round and round, twenty-four hours a day.

In my meditation camps I used to have a special meditation. The meditation was that for one hour everybody was to sit relaxed and say whatsoever came to his mind – just to become a spokesman of his own mind, just a loudspeaker – and to do whatever he felt like doing, no inhibition, for one hour. And it was such a joy, and people were doing such great things! Such good people...you would have never imagined. One man... I would never have thought that he would do this, he was continuously phoning, just sitting in front of me. And he was a man of the age of near-about sixty, a rich man, continuously phoning: "Hello, hello!" Later on I discovered that that's what he did; his whole business was the stock market. And he used to sit just in front of me, so once in a while he would look at me and smile because he would see that what he was doing was not right, what he was talking was nonsense. But what to do? – this was the meditation one had to do!

Jayantibhai is sitting here. One of his friends – they are old friends, they are still friends, and very deeply related – simply stood up and started pushing Jayantibhai's car down the hill. It was the car in which I used to come to the camp, and he was going to push it down the hill – it would be finished! And he was Jayantibhai's great friend. I had to tell a few people, "Stop your meditation. Just catch hold of that man; otherwise that car is finished. And he knows it is his friend's car, and he knows that I will need it, that I have to go..."

Somehow he was prised away from the car, but he was so angry that in his anger he climbed up the tree that was just in the middle where all the meditators were sitting, and he started throwing his clothes from there, he became naked. He is such a serious, silent person – you cannot imagine that he can do such things. And it was such a difficulty to bring him down: "The meditation is finished, you come down," but he wouldn't listen, it was too difficult for him to come out of the meditation.

These things go on in the mind, but you don't do them. Finally I had to stop that meditation, because it was dangerous. It was very beautiful to throw out your garbage, it was very cleansing, but it was dangerous – people may start hitting each other. It happened in one place. People were meditating, and one *sardarji* started hitting...not that anybody was his enemy or anything. He made such long jumps to hit people that the whole of the grounds were empty; all the meditators were standing around the edge of the grounds, and the *sardarji* was alone inside.

I said, "*Sardarji*, now sit down. Everybody has gone."

He said, "What came over me, because I am not a violent man?" And the people of his town also reported, "He is a very good man. What came to his mind?"

I said, "It must have been coming to his mind every day; it is just that the chance was not there. Today he got a chance. He alone finished all the meditators!" And there were at least five hundred people.

I asked him later on, "Did you not realize what you were doing?"

He said, "I realized that what I was doing was not right, and that these people have done no harm to me. Most of them are unknown to me. But from my very childhood I have had dreams of beating people, cutting their heads off. Even in the day, when I close my eyes I have always had this: that I alone am enough for hundreds of people. You have seen it yourself – five hundred people, great meditators, all forgot their meditation."

I said, "And do you think you are sane?"

He said, "That's what I have been asking after your meditation. This thing is in my mind...any day, something goes wrong, goes beyond my control and I will be insane. Insanity is there, it is just repressed."

There are only two kinds of people in the world: normally insane people and abnormally insane people.

One man became mad – and mad people are very inventive because they don't have any fear of anybody; no question of respectability, no question of what others will think about them. They become very fearless, and they start doing their thing, what they had always wanted to do but were suppressing. This man had this idea that some strange, slimy creature was rolling all over him, and the whole day he was throwing it off of himself. His family said, "What are you doing? – because we don't see any slimy creature or anything."

He said, "You cannot see it. I was also in your situation before; I had suspicions about it but I had never seen it. Now it seems my third eye has opened. I can see it!" and he would go on throwing it off.

They said, "You are just... Are you going to the business, to the office, or not?"

He said, "How can I go? And it is so disgusting – it crawls on my face, it goes on into my hair...I cannot go anywhere."

So finally they took him to the psychiatrist. The psychiatrist said, "Don't be worried, I have seen such cases. Come here and sit down."

He sat there, and he was continuously throwing off the creature. The psychiatrist said, "There is nothing; you just have an idea, you have become obsessed with an idea."

He said, "Obsessed? I will show you."

He took his chair close to the psychiatrist. And the psychiatrist said, "What are you doing?"

And the man started throwing his creatures onto the psychiatrist, and the psychiatrist said, "Stop! Don't throw those creatures on me. What kind of fellow are you? Have you come here for treatment or have you come here to make me sick also? What a disgusting fellow."

He said, "Now you see, it is not an idea."

The psychiatrist said, "I do understand, it is not an idea. I can see them; it seems my third eye is also opening! Just don't come again. You can try another psychiatrist; he lives just opposite me. He is my enemy, and when I find cases like you, I send them to him. But forgive me – this is your fee, take it back. But don't drop your creatures here! Take them to the other psychiatrist every day – that is his office. And if you want something, I will pay your fee. Whatever fee you have to give to the psychiatrist, I will give to you. But open his third eye just the way you have opened mine. You are great – there are yogis who are trying hard to open their third eyes and nothing opens, and within minutes you have opened my third eye."

And as the man was going out, he looked back. The psychiatrist was throwing off those creatures.

Everybody is in the same boat. Just a few are sitting in the middle, a few are sitting at the very edge, can fall into the river easily. It is not your question. No question is yours. Remember, all questions come out of your normal insanity. So when you hear that somebody else has asked your question, don't be puzzled. These are the same slimy creatures; it is not your monopoly. They also have their own. If you remain silent, you will find that every question that has ever bothered you is being asked by somebody else, by someone else – because we are not islands; we are all connected, we are one continent. And we are continuoually broadcasting our ideas, even without saying anything to anybody sitting by our side. Neither are you trying to say something to him, nor is he trying to listen to you, but those ideas are radiating.

It is something to be understood: that most of your ideas are just uninvited guests, which you pick up from just anywhere. They are in the air, and once they get into your head you think, "It is my idea." And if you listen carefully, every answer is for you. Even if the question was not yours, even if you were not able to recognize any resemblance of the question to any question in your mind, the answer is certainly for you – as it is for everybody else. My work is not what you call retail; it is wholesale. Now, if I go on doing retail work, it will be too big a job in too small a life; I cannot help many people. I do a wholesale job. My answer is for you, whether you have asked or not. Perhaps you may ask tomorrow or the day after tomorrow; just wait but remember the answer. The question will come. The question may be coming, already arising from your unconscious layers; it has just not reached in time. So keep the answer; the question is bound to come.

I am answering your questions just to kill them, just to destroy them, so that I can help you to go beyond questions and beyond answers into a state of silence where there is no question and no answer. That space is the space of all miracles, of all mysteries. That magical space I call true religion.

To enter into it is to be a religious person.

Osho,

When sitting here with you, I try to watch and to be as aware as possible. My mind runs on, wondering if this space is right, whether I should be the watcher or be lost into you. At the same time, I try to relax and ignore all this.

Somehow, despite all these gymnastics, a moment comes when melting happens, and I become so soft and receptive, so very simple and flowing.

Osho, how can I get out of my own way so that I don't waste so much of this precious time with you?

There are things which are really simple, but become very complicated because of you. Now sitting here, you can simply relax and enjoy – but no, you make a problem out of it: whether to relax or to merge or to watch. And in all this you are missing the train. There is no need to do anything here. Just relax and listen, and out of that listening a few insights will come to you. Use those insights in your life.

When somebody insults you, watch it – as if you are just the watcher, he is insulting somebody else. That's truly the case. Or you are sitting by the side of the ocean – merge with the beauty of the sunrise, don't bring the watcher in, because beauty is something which has to be enjoyed. And anger is something which has to be dropped. So different methods have to be used in different situations.

Lying on your bed, you have nothing to do – just relax. The whole day you have been active, you have been doing a thousand and one things. Now is the time to forget it all and just let your whole energy relax and be refreshed. Relaxation, merging, watching – all are different techniques for different situations. And if you are trying all the techniques in a single situation, you will simply miss the whole point and you will not be able to do either this or that. Still, you are fortunate that doing such a stupid thing, you finally find relaxation. Perhaps you get tired, because enough is enough – merging, watching, relaxing. You get tired, so relaxation comes on its own; you feel soft. It is good.

In India we have a proverb that if a person gets lost in the morning and comes home by the evening, he should not be called lost. At least he has come back – for the whole day he has been wandering and doing all kinds of stupid things. But when you see that relaxation comes and you are soft and things become beautiful, why not do it from the very beginning? Or is that introduction a necessity?

If you have read George Bernard Shaw's dramas, his introductions are very long, longer than the drama. The drama is very small, and the introduction is three times bigger. Every friend, well-wisher, told him, "This is unnecessarily tiring. If we miss the introduction and just read the drama, then it feels that perhaps we are missing something: the man has written such a big introduction, there must be something in it. And if we read your introduction, it is so tiring that by the time we come to the drama we feel like throwing the book away – you have tortured us so much."

There is no need of long introductions, just a preface. So it is okay if for a minute or two you do merging, relaxation, watching – finish it quickly so you feel satisfied that the introduction part is done. Then come to the real drama, relax and enjoy.

Things are simple. But somehow the mind wants to make them unnecessarily complicated, because unless they are complicated, the mind is not of any use. The mind is useful only when something is complicated, then the mind is needed. When the thing is simple, the mind is not needed at all. And life is so simple that if one is courageous enough to live it, mind can be abandoned completely. And to abandon the mind and to live life spontaneously is what I call sannyas.

Moment to moment, we will see. Why go on doing rehearsals? When the moment comes, your consciousness will face it and respond to it. But people are preparing so much that almost their whole lives are used up in preparations.

I have heard about a German professor. He wanted to have the biggest collection of philosophical, religious, spiritual literature. And he was a very rich man too, so he wandered around the earth collecting all kinds of scriptures. There are three hundred religions in the world, and there are hundreds of philosophies, and each philosophy has hundreds of books in different languages. And he had translators translating them all into German. This was all preparation for when he would start reading.

But by the time he was ninety he was still collecting books. Somebody told him, "Now it is time that you should start reading. The preparation has gone on too long, and you have thousands and thousands of books. We don't think you will be able to read all of them. Your life is just at the very end, maybe a year or two more."

But the man said, "But my collection is not complete yet."

So he started collecting more forcibly, put more men into collection, into translation. Finally he fell sick, and the doctor said, "He is not going to survive more than seven days."

He called all the scholars who were translating his books: "Now stop translating. Just try to find small summaries from every scripture, because I have got only seven days and I want to know what is written in all the scriptures. So just prepare small summaries of all the scriptures."

But the scholars said, "You have collected so many scriptures, even summaries will not be possible. We will try, but in seven days all the summaries will not be ready."

The last day came. He inquired again, "What has happened?"

They said, "We are trying."

He said, "Forget all about it. Do one thing: just make one small note summarizing all the scriptures. Because there is no more time; I feel that I am going. So be fast and be quick."

They said, "How can we be fast and quick? We have to look into scriptures to find the very gist, the very essential center of all of them. It will take a little time."

The whole day passed, and by the evening they had come to a conclusion, a small summary of a few pages. They reached him; the man was almost drowning. He said, "That many pages won't do. Just make it half a page, just a small summary that can be printed on a postcard. I don't have time for all these pages."

So they rushed back, again they summarized. Now it meant nothing, because all those scriptures, summaries and summaries... And by the time they came back, the man was dead.

His wife said, "It is a very sad thing. You can at least shout loudly in his ear; perhaps he may be able to hear. He is just going down."

The doctor said, "Now it is useless. But you can try, there is no harm in it." So one scholar shouted the summary of all the scriptures. But the man was dead already, and the doctors were saying, "Now he cannot hear."

His whole life went into preparation. And this is not the story of one strange, weird man. This is the story of all normal people: preparation, preparation, preparation. They forget completely, that...preparation for what? We are not certain even of the next moment. Preparation for what! Either live or prepare. If you want to live, live now. Or prepare for tomorrow – and remember, tomorrow never comes. What comes in place of tomorrow is death. An intelligent person lives his life. He does not bother about preparations, disciplines.

You are here with me. Live this moment to its totality, to its very intensity. Perhaps out of that totality and intensity, you may get the taste that will go on lingering with you into the next moment. And once you have known that a moment can be lived with totality and intensity, you know the secret, the very secret of life. You are always given a single moment; you are not given two moments together. If you know the secret of living one moment, you know the whole secret of life, because you will always get one moment, and you know how to live it, how to be totally in it.

Your question reminds me about one of my old friends, a centipede. A centipede has one hundred legs; hence, the name centipede. The name comes from ancient Sanskrit, *shatpadee*. Just one morning, early in the morning as the sun was rising, the centipede was going for a morning walk. A philosophical rabbit, watching the legs, could not believe – he said, "My God, this centipede is going to be in trouble soon. How is he going to remember which foot first, which foot second...one hundred legs! He is bound to be in trouble."

The rabbit came close and said to the centipede, "Uncle, I am a philosophical rabbit – just a student, an inquirer about truth."

The centipede said, "That is all right, but what is the problem?"

He said, "The problem is: how do you manage one hundred legs?"

So the centipede said, "I never thought about it. And no centipede has ever thought about it; there is no mention of it in our scriptures. We have been managing perfectly well. But your question is valid. Just sit. I will try," and he could not go even two feet. Puzzled, he fell down.

And he was very angry at the rabbit. He said, "You rascal, never again ask any centipede your philosophical question, because now I am in trouble. And the question has got into my head; now I cannot walk without thinking about how it is happening – which one? And one hundred legs... My life is finished, but be kind enough not to ask such questions to anybody else. I will try to forget this question. I don't know...if I can forget it I can live; if I cannot forget it, I am finished."

Now you are trying to be in my presence, relaxing, merging, watching... You will get into trouble. Forget all nonsense; forget all philosophical questions. Here, just be. Simply be, and out of that being grows an understanding that will give you the insight into where to merge, where to watch, where to relax. Here, you are to just get a taste of being – of being fully alive, silent, joyous – and everything else will come out of that.

11 Harmony: The Birthplace of Love

Osho,
The fruit falls on the ground when it is ripe. One day you will leave us, and it will be impossible to have another master in your place.
How can anybody else be the substitute for the Master of Masters?

Osho, when you leave the physical body, will your meditation techniques help our inner growth as they do now?

My approach to your growth is basically to make you independent of me. Any kind of dependence is a slavery, and spiritual dependence is the worst slavery of all.

I have been making every effort to make you aware of your individuality, your freedom, your absolute capacity to grow without any help from anybody. Your growth is something intrinsic to your being. It does not come from outside, it is not an imposition; it is an unfolding.

All the meditation techniques that I have given to you are not dependent on me – my presence or absence will not make any difference – they are dependent on you. It is not *my* presence, but *your* presence that is needed for them to work. It is not my being here but your being here, your being in the present, your being alert and aware that is going to help.

I can understand your question and its relevance. It is not irrelevant. The whole past of man is, in different ways, a history of exploitation. And even the so-called spiritual people could not resist the temptation to exploit. Out of a hundred masters, ninety-nine percent were trying to impose the idea that, "without me you cannot grow, no progress is possible. Give me your whole responsibility." But the moment you give your whole responsibility to somebody, unknowingly you are also giving your whole freedom.

And naturally, all those masters had to die one day, but they have left long lines of slaves: Christians, Jews, Hindus, Mohammedans. What are these people? Why should somebody be a Christian? If you can be someone, be a Christ, never be a Christian. Are you absolutely blind to the humiliation when you call yourself a Christian, a follower of someone who died two thousand years ago? The whole of humanity is following the dead. Is it not weird that the living should follow the dead, that the living should be dominated by the dead, that the living should depend on the dead and their promises that "we will be coming to save you". None of them has come to save you. In fact, nobody can save anybody else; it goes against the foundational truth of freedom and individuality.

As far as I am concerned, I am simply making every effort to make you free from everybody – including me – and to just be alone on the path of searching. This existence respects a person who dares to be alone in the seeking of truth. Slaves are not respected by existence at all. They do not deserve any respect; they don't respect themselves, how can they expect existence to be respectful towards them?

So remember, when I am gone, you are not going to lose anything. Perhaps you may gain something of which you are absolutely unaware. Right now I am only available to you embodied, imprisoned in a certain shape and form. Right now you have to come to me. When I am gone, where can I go? I will be here in the winds and in the ocean; and if you have loved me, if you have trusted me, you will feel me in a thousand and one ways. In your silent moments you will suddenly feel my presence. Once I am unembodied, my consciousness is universal.

Then, you will not need to seek and search for me. Wherever you are...your thirst, your love...and you will find me in your very heart, in your very heartbeat.

Osho,

Being on my own in the marketplace, I felt myself becoming very mechanical and unaware in my activities. Now, being in your presence and going inside, my body-mind speed is slowing down, and self-consciousness is arising. This state of self-consciousness gives a lightness, and one wants to stay in it more and more. When I look at you, I see a grace that is pointing far beyond.

Osho, can you speak on the self-consciousness of the disciple, and the grace of the master?

It is good that you are becoming aware of a very essential phenomenon: that in the marketplace you had become mechanical, robot-like. Coming here, you are more relaxed. The speed of the mind is slowly, slowly getting less. And as your awareness is becoming clear, your mechanical-ness is disappearing. You have to see that awareness and mechanical-ness cannot exist together; there is no coexistence possible between those two factors.

In the marketplace you are not expected to be aware; you are expected to be efficient. Efficiency is a quality of machines, machines are more efficient than human beings. Because efficiency is required, you become more mechanical, and as you become more mechanical your awareness disappears. And your awareness is your real being. By efficiency and mechanical-ness, you may succeed in earning more money, more power, more prestige, more respectability, but you will lose yourself. And you are losing yourself very cheaply; what you are gaining in return is worthless. Do you know how many people have lived before you on this earth? Do you realize the fact that millions of them were successful people? Millions of them were famous in their time, and now people don't even remember their names. They have disappeared like dreams, without leaving any trace behind. We are also going to disappear in the same way.

The only people who have died and yet continue to live on in people's love, in people's trust, are not the very successful: the emperors, the world conquerors, the richest. Those few people who, in spite of their deaths, still beat in the hearts of man belong to a totally different category: they were the people of awareness, people with soul. Their impact has been so deep that it will remain unto the last man. Gautam Buddha, Lao Tzu, Kabir, Christ, al-Hillaj Mansoor – these people cannot be forgotten. They will go on living in the deepest parts of your being for the simple reason that they never compromised their awareness for the expectations of the marketplace.

So the first thing: you have become aware. Make your awareness sharper, and next time you go to the marketplace there is no need to become robot-like. Perhaps you will not be as efficient as robots – so what? Perhaps you will not be as successful as the mechanical ones – so what? Let them have their day, and then they will disappear like soap bubbles. Don't feel jealous of them. Be compassionate towards them, and remain contented with your awareness.

Risk everything for awareness, but never risk awareness for anything. This is the commitment of a sannyasin: that he is ready to lose his life but not his awareness; he has found a value which is higher than life. There is no other value which is higher than awareness. Awareness is the seed of godliness in you. When it comes to its full growth, you have come to the fulfillment of your destiny. As your awareness goes deeper, your actions may not be efficient but they will have a new quality, the quality of grace, which is far more valuable. No machine can have the quality of grace. Your actions, your words will have a beauty of their own. The way a man of awareness lives, each moment is filled with tremendous grace and beauty. It is reflected in his actions, even in the smallest actions – just in the gesture of his hand or just the way he looks; in the depth of his eyes or the authority of his words or the music of his silence. His very presence is a celebration.

In comparison to such a man, emperors are beggars; they have everything of the world, but inside they are empty. The temple may be made of gold, but inside the master of the temple is missing.

Every day the disciple becomes more and more graceful, more and more alert; and with all these qualities, a deep gratefulness towards the master is a necessary outcome. It is not that you have to *do* it. If you do it, it is phony. If it comes on its own accord, then it has authenticity. And as your gratefulness grows, you become more available, more open. The master can pour his whole being into you, all his blessings, his whole benediction.

Osho,
I sense something wonderful, something incredible happening to you over there in your chair. And more and more over the years, I sense something really wonderful happening within me over here. For me, it is not enlightenment – I know that. But it is like a harmony with you.

Osho, can you say something about how I can reach through the smoke of the mind to bring this wondrousness, this beautiful feeling of giftedness out into the open so that it can grow?

The phenomenon of harmony is one of the most mysterious experiences possible. It means that two bodies are still two bodies, but the two souls within them are no more two. One soul within two bodies: that's exactly the meaning of harmony. It is the most exquisite experience.

Ordinarily we are living in conflict, in disharmony. The husband is living in disharmony with the wife – they call it living together. But unless this oneness arises, their togetherness is nothing but an underground conflict, erupting at any moment for any meaningless, silly reason. Both are sitting on volcanoes. Parents are feeling a generation gap between themselves and their own children. There seems to be no common ground of understanding; harmony is a faraway goal. They don't even understand each other's language – not that they speak different languages, but their visions are different, their attitudes are different, their approach towards life is different – and there seems to be no way to come to any conclusion. Parents and children are no longer on speaking terms because each time they speak it turns out to be a fight.

The same thing happens with husbands and wives. When they

are newly wed, things are hot: they fight, the wives throw things, break plates, cups and glasses, throw pillows. The husbands behave in the same way – they beat the same woman they used to think they could not live without. They not only beat her, they even imagine many times killing her; otherwise, the wife is going to kill him. It is only a question of who takes the initiative; it is a cold war. Slowly, slowly, things get cooler: no more pillow fights, no more breaking of cups and glasses and saucers. But that does not mean that they have come to a harmony. That simply means they have understood the stupidity of it all; it is better to be silent. The husband simply goes on reading the same newspaper. On Sunday it is a little difficult; they avoid each other, they don't want to be left alone together.

One of my friends – a very rich man – asked me when he became fifty, "I have enough money. I have only two girls, who are married. And it is very difficult because only my wife and I are left in the house."

But I said, "You should be happy. I thought this was a love marriage."

He said, "Now I don't use that word *love* at all; it is that word that has destroyed my life. So just because of the wife, I continue with the business and the industries – just to avoid her, because otherwise there would be no need."

I said, "Then find a beautiful hill station, and move there and live peacefully."

He said, "But...alone with this woman on a hill station? You are suggesting a murder!"

I said, "What are you talking about? Who is going to murder whom?"

He said, "That depends on who takes the initiative first. With this woman alone – no! If you are willing to stay with us, I could be safe, I could go to any hill station. Without a friend, we don't even go to see a movie. The friend has to sit between the two of us; otherwise, something...and anything is enough to begin a quarrel."

I said, "I never see you fighting."

He said, "That's true; for years, everything has gone

underground. But we are fighting. Inside myself, I am beating her; inside herself she is beating me – but not to make a show. What will people think, what will the servants think?"

They were not sleeping in the same room. I asked the wife why. She said, "No, there is not much of a problem. It is because he snores."

I said, "I have slept in the same room with him many times. I have never heard him snoring."

I asked my friend, "What is the matter? Your wife says you snore."

He said, "Yes, I snore – just to keep her in the other room. I never snore in my sleep! That's why you have not heard it. I have to make an effort to snore – it is a very difficult art, one has to learn it – just to give her an excuse. She wanted to sleep in the other room, but some excuse was needed. And it is perfectly peaceful to be here. She is there, and I lock the door from inside, because she may come in the middle of the night; some idea may come to her and a quarrel will start."

People are not living in harmony. *Harmony* is an empty word, and for most people, unfortunately, it remains empty. They know only fight, anger. Harmony means you are dropping your ego, you are saying, "I would like to be with you so deeply one, that this very idea of I is no longer needed."

A few people have lived in harmony; and particularly the master and the disciple cannot have any kind of relationship without harmony. The master is without ego; the disciple just has to drop his ego, and two consciousnesses become one, and a great music vibrates – in both persons, one music. It has happened in other relationships too, but very rarely. I am reminded of a strange book in Sanskrit. Its name is *Bhamiti*. It is a strange name because it is a commentary on one of the most philosophical treatises ever written, the *Brahma Sutras* of Badarayan.

Badarayan is perhaps the greatest philosopher the world has produced, and he has written these small maxims, *Brahma Sutras*: maxims about the ultimate. There is no other book in the whole world on which so many commentaries have been written –

thousands and thousands of commentaries, because the maxims are so small, so condensed that unless somebody opens them, explains them, interprets them, you will not be able to find their meaning.

Brahma Sutra is a strange book. No other book has had the same fate as Badarayan's *Brahma Sutra*. Commentaries have been written, but the commentaries were also very difficult to understand, so commentaries upon commentaries were written. But still these were not so simple either, so commentaries on those commentaries... This is the only book in which you will find a series of commentaries; the original is lost. And for thousands of years in India, people have been writing commentaries on the commentaries to bring its meaning to the masses.

One of the commentaries, one of the best commentaries on the *Brahma Sutras*, is *Bhamiti*, and it is strange, because Bhamiti is a weird name for a commentary. Bhamiti is the name of a certain woman, and to give that name to the commentary... The commentary was written by a great philosopher, Vachaspati, whose wife's name was Bhamiti. It took him twelve years to write the commentary, and he decided that the day the commentary was complete, he would renounce the world and go to the Himalayas. One day, in the middle of the night, the commentary was completed. He took the candle, in whose light he had been writing the commentary, to go to his room. And on the way there, he found a woman and he asked, "Who are you and what are you doing here?"

She said, "My lord, you were so immersed in writing the commentary, you forgot completely that you had married me. I am your wife."

Vachaspati said, "I remember. And I also remember that every day... Just show me your hand, because I can recognize your hand. You were the one who put the candle by my side every day as the sun was setting. I know this hand. But it is too late; I have decided that the day the commentary is complete I will leave the house. You should have reminded me."

Bhamiti said, "It would have been very unloving to disturb you;

I was waiting. And don't be worried – if you have decided to leave, you can leave without any worry. I will not come as a hindrance to your decision. It is enough that I can see that you are worried for me. This will be enough for my whole life, that you had a certain love."

Vachaspati said, "You are a great woman. It is very rare to find such a woman. It is easy to find many commentators of my quality, but to find a woman of your quality – such love, such trust, such waiting, such patience. And such greatness of heart: just your concern that it is getting late is enough for you, as if there is no expectation. I will call my commentary Bhamiti, so that whoever reads this commentary is bound to be surprised by the name" – because it has no relevance; the commentary is on the *Brahma Sutras* – and, Bhamiti...?

"But without you, and without your love, and without your patience, and without your silent waiting... You never came in front of me, and you are so beautiful that it is certain: if you had come in front of me, it would have been a disturbance. I might have forgotten about the commentary; I might have delayed completing it, just to remain with you."

But Bhamiti said, "I have received more than I deserve. You should not wait in the house any longer. Let me have the pride of having a husband who has followed his decision, even though now I can see you are hesitating. Don't hesitate. I will not allow you to remain in the house; you have to go to the Himalayas, because if you remain in the house, I will not be able to give you the same respect."

This is a tremendous, unbelievable story. Vachaspati left for the Himalayas, but he could not forget Bhamiti – such a quality, such grace and such beauty, something beyond human qualities. Only such people have given proof that there is something more than human qualities, something which can only be called divine. Vachaspati remains a great scholar, but Bhamiti proves to be a far more divine personality.

So once in a while there have been, in other relationships, people who have felt harmony with each other, but that is extremely rare, accidental and exceptional. But as far as the master and disciple relationship is concerned, it is a basic necessity; without it, there is no relationship. A musical oneness, such a deep love that it consumes your ego. There are not two persons in relationship but only a harmonious whole, an energy field. And once you have experienced it with a master, you can experience it in your other relationships too, because the principle is the same. And if you can experience it in all your relationships, many harmonies around you, your life becomes truly a divine gift, an orchestra. Then the master-discipleship was just the learning of a certain knack; you can use it with your wife, with your husband, with your children, with your parents, with your friends. You can spread it all over the world. You can feel it with the trees, with the stars; it is only a question of knowing the knack.

The secret is how not to be, how to disappear as an ego. Then whatever you touch creates music, whatever you touch becomes gold.

Osho,

After leaving Rajneeshpuram in November last year, I experienced that it became nearly impossible for me to find out what I was going to do. In the beginning it was a bit frightening, but very soon I saw more and more that just waiting was enough, and many beautiful things started happening to me, without my going for it.

Is this how being with you works?

It is not only the way things happen around me, it is the way of the whole of existence. You just wait, and everything happens at its right moment. Wait and watch. Don't fall asleep – because in waiting that is very natural, to fall asleep. Nothing to do one falls asleep. Then things will be happening but you will not know. So wait and watch.

Life has been disturbed by the so-called do-gooders who, around the world, are continually preaching, "Do this, do that, do service to the poor." Doing has been raised so high that we have completely forgotten the art of waiting. And, certainly, there are things which can happen only if you do them. For example, you cannot simply wait and grow rich. There are people who even teach that. One American thinker, Napoleon Hill, has written beautiful books, a master writer. I have always liked one of his books, *Think And Grow Rich*, although it is absolute nonsense. But he writes well. And there are people who believe that all that you have to do is simply wait; sow the seeds of thinking that a Cadillac car should come into your garage, and just wait. And one day, suddenly a Cadillac car comes, delivered to you. There are people who believe this – that thinking has so much power.

In America there is still a Christian sect... Half a century ago it was very important because a large number of people believed in it. The sect calls itself "Christian Science." And the science is that you need not do anything, you have just to think. God is the doer. You think, pray, wait; just give time to God. And what do you think, that a Cadillac is a bigger thing than the whole universe. God can create the whole universe and he cannot create a Cadillac car.

I have heard a story that a young man was going to college and was met by an old woman. She asked, "What happened to your father? He is not coming to our Sunday meetings." They were Christian Scientists.

The boy said, "He is sick."

The old woman laughed. She said, "Nonsense, he must be thinking he is sick. It is thinking that matters. Just tell that old man, that 'For your whole life you have been a member of Christian Science and still you have not understood a simple thing. Stop thinking that you are sick, and you will not be sick.'"

The boy said, "I will deliver the message."

After a week, again the old woman met the boy and said, "What happened? – because he has not come even this week to the weekly meeting of the Christian Scientists."

The boy said, "Madam, now he thinks he is dead. And not only does he think he is dead, the whole neighborhood thinks he is dead, so they have put him in the grave. I tried to persuade them, 'Wait! He may be thinking' – but they think that I am mad."

There are things which will go on happening without your doing;

you just have to wait – and there are things which you have to do, only then will they happen. And slowly, slowly, the things that happen by doing have become more important: they are your material possessions, your money, your power, your prestige, your palaces, your empires. They won't happen just by waiting. By waiting, you will not become Alexander the Great. So, because things which happen only by doing became important, humanity has completely forgotten the whole area of things which happen.

Love happens, you cannot do it – although all over the world people have been trying to do that. And it is so strange that the world has not yet recognized the utter failure... Parents, for centuries, have been arranging marriages for their children. Astrologers are asked, palmists are asked, everything else is inquired about – the family, the wealth, the character of the people – but nobody asks the boy and the girl whether they love each other. Love is not a subject of inquiry at all. It is taken for granted that once they are married, they will love. For thousands of years humanity has been doing that, and certainly when a small boy and girl are married, they start being like brothers and sisters also – fighting, playing with each other, quarreling. They never come to know what love is; they think this is love. They produce children, they buy ornaments for their wives, the wives try to make the life of the husband as difficult as possible – in every way they help each other.

It is only just in this century that people started saying, "Unless we are in love, we will not marry" – and that, too, only in a few advanced countries. But love is a question about which you cannot do anything. Either it happens or it does not happen. It is not within your control. Love marriage came into existence but is not going to survive, for the simple reason that love comes, happens, and one day suddenly goes. It was not in your hands to bring it; neither is it in your hands to keep it.

The arranged marriage failed because the insistence was that you should love your wife, you should love your husband. It was a "should." And you could not even conceive how you could love; at the most you could pretend, you could act. But love is not a pretension, is not acting. You cannot do anything. You are absolutely powerless as far as love is concerned. The old marriage has failed. The new marriage is failing because the new marriage is simply a reaction to the old marriage. It is not out of understanding, but only out of reaction, revolt – "love marriage."

You don't know what love is. You simply see some beautiful face, you see some beautiful body and you think, "My God, I am in love!" This love is not going to last, because after two days, seeing the same face for twenty-four hours a day, you will get bored. The same body... You have explored the whole topography, now there is nothing to explore. Exploring the same geography again and again, you feel like an idiot. What is the point?

This love affair, this love marriage is failing, it has already failed. The reason is that you don't know how to wait so that love can happen. You have to learn a meditative state of waiting. Then love is not a passion, it is not a desire. Then love is not sexual; then love is a feeling of two hearts beating in the same rhythm. It is not a question of beautiful faces or beautiful bodies. It is something very deep, a question of harmony. If love arises out of harmony, then only will we know a successful life, a life of fulfillment in which love goes on deepening because it does not depend on anything outer; it depends on something inner. It does not depend on the nose and the length of the nose; it depends on an inner feeling of two hearts beating in the same rhythm. That rhythm can go on growing, can have new depths, newer spaces. Sex can be a part of it, but it is not sexual. Sex may come into it, may disappear in it. It is far greater than sex. So whether the person you love is young or old does not matter. Every woman has thought once in a while... Many women have been asking their lovers, "Will you also love me when I become old?"

I know about one of my friends – he asked me, that's why I know – that the girl he loves is continually asking him, "Will you love me when I am old?" He asked me, "What should I say?"

I said, "Why are you bringing me unnecessarily into this trouble? This is your business. You say anything. What do you feel?"

He said, "If she becomes like her mother, I cannot love her. And most probably she *will* become like her, so that is the only fear."

So I said, "Say it clearly, that 'Your old age is not the question;

but if you become like your mother then just forgive me, I will not be able to love you.'"

He said, "But then everything will be finished, because then her mother will be angry, and the whole thing depends on her. I am persuading her mother. The father is dead; she is the only one to decide about the marriage. Secondly, the girl will also get angry, because she also knows that she will become like her mother. All the symptoms are there."

I said, "Then keep quiet. Then when the difficult times come, see me again."

He said, "But that girl is so insistent. She wants to know before marriage."

I said, "It is simple. You start asking her, 'When I become old, will you love me?'"

He said, "That's good, because I am going to become old just like my father, and she hates my father just like I hate her mother. That's absolutely right."

And he told her, and she said, "Never! If you become like your own father, I am not going to love you. I will divorce you immediately."

The boy said, "Then when the difficult times come, we will see what to do."

Why bring in these questions from the very beginning? But all your love is dependent on such small things – the size of the nose, the eyes, the color of the hair, the proportions of the body. These things have nothing to do with love. Love is a feeling of harmony with an individual, of accordance.

So it is not only with the relationship of the master and the disciple; in all your relationships, if you wait and watch for a harmonious moment with existence, you will find that things are happening that you could never have been able to do. Many flowers are possible, many poems and songs are possible. Many stars are born out of harmony, waiting, and being alert. Things are happening, but you have to be conscious. Many times things are happening but you are not conscious. You miss what was your very right, just by being sleepy.

My teaching is basically of let-go. Things that happen only by doing are mundane. I am not against them, but they are not the essential part of your life. If you want to have a beautiful house, you will have to build it; it is not going to happen. Whether you are a Christian Scientist or you believe in *Think And Grow Rich*, nothing is going to help. But these are non-essential things. Essential things: love, joy, cheerfulness, a sense of humor, peace that passeth understanding, an inward journey to find yourself, these are the essential things which you cannot do, which you have to learn to allow to happen.

So keep a clear-cut idea: what has to be done should be done, and what has to be allowed to happen should be allowed to happen; never interfere with it. And also remember, the essential is that which happens on its own, and the non-essential is that which you do. Your doing cannot be anything sacred. That's why I say that all the temples and all the churches, all the statues of God made by man are mundane. Whatever is made by man cannot be higher than man.

It is a simple arithmetic: What is higher than man always happens, it is beyond your doing. You are always at the receiving end. You have to be just open, receptive, grateful to existence.

Osho,

Being with you in discourse, I feel so nourished, and have finally found the rest I had longed for.

Being in the west, I didn't even feel how much I was missing being in your presence. How could I forget the beauty of being with you?

Please comment.

Man's memory is not very great. He forgets easily.

Just a few examples will help you. You all have been children. How much do you remember the innocence that you had? In fact, a strange fact has been discovered by the psychologists: that if you go backwards trying to remember, you reach only to the age of four, at the most to the age of three. But those three or four years in the very beginning were the best – no responsibility, no worry, no tension. Life was simply a romance, a sheer joy, but people don't remember it.

And it is very strange that everybody's memory stops nearabout the age of three or four. It seems the best in us is not recorded. Perhaps it is a biological strategy that you should forget it; if you remember it, then for your whole life you will feel you are missing. You are missing because you have seen the most beautiful moments, and now everything will be dull, pale, dead. It will not have that luster, that joy, that liveliness. Perhaps it is a strategy of biology not to record those beautiful moments.

Even in later life... You will be surprised to know that the mind functions in a very strange way: it records everything that is miserable very quickly. Somebody has insulted you – you will never forget it for your whole life. So many people have respected you, you have forgotten. One person has insulted you and you cannot forget. It seems that the ugly, the dark, the humiliating, the tragic have a priority as far as remembrance is concerned. All that is good, all that is beautiful is simply forgotten; they leave no marks on your memory.

Politicians have been using it, priests have been using it in exploiting humanity from the very beginning. They say that in a democracy two parties are needed. Democracy has nothing to do with two parties. Two parties are needed for a totally different reason, which is psychological. One party is in power for five years; in those five years everybody goes against that party – because it has promised paradise and you are living in hell, and it has forgotten all those promises. The opposition party goes on provoking you: "What happened to the promises of these people? We could have fulfilled your promises." In the next election, those who were in power lose power and the other party that was powerless comes into power. In five years' time, they are finished. But in five years, people have forgotten the first party, and the first party is again promising a paradise, and they are listening to them and believing them.

It has been found that the masses have a memory of five years at the most. That's why elections have to be decided every five years; there is no other reason. So in five years' time the masses forget the first party's crimes, the first party's stupidities, the first party's lies;

they all become saints again. That's why two parties are needed. One party will be in difficulty, because if they are continuously in power you cannot forgive them. People will start revolting, killing those who are in power. So this is a very psychological way of keeping people satisfied: "Don't be worried, it is only a question of two years more. Then these people will be gone and the good people will be coming" – and they all belong to the same category.

I have never voted in my life for the simple reason that I could not see any difference between two idiots, who is a lesser idiot. I could not find a way, so I thought it was better not to get involved in it. At least nobody can blame me: "You have chosen this idiot." I have never chosen anybody. Choose anyone and you have chosen the wrong person. Just look forty years back in India: whoever you choose, you always choose the wrong person, and whoever you choose again you will choose the wrong person – because they are the same people. It is just like a football match: two parties, two groups are playing football, and you are the football. You are going to get kicks from everywhere. Wherever you go, you will get a good kick.

You are asking me why we tend to forget the beautiful moments. It is natural, because the mind is not interested in taking note of the flowers, it is interested in taking note of the thorns. Anything that hurts, it immediately takes note of. Who cares about a flower? You remember your enemies better than your friends. Just watch your mind and you will be surprised that you remember your enemy more than you remember your friends. You can forget your friends, but you cannot forget your enemies. This is your insane mind.

A saner mind will look at things from just the opposite direction; it will count the blessings, it will count all that is beautiful, it will keep note of all it has to be grateful for. And then, naturally the life of such a person will become a life of blessings, surrounded by all beautiful experiences.

It is only a question of changing a small structure in your mind.

I have always loved a story:

It happened in a synagogue which was also a monastery for the

Jews, and the chief rabbi was a very strict person. Two young Jews were walking in the garden of the monastery. They used to get one hour in the morning, and one hour in the evening to go into the garden. Other times, they had to study the scriptures and do other disciplines. They both were thinking, "Should we ask the chief if we can smoke while we are in the garden?" Both were chain smokers, but in the monastery, inside the synagogue, smoking was impossible. It was a crime. They were suffering, so both decided that although it was putting your hand in the lion's mouth, the effort should be made: "That chief rabbi is a dangerous man; how he will react, only God knows."

The next day, one of the two was coming out of the synagogue with tears in his eyes, both angry and sad. And then he saw the other fellow, who was sitting by the side of a beautiful rose bush – smoking! He said, "My God, have you started without asking?"

The other man said, "No, I have asked."

He said, "What kind of man is this? I asked him also, and he shouted at me so loudly: 'You rascal! What do you think – this is a synagogue or hell? If you want to smoke cigarettes, go to hell!' So how is it that he allowed you?'"

The other man smiled and he said, "What was your way of asking?"

He said, "What has that to do with it?"

The other man said, "Just tell me, how did you ask?"

He said, "I simply asked..." Because these two hours were called hours of prayer, they were allowed to go into the garden for two hours of prayer.

So he answered, "I simply asked, 'Can I smoke while praying?' And he shouted so loudly and it seemed he was going to hit me!"

The other man said, "Calm down. You asked in the wrong way. I asked him also; I asked him, 'Sir, can I pray while smoking?' and he said, 'That's perfectly good, there is no harm in that.'"

Just a slight change, but it makes lot of difference.

Start collecting all that is happening to you that is beautiful. And it is happening to everybody. And anything that is not beautiful is not worth remembering, not worth collecting. Why make yourself burdened with rubbish when you can be full of flowers and fragrance? You have to make a little change in your natural biological mind.

Meditation can do it very easily. One of the essential parts of meditation is to look at the good side of things, to look at the good side of people, to look at the good side of incidents, so that you are surrounded with everything good. Surrounded with all beautiful things, your growth is easier.

But people are strange. You may do one thousand favors for a person and just do one unfavorable thing; he will forget the one thousand favors and he will remember that one unfavorable thing that you did. That he will carry for his whole life. This is how people are living: in revenge, in anger, in despair, feeling rejected by life, feeling like outcasts of existence.

But the whole thing is that you are collecting the wrong things. Life is full of both. You can see that one day is sandwiched between two nights, and you can also see two beautiful days sandwiching one small night. Choose how you want to feel – to be in heaven or hell. It is your choice.

12 The Three Initiations: Student, Disciple, Devotee

Osho,
Is it true that to be in communion with the master is the initiation?

The word *initiation* is very significant and profound. There are three initiations: first, when a student becomes a disciple; second, when a disciple becomes a devotee; and third, when the devotee disappears in the master. To understand the whole process, all three steps have to be understood.

Everyone begins as a student, as an inquirer into what this life is all about, with a curiosity to know the mysteries that surround us. But the desire is for knowledge, and hence is superficial. Because the desire is for knowledge, it is of the mind. And mind is the periphery of our being, the most superficial part of our individuality.

The student has questions, but he has no quest. His questions are easily answerable, he is easily satisfied – just borrowed knowledge is enough for him. He does not yet need a master; he only needs a teacher. He accumulates answers, becomes an intellectual, but does not become intelligent. The accumulation of answers happens in the memory part of the mind, and the part that functions in accumulation is mechanical, it has nothing to do with intelligence. It is possible to find very educated, cultured, sophisticated intellectuals behaving in life in a very unintelligent way. They are very efficient whenever some question is asked for which they are already prepared. But if life raises a new question for which they are not prepared, they are completely at a loss, they are as ignorant as one can be. And the problem is, life goes on posing new questions, new challenges.

Memory is good in the marketplace; memory is not good as a lifestyle. And all your universities only teach you how to memorize. It has been found that the people of very great memory are generally unintelligent people. In the life of one of the British viceroys, Curzon, there is mention of a very significant incident – and it is a historical fact. Curzon had heard that there was a man in Rajputana whose memory was just unbelievable. The man knew only his local dialect, Rajasthani, a dialect of Hindi; he did not know any other language. But that did not prevent him from memorizing any statement in any language, and in such a way that it seemed almost superhuman. He was called to the court of the Viceroy Curzon; a special meeting was arranged. Thirty scholars, knowing thirty languages, were to examine the man and his memory. Among those thirty scholars, there was not a single one who understood the man's mother tongue, and all those thirty languages were foreign languages for the man.

And the arrangement was so strange – it had never been made before and I don't think it will ever be made again. The arrangement was such that each of those thirty scholars was to deliver one sentence in his own language to the poor villager from Rajasthan. But the sentence was not to be delivered to him in one piece. The villager would go to one person who would give him the first word of his sentence. Then a bell would be rung. Then the villager would move to the next person, who would give him *his* first word. In this way he would go round and round. After thirty persons, he would come again to the first person to get the second word of his sentence, and after each word a big bell would ring to confuse him.

The scholars were not certain that they would be able to

remember their whole sentence for the whole time, because it was going to take so much time. They all had their sentences written in front of them, and they were marking off each word they had given. And this man went on and on, round and round, taking their words, and accumulating in his memory system the sentences which were given to him in pieces. After all the scholars had given their sentences, he repeated thirty statements in thirty languages, of which he knew nothing. He knew nothing about what they meant. He was so correct that all the intellectuals were puzzled. They could not remember their own sentences, they had had to write them down. They could not remember whether they had given the fifth word or the sixth – they had had to mark it. And this man was uneducated – he could not even write.

Curzon was amazed. He praised the man, and rewarded him. But it was found by talking with his fellow villagers that he was an idiot. Just as far as his memory was concerned, he was simply great – but any simple question in life, any simple situation in life, and he was not able to solve it, he was not able to answer it. They said, "He is known in our village as 'the great intellectual idiot.'"

It is a well-known fact that a student is interested in collecting knowledge. His questions are easily satisfied. His mind functions like a computer. But once in a while, a student falls into the trap of a master. He is not in search of a master, he does not know any difference between the words *master* and *teacher*. In the dictionaries both words mean the same. But in actual life, a teacher simply transfers knowledge from one generation to another generation – it is not his own experience. The master does not transfer knowledge from one generation to another generation; what he gives out is his own realization.

But if the student is caught in the trap of a master, then it is very difficult to get out of it because soon it becomes clear that knowledge and knowing are two different things; questions and quest are two different things. Questions are simply curiosities; quest is a risk, is a pilgrimage, is a search.

A question is easily satisfied by any logical, rational answer. The quest is not satisfied by logical or rational answers; the quest is like thirst. You can go on repeating that, scientifically, H2O means water, but that is not going to quench the thirst. It is an answer, and a perfectly good answer. If somebody is asking what water is, as a question, it is very simple to answer it. But if somebody is asking about water because he is thirsty, then H2O is not going to help. Then, only real water will do. Quest means thirst, hunger. No borrowed knowledge can satisfy it. And the master slowly makes the student aware that if you are really a man, then just to be curious is childish. Maturity demands that you should go on a quest, that you should not ask only for knowledge, you should ask for ways and means and methods so that you can know – not knowledge that has passed from generation to generation. No one knows whether somebody invented it, whether it is fiction, whether somebody realized it or not, how much is lost in transferring it, how much is added, how much is edited out. Knowing means "I want a personal experience."

A genuine seeker has no questions, but a tremendous thirst.

This is the first initiation: when the master changes the student's focus from knowledge towards knowing, from memory towards intelligence. And it is not an ordinary phenomenon, it happens to only a very few fortunate ones. Millions of people simply remain curious, childish, immature for their whole life.

Once the emphasis has moved from knowledge to knowing, your concern is no longer with the past; your concern is with the present. Your concern is no longer with the great philosophers, wise people; your concern is about your own consciousness. For the first time you become interested not in objects but in your subjectivity, not about other things but about the one who wants to know: who is this who wants to know?

This is the first initiation: the student dies, and the disciple is born. The second initiation is when the disciple also disappears – into a devotee. A disciple is still interested in gaining methods, disciplines, ways to know himself. The master has to be used; hence, he is grateful. But he is the end, and the master is the means; he is using the master for his own ends. As he comes closer to the master, the master takes him into the second initiation. And the second initiation is that unless you drop this obsession with yourself you will never know yourself. It appears contradictory; it is not. Your very obsession is preventing you; it is egoistic. You drop the ego, surrender the ego; you forget yourself, and in the very moment you forget yourself you will find yourself.

From knowledge to knowing, the student was never interested in himself. He was interested in things, objects, the whole world. The first initiation brought him into a new world of interest about himself. The second initiation takes away the ego; the second initiation teaches him love. If you can love, you will know yourself without any difficulty, because knowing oneself is a byproduct.

Only in loving light does the darkness within you disappear. Love is light, and the flame of love has to be taught.

The master loves; his presence is love. His very presence is magnetic. Without saying a word... Just to be close to him, you will feel a certain pull, a certain love, a trust. And you don't know the man, you don't know whether he is trustworthy or not. But you are ready to risk. The presence of the master is so convincing that there is no need of any argument to prove it.

I was a teacher in the university, and each year on Teacher's Day the university professors used to have an intimate meeting to discuss problems that they were facing. And every year the basic and the most troublesome problem was that the students didn't respect them. When I joined their meeting for the first time it was my first year in the university. They were all condemning the students, they were condemning modern society, the Western world, because these have taken away all respect. One of the professors – an old man, a very respected professor, he was the dean of the faculty of arts – said, "It is so shameful, particularly in a country where there have been students like Ekalavya." I will have to tell you the story so you can understand. It is an ancient Indian story.

There was a great master archer, Dronacharya. Princes, rich people, high caste Hindus and warriors used to come to him from faraway places to learn archery.

The Hindu society is divided into four classes. It is the ugliest division that exists in the whole world, and it has existed for five thousand years. A fourth of Hindu society are not treated like human beings; they are called *sudras*, untouchables. They are not even worthy to be touched. If by accident you touch a *sudra*, you have to immediately take a shower to clean yourself. Not only the *sudra*, even the shadow of the *sudra* is untouchable. If a *sudra* passes by and his shadow touches you, you have to take a bath.

This young man, Ekalavya, was born a *sudra*. But he wanted to become an archer, and he started learning archery on his own. He knew perfectly well – his elders told him – "No teacher is going to accept you."

He said, "Before I go to any teacher, I will learn so much that it will be almost impossible for him to reject me." And he disciplined himself, and when he thought that now he knew enough, he went to the greatest archer of those days, Dronacharya.

Dronacharya was amazed, seeing that the young man had learned on his own tremendously well. But still, Dronacharya was a brahmin, the highest Hindu caste, and it was impossible to accept Ekalavya as a disciple. He rejected him.

But Ekalavya was made of a different kind of mettle than ordinary human beings are made of. He went into the forest and made a statue of Dronacharya. And just in front of the statue, he continued learning on his own. Soon the word started spreading all over the country that Ekalavya had become a master archer, just by the side of the statue of Dronacharya.

Dronacharya had an ambition, and that ambition was that one prince who was his disciple, Arjuna – and he was a great archer – should become the greatest archer in the history of man. But this Ekalavya was disturbing everything, he was becoming more famous.

Dronacharya went into the forest... And this is the point to be noted – that's why the dean of the faculty of arts had quoted the name of Ekalavya.

Ekalavya had been rejected by Dronacharya. Any ordinary human being would have felt insulted, humiliated. But on the contrary, he made a statue of Dronacharya – because he has chosen him as his master. It does not matter whether Dronacharya accepts him as his disciple or not – he will *have* to accept him. What matters is how deep *his* acceptance is of Dronacharya as his master.

And when Dronacharya came, he fell at his feet. And Dronacharya saw what he had learned. Certainly he was far ahead of Arjuna, and Arjuna was not going to be the greatest archer, which was the deep ambition of Dronacharya. This man had rejected Ekalavya, and now he said to him, "You have been learning here in front of my statue. You have accepted me as your master."

Ekalavya said, "I have always thought of you as my master, even when you rejected me. I have not taken any note of your rejection."

Dronacharya said, "I accept you as my disciple, but then you will have to pay the fee. Every disciple has to pay the fee to the master – and you have not given even the entrance fee, and you have already become such a great archer."

Poor Ekalavya said, "Whatever you ask, if I have it I will give it to you. I can give my life. You are my master; just say it. But I am a poor man, so just ask for that which I have."

Dronacharya said, "Yes, I will ask only that which you have. I want your right-hand thumb. You cut it off, and give it to me."

This is an ugly story. The strategy is that once his right-hand thumb is cut off, his archery will be finished, he would no longer be a competitor to Arjuna. Dronacharya accepted him as his disciple just to get his thumb.

And Ekalavya, without saying a word, simply took his sword and cut off his thumb. He gave it to the master and said, "If you want anything more, just tell me."

This story, you have to remember in the background. The dean was saying: "This country, which has produced students like Ekalavya – who respected a master like Dronacharya who rejected him, insulted him – has fallen so low that students are not respecting teachers at all. Something has to be done."

I was very new. It was my first meeting with all the professors from all the departments. I had to stand up, and I said to the old man, "You have raised a few questions. One: this is certainly the country of students like Ekalavya, but this is also the country of teachers like Dronacharya – ugly, cunning, inhuman. Why do you go on forgetting about him? – who has behaved in the most inhuman way possible: first, you are rejecting a poor young man because he is condemned by you as an untouchable. Secondly, when he achieves on his own, you are willing to accept him as your disciple – in the forest, where nobody knows what is happening. And that too for a certain reason, so that you can cripple his right hand to destroy his archery, so that your ambition of making Arjuna the greatest archer in the world can be fulfilled.

I said, "You should not forget that it is because of teachers like Dronacharya that teachers in India have lost their respect. You represent Dronacharya – on what grounds do you want students to respect you? And you are not even conscious of the fact you are mentioning Ekalavya. As far as I am concerned, I don't see... I also have students, and I am a new professor. I have not seen a single student being disrespectful towards me. I love them; I respect them. Love resonates love in the other, respect creates respect in the other – these are resonances. If I had been in the place of Ekalavya, I would have cut off the head of Dronacharya! That's exactly what he deserved."

The old man was in such a shock and so shattered he was almost trembling. I said, "Sit down because you are trembling, and if a heart attack or something happens I will be responsible for it. Please sit down. I am not going to cut your head off; although you also need to be treated in the same way. You want students to be Ekalavyas – what about the teachers?"

The master is not a teacher. He loves; it will be better to say he *is* love. He respects; it will be better to say he *is* respectfulness. Naturally he creates a gravitational field of love, respect, gratitude. In this gravitational field, the second initiation happens. The disciple is no longer interested in knowing about himself. His only interest is in how to be dissolved into the master, how to be in harmony with the master. And the day the harmony comes to its peak, the disciple disappears; the devotee is born.

The devotee is miles away from the student. The whole journey has taken such revolutionary changes. The devotee is on the verge...the life of the devotee is not long. The longest life is that of the student. In the middle is the disciple. And the life span of the devotee is very small. It is something like a dewdrop on a lotus petal in the early morning sun, slipping slowly, slowly towards the sun into the ocean. The dewdrop is just that small fragment of time that it takes to slip from the lotus leaf into the ocean.

The devotee's life is not long, it is very short – because once you have tasted the harmony you cannot wait to taste oneness. It is impossible to wait. The dewdrop runs fast, drops into the ocean, becomes one with the ocean.

There are two ways to say it. Kabir, one of the great mystics of India, is the only one who has used both ways. When for the first time he slipped into the ocean, he wrote a small statement in which he said, "I had been searching for myself, but, my friend, instead of finding myself, I have disappeared into the ocean. The dewdrop has disappeared into the ocean."

After almost twenty years, when he was on his deathbed, he asked his son, Kamal, "Bring the notes you have been taking of my statements. Before I die, I have to correct one thing." He said, "I said in one place that the dewdrop has disappeared into the ocean. Change it. Write down, 'The ocean has disappeared into the dewdrop.'"

His own words are tremendously beautiful. The first words are: *Herat herat hey sakhi rahya kabir herai, bund samani samund mein so kat heri jai*. And the second: *Herat herat hey sakhi rahya kabir herai, samund samana bund mein so kat hero jai*. In the first, the dewdrop has disappeared in the ocean. In the second, the ocean has disappeared into the dewdrop – perhaps two sides of the same coin.

This is the third initiation, and only after the third initiation is there communion – because there is union, there is no longer separation, there is at-oneness.

The path of a mystic begins as a student, ends as a master, begins as a dewdrop, ends as an ocean.

Osho,

The closer I am to you physically, the more I get lost in your presence and forget about the person that I think I am. It feels as if magnetic energy is coming from you that pulls me strongly towards you.

What is happening?

That which should be happening is happening. You are coming closer to my presence. You cannot keep your person intact. You cannot have both my presence and your person. If you want your person, you will have to lose my presence; if you want my presence, you will have to lose your person, they cannot coexist.

But what is your person? Have you ever thought about it? It consists of all your miseries, anxieties, despairs, nightmares; it is your hell. Have you ever given thought to a simple phenomenon? Since the very beginnings of man, why have human beings been so much interested in intoxicating drugs? In Rig Veda, the oldest book in the world...even the so-called seers of the Vedas are interested in a certain drug called *soma*.

One of the most intelligent persons of this century, Aldous Huxley – who was very well acquainted with the East, particularly eastern mystics – finally ended up experimenting with LSD. He wrote that in the coming century, the finest form of LSD will be called soma, in remembrance of the Rig Vedas' soma. He was absolutely convinced that LSD had come very close to soma. And perhaps he is right, because the *rishis*, the seers of the Vedas, after drinking *somrasa*, the juice of a plant called *som*, have described their experiences and what happens to them – how much peace, how much serenity, how much joy. All their experiences are exactly the same as those Aldous Huxley described when he came out of his first LSD trip.

All the cultures, all the religions have been condemning alcohol, opium, hashish, marijuana, but their condemnation seems to have no effect. Humanity goes on taking drugs, and nobody bothers to ask: "If so many wise people are against it, why are people taking these drugs?" And the strange thing is that so many of these wise people who are against it are taking drugs themselves – perhaps in different ways.

In one country, marijuana may be illegal, hashish may be illegal, LSD may be illegal, but alcohol is not. And alcohol is more dangerous than any of the other three. Why isn't alcohol illegal? – because Jesus used to drink it. Christianity cannot make it illegal; otherwise Jesus would be proved a criminal – and not an ordinary criminal – because he was even turning water into alcohol.

And the countries that have tried... For example, India, which is not a Christian country, has tried hard to prohibit alcohol, but has failed. Prohibition makes things even worse. People start making alcohol on their own, in their own homes. And thousands of people have died from poisoning because they don't know what they are drinking. It is being sold underground, and they don't know how it is being prepared. And finally those prohibitions had to be withdrawn.

One thing that I want to make clear to you is that all the people who have been against the laws and governments and religions and who are still going for drugs have a certain argument. And that is that they want their personality to be forgotten. Their person is so painful, so ugly, that they are ready to commit any illegal act, just to forget it for a few hours. The influence of intoxicating drugs proves only one thing: man, in his ordinary personality, is living in despair. He wants, for a few hours at least, to forget all about the worries and the problems and the anxieties, and there seems to be no other way.

What do you want to protect your person for? Your person is your problem.

And if you are intelligent enough, and you can find some presence where your person starts melting and disappearing – without any intoxication, without any drugs – then can you conceive of a greater blessing? Let the person disappear; it is simply a burden, a torture, a pain in the neck for which there is no medicine. What do you think, Amrito – is there any medicine for a pain in the neck? I have never heard of it. I am asking my physician, and he is a knowledgeable physician, he is a member of the Royal Society of England.

Let the person disappear, evaporate.

The disappearance of your person is not *your* disappearance, remember; on the contrary, it is your appearance. As your person disappears, your personality falls away, your individuality, your individual arises. To have a personality is hypocrisy. To be an individual is your birthright. And the function of the master is to take away everything that is not you, and leave only that which is essentially yours, given by existence itself.

I can understand, there arises a fear. You have lived with the person for so long, you have become identified with it. When it starts disappearing, a fear arises: "What is happening? Am I going to disappear?" Now, what is true is not going to disappear, and what is untrue *needs* to disappear. So be courageous.

And when your personality leaves you, say good-bye to it forever: "Don't come back. Find somebody else; there are so many people all around" – because there are people who are not so poor as to have only one personality. They are rich people, they have many personalities: when they are with their wife they have one personality, when they are with their girlfriend they have another personality – the same personality won't do. They go on changing constantly. It becomes almost an autonomous process.

George Gurdjieff, one of the great masters of this age, used a few techniques. One of the techniques was to make you aware of your personalities. He himself was such an expert that you could be sitting on his left side and your friend could be sitting on his right side, and to one he would show an angry face and to the other his face would appear really blissful, peaceful, very loving. And when they meet, one will say, "What a man! I was so afraid; he was so angry the whole time." And the other will say, "What are you saying? He was so loving, and smiling." And only later on would you discover that he had been playing a game. He had learned the art of changing personalities to such an extent that he could use two personalities at the same time. Gurdjieff could show half of the personality to the wife, and half to the girlfriend!

But a long training... There is no need. Whether you have one personality or many, they are all junk. Just leave them, just be simply yourself. In the beginning it may feel a little awkward, as if you are naked – in a certain way it is a kind of nakedness. But soon you will understand the beauty and innocence of simply being yourself.

My grandfather died. We were great friends; in my whole family, we were the only friends. No one was at ease with me, and no one was at ease with him. He was very old, but a troublemaker. But with me he was perfectly happy. We used to go together to the river, to the temple, to public meetings, and he would tell me, "Create trouble. Ask some question just to make that leader feel embarrassed."

He was a nice, beautiful man. He died. So the whole family was sad, people were crying. I went to a nearby sweet shop, and I said to the owner, "Give me all the beautiful sweets that you have prepared today – the whole lot."

He said, "Are you mad? Your grandfather has died. Haven't you heard?"

I said, "That's why! In death – celebration! We were great friends, you know?"

He said, "I know, but your father, your uncle and the others will kill me. They will say, 'He is a rascal, but you... Why did you give him sweets? Is this a time for celebration?'"

I said, "Are you going to give them to me, or should I create some trouble?"

He said, "No, I don't want any trouble. You can take them, but it is your responsibility."

I said, "I always do everything on my own responsibility."

By that time a few people had gathered. I said, "All these people are witnesses; I am taking these sweets on my responsibility. This man is absolutely innocent. In fact, he has been trying to prevent me because he does not understand at all that my grandfather has gone to heaven and this is a time to celebrate."

And I sat in front of my house distributing sweets. My whole family gathered and they said, "What are you doing?"

I said, "Simply celebrating."

They said, "Is this a time for celebration?"

I said, "To be sincere, you are all feeling good that the old fellow is dead. Except me, nobody is sad. But you are all hypocrites."

My father said to them, "Don't talk so loudly, you will gather a crowd; and if you gather a crowd, he is always the winner." He told me, "Do whatsoever you want to do. He was your grandfather, and if you want to celebrate, celebrate."

But whoever I gave the sweets to would say, "But this is not the time."

I said, "This *is* the time, because my whole family is celebrating except me – and they are all sitting sad, with crocodile tears. That is all nonsense. I know them, and because they have to hold on to their hypocrisy they cannot celebrate. So I have to do this job – although I am the only person who is sad, because he was my friend. And everybody is saying that he has gone to heaven – then why not make it a celebration? If he had gone to hell, then it would be perfectly okay. Sit with long faces and tears, and don't eat for two or three days, and make as much fuss as you can. But if he has gone to heaven, then why are you feeling jealous? Just celebrate, enjoy."

Late in the night my father told me, "The whole day I have been thinking that perhaps you were right. We were not sincere. We were all feeling relieved because he was always a trouble – in everything he created trouble."

In the shop they avoided him. He would come into the shop, and they would send him somewhere else because he would tell the customers, "He is cheating you" – his own son – "He is cheating you. That cloth is not worth twelve rupees, it is just worth eight rupees. If you wait a little, I will give it to you for eight rupees. Otherwise, it is...if you have too much money to throw away, throw it."

So in the shop, all my uncles, my father, everybody tried to get rid of him: "Customers are coming, send him away – anywhere, whatever he wants to do. But if he stands here, he will tell the truth."

And if I was there, I would tell the customers, "Just wait a little, my grandfather is coming. Then you will get the same thing for four or five rupees less."

So not only were they getting rid of him, as I would enter the shop they would tell me, "Just go to the post office."

I said, "You harass me unnecessarily. Collect all your post in the evening and I will go every day. But I cannot do this the whole day long. Whenever I come: 'Go to the post office, just one postcard...drop it at the post office.' And this is just a trick, nothing else. I will go only when my grandfather is in the shop. At least one of us has to be here; otherwise the customers are going to be cheated, exploited."

So my father said, "You were right. We were all feeling relieved, and all our tears were false. But you made it too open a secret, distributing sweets to the whole town and telling people that 'My whole family is celebrating.'"

I said, "If I was right, then you should drop these masks. Even at the death of your own father, you cannot drop your false faces. When are you going to be true?"

All your personalities are absolute cover-ups, hiding your individuality. So it is perfectly good if it is happening that you are coming closer and you feel a magnetic pull. Don't resist; help it. Let those personalities die. Their death is going to become your new life, a life which will be a joy, an innocence, a luminosity, a constant dance of the heart. Just a little courage... Don't ask what is happening. Let it happen, and see. What I am saying is nothing; what will happen will be a thousandfold more.

Osho,

I love you so much, and still – how can it be that so many questions, which come to my mind, are reflecting the dark side of me? I am afraid to bore you, but somehow these questions often feel as if they are the most honest and authentic to me.

Please comment.

One thing to be constantly remembered is not to judge what is dark and what is light, what is right and what is wrong, what is good and what is evil – because the moment you judge, you start repressing. You don't want to show anything that you judge as dark, as evil, as bad. Then you have chosen only half of yourself; it is as if you have chosen only the day and you have denied the night. But the night has its own beauties. Its darkness is also a beauty – it has a depth, a silence, a serenity, the stars. If the day has its beauty, the night has its own beauty; they are both unique and they are complementary.

What you have been doing is to ask questions which look good, and you repress those questions which you feel and judge to be bad. Naturally, your so-called good side is exhausted by and by, and only the side, which according to you is bad, remains inside. Then you are boiling with all that is black. Days are finished; only nights remain, and now you feel very much afraid to open yourself because anybody will see simply darkness and nothing else. And at the same time, you feel that it is absolutely sincere, it is part of you. It is not something insincere, but the whole problem begins in your judgment. Judgment is one of the crimes.

We go on judging other people, and we do the same with ourselves. We go on judging our thoughts, our actions, what is good, what is bad, what should have been done, what should not have been done; and we are constantly creating conflict and duality.

Here with me you have to create a oneness, a beautiful harmony between day and night, between life and death. You have to create wholeness between any things that seem to be polar opposites. And then you will not feel, bringing out anything, that it will expose you; it will simply show your wholeness. Just think of a rosebush. If the rosebush starts worrying about the thorns and starts suppressing them, the whole energy of the rosebush will be involved in suppressing the thorns. It may not be able to bring roses – or even if it does they may not be worth bringing – they may be crippled, almost dying from the very beginning.

But once you accept that thorns are part of the rosebush, as roses are... From my very childhood I have seen thorns in the rosebushes as the bodyguards of the roses. And they *are* bodyguards; they protect them. They come from the same roots; they are part of the same bush, they live on the same juice. They are brothers and sisters; they live in deep harmony, there is no conflict. Have you seen the thorns and roses fighting with each other? Have you seen any rosebush being embarrassed that it has thorns? Thorns have their own beauty.

The mind that continuously goes on judging creates anguish in you. But we are taught to judge. Even those with whom we have no concern, we go on judging: this man is good, that man is bad. What business is it, what concern is it of yours? And if you knew the whole story of the man, perhaps you would have said that this act you had thought was bad was absolutely inevitable. Without this act there would have remained something incomplete in the whole story. You know only parts – as if you take out a page from a novel, and you judge the whole novel from the page. It is sheer stupidity. First, go through the whole novel.

And as far as human life is concerned, nobody can go through the whole of a single human life. It is so vast, compressed in such a small time, seventy or eighty years, with so many complexities, complications that if you could see it as a whole you would not say that something was bad; it fits perfectly in the whole pattern of the person's life.

And anyway, who are we? Who has made us judges? Once the mind learns the trick of judging, it goes on. Then you are continually judging inside: this is good, this is bad. Then you show always the good side, and keep the bad side to yourself. Slowly, slowly, the good side is shown so much everybody is bored with it. *You* are bored with it. And you cannot show the bad side, because it is bad.

Show your wholeness; just your good side is bound to be boring, too flat. With your black parts it becomes juicy; it becomes more interesting.

It is said that "a good man has no life" – and I agree with this statement, whoever made it. What can a good man have? A bad man has a life! If you are whole, you will have more alive expressions – not flat, not boring, but always full of surprises. Not only surprising others but even surprising yourself: "My God, I was able to do this too?"

Life should be lived with as much wholeness as possible. That's the only way to live, to love, and to have a good laugh in the end. And don't be worried about what is right and what is wrong. Just for example, God created the world. Of course, if there was no Devil, there would have been nothing at all in the world. Although the whole credit goes to God, it should go to the Devil, who persuaded Adam and Eve to eat the fruit from the tree of knowledge. He is the first revolutionary, the first rebel, the first man to bring some aliveness into the world; otherwise, Adam and Eve would still be chewing grass. In the Garden of Eden what else will you do? God has said not to eat from the tree of knowledge, not to eat from the tree of eternal life – what is left? Knowing is prohibited, living is prohibited – just sit silently like buffaloes and chew grass.

It is by the mercy of the Devil that you see this whole world. God has not created it. God created a world which consisted of Adam and Eve just like animals. This whole humanity, these great people – Gautam the Buddha, Jesus Christ and Moses, Mohammed and Mahavira – you would never have heard of them; they're all because of the Devil.

It is significant to remember: *devil* comes from a Sanskrit root which means divine. It comes from *dev* – from the same root comes *divine*, from the same root comes *devil*.

The Devil has done such divine work. This whole creation is a deep partnership between God and the Devil. Neither can God do it alone, – because he can only create flat things, – nor can the Devil do it alone, because he can only revolt, he is a revolutionary. First something has to be there to be revolutionary against. God is needed for the Devil to revolt against, and then the dynamics start turning, and the wheel of life and death, day and night, good and bad...

Remember, life consists of opposites.

And don't try to judge; just live the whole, whatever it is. I teach you wholeness, and you go on judging parts. Parts are not of any use. It is the whole, where parts lose their personalities and function in the way an orchestra functions. I myself have never thought that anything is good or anything is bad. Not for a single moment have I thought that anything is bad or good; they are both together and they can exist only together. If you want to live, live them in their togetherness.

The people who are afraid of their togetherness started teaching, "Renounce life, escape from life, because here you cannot avoid the bad. Whatever you do, even if you do good, you cannot avoid the bad."

You will be surprised to know that in India, Jainism has a sect called *Terapanth*. Mumbai has many followers of the Terapanth. It is a very logical but very strange ideology. It says that if somebody falls into a well you should not take him out. He may be shouting and you are by the side of the well and there is nobody else there – you simply go on as you are, unconcerned. It seems strange. A philosophy of non-violence, and a man is dying and they are saying that you go on, unconcerned. But their reasoning is worth noting: they say you can save the man but if tomorrow he murders somebody, then you will be responsible too. And what is the guarantee about his tomorrow? It is better not to get involved. In the first place he has fallen in the well. It must be because of some evil act in his past life; otherwise why should he fall into the well? Now, he is receiving the punishment for his action, and you interfere in it, you interfere in the great law of action. Secondly, if he murders somebody tomorrow, then you will share the evil act. It is better to move on silently, not to bother about what is happening to him.

These are the people who have been judging. Now, judgment has gone to the extreme. Somebody is thirsty; don't give him water. Somebody is hungry; don't give him food – because you don't know what he is going to do. You get involved in his life by giving him water; otherwise he may have died. By giving him water you keep him alive. Now whatever he does, you are going to share in it. You have not done a bad act, but life is not so simple – it may turn into a bad act. It looks very logical, but very inhuman; it looks very rational but very uncompassionate, without any love. But this is the logical end of judging things.

I want you to drop judgment and live a life without judgment, in its wholeness. And you will be surprised that wholeness is neither good nor bad.

Wholeness is transcendental; it is beyond good and evil.

There is only one man in the whole history of humanity, Friedrich Nietzsche, who has written a book, *Beyond Good And Evil*. And my insight and understanding is that he is the only man who has seen judgment to its logical end.

An authentic person should live beyond good and evil. He does not care what is good, what is bad. He lives with intensity and totality, and whatever the moment allows him and he feels to do, he does it. But all the religions and all the theologians and all the saints are sitting and thinking about whether this is right or wrong. And if you listen to them, you will find it impossible to live; everything seems to be wrong.

I have looked into all the scriptures of the world just trying to find out: perhaps there may be one thing which is not condemned by somebody. But there is not, somebody or other is against everything. And there are things that somebody or other is for. There is no ultimate criterion to decide what is right and what is wrong.

As far as I am concerned and my people are concerned, they should live wholeheartedly – live the day and live the night too. Don't miss anything. Make your life such a complementary whole that everything fits together and makes it a piece of art, a beautiful phenomenon.

13 The Only Holy Approach

Osho,
When I close my eyes, I feel such an enormous presence, such a vast isness, such a beatitude. But it is a fullness not an emptiness. Could you please say something about the difference between this fullness, and the emptiness or nothingness, which you are speaking of?

The fullness that you are experiencing and the nothingness that I have been speaking about are just two names for the same thing seen from two different perspectives. If you look at it from the world of miseries, anxieties, darkness and death, it is nothingness – because all these things are absent. Your whole so-called world and its experiences are no more in it. But if you look at what is left, or at what is revealed because of the absence of misery and darkness, then you are full of blissfulness, full of light, of enormous presence and beatitude, a great benediction. It is fullness. It is empty of the world and full of godliness, it is empty of all your falsities and full of your essential reality. Those two words are not contradictory; they are indicating the same experience from two different perspectives.

It is significant to understand that there is only one person, Gautam Buddha, who has used nothingness, emptiness, for the ultimate experience. All other mystics of the world have used fullness, wholeness, as the expression, the indication of the ultimate experience.

Why did Gautam Buddha have to choose a negative term? It is significant to understand – for your own spiritual growth, not for any philosophical reasons. I do not speak for philosophical reasons. I speak only when I see there is some existential relevance. The idea of fullness, the idea of God, the idea of perfection, the idea of the absolute, the ultimate – all are positive terms. And Gautam Buddha was amazed to see the cunningness of human mind.

The innocent mystics have simply used the positive words because that was their experience. Why bother about the misery which is no longer? Why not say something about that which is now? The innocent mystics have spoken out of their isness. But throughout the centuries the cunning minds of people around the world have taken advantage of it. To the cunning mind, the idea of fullness and the positive terms indicating it became an ego trip: "I have to become God. I have to attain the absolute, the *brahma*; I have to achieve the ultimate liberation." The "I" became the center of all our assertions. And the trouble is that you cannot make the ultimate experience a goal for the ego. Ego is the barrier; it cannot become the bridge.

So all the positive terms have been misused. Rather than destroying the ego, they have become decorations for the ego. God has become a goal; you have to achieve the goal. *You* become greater than God. Remember, the goal cannot be greater than you. The achieved cannot be greater than the achiever. It is a very simple fact to understand. And all the religions have fallen because of this simple innocence of the mystics.

Gautam Buddha was the most cultured and the most educated, the most sophisticated person ever to become a mystic. There is no comparison in the whole of history. He could see where the innocent mystics had unknowingly given chances for cunning minds to take advantage. He decided not to use any positive term for the ultimate goal, to destroy your ego and any possibility of your ego taking any advantage. He called the ultimate, nothingness, emptiness, *shunyata*, zero. Now, how can the ego make zero the goal? God can be made the goal, but not zero. Who wants to become zero? That is the fear; everybody is avoiding all possibilities of becoming zero, and Buddha made it an expression for the ultimate.

His word is *nirvana*. He chose a tremendously beautiful word, but he shocked all the thinkers and philosophers by choosing the word *nirvana* as the most significant expression for the u timate experience. Nirvana means blowing out the candle.

The other mystics have said that you are filled with enormous light, as if thousands of suns together have suddenly risen inside you, as if the whole sky full of stars has descended within your heart. These ideas appeal to the ego. The ego would like to have all the stars, if not inside the chest then at least hanging on the coat outside the chest. Enormous light...the ego is very willing.

To cut the very roots, Buddha said the experience is as if you were to blow out a candle. There was a small flame on the candle giving a small light – even that has gone, and you are surrounded with absolute darkness, abysmal darkness.

People used to come to ask him, "If you go on teaching such things, nobody is going to follow you. Who wants darkness, enormous darkness? You are crazy. You say that the ultimate experience is ultimate death. People want eternal life, and you are talking about ultimate death." But he was a very consistent man, and you can see that for forty-two years he hammered on the genius of the East without ever compromising with the ego.

He also knew that what he called darkness was too much light; that's why it looked like darkness. If one thousand suns rise in you, what do you think, that you will feel enormous light? You will feel immense darkness; it will be too dazzling. Just look at *one* sun for a few seconds and you will feel your eyes are going blind. If one thousand suns are within you, inside the mind, the experience will be of darkness, not of light. It will take a long time for you to get accustomed, for your eyes to become strong enough to see: slowly, slowly darkness turning into light, death turning into life, emptiness turning into fullness.

But he never talked about those things. He never said that darkness would ever turn into light. And he never said that death would become a resurrection at some later point, because he knew how cunning your ego is. If that is said, the ego will say, "Then there is no problem. Our aim remains the same; it is just that we will have to pass through a little dark night of the soul. But finally, we will have enormous light, thousands of suns."

Gautam Buddha had to deny that God existed – not that he was against God, a man like Gautam Buddha could not be against God. And if Gautam Buddha was against God, then it was of no use for anybody to be in favor of God. His decision was decisive for the whole of humanity, he represents our very soul. But he was not against God. He was against your ego, and he was constantly careful not to give your ego any support to remain. If God can become a support, then there is no God.

One thing becomes very clear: although he used, for the first time, all negative terms, the man must have had tremendous charismatic qualities. He influenced millions of people. His philosophy is such that anyone listening to him would freak out. What is the point of all the meditations and all the austerities, renouncing the world, eating one time a day – and ultimately you achieve nothingness, you become zero! We are already better – we may be miserable zeros, but at least we *are*. Certainly, when you are *completely* a zero there cannot be any misery; zeros are not known to be miserable – but what is the gain?

But he convinced people, not through his philosophy, but through his individuality, through his presence. He gave people the experience itself, so that they could understand: it is emptiness as far as the world is concerned; it is emptiness for the ego. And it is fullness for the being.

There are many reasons for the disappearance of Buddha's thought from India, but this is one of the most significant. All other Indian mystics, philosophers, and seers used positive terms. And for centuries before Buddha, the whole of India was accustomed to thinking only in the positive; the negative was something unheard of. Under the influence of Gautam Buddha they followed him, but when he died his following started disappearing, because the following was not intellectually convinced; it was convinced because of his presence.

Because of the eyes of Gautam Buddha they could see: "This man, if he is living in nothingness then there is no fear, we would love to be nothing. If this is where zero-ness leads, if by being nothing such lotuses bloom in the eyes and such grace flows, then we are ready to go with this man. The man has a magic." But his philosophy alone will not convince you, because it has no appeal for the ego.

And Buddhism survived in China, in Ceylon, in Burma, in Japan, in Korea, in Indochina, in Indonesia – in the whole of Asia except India – because the Buddhists who reached there dropped negative terms. They started speaking in positive terms; then the ultimate, the absolute, the perfect, the old terms, returned. This was the compromise. So as far as I am concerned, Buddhism died with Gautam Buddha. Whatever exists now as Buddhism has nothing to do with Buddha because it has dropped his basic contribution, and that was his negative approach.

I am aware of both traditions. I am certainly in a better position than Gautam Buddha was. Gautam Buddha was aware of only one thing: that the ego can use the positive. And it is his great contribution, his courageous contribution, that he dropped the positive and insisted on the negative, emphasized the negative – knowing perfectly well that people were not going to follow this because it had no appeal for the ego. To me, now both traditions are available. I know what happened to the positive: the ego exploited it. I know what happened to the negative. After the death of Gautam Buddha, the disciples had to compromise, compromise with the same thing which Gautam Buddha was revolting against. So I am trying to explain to you both approaches together: emptiness as far as the world is concerned and fullness, wholeness as far as the inner experience is concerned. And this is a total approach, it takes note of both: that which has to be left behind, and that which is to be gained.

I call my approach the only holy approach. All other approaches up to now have been half-half. Mahavira, Shankara, Moses, Mohammed, all used the positive. Gautam Buddha used the negative. I use both, and I don't see any contradiction. If you understand me clearly, then you can enjoy the beauty of both viewpoints, and you need not be exploited by your ego or be afraid of death and darkness and nothingness. They are not two things. It is almost as if I were to put a glass of water in front of you, half full and half empty, and ask you whether the glass is empty or full. Either answer would be wrong, because the glass is both half full and half empty. From one side it is empty, from another side it is full.

Half of your life is part of the mundane world, the other half is part of the sacred. And it is unfortunate, but there is no other way – we have to use the same language for both the mundane and the sacred. So one has to be very alert. To choose the mundane will be missing; if you think of the mundane, you will find the sacred life empty. If you think of the sacred, you will find it overflowingly full.

Osho,

As you were talking about Indian and western sannyasins, I felt what you were saying was true – sometimes the Indians are too much of the heart. It is hard to say no to them, yet you cannot say yes to their expectations and theories. They are deaf.

Will you please explain why this is so?

The question has many parts. The first part: that the Indians are sometimes too much of the heart, that statement is wrong. One can never be too much of the heart; that is existentially impossible. The heart and its qualities are such that you can always have more of them. And there is no limit – not even the sky is the limit. But I understand your problem. You are saying that you are finding it difficult in certain moments, the people of the East are much too loving; you cannot say no to them and you cannot say yes either.

I am reminded of when I came to Mumbai for the first time, I was invited for lunch, I was new, and the people who had invited me here were new. None of us knew each other.

The man had come to Mumbai just two or three days before. He is one of the most beautiful men I have met in my life. Along with me, he had invited at least twenty more people. It was beautiful food, but the way they were forcing everybody to eat was just unimaginable. They were three brothers; two of the brothers would hold the person, and the third one would force him: "One *laddu* more."

And the person would be trying to say, "I will die! Leave me!"

They would say, "Just one." And this was something unending.

Even the women of the house were helping. People were trying to run out of the room and the women were standing in the doorway.

I asked the man, "Your love is good, and your sweets are good, but there is a limit. That man is saying he will die – and you are not concerned about his death, you are concerned about forcing more food on him."

What he said to me I have not forgotten. He said, "If we don't do this, my father's soul will be very unhappy."

I said, "My God! Is your father's soul also present here?"

He said, "No, that is not the question. This is our heritage. In my father's day, this was the routine: unless the guest starts fighting and beating you, don't leave him alone. Things have to come to that end."

I said, "Listen, don't do this thing to me – because I cannot beat you, and neither do I want to fight."

They said, "But our father's soul..."

I said, "You are idiots! Your father's soul must have been born again by now. When did your father die?"

They said, "It must be twenty years."

I said, "He must be in a college somewhere studying. Forget about him, he has nothing to do with it."

He said, "If you say so, but we will feel very guilty."

I said, "If you force anything on me, I am not going to come to Mumbai again."

With tears in his eyes, he took hold of my legs. He said, "That's perfectly good. I will not force you. Just one *laddu*, no fight, but please continue to come. And promise me that at least whenever you come...one lunch at my house, and we will never force you. Just have one more *laddu*."

I said, "But you *are* forcing me! This is another strategy – tears, holding my leg; it is no different from holding my neck. It is even worse, because I feel that although it will create trouble for me – you have forced so many sweets on me – looking at your tears..."

He said, "What can I do? Just thinking of my father's soul..."

I said, "Drop your father's soul! Do you promise me that if I take this *laddu* you will not ask anything?"

He said, "I absolutely promise."

But I was not aware of the strategy. It was one brother's promise – they were three brothers, with three wives.

I said, "My God, it seems soon my soul is going to meet your father's soul! If you have any message, I will deliver it to him. And I will never come again."

And they were all sitting on the floor, holding my leg – "You have to come."

Love is one thing; this is not love, because love would take care of me, see that I don't fall sick. They were taking care of their father's soul; they were not concerned with me. So I can understand your question, that sometimes their love is too much, their heart is too much. You cannot say no and you cannot say yes either.

But you have to be very clear with the people in the East. Accept their love, be grateful for their love, but when it goes against your reason, *no* is not something that cannot be said. It is not necessarily against love. You are simply protecting yourself, and you have the right to protect yourself. And if you cannot say yes, don't say yes.

And remember: what they are doing is not love, but some formality, some tradition, some convention. This is not part of love. They are fulfilling their own traditional, conventional, orthodox views. If it were love then food would not be forced; then the guest would be served and allowed to eat whatever he felt like eating, and however much he wanted to eat. Love will give that freedom.

It is not heart. The dividing line is very fine – that's why you cannot understand how to say no. The person is so loving that it seems better to suffer a little, but not to say no. But this is not his love. Love never enforces anything on anyone. Love never tries to dominate, to dictate. You call this love? – two persons are holding onto the man's hands and the third person is forcing a *laddu* into his mouth, and the man is saying, "I will die! What are you doing? If you had told me that this was going to happen I would have never come." But they have a certain idea. It has been happening in their family for centuries – unless a guest starts beating you, you are not a host, not worth the name. A strange idea!

You have to say no. And if they need beating, then it is better that before they force the food, you start beating them. If that is the only thing that will stop them and satisfy them and their father's soul, then beat them before they make you sick. Be alert, and understand clearly the idea of love. It is non-interfering. It is non-enforcing – about *anything*. Love is authentic only when it gives you freedom.

I am reminded of a strange Eastern story that will show you what love is.

A man is in great love with a woman. The woman says, "I am ready to marry you, but there is one condition."

If the man had been aware of a simple fact, that love never makes conditions, he would have said good-bye to the woman at that very point. But he was mad, really blindly in love. He was ready to do anything. He said, "Any condition, and I am ready to do it."

The woman said, "My condition is difficult."

The man said, "Whatever the condition is, don't be worried. You just say it."

The woman said, "Go home and kill your mother. Bring her heart on a plate and present it to me. Only on this condition will I marry you, because only this will give me proof that you really love me."

Blind lovers can do anything. They are blind, not only in this story but all over the world. He went home, he killed his mother, and he put her heart on a plate. He rushed. He was in such a hurry to reach the woman that he stumbled on the road and fell. The plate broke and the heart was all over the street in small pieces.

And a voice came from those pieces: "My son, are you hurt? I am sorry, but it wasn't my fault. Try to gather the pieces; go home and get another plate, and go to your sweetheart."

Listening to this, it was as if he suddenly awoke from a dream. What was he doing? What had he done? And his mother had not complained, was not even angry. On the contrary, she had inquired,

"Are you hurt? – because you've fallen on the ground. I have always been telling you to go slowly, but you never listen to me. Now collect all the pieces and go back home."

He collected the pieces, went home, and forgot all about that woman.

The woman waited and waited. One day passed, another day passed. She said, "What happened?" She went to the man's house, found that he had killed his mother. She said, "What happened then? Where is the heart?"

It was on a plate, in fragments. He said, "This is the heart, but something happened on the road that made me turn back. I knew for the first time what love means. I am grateful to you; otherwise I would have never understood that my mother was so concerned about my welfare. And I cannot forgive myself, that I killed the woman with my own hands. As for you, who asked such a condition..."

Love makes no conditions. Love gives you freedom to be yourself, helps you to be yourself. Even if it goes against his own interest, still, a loving person will suffer himself, rather than make the loved one suffer.

Another ancient story:

A woman loved her husband, but the husband never paid any attention to her. He was in love with a prostitute, knowing perfectly well that prostitutes don't love – because there were many other customers. He was only a customer, not a lover. And in his life he had seen that the day the customer's money is finished, the prostitute's door is closed for that man.

He had destroyed his health, he had destroyed his money; now he was dying. Just as he was dying, his wife asked him, "If you have any last wish so that you can die contented..."

He said, "Yes, I have a wish, but I am ashamed to say it to you."

She said, "Don't be ashamed. This is not the time to be ashamed. I love you as you are, there is no question of feeling ashamed."

He said, "My only wish is to see the prostitute just once more before I die."

The woman said, "There is no problem."

He had lost all their money; there was no money in the house. She had to carry the dying man on her shoulders to the prostitute's house. She knocked on the door.

The prostitute opened the door and could not believe it. She said, "Am I hallucinating? Is this real? You are the wife of the man..."

The wife said, "Yes, I am the wife and also the lover of the man."

The prostitute said, "Then why have you brought him here? He destroyed your life, he spent all your money and he was mad after me. And to me, once the money is finished, all relationship is finished. He was only a customer. This is a marketplace and he knows it. You are a strange woman."

She said, "But this was his dying wish. He wanted to see you, and I love him so much that I could not say no. In his happiness is my happiness, and if he can die contented I will feel I have fulfilled my duty, my love."

No complaint about the man, about his whole behavior. No jealousy against the woman. Love knows no jealousy, love knows no complaint: love is a deep understanding. You love someone – that does not mean that the other should love you also. It is not a contract.

Try to understand the meaning of love. You will not be able to understand the meaning of love by your so-called love affairs. Strangely enough, you will understand the meaning of love by going deep into meditation, by becoming more silent, more together, more at ease. You will start radiating a certain energy. You will become loving, and you will know the beautiful qualities of love. It knows to say yes, it also knows to say no. It is not blind. But it has to come out of your meditation – only then does love have eyes; otherwise love is blind.

And unless love has eyes, it is worthless. It is going to create more and more trouble for you – because two blind persons with blind expectations are not only going to double the troubles of life, they are going to multiply the troubles of life.

So be silent and be alert. Be loving.

And you can say no with great love. No does not mean that you are un-loving; yes does not mean that you are loving. Sometimes yes may mean that you are simply afraid, it is out of fear. So it is not necessarily that love means yes and you cannot say no. Love with eyes knows when to say no, when to say yes. Love neither interferes in anybody's life nor allows anybody else to interfere into one's own life. Love gives individuality to others, but does not lose its own individuality.

And it is not a question of Western or Eastern – what I am saying is applicable to all. Just because you have asked the question as if the problem is because you come from the West... It has to be understood well: it is not a question of your coming from the West; it is a problem because reason and heart are always in conflict. And the West is more rationalist, but the West has spread all over the world through its empires and through its educational systems. Now it is very difficult to find a purely Eastern man. The West has poisoned everybody. Reason has become supreme. So try to understand it in terms of reason and heart, not in terms of West and East. Because even in the East, for the people who are living in their reason – and all people who are cultured, educated, are living in their reason – the problem is the same.

The heart has its own language, reason has its own language, and they are not necessarily always in agreement. Most probably they are in disagreement, because reason thinks in a different dimension.

I am reminded of Albert Einstein and his wife, Frau Einstein.

His wife was a poet. And he was just the wrong person to be married to: a mathematician, a physicist. In mathematics, one plus one is always two. In love, one plus one is always one. Languages are so different.

And Frau Einstein was a talented woman; naturally she wanted to show a few of her poems to Albert Einstein, and would have enjoyed being appreciated by the world's most famous mathematician, physicist, scientist. But she could not see any emotion moving on Albert Einstein's face, or any changes in his eyes. He listened to her poems as if he were a stone statue.

She had written a beautiful piece, talking about the beloved and comparing the face of the beloved with the moon. At that point, Einstein said, "Enough! Stop! This is too much. You don't understand anything about the moon. Do you know its proportions? If a moon were put on a man's body as a head, your beloved would not be found again, he would be crushed to pieces. And who told you that the moon is beautiful? It is a dead rock, with no water, no greenery, no flowers, no trees, no birds. Who told you that the moon is beautiful? What do you mean by beauty?"

The wife was shocked, she could not believe that such a great scientist would talk in such a way. But he was not joking – that's how reason thinks.

Reason cannot understand poetry; it is not its way – it is very prose.

Frau Einstein has written in her memoirs, "That was the first and the last time I ever mentioned poetry to him. It would be better to talk to a rock; perhaps the rock might respond better than this man."

The question is not of East and West. The question is between the heart and the reason. In the East, the heart has been predominant, but it has created a problem which nobody has discussed. I have been looking through ancient scriptures, literature, commentaries – has anybody ever thought about this problem or not? – because it is so significant it cannot be ignored. Because the East is leaning too much towards the heart, it has not developed rationality to its fullest – but still it goes on talking about theories, reincarnation, heaven and hell. If you were to say that these are mythological, there would be no problem, but people insist that these are rational hypotheses.

And your question is relevant. It becomes so difficult to talk with the Eastern person because he goes on talking about theories which look absurd, stupid, illogical. But to him they seem absolutely valid because he has never been trained in reason. His validity is of the heart.

I will give you few examples so you can understand: Jainas say that once a snake bit Mahavira on his foot, and instead of blood coming out, milk came out. Now, if you say it is a myth, a parable, a poetry, there is no problem.

The first time I spoke in Mumbai, a Jaina monk, Chitrabhanu, had spoken ahead of me. And he mentioned this fact, and gave the reason why milk came out: because Mahavira is so full of love that even when a snake bites him, it is because of his love and compassion that milk comes out – just a little breakfast for the snake: no anger, no violence. And for twenty-five centuries Jainas have been writing in their books that this is factual.

I was to speak after Chitrabhanu, and I said, "If it is factual then many things have to be explained: it means that Mahavira's body was filled with milk instead of blood. And the snakebite happened when he was nearabout fifty, so for fifty years... All the milk would have certainly turned into curd. And he used to walk naked, on foot. In fifty years' time, the curd would have turned into butter! And in such heat, in such a hot country, butter is going to become ghee."

So if ghee had come out of his foot instead of blood, there would be some rationality to it – but milk? And this is so stupid, that a man is full of curd, he would stink of curd! Fifty years filled with curd and butter and ghee – just think of that poor man. In the hot season, he wouldn't perspire; he would start flowing with ghee!

So I said, "This is nonsense. The only possibility is: milk comes out of a woman's body, and she has a certain mechanism in her breast to transform the blood into milk. A rational mind could accept it, that Mahavira had the same mechanism in his feet. His feet were nothing but breasts. And strangely, was he expecting that the snake was going to bite him on the foot? Most probably he had breasts all over, so that wherever the snake bit, milk would come out."

And even a woman's breast will not give milk unless she has given birth to a child. So I said, "This goes on and on into difficulties. It is better to accept that this is simply poetry. Don't make it history. Don't try to theorize it, don't try to make it scientific. Simply say that it is a poetic way of saying that he was so loving... How to say it in poetry? – so we have expressed it by saying that milk came out, just as the milk comes out of the mother's breast, in love."

Milk has a certain association with love, because the child receives the milk and love from the same breast – that is his first experience in the world. And that's why humanity is so obsessed with the breast. Painters go on painting breasts and breasts, sculptors go on making breasts and breasts. Poets, novelists, all kinds of creative people are obsessed only with one object, and that is the woman's breast. The reason is clear: it is the child's first experience of love, of warmth, of the human body, of the other, of the world. It contains so much. So just to give expression to a feeling of love and warmth, milk has been used as a symbol.

But no Jaina is going to agree with me, because then the miracle is lost. Poetry is not a miracle. The miracle is in the historicity of the fact. So you are right in questioning how to deal with these people. They are so loving, they are so full of heart, but they go on talking about such nonsense: esoteric, occult.

And everybody in the East knows so much that it seems that all are realized souls! Where to stop these people, and where to say no to these people? You have to be very clear, very loving, but without any compromise. The moment you see that these people are going into fictions and creating stupid theories – and their scriptures are full of them – you have to stop them. That is one of the misfortunes of the East, that people have forgotten completely that poetry is not history, that poetry is far more significant than history. Then theorizations, rationalizations are meaningless, and the effort to prove them as if they are scientific truths makes the whole East a laughingstock.

My own approach is very simple: you have to be alert not to allow the heart to start overpowering your reason, just as you have to be alert that your reason does not overpower your heart. Their functions are separate. Reason should function in the world of objects, and the heart should function in the world of human consciousness. And the moment they overlap, there is going to be a certain kind of mess.

And whenever you feel it, that the man is so loving, how to say no to him? – don't be worried. It has been my whole life's difficulty – because everybody in India is so full of knowledge, and all that knowledge is simply holy cow dung, there is nothing in it. But these people are good; this is the problem. The people are good: very generous, very loving, very helpful. Only their hearts have overrun their heads, so whatsoever they are saying, you have to be a little alert.

And when you say no to them, they feel hurt; they think their love is rejected. So you have to be very careful and very articulate. It is a difficult task – it was for me, because with my family, my teachers, my professors, everywhere I was in difficulty. Because I could not see how a well-educated professor could be talking such nonsense, without even being aware at all that what he is saying is nonsense. And he was a good man, there was no doubt about his sincerity. It was simply that his reason was retarded. Only the heart had grown, and it had its beauty. But the heart was leading the reason, so they were talking all kinds of nonsense.

I had to stop them – "Wait a minute. You cannot say this rationally. Either accept it as a poetry or withdraw it."

But the result was that I was expelled from this college, from that university – and they had no reason. The vice-chancellor said to me, "We don't have any reason to expel you, you have not done anything that demands such punishment as to expel you. But you should understand our difficulty: you are creating such trouble to so many professors that they are threatening to resign if you don't leave this university. And we cannot afford it, those are our very respected professors."

And I said, "First you should call them and ask them what the problem is, why they are so angry with me."

And the professors said, "It is not a question of being angry with you. You simply raise questions which make us feel embarrassed before the whole class. And people laugh, and we cannot answer. You are destroying the respectability we have established over thirty years, forty years – you, within half an hour, destroy the whole of it. People lose all respect for us."

And I said, "Have I ever shown any disrespect to you?"

They said, "You never show any disrespect. That is not the question, the question is that we cannot change now. Our whole lives we have lived with certain theories. And we have believed them to be scientific; we have never suspected them. Suddenly you come here, and on each point you create a question and we are at a loss."

One of the professors was a celibate, and he was continually preaching celibacy, that the only spirituality is to be celibate.

I asked him, "I have been in your home, and I see Rama there with Sita, the Hindu god Rama standing with his wife, Sita. What kind of celibacy is this fellow following? And out of this celibacy two children are born – you should throw this fellow out of your house! But you worship him, and in the university you talk about celibacy. Do you see the contradiction or not? All your Vedic seers were married people, all your Upanishadic seers were married people. You read Shrimad Bhagavadgita every day, and this fellow Shri Krishna had sixteen thousand wives – what kind of celibacy is this?"

Now this man took my hand and told me, "Come with me to the vice-chancellor. This is too much – now either you are going to remain in the university or I am going to remain in the university."

But I said, "I have simply asked a question. You can satisfy me by giving a satisfactory answer. Or, you can say that you are greater than all these people because you are celibate and they were not. But why are you worshipping them? They should worship you."

On the way, he asked me, "Should we go to the vice-chancellor or not?"

I said, "It is up to you. Because the whole question will be discussed, and I will insist that the vice-chancellor have a look in your house. You have made a temple where Rama is standing with Sita and Krishna is standing with Rukmini – which is absolute hypocrisy; he was married to this woman Rukmini but he never lived with her. How could he manage it? Sixteen thousand wives stolen from other people's houses...he was married to only one woman; the remaining ones were all stolen, forcibly taken. Whenever he saw a beautiful woman, his soldiers would take her – no consideration of the husband or the children or the old parents, no consideration at all. And still, the hypocrisy is that you are putting poor Rukmini next to Krishna. I will take the vice-chancellor to have a look in your house and things can be decided then and there."

I said, "There is no need for you to resign. Simply don't be celibate, get married! The problem will be solved – neither I will have to be expelled from the university nor will you have to resign. And if you feel shy, I will find a good wife for you."

He said, "Stop! Don't talk like this, you are almost persuading me. This is seduction."

I said, "Then come on and see the vice-chancellor."

And we went, and the vice-chancellor listened, and he told me, "You are not wrong, but what can we do? As far as Indian logic is concerned, this man is the best in the whole of India. We cannot..."

I said, "Just think – this man is absolutely illogical. How can he be an expert in Indian logic? His behavior is so illogical: a celibate worshipping married people."

But the vice-chancellor said, "You had better choose some other university. I will recommend you. I will not expel you, I will recommend you as highly as possible." But no university was ready to accept me, because my fame had reached ahead of me already: that fellow is coming to be admitted to the university or the college.

In India it is a problem – people are not rational. Even those who pretend to be rational, their behavior is very irrational. They will be very loving, but don't allow them to destroy your reason. The heart has to grow, reason has to become sharp – because both have to fulfill their functions in the totality of your growth.

A man with a great heart *and* a great intelligence without any conflict between them, is truly a genius. And everybody has the possibility, but everybody is either dominated by logic or dominated by the heart. Everybody is living a lopsided life.

Have you seen any advertisements for circuses? When a circus comes to a town – I have seen it in many towns – they have bicycles, with one wheel small and one wheel big. And the big wheel's center is not in the center; it is off-center. So the man riding on the bicycle comes up, goes down, comes up, goes down – naturally he attracts everybody's attention: "What is happening?" A man suddenly comes up and goes down, and he is a joker, wearing the joker's dress and the name of the circus, and the timings and the tickets and everything.

A single man will attract everybody: a simple device.

But seeing that kind of advertisement, I saw that this is the situation of almost every man. You have two wheels, the reason and the heart. Somebody's heart is big and their reason is small – then he goes up and down. Somebody's reason is big and his heart is small – then he goes up and down. Everybody is going up and down – and for whom are you advertising? And it is not easy to sit on that bicycle; I have tried it. It is a very difficult job. But people are living this way – unbalanced.

You need a balanced life in which reason and heart move in harmony, supporting each other, helping each other. So whenever you see that anybody – either from the East or from the West – is disturbing your harmony, stop him. Stop him lovingly, there is no need to be rude. But don't be silent, because to be silent is to be rude. You have allowed that man to move in a wrong way, you were not compassionate enough.

14 Don't Be a Missionary, Be a Message

Osho,
You heard my prayer and called me to you on the 8th of August.

As I entered your room, I experienced you as a large ocean, an emptiness that I have never experienced before. I saw your beautiful being, and I was immersed in that emptiness and beauty. I felt that the ocean's emptiness was flowing into me from you.

After that day, new songs and melodies are coming from that emptiness of yours, and I don't know anything.

Osho, please explain how this can happen so easily in the master's presence. Is it so simple? It doesn't feel possible for me to exist in this life without having had that meeting – is that so? I feel that such a feeling might not have otherwise happened to me for many lives.

Please explain the meeting of the master and the disciple.

The most obvious in life seems to be the most difficult; the most simple seems to be the most complicated.

The reason why it happens so is because the mind is not interested in the obvious. It wants the challenge of the impossible; only with the challenge of the impossible can the mind fulfill its ego. With the obvious, there is no space for the ego to grow or even to exist. The obvious is the grave of the ego. The simple we take for granted because it is so simple. Only the far away, the distant, catches our eye, invites us for a journey. Because of this, people have gone around the earth – people like Columbus. People have gone to the moon, people are trying to go to Mars, people are thinking to reach some day to the most distant stars. Nobody bothers to enter into himself, and to see the most miraculous, the most mysterious, the most fundamental principle of life, the very source of life – it is so close, so obvious, so simple.

People may not find anything on the moon; they have not found anything, but they have become great historical figures. Edmund Hillary has not found anything on Everest, but his name will remain a landmark forever. I have always been surprised that for at least one hundred years people from all the Western countries have been coming to climb the highest peak of the Himalayas: Everest. No Indian has bothered about it; for the Indian it is so obvious. The more difficult a thing is, the more attractive it is; the more unattainable, the more mind becomes obsessed.

I have heard...

A great psychologist was visiting a madhouse. The superintendent of the madhouse was taking him on a tour, satisfying his curiosities and questions about the inmates. He became immensely interested in one inmate; behind the bars, in his cell, he was standing naked. On the wall there was a small picture of an ordinary woman, and he was standing in a worshipful mood, tears flowing from his eyes. The psychologist asked, "What is the matter with this man?"

The superintendent said, "Don't disturb him," took him a little way away, and said, "He does not like to be disturbed in his prayers, and he is praying almost the whole day."

The psychologist said, "Whose picture is that?"

The superintendent started laughing. He said, "It is nobody, it is just an ordinary woman. He was in love, but because they belonged to different castes, the father of the woman refused; he became mad and the woman became a goddess. Unattainable, one ordinary woman became a goddess. Now he worships and prays, 'What has not happened in this life, perhaps through prayer and worship may happen in the next.'"

The psychologist said, "I have never come across such a case."

The superintendent said, "Just wait a little more."

In the next cell there was another man who was hitting his head against the wall, and two guards were holding him. The psychologist said, "What has happened to him? Why does he want to hit his head on the wall?"

The superintendent said, "He has gone mad. He wants to commit suicide, and it is such a problem to watch him continuously – he hurts himself."

"But what is the cause of his madness?"

The superintendent said, "That's why I was telling you to just wait a little. He got married, and the marriage has been such a disaster that he is in the madhouse. He wants to commit suicide. Because sooner or later he will be sent out of the madhouse, and again be in the hands of that woman. But it is the same woman! And to avoid her, he wants to commit suicide."

The psychologist said, "My God, it is the same woman the other man is praying to get in his next life, because he missed the train this time! And this poor fellow did not miss this time – now he wants to jump out of the train. He can't even wait for the station to come."

Logic is a complicated phenomenon Life is not logic. Life is closer to music than to mathematics, because mathematics is of the mind, and life throbs in your heartbeats. Life is love.

Love is simple, innocent communion.

Ashok Bharti, you love me and that opens the door for all the mysteries possible. People say love is blind because they do not know what love is. I say unto you, only love has eyes; other than love, everything is blind. Once your eyes of love are opened, things which you have never dreamed of start becoming realities; new songs that you had never thought yourself capable of, new poetries, with such insights that you cannot believe that you have written them.

This is the reason why all the ancient scriptures don't have the names of their authors – because the authors could not believe that they were the writers of the Upanishads, of the Vedas. They could not believe it. At the most, they have been vehicles; they were possessed. Some universal energy has taken possession of them, and what they have written has nothing to do with them. They have not signed the scriptures that they have written.

It is very difficult to find out who are the sculptors of the most beautiful ancient statues of Gautam Buddha, which have never again been equaled. The grand architecture of the caves of Ajanta, Ellora... It seems almost superhuman work, and the people have not even signed their names because they never believed that they were doing it. They experienced that existence was using them as instruments, and they were blessed and grateful that they had been chosen to be instrumental. Existence had been compassionate towards them; they were rewarded enough.

Ashok Bharti is a poor man, but has a very rich heart; and to have a rich heart is the only real richness in the world. He has the potentiality of becoming a great singer, a great poet, a great composer, but he was not aware of it. He had come just to see me; he's my old sannyasin. And knowing that to me, religion means celebration, he brought his *khanjhari* – just to sing a song to me, what else to bring as an offering? He was very shy in asking, "Can I sing a song in your presence?"

I said, "This is the most beautiful present anyone could have brought to me. You can sing every day." And I have been watching him for almost one month – the depth, the significance, the meaning of his songs has been deepening. His courage is growing, he is no longer hesitant, he is not worried that so many people are watching. He is not a public singer. He's just like everybody else, a bathroom singer.

It is strange: in bathrooms you will find the great singers of the world, but the moment you bring them out of the bathroom they become dumb. Everybody is a good conversationalist. The whole world is agog with people talking to each other, but just put somebody on a pedestal, and he looks at the crowd watching him and his heart starts sinking. These are the same people he has been talking to separately, privately. But to be observed by thousands of eyes, a fear arises, "If something goes wrong, I will become a laughingstock before so many people."

I have been watching Ashok. The first day there was that fear. Slowly, slowly, the fear has disappeared, on the contrary, a fearlessness, a strength... And he has been creating his own songs, tremendously beautiful – not composed by the mind, but arising out of his love and out of his heart. They have a totally different beauty. It is true, that if you love me you will feel in my presence as if you are disappearing into a vast emptiness or into a vast fullness. Beyond the human mind, emptiness and fullness mean the same thing. Love makes you empty – empty of jealousy, empty of power trips, empty of anger, empty of competitiveness, empty of your ego and all its garbage. But love also makes you full of things which are unknown to you right now; it makes you full of fragrance, full of light, full of joy.

An ancient story is:

A king is getting old; he has three sons, and all are intelligent. They are triplets, born together, so there is no question of who is the eldest. Otherwise, there would have been no problem; the eldest son would have been the successor. The problem was, who out of the three is going to be the successor? They are all of the same age. In horse riding they are all of equal efficiency; in archery they are equally great. In every field it is impossible to decide who is the best of the three.

He asked his master, an old wise man living in the forest, "I am getting old, and somebody has to succeed me and take care of the kingdom. And I am in great difficulty; can you give me some idea how to choose the right person?" And the wise man gave him some advice.

The king came back, and he gave an equal amount of money to all three sons and told them – because they all had their own palaces – "With this money, you have to manage to fill your palaces completely. And after seven days I will come to see. Whoever succeeds in filling his house totally, better than the other two, is going to succeed me as the king of the kingdom."

They were puzzled, because the money was not that great. They thought of many things, but the palaces were big – how to fill them completely? The first prince went to the municipal corporation and asked, "From today, all the trucks that throw the garbage of the town outside the city should throw it into my palace – because with that money this is the only possible way to fill the palace completely."

He filled the palace completely. The whole neighborhood was angry; even the traffic on the road stopped – because it was stinking. But they could not do anything – he was the prince, and it was a question of a certain test. The king himself has asked.

The second prince was very worried, asked many people... But they said, "With such a small amount of money it is very difficult. What your brother has done... He has filled the house; you can do something similar. Just purchase cheap grass...fill the house." He purchased the cheapest quality of grass, which even animals were not ready to eat, but still the house was not full; it was only half full.

They were both worried about what the third brother was doing, because he looked absolutely unconcerned. Six days had passed and he had not done anything. And the seventh day came, and by the evening, as the sun set the king came with the wise old man.

It was impossible to come close to the first son's house. The king said, "This idiot, he has really filled the house – but with garbage! It is disgusting, I am feeling sick."

But the old man said, "You had asked...and we have to go and see. Just have a little patience. You need not stay long; just have a look to see whether he has filled the house or not."

They saw it.

They went to the second son's house. It was not better, but it was not worse either. It was rotten grass, but the house was only half full.

The king was very disappointed – so much so that he thought that it would be better not to go to the house of the third prince, because these idiots... What they have done is not worth seeing.

But the wise man said, "You have to go, because the decision has to be taken."

They went to the house of the third young man. They entered

the house, and they were puzzled – because it was absolutely empty. He had even removed the furniture, the paintings, the statues, other things of the house; everything had been removed. The house was utterly empty.

They asked the son, "What have you done?"

He said to the father, "Just see, it is full."

The father looked around. He said, "It is absolutely empty, you are befooling us."

The wise old man said, "Don't be angry with him; it is full, but it is full with something that you are not acquainted with. What he has done is that he has just purchased candles and put the candles all over the house – it is full of light."

Light is not material; it is not objective. The word *objective* is beautiful, it means that which objects to you. You want to go through the wall. The wall will object, will prevent you; the wall is objective. Light is immaterial. It is a strange phenomenon on the earth. In a sense it is outside you, can be called objective, but in another sense it is not creating any objection – you can pass through it, it is immaterial.

It was thought for centuries that light had no weight; just recently they have discovered that it has weight, but it is almost negligible. When the sky is without clouds and the sun is burning hot, all the rays that fall on five square miles will have some weight that can be detected. If we could collect all those rays, they would give you a little sense of weight. So in a way, light is part of the objective world, and in a way it is part of the non-objective world.

The old man said, "You don't understand the boy."

And the boy returned most of the money. He said, "This was too much. I could have filled the house in many other dimensions also. I could have brought music into the house, which has no weight. I could have brought incense into the house – the fragrance has no weight, and it would fill the house. But I thought that would be doing too much. This is enough. And why waste your money? Take your money back; a small part of your money was enough."

When you are in love, in a way you feel as if you are disappearing into emptiness as far as the material world is concerned. But on the other hand, you are entering a new kind of fullness: immaterial, spiritual, not of this world. But this is not the only world. Something transcendental, something from the beyond...

And I can see your love. This whole month it has been growing, as if spring has come to you, new green leaves, new flowers, a new perfume, and your heart is full of new visions. Just continue dissolving into love.

That's the meaning of disciplehood: dissolving into the love, dissolving into the presence of the master, just becoming one with his heartbeats. And songs will shower on you, and flowers of unknown, inexperienced fragrances will grow in you. You are on the right track. Just don't look back – and don't stop anywhere, because this is a journey that only begins but never ends.

Osho,

I wonder whether as your disciple I can be utterly selfish, to find my way to enlightenment whatever I am doing, or do I have to fulfill a certain function for you to spread your vision?

It has to be understood very clearly that nobody has a duty to spread my vision, my message, to the people. I hate the very word *missionary*. They are the ugliest creatures on the earth. I don't want to create missionaries.

You have to be utterly selfish, concentrated on only one aim: becoming enlightened. Of course, as you become enlightened, your light will start reaching to others. My message will start vibrating through you, through your love, without any effort on your part. It has never been said: "Be utterly selfish." All the religions of the world have been teaching, "Be altruistic," and they all have failed, because their very foundation was wrong. You don't know what truth is, and you start spreading the message about truth. You are lying.

I have asked Christian missionaries, "What is your experience?" They don't have any experience. What they have are degrees from theological colleges. Somebody is a DD, a doctor of divinity. Because he has written a thesis, he has become a doctor of divinity – and he knows nothing about divineness, he has never tasted anything that he can call divine. He has never had a single moment in his life when he has touched the beyond; he had no time – he was reading books and writing his doctoral thesis. He was concerned with words, not with experiences.

I lived in Jabalpur for at least twenty years, and Jabalpur has Asia's biggest Christian theological college. It prepares missionaries – that's its function.

The principal was very interested in me. I asked him, "Be sincere, do you really feel that you have something more than the body and the mind? Have you experienced anything of the soul?"

He said, "I have read about it, and I trust that the people who have written about it are not lying."

I said, "It is possible they were also in the same position as you are, that they had read other people whom they believed could not lie – but you cannot be certain unless you experience. And what about your professors? And you are preparing three thousand missionaries per year; you are giving them degrees to go all over Asia to convert other people to Christianity. This whole game is hypocrisy. None of your teachers, none of your students has any taste of meditation; none of them has encountered God. And I think none of them is ready to be crucified like Jesus Christ."

I asked him, "Are you ready to be crucified like Jesus Christ?"

He said, "What kind of question are you asking? I have children, I have my wife, I have my old parents."

I said, "Jesus also had his old parents. And you are almost sixty; he was only thirty-three. Then why are you hanging a golden cross on a golden chain around your neck? Because as far as I understand, the neck has to be put on the cross – not that the cross is golden, hanging around your neck on a gold chain."

He said, "I was thinking that one day I would ask you to speak to my college students" – they had almost five thousand students – "but now, I have dropped that idea. You can disturb the whole thing."

And the same question, you are asking me. I am not converting you. I am trying to explain to you how to transform yourself, how to become more luminous, how to become more alert, more conscious.

And if that consciousness brings you experiences which are not available ordinarily, and those experiences have an intrinsic quality that they have to be shared, then share them. But don't try to impose any ideology on anyone.

You love me. Naturally the desire arises that others should also love me. But the only right way is that you should come to a state that others start loving you. I can be connected through you to others, not by your words, but by your life. You are not to be a missionary. You have to become a message yourself. People should ask you, "What has happened to you? Why do we feel such a magnetic attraction towards you? Why do we feel that you are hiding some treasure from us? Why do we feel that you have moved far above our ordinary visions?"

Then share your experience; there is no need to convert anybody. And when somebody comes on his own accord to be transformed, to learn the whole science of living in a new way, it is totally different. When you go to people to somehow convince their minds that your ideology is better than their ideology, it is possible that you may convince a few people with your ideology, but it is not conversion. They remain the same. The Catholic, the Protestant, the Hindu, the Mohammedan, the Jew, the communist – what is the difference in their lifestyle? If you insult any of them, they are going to react in the same way.

I am reminded of a beautiful story...

Gautam Buddha is passing near a village, which consists only of high caste brahmins. They are very much against Gautam Buddha; they have all gathered outside the village to condemn him, to abuse him. He stands there listening to their abuse, their allegations, their lies. Even Ananda, who has been with him all these years, feels angry because they were born into a royal family; they were warriors, their whole training was to fight. But because Gautam Buddha is present, he controls himself; otherwise he would have killed one or two people then and there.

Gautam Buddha said to them, "You see that the sun is going to set soon, and we have to reach the other village before the sun sets. If you have not finished all that you wanted to say to me, I will make a point that when I return I set aside enough time to listen to you again. And in two days, I will be returning along the same route. So it will be very kind of you if you can wait just two days."

One man from the crowd said, "You don't seem to be disturbed at all. And we are not just saying things to you, we are abusing you, insulting you."

Gautam Buddha said, "You have come a little late. If you had come ten years before, you would not have gone back alive. I am also a warrior. There would have been bloodshed here; not a single man in this crowd would have gone back alive. But you have come a little late.

"In the village just before this village, people came with sweets and fruits. And we said, 'We eat only once a day, and we have taken our food, so it would be very kind if you would take these things back with you. We are grateful.' What do you think they did with those sweets and those fruits?"

Somebody said, "They must have distributed them amongst themselves; they must have eaten them."

Buddha said, "You are intelligent. Do the same: whatever you have brought, I don't accept; take it back. Because unless I accept your insult, you cannot insult me; it is a two-way affair. It is your mouth, you can say anything – but unless I accept it, you are just talking into the air. Just go home and say all these things to each other – enjoy. And I will be coming again after two days, so be ready."

They were shocked, and they could not believe: what kind of man is this? When they moved on, Ananda said to Buddha, "This is too much. There were moments when I was going to jump and hit the man. Just because of you, I tried to control my temptation."

Buddha said – and remember it – he said: "What those people were saying has not hurt me. What *you* are saying hurts me. You have been with me for so many years, and yet you are not aware enough to know what to take and what not to take? Can't you discriminate?"

I want you not to become missionaries. I want you to become

messages.

And that is possible only if you are utterly selfish, so that before you start helping others, you have helped yourself; before you start enlightening other people, you are enlightened yourself. That's what I mean by being selfish. Whatever you want to spread must be your living experience.

Osho,

These days here with you are certainly the most beautiful. Doing nothing, so much time to sit silently in the garden, in my room, and watch the trees dancing in the wind, sparkling in the sun. So much beauty.

My mind is finally getting used to the idea of being turned off. I am so peaceful, so happy. Now, today, again going inside on this path of silence, with thoughts drifting away and emptiness surrounding me, I am aware of a tension inside me as if I am holding on to something.

Osho, what am I holding on to, and how do I let go?

It is not difficult to find out what you are holding on to, what your subtle tension is inside. You are feeling peaceful, you are feeling silent, you are feeling blissful as you have never felt. Hence, side by side, a fear must be lurking inside that soon you will be going from here and will this peace, this silence, this blissfulness remain a part of you? Or the moment you are away from me, will it disappear? This fear is not only within *you*, it is in every disciple's mind, that when you are here it is one thing and when you go back to the marketplace, into the world, you will find it more miserable, more saddening than before because now you have something to compare it with.

Have you seen...? By the side of the road you are standing in darkness, and a car passes with its headlights on. The darkness disappears for a moment. The car has gone, but strangely enough after the car has gone the darkness is greater than it was before the car had come. You have seen the light; now there is a comparison.

This fear is natural. Only one thing can be done about it, and that is not to repress it but let it surface. You are repressing; that's why you are not finding what it is that is troubling you somewhere inside. Allow it to surface. Experience that fear also. Accept the fear, and accept the challenge of the fear. Tell your mind, "It does not matter where I am. Whatever I have experienced, it is *my* experience and I can create it again." It may have been triggered in my presence, but it is not my experience, it is your experience. Let it be deeply settled in you that it is your experience, it has nothing to do with me. I may have been a catalytic agent, but the experience is yours. And now, once it has happened, you can create it again anywhere in the world. Maybe in the beginning you will find it a little difficult, because you have become accustomed, and associated it with my presence. But it is not dependent on my presence.

It is just as if you light a candle with another candle – but once the candle is lit, it has its own flame. Perhaps in the beginning it needed to be close enough to another flame, but once it catches the flame, it has its own; it is no longer dependent. And when you go away, you will experience what I am saying – but give it a chance. Don't decide that "Now it cannot happen because the master is not here."

The master was needed to make you aware that it is something within you. Now you have seen it. Close your eyes anywhere, and you can recreate the silence, the beauty, the bliss. You can even recreate the presence of the master – that is the most difficult part, but not impossible. It depends on how intense is your love, how deep is your trust.

But no need to try it; first try those things which you can create within yourself. And once you have created all those things then you can try the tremendously beautiful experiment of creating the presence of the master.

So don't be worried; just bring your fear to the surface. And it is not only in you; it is in everyone. It is something in the nature of things. So don't give it too much importance either; just accept it as a natural phenomenon which will disappear by your little experiments away from me.

I guarantee it will disappear, because I have guaranteed it to thousands of my sannyasins and it has disappeared from their lives. There is no reason why it should not disappear from your life. The principles are the same; there are no exceptions.

Osho,

I seem to be so unconscious so much of the time, so very unaware and just simply involved in life and loving living it.

When you speak about the totality and intensity of the search, and how nothing else really matters, and how important it is to let nothing become a distraction, I fear I will never manage it.

In my heart I feel nothing else does matter, yet I am not living in this awareness all the time and in every situation.

Would it be good for me to try to bring this awareness to each and every moment, even if it requires intense effort? If you feel this is good for me, I will try it even though I am afraid I may lose some of the fun and spontaneity and ease of just living, and even though I don't know if I can manage it.

The question is significant for everybody. Because I am speaking to so many people – not only those who are present here, but also to those millions who are not present here but will be hearing my words or reading my words. It becomes a very difficult affair, because people are different in many ways. And certainly no two persons are the same. And the danger is that you may start doing something which is not meant for you.

A simple criterion should be remembered: whatever feels good for you – blissful, peaceful, spontaneous, happening on its own accord – that is your path.

But I have to speak also to those people for whom nothing is spontaneous, for whom the most difficult thing is to relax, for whom the most impossible thing is just to sit and not to do anything. They also need every help. To them I say, "Live with total intensity, with total effort" – because that is the easiest thing for them. And whatever is easy is close to truth.

Maitri, for you that would not be the easiest thing. You would have to make effort against *yourself*; it would not be natural, it would not be spontaneous. You would be forcing yourself, and this will destroy the whole beauty and the peace and the silence that you are already feeling. If you are feeling silence, peace, a beautiful energy through spontaneity, through relaxation, through let-go, then that is your way.

Everybody has to find out what is close to his heart. I am speaking for many people of many types. You have to find out what is right for you. If you start doing everything that I am saying, you will get in a mess. You simply do that which your heart supports. And remember, the heart is never wrong. The mind can be right, can be wrong. The heart is always right, there is no question of its being wrong. So whenever your heart feels at ease with something, then go with it – root and all. Then don't look back and don't bother about what others are doing. Let them do *their* thing; you do *your* thing.

Because the religions of the past emphasized only one method, naturally that religion became only for one type of people. It is because of this that there are three hundred religions on the earth. And I want only one religiousness. All those three hundred religions have some kind of truth and some kind of validity to them. But they are specializations of a certain method, applicable to certain people – and that has made the whole world irreligious.

For example, effort is the way for Mahavira. Even to mention the word *let-go* is to support laziness. Mahavira is not his name; his name was Vardhamana. He is called Mahavira because his attitude and approach is that truth has to be conquered. It is not a love affair; it is a war. And Mahavira has won the war; that is why he is called the great warrior. Mahavira means the great warrior.

Now, it creates trouble. His method is suitable only to a certain type of person, the warrior type. But because of his own teaching, his followers – who all came from the *kshatriyas*, the warrior race in India – had to drop their profession of being warriors, because that is violence. Now they were in trouble – what to do? They could not be brahmins because a brahmin is only born. You cannot become a brahmin by studying or by doing anything, there is no way. A brahmin is only born, you cannot be converted into a brahmin. So these people could not be brahmins. These people could not be sudras, untouchables, because they were high caste Hindus, second only to brahmins. They had their own pride. The only way for them was to become businessmen. So all the Jainas in India are businessmen.

They could not become cultivators, gardeners, because in cultivation or gardening you will have to cut trees, and that is violence, because trees have life. So all other areas are rejected.

And these business people are not trained like Mahavira. He was trained in his youth as a warrior, as a fighter, and he brought his fighting qualities to his search for truth. Now, these business people are not trained for fighting. If somebody comes and says that truth can be purchased, they will be ready. But "truth has to be conquered"? – that just seems to be out of reach. Conquered – that is beyond their scope. All they can do is worship Mahavira. Twenty-five centuries have passed, and Jainas have not been able to produce another man of the same caliber as Mahavira. What is the reason?

He represented one type, and he preached for one type, but it was an accident that the people who followed him were not of that type and cannot be of that type. So they have remained in a limbo, they cannot move anywhere. Business they can do, and they have created the most beautiful temples in India, the most beautiful statues. Worship they can do. But fighting – that is simply not possible.

So a strange phenomenon... The teacher they followed was of a different type. They were impressed by his unique quality; he was a man of steel. But his followers can only praise him; they cannot do what their teacher has done. And this is not only with Jainas, this is the situation with every religion.

And there is no necessity that your child will be of the same type as you are. But by a certain calamity we have accepted the idea that religion comes by birth. This is simply stupid. It is as if a doctor's son becomes a doctor because he is born to a doctor. He need not go to the medical college – what is the need? And if he is the son of a doctor whose wife is also a doctor, then there is no question – in his very blood and bones he is a born doctor, he needs no certificate.

It is good that we don't do this. But in religion we *have* been doing it. I have seen people who were born into a religion where devotion is not allowed. It is not for the devotional type, but the person *is* of the devotional type. Somebody is the type who can easily move with a negative approach, and for somebody else a negative approach is simply impossible; unless something positive is there, he cannot take a single step.

My own suggestion is that religion should not be something decided by birth. A religion should be decided by the person himself, according to his feelings. Wherever he feels good, growing, wherever he feels joyous, wherever he feels a certain magnetic attraction, that is his path. It does not matter whether that is the religion he is born into or not; that is the religion he is born for. But that is possible only if everybody is freed from religious slavery, and we allow our children to be acquainted with all kinds of religions, all kinds of methods. And if we tell them to feel, to move with different kinds of people: "Go to different temples, go to different schools, go to different masters, and feel your way." And wherever he feels that this is his nourishment, then the parents have to bless him to go on that way.

It does not matter if you feel nourished in the company of a Mohammedan Sufi, it does not matter if you feel nourished in the company of a Buddhist monk; the whole question should be decided by your own heart. And the heart never leads you wrongly. If you allow it, it will give you clear-cut indications that you are on the right path. Peace, silence, bliss, benediction – all will be coming more and more, and the scope will become wider and wider.

Osho,
Who is the blessed one?

The one who is asleep in you is the blessed one, but unfortunately he is sleeping and snoring. He has to be awakened, and the moment your sleeping consciousness becomes wakeful you start feeling blissfulness. The highest peak of your bliss makes you feel to go beyond humanity. That is the moment of being the blessed one; you have become part of the universal blissfulness. But people are so asleep.

I have suffered so much from people's sleep because I used to travel continually in India. Mostly I was in an air-conditioned coupe, but sometimes there was another person in the coupe also. And sometimes a coupe was not available so there were four persons.

Once it happened, I was coming from Calcutta in a four-person room. And I have seen many snoring people, but I will not forget those three fellows. They had a certain harmony: one would snore and the other two would remain silent, and then as he would stop, the second would snore louder than the first and the other two would remain silent. Then as the second would stop the third would snore loudest of all, and the other two would remain silent. And the circle went on.

I heard this for one hour and then I said, "This is impossible. I don't want to interfere in anybody's life, but these three people are interfering in my life." So as the third stopped, I snored so loudly that all three became awake. And they saw me snoring with open eyes, so they could not believe it. They looked at each other like: "What kind of man is this? His eyes are open." And I was not blinking my eyes. All three got up from their seats and came close to me.

I said, "Listen, if you want to sleep, stop this harmony that is going on. Otherwise, I will not allow *any* of you to sleep."

One said, "But you are awake and you are snoring?"

I said, "What else to do? – because I cannot sleep, so the question of sleeping and *then* snoring does not arise. You don't allow me to sleep. First let me sleep. Then perhaps I may fall into the harmony, something may happen, but first let me sleep. And how are you managing it?"

They said, "We three are brothers."

I said, "You are great brothers."

They said, "What to do? It is such a difficult matter, even in our family. Our wives don't sleep in our rooms; we three brothers have to sleep in one room. So, slowly, slowly, a certain harmony has arisen."

I said, "That's perfectly good, but in just one night it will be very difficult for me to get into the harmony. Something has to be done."

So we had to come to a conclusion that those three fellows would play cards while I slept for a few hours, and then they would have their harmony and I would sit and listen. But listening to them was also beautiful, because how were they managing any sleep?

Everybody is carrying the blessed one, but it needs to be awakened.

The blessed one is not a certain talent. It is not like being a musician. A few people are musicians but not everybody can be; a few people are painters but not everybody can be; a few people are poets, dancers, actors, writers – these are talents.

The blessed one is not a question of talent. It is your very nature. It is your self-nature; it is your intrinsic quality.

It is up to you how long you want to be miserable and asleep – you are free. The moment you decide that enough is enough, you will have the same experiences as any Gautam Buddha or Ramakrishna or Raman Maharshi – these are not talented people. Kabir or Raidas or Farid – these are not talented people, they are just ordinary human beings. But as far as their blissfulness is concerned, they have reached to the same peak as Gautam Buddha.

It is your birthright.

15 Let Your Trust Grow

Osho,
Every time when people ask me, "What is Osho in your life?" – I answer that you are my master. But the people don't understand, even if I try to explain. What is the reason for it? Why can't I explain it with success?

Life is beautiful because there is so much which cannot be explained. It would have been a disaster if life consisted only of things which can be explained. Just think for a moment, if everything could be explained, then there would be no mystery, then there would be no poetry, then there would be no secret. Then everything would be utterly flat and boring. Life is not boredom because there are dimensions in it that you can go on exploring, yet you can never come to explanations. You can experience much, yet that which you have experienced cannot be translated into words.

You fall in love. Since the very first man, millions of people must have fallen in love, yet love is still a mystery, you cannot reduce it to knowledge. The moment you try to reduce it to knowledge, it slips out of your hands. And it is good that it is so miraculous that generation after generation, millions of people go through the experience; they know what it is yet they cannot say what it is.

All that can be experienced is not necessarily explainable, and all that can be explained is not necessarily experienceable. Mathematics can be explained easily, but there is no corresponding experience. Science can be explained easily, but even the greatest scientist is not transformed by his knowledge. But an anonymous poet not only gives birth to poetry, he also goes through a deep revolution, a rebirth. His poetry is not just a composition of words; it is the juice of his very life. The greatest poets have not been able to explain their own poetry.

Once Coleridge was asked by a professor of literature... The professor was teaching at the university and he came across a point in one of Coleridge's poems where he was doubtful about the meaning. He was a sincere man. He told the students, "You will have to wait at least one day. Coleridge lives in my neighborhood; I can ask him exactly what he means."

The professor went to Coleridge that evening. Coleridge said, "You have come a little late."

He said, "What do you mean – a little late? You are still alive."

Coleridge said, "It is not a question of my being alive or not. When I wrote these lines, two persons knew the meaning; now only one knows."

Naturally, the professor inferred that the one person could not be anyone else but Coleridge. He said, "So I have *not* come too late. Tell me what the meaning is."

Coleridge said, "You have not yet got the point. When I wrote those lines, two persons knew the meaning: Coleridge and God. Now only God knows!

"I myself have been wondering. Many times I have read it and wondered: what is the meaning? It is groovy – but very slippery. You feel that you are just about to catch it and it has gone just like a breeze. I am sorry. I have certainly written these lines, and I know there is *some* meaning, and I feel it, but you will have to forgive me. I cannot even explain it to myself, how can I explain it to you?"

It is not only so about poetry. Anything significant in life...

Picasso used to get very angry whenever anybody would ask the meaning of his paintings. And he was not an angry man. He was a very beautiful, loving person. But the moment you ask the meaning of his painting, you have touched him from the wrong side. He would immediately get very angry. He would say, "This is strange. Nobody asks a roseflower what its meaning is. Nobody asks the stars what their meaning is. Nobody asks a bird on the wing what its meaning is. Nobody asks a sunrise or a sunset what its meaning is. People simply enjoy the beauty; nobody bothers about the meaning. Why are people after me? I am a poor painter. All that I can say is that it is beautiful. But that is not its meaning; it is its impact on a sensitive being."

Meaning is rational, and the experience of mystery is supra-rational.

Your question is significant, and it must be the question of many other disciples. People ask you what the relationship is between you and me. Just to say that I am your master neither satisfies them nor satisfies you. How can it satisfy them when it does not even satisfy you? – because it is not just a relationship like somebody is your father and somebody is your mother and somebody is your brother. Once you have said that somebody is your father, everything is explained. Nobody bothers you anymore that, "What do you mean by father?" and...

The relationship with the master is not of the same category as all other relationships. It is intrinsically different. It is love, but not only love. It is love with a center of trust. Love alone is unexplainable, and now it has joined hands with an even greater mystery. Trust is absolutely something of another world.

In this world, there is distrust in everybody. Even in people who love each other, there is no trust. There are friends who can, if there is need, die for each other – but there is no trust.

In the Middle Ages it used to happen:

A very strange and ugly thing was in existence in Europe. Whenever a warrior would go to war, he would put a lock on his wife so that she could not make love to anybody, and take the key with him. A strange device it was – those locks are still exhibited in the museums of Europe. You cannot even trust your wife! And if you cannot trust your wife, do you think a master key cannot be found? The goldsmiths who made the locks also made extra keys.

One prince was going to war. His only fear was about his beautiful wife. He was afraid that if the key were lost in the war then for the rest of his life he wouldn't be able to make love to his own wife. So he thought it would be better to give the key to one of his best friends. They were so close that they would have died for each other, so there was no question of distrust.

He gave his friend the key and told him, "When I come back I will take it back. So keep it safe."

He had gone not more than half a mile out of the town on his horse, when he heard a fast horse approaching him from behind. He looked back, and his friend was coming, shouting, "Wait!"

He said, "What has happened?" Just five minutes ago he had left him perfectly healthy, and there had been no problem. The friend said, "You gave me the wrong key!"

In this world, there is no trust at all. When love is joined with trust, it becomes even more difficult to explain it. It becomes more mysterious. And thirdly, as love and trust grow to their optimum, something comes which can only be called surrender. It is not a good word, but there is no other word as a substitute.

Surrender makes the whole thing absolutely not of this world. You cannot give any reason; you cannot give any explanation. The only way is: whoever asks, tell him that it is something like a thirsty man finding water in the desert. His every fiber is just thirst, and the water quenches all thirst. A great peace descends. The master is not a person. The master is only a presence. If you are thirsty enough for the unknown, you can drink out of this presence and be quenched.

Anybody who asks you the question, tell him, "Come with me. There are a few things which cannot be explained, but I can take you to the place where perhaps you may also experience them. Your question itself shows that there is some interest in you – perhaps a deep, hidden desire. Who knows? – it may become aflame in the presence of the master. Who knows? – surrounded by disciples and their love and their trust and their surrender, and the presence of the master, something may transpire in you. One thing is certain: if something transpires in you, you will become dumb the way I am dumb."

Accept your dumbness, but create a quest in the person who is asking only for a verbal answer. Use that situation. A verbal answer is of no use. Just say, "I have experienced something which is untranslatable into any language, but I can take you to the river. You yourself can drink. Your experience will be the only explanation."

And I repeat again: Life is beautiful because there are so many unexplainable dimensions to it. That is its richness. If everything is explained, all juice will be lost; you will be fed up, bored to death with a life, which is explained. What transpires between a master and a disciple is one of the peaks of unexplainable experiences. Don't destroy it with any explanation. It is a crime to destroy the unexplainable by bringing it to the level of explanations, because you have killed. It is almost like a bird on the wing in the sky – it is so beautiful in its freedom; the whole sky belongs to him, all the stars belong to him: no limits, no barriers. You can catch hold of the bird; you can make a beautiful golden cage and you can put the bird in the cage. But remember, it is not the same bird that was flying in freedom in the sky under the stars. Factually it is the same bird, but spiritually no – because where is the freedom and where are the stars? Where is the sky? Your golden cage cannot replace what you have taken away from the bird. It has lost its soul.

The same happens when you try to explain something which is unexplainable. You bring it into the cage of language, of words – beautiful words, but the soul has disappeared.

Don't do it. I know it feels a little awkward when somebody asks and you cannot answer – you feel embarrassed. It is better to feel embarrassed. But don't commit a crime against the mysteries of life. Tell the person, "I am feeling embarrassed because I cannot say it. Not that I don't want to say it – I would have loved to say it to you but I cannot, because saying it means killing it. I can take you to the window from where you can see the open sky; I can take you to the man. Perhaps your heart will start dancing in the same way my heart dances within me, and in deep silence, you will understand what it means to me. But only when it starts to mean something to you."

People will be asking you many questions. Use their questions to invite them towards the same light, towards the same bliss, towards the same truth. Don't answer – because you cannot answer, and whatever you say will fall flat. Resist the temptation of being knowledgeable. Accept your inarticulateness. But invite the person. Perhaps out of ten, one may turn up. And one never knows – by coming here, he may turn on!

Osho,

I am old, and had been a Buddhist for over thirty years before I came to Pune. But still I feel as if I am at the beginning, confused with lots of doubts.

On the other hand, something inside me knows about your silence, and that "something" is not irritated at all. It is like a robe of trust, but I am not able to believe.

Could you please say something about the difference between trust and belief?

Trust and belief have a very similar appearance, but they are diametrically opposite realities.

Belief is a false coin. It pretends to be real; it tries to play the role of trust. Millions of people are caught in the net of belief, because it is cheap. Trust is costly, very costly. Trust is costly because it is risky; it is dangerous. It means you are opening yourself, becoming vulnerable to somebody who can do you harm. You are dropping all your defense measures. You will be defenseless – you can be exploited, cheated, destroyed.

Everybody has a defense system around himself, just to protect himself from others. Life is competitive. Everybody is running after the same goals, and you cannot remain loving, compassionate, kind, in a competitive world or you are going to be a failure. In this competitive world, the people who succeed are the people who are ready to sacrifice anybody, to destroy anybody. They go on climbing on people as if people were stepping-stones. They care about only one thing, and that is success. Naturally, everybody has to be ready not to be trampled, killed. Trust means going against the current of the competitive world. In the competitive world, trust is simply impossible.

Machiavelli wrote one of the most significant treatises on diplomacy, *The Prince*. Strangely enough, his great, great granddaughter is a sannyasin – Machiavelli would have never dreamed that his blood would one day trust somebody. Machiavelli has written in *The Prince* – it is a small treatise for every politician – maxims to be followed if you want to succeed: Don't trust anybody, but let everybody believe that you trust them. Don't say anything to a friend that you would not say to an enemy – because no one knows, the friend may turn into your enemy tomorrow. Don't say anything against your enemy that you would not say against your friend – because in this competitive world, the person who is an enemy may become a friend, the person who is a friend may become an enemy. Basically, keep yourself completely closed and secretive. If you say something, say it in such a way that it can be interpreted either way, for or against. Don't say anything which has only a single meaning, because every day you will have to face a new reality and you will have to change your meaning.

Machiavelli is the real leader of the world – not Jesus Christ or Gautam Buddha. It is a strange world. Here, the *real* leaders are not worshipped, but they are followed. Here, the *unreal* leaders are worshipped – but not followed.

When love and trust meet, their ultimate byproduct is surrender. You relax into the master, into his being, without holding anything. It is certainly only for those who are ready to take a risk.

But belief is very cheap. Everybody is a believer – somebody is a Hindu, somebody is a Mohammedan, somebody is a Christian. Belief comes in all sizes, all shapes, all colors – you can choose. And you don't have to pay anything for it. Generally you get it with your mother's milk, free of charge.

Secondly, belief is always in an idea, and trust is always in a presence.

That is a very delicate difference. Belief is theoretical; trust is existential.

You can change your belief without any trouble; it is just like changing your clothes. From a Hindu, you can become a Christian; from a Christian, you can become a Mohammedan; from a Mohammedan, you can become a communist. There is no problem, because belief is only of the mind. If anything is more convincing, more logical, you can change it. It has no roots in your heart. Belief is like plastic flowers, which look like flowers from far away. They don't have any roots, they don't need any care – no manure, no chemicals, no watering, no gardening, nothing is needed. And they are permanent "people," they can remain with you your whole life long – because they were never born, so they will never die. They are manufactured. Unless you destroy them, they will remain.

Trust is a real rose. It has roots, and roots go deep into your heart and into your being. Belief is just in the head. Trust is in the heart, in your deeper world of being. To change trust is almost impossible – it has never happened, it is not known to have happened in the whole of history. If you trust, you trust; there is no possibility of its changing. And it goes on growing because it has roots. It never remains static; it is dynamic, it is a living force. It goes on growing new foliage, new flowers, new branches. Belief is a dead thing, a plastic flower; it never grows.

Hindus may have believed in a certain thing for ten thousand years – it is still there, the same; it never grows. "The cow is the mother" – Hindus have believed it for ten thousand years. The belief has not grown even to include the fact that the bull is your father! It is static. And if you mention to any Hindu that the bull is his father then *he* will become a bull, and prove that certainly the bull *is* his father! But he will not believe it; he will behave exactly like a bull, but he will not accept the fact.

All beliefs are old; all beliefs are dead. No belief grows even a single leaf. Belief is ideological, philosophical, but it is not a force that transforms your being. It can make you a great scholar, it can make you a great philosopher, theologian, but it can never make you a new man, young and fresh; it cannot give you any experience. It can bring you degrees from the universities and awards and Nobel Prizes. It can do everything, but it will not change anything in your interior, that will remain empty.

The question is even more important because it is coming from a person who has been a Buddhist for thirty years. After being a Buddhist for thirty years, the person comes to me, feels a certain trust in me, falls in love. Naturally, there is a conflict, which is bound to happen. His mind is full of thirty years of Buddhist ideology – that is the belief system – and the heart is growing fresh sprouts of trust. The person is bound to be in great difficulty. The beliefs are pulling in one direction and the trust is moving in another direction. The beliefs have a certain weight because they are thirty years old, but the trust, although it is new, has a force of its own because it is alive. The beliefs are thirty-year-old corpses. They have weight, but they don't have any force. The person is bound to be split.

Things can be solved very easily. The first thing to remember is: if Buddhism was enough, there would have been no need to come to me. Being a Buddhist for thirty years has not done anything to you. You can be a Buddhist for thirty lives, but a belief never changes your reality. The length of time makes no difference. So the first question you have to ask yourself is why, after thirty years, you had to seek and search for some new source, for some new light, for some new indication. If you are courageous, you need not get into a conflict; you can simply see that those thirty years have gone to waste. But what is gone is gone; now don't waste any more time on it.

And remember, I am not saying that Buddha is wrong. I am simply saying that Buddha was right only for those people who could drink out of his presence, for whom he was a master. But for you, he is only a belief.

It is better to get rid of those thirty years and whatever information you have collected in you, because that is a burden and a hindrance to your spiritual growth. If you can dare not to be a Buddhist, I promise you that there is a possibility of your being a buddha. Why be a Buddhist when there is a possibility of being a buddha? Why settle for such dead theories when living waters are available? To be a buddha is beautiful. To be a Buddhist is stupidity.

Buddha was not a Buddhist; remember, he never heard the word. Nobody called him a Buddhist. Jesus was never a Christian. So one thing is certain, that no Christian remaining a Christian can find the experience that Jesus found. If any Christian wants to experience what Jesus experienced, the first thing to do is to get rid of Christianity – because Jesus was not a Christian.

Your belief system has to be completely thrown out, so that your juices are not divided and your whole energy moves into your trust. Your trust is growing, but under a heavy burden, under a tension. It can grow in a relaxed way, under open sky. Just say good-bye to those beliefs that you have been carrying, and let your trust grow.

What Buddha has been to his disciples, his theories cannot be. Theories are mere words. They don't have the charm and the grace and the charisma; they don't have that magnetism.

And when you are here and the possibility is available for you to become awakened, to become a buddha, I don't think that it is a bad bargain: dropping Buddhist theories in favor of becoming Gautam Buddha himself. In twenty-five centuries, how many buddhas have been produced by the Buddhists?

One English Buddhist – Bhikkhu Dharm Rakshita, a very devoted man – dropped Christianity, was converted to Buddhism and became one of the topmost scholars of Buddhist literature. He had an ashram in Kalimpong. He used to go once in a while to attend Buddhist conferences, and he made it a point that whenever he came down from the Himalayas he would find me and come to be with me for a day or two.

He was an internationally known Buddhist scholar. His books are rare as far as the accuracy of his translations is concerned. I used to ask him, "Dharm Rakshita, you have devoted almost fifty years to learning Buddhist theology, translating Buddhist literature – but have you got any taste of buddhahood?"

And tears would come to his eyes. He would say, "Please, don't ask that question. You are the only person who asks that. Nobody else seems to be interested. They ask about literature, they ask about principles, philosophies and everything, but nobody asks, 'Has fifty years' concentrated effort brought anything to your being – or has it brought only a dozen books and world fame? Are you satisfied?'"

One night he said to me, "You met me too late. I am old, I have wasted my whole life. And now it is very difficult for me to drop all that garbage that I learned with great effort, and to begin from *ABC*, from complete scratch. But whenever I can manage it, I just come to be near you. And whenever I am near you... I don't know how it would have been to be with Gautam Buddha, but I feel it must have been something like this, the same taste. It is too late for me to change now, but at least at the very end of my life I will not be dying just a scholar, I will be dying as a seeker. I could not do it in this life, but you have created a thirst. Perhaps in my next life I may not get lost in the jungle of theories, and I may try to enter into myself."

You have a rare opportunity here. Nothing like this has ever existed in the world before. Because I don't have any prejudice – you can become a Christ here, you can become a Buddha here, you can become a Mahavira, you can become a Lao Tzu. I don't have any prejudice because I know these are only different names. Behind them is the same universal consciousness.

So don't be bothered about your beliefs; just drop them. Trust is enough, more than enough. It is enough nourishment for your pilgrimage.

Osho,

Inside of me there seem to be so many questions, but when I try to ask you one of them, they all seem to have gone, and I don't know even if I really wanted to ask you something. But still the feeling of question remains.

Please, can you explain where this feeling comes from?

It is very simple. You don't have a question; you have a quest. And you are not aware of the distinction. Your quest is not clear to you; it is clouded. You think perhaps there is some question, so you make many questions and they disappear but you are left with a vague feeling that something similar to a question is still there. What is it? All questions are like leaves. The quest is like the roots.

You are fortunate, because at first people have to ask thousands of questions; then, by and by, one by one, the leaves disappear. Then branches come, then the trunk, and then finally they realize that the real thing is the quest. You are fortunate that you have only roots.

But with roots the difficulty is that they are always underground, so you don't see where they are. You try somehow to make questions, but they disappear because they are not connected to your roots.

A quest is the most significant thing for a seeker. A quest means you want to know, you want to experience, you want to be the truth itself. A question wants to be answered. A quest wants to become the answer itself. Questions are many; the answer is one. And you are in a position that if you simply meditate, you will not come across a question, you will come across the answer. And the answer is not something separate from you. You are the answer.

Just go to your very center. It is there for you, waiting for thousands of lives. Don't let it wait any longer. Sometimes it also gets impatient. Because of that impatience, it starts creating questions. Questions only show impatience.

But your position is very clear; you don't need to ask anything, you simply have to go deeper and deeper into silence, and you will find it.

Osho,

Before coming into contact with you, professor Joshi of Kathmandu was spiritually guided by a buddhist lama. This lama left his family and village when he was young and traveled for forty years in Tibet, Burma and Thailand, meditating and seeking truth.

At the age of sixty, one evening the lama quietly returned to his village and joined the family and his old life. But his grace and silence attracted many seekers, and now he is famous as an *Avatari* Lama. The professor was highly impressed by the lama, and out of love presented him with your book, *Anta Yantra*. The lama could not read Hindi or English, so he requested Mr. Joshi to read some passages to him and to show him your picture.

When he saw your picture, the lama said: "Osho comes from the land where I go every day in my meditation. This time he has come with full glory, (sixteen *kalas*) – which happens only in the incarnation of Krishna or Buddha. Now there is no need to come to me for guidance; follow Osho, he is the right master."

Osho, how can people see so much just in your picture, which we disciples cannot realize even after such a long association?

It is not a question of long association. It is a question of deep insight. You don't have that meditative perspective. You can see only what the ordinary eyes can see. But as a person becomes more meditative, he starts growing his sensitivities to such depth and such height that he is able to see things which are invisible to us. Life is not only what is available to our five senses.

Just think, for example, if you were all blind, you would never come to know that there is something like light – although the light will be all around you. But just the existence of light is not enough; you need something to perceive it.

One fact scientists have been concerned about is that on at least fifty thousand planets there is a possibility of life. One thing is certain: that on these different planets, life must have grown in different ways, because the climate would be different, the whole situation would be different. It is possible that on some planet there may be animals that have more than five senses. Right now it is only a hypothetical question, but it is significant; the possibility is there. If there are animals on some planets that have seven senses or eight senses, then they must be able to perceive two or three things more than we can perceive. And we cannot even imagine what those things might be, because even in imagination, we can only imagine that which we have seen. We cannot even dream about it, because our dreams are only reflections. You cannot be so creative in your dreams as to create something new. All that will be reflected are those five senses. Before x-rays were developed, we had no idea that there are rays which can enter into your body and photograph your insides.

The people who have been working on meditation for centuries have come to know many things, but because they are not scientists they have never tried to prove them objectively. For example, in the East it has been known for centuries that a man of meditation can see if somebody is going to die within six months or not. And the thing is so simple that it need not be even a question of meditation; you yourself can know whether you are going to die within six months or not. The day you stop seeing the tip of your nose, that means only six months are left – because at the time a person dies, his eyes turn up, and they start turning up six months before that, very slowly, very slowly. From six months beforehand till his death, he cannot see the tip of his nose. That is known to villagers, who have no meditation or meditative understanding. The lama has been meditating for forty years; he can see in my picture things which you cannot see.

I am reminded of Ramakrishna. A painter made his portrait, and he brought the painting to show Ramakrishna, to see whether he liked it or not. The disciples were also gathered there.

Ramakrishna looked at the painting and touched the feet of the painting. His disciples – Vivekananda and others – felt embarrassed: "What to do with our master? – because he does such things that even we look like fools. Now it is his own picture, and he is touching its feet. We had no idea that he would do this; otherwise we would have prevented him. And now he has done it, and people are laughing and smiling and looking at each other."

There were many observers there who were not disciples. They asked, "They think this man is a realized soul? He seems to be insane! Even an insane person will not touch his own feet; at least he will recognize that 'This is my own portrait; I cannot touch its feet.'"

The painter was also shocked, but he was not a disciple. So he gathered courage and said to Ramakrishna, "I cannot believe my eyes. This is your own portrait and you are touching your own feet! It looks a little awkward."

And Ramakrishna's eyes were full of tears of joy. He said, "It is my picture, I know, but I am not touching the feet because it is my picture. I am touching the feet because you have caught my state of *samadhi* in the picture. And when I see a picture of someone in *samadhi*... It does not matter whether that picture is of me or somebody else, that is irrelevant. What matters is that the picture is of a self-realized consciousness; then I have to touch its feet. And I cannot see why you are all looking so embarrassed."

Now they all felt *more* embarrassed: "We are such idiots. We don't understand; we should at least keep quiet. If we don't understand, then it is better not to show any emotion. He has done something which nobody has done before, but his reason is so valid."

The lama must be doing well in his meditations. If he can see what he has seen in my picture, that validates that he is on the right path, that his meditation is bringing flowers, that he is very close to the home.

Osho,

I have heard you saying, "I love": I have heard you saying "I hate." What do you mean?

Osho, tell me the truth, for my feeling is that there is nothing up there – not even love, not even compassion.

Do I have to tell you the truth? It is a little bit difficult for me because it is not my habit – but the truth is there is no love, no hate.

Up there is absolute silence.

16 Rising in Love: A Partnership in Meditation

Osho,
I'm experiencing more and more a harmony, a quietness, an ease, an abundance in myself, moments in which I feel so vast and rich, like the universe, and so close to you. I dive into it and disappear, and see that this again was just an opening, a door to another dimension on this ongoing, never-ending journey you are taking me on, my beloved master.

And I can find no words to express how much I feel, that I can be with you.

Being together with a man I find these most beautiful and precious moments so rarely; it seems most of the time is wasted in loving, and finding ourselves and each other. Why is it so difficult for me to be in this harmony together with a man, and even take him with me into this unknown?

Or is it something which can happen just between you and me?

There are a few very fundamental things to be understood: first, a man and a woman are on the one hand halves of the other, and on the other hand, opposite polarities. Their being opposites attracts them to each other. The farther away they are, the deeper will be the attraction; the more different from each other they are, the more will be the charm and beauty and attraction. But there lies the whole problem.

When they come close, they want to come closer, they want to merge into each other, they want to become one, a harmonious whole – but their whole attraction depends on opposition, and the harmony will depend on dissolving the opposition. Unless a love affair is very conscious, it is going to create great anguish, great trouble. All lovers are in trouble. The trouble is not personal; it is in the very nature of things.

They would not have been attracted to each other... They call it falling in love. They cannot give any reason why they have such a tremendous pull towards each other. They are not even conscious of the underlying causes; hence a strange thing happens: the happiest lovers are those who never meet. Once they meet, the same opposition that created the attraction becomes a conflict. On each small point, their attitudes are different; their approaches are different. Although they speak the same language, they cannot understand each other.

One of my friends was talking to me about his wife and their continuous conflict. I said, "It seems you cannot understand each other."

He said, "What to say about *under*standing her, I cannot even *stand* her!" And it was a love marriage. The parents of both were opposed to it; they belonged to two different religions, their societies were opposed. But they fought against everybody and got married – just to find that they had entered into a constant struggle.

The way a man looks at the world is different from a woman. For example, a man is interested in faraway things – in the future of humanity, in the faraway stars, whether there are living beings on other planets or not. A woman simply giggles at the whole nonsense. She is only interested in a very small, closed circle – in the neighbors, in the family, in who is cheating his wife, whose wife has fallen in love with the chauffeur. Her interest is very local and very human.

She is not worried about reincarnation; neither is she concerned about life after death. Her concern is more pragmatic. She is concerned with the present, here and now. Man is never here and now. He is always somewhere else. He has strange preoccupations: reincarnation, life after death.

If both partners are conscious of the fact that it is a meeting of opposites, that there is no need to make it a conflict, then it is a great opportunity to understand the totally opposite point of view and absorb it. Then the life of a man and woman together can become a beautiful harmony. Otherwise, it is continuous fight. There are holidays. One cannot continue to fight twenty-four hours a day; one needs a little rest too – a rest to get ready for a new fight.

But it is one of the strangest phenomena that for thousands of years, men and women have been living together, yet they are strangers. They go on giving birth to children, but still they remain strangers. The feminine approach and the masculine approach are so opposed to each other that unless a conscious effort is made, unless it becomes your meditation, there is no hope of having a peaceful life.

It is one of my deep concerns: how to make love and meditation so involved in each other that each love affair automatically becomes a partnership in meditation – and each meditation makes you so conscious that you need not fall in love, you can rise in love. You can find a friend consciously, deliberately. You feel a deep harmony with me, moments of peace, love and silence, and naturally the question has arisen in you that if this is possible with me, why is it not possible with the man you love?

The difference has to be understood. You love me, but you don't love me in the same way you love your husband, your wife. Your love towards me is not biological; with me your love is a totally different phenomenon – it is of the spirit, not of the body. And secondly, you are connected with me because of your search for truth. My relationship with you is that of meditation. Meditation is the only bridge between me and you. Your love will deepen as your meditation deepens, and vice-versa: as your meditation blossoms, your love will also blossom. But it is on a totally different level.

With your husband, you are not connected in meditation. You never sit silently for one hour together just to feel each other's consciousness. Either you are fighting or you are making love, but in both cases, you are related with the body, the physical part, the biology, the hormones. You are not related with the innermost core of the other. Your souls remain separate. In the temples and in the churches and in the courts, only your bodies are married. Your souls are miles apart.

While you are making love to your man – even in those moments – neither are you there, nor is your man there. Perhaps he is thinking of Cleopatra, Noorjahan, Mumtaj Mahal. You are also thinking... And perhaps that's why every woman keeps her eyes closed – not to see her husband's face, not to get disturbed. She is thinking of Alexander the Great, Ivan the Terrible. And looking at her husband, everything falls apart. He looks just like a mouse.

Mulla Nasruddin and his wife were quarreling one morning. She said, "Outside the house you walk as if you are a lion, and inside the house you look just like a mouse."

Mulla Nasruddin said, "That is absolutely wrong. Put yourself right. I am not a mouse, I am a mousetrap. *You* are a mouse. Mousetraps don't run after mice to catch hold of them. The mice themselves come and get caught, and that's how it happened with us."

Mulla Nasruddin was not courageous enough to approach this woman. He was afraid from the very beginning. Every man is afraid because he has seen what has happened to his father, what has happened to his grandfather. He has seen what is happening to every neighbor. Every man is afraid. Mulla was very much afraid; he never approached any woman. It was this woman who caught him. So he said, "Remember, I am a mousetrap, that is true, but I was just sitting in my place. *You* got into *me*, it is your responsibility."

But it does not matter who catches who, who takes the initiative. Even in those beautiful moments which should be sacred, meditative, of deep silence – even then you are not alone with your beloved – there is a crowd. Your mind is thinking of somebody else, your wife's mind is thinking of somebody else. Then what you are doing is just robot-like, mechanical. Some biological force is enslaving you, and you call it love.

I have heard that early in the morning, a drunkard on the beach saw a man doing pushups. The drunkard walked around him, looked very closely from here and from there, and finally said, "I should not interfere in such an intimate affair, but I have to tell you that your girlfriend has gone. Now don't exercise unnecessarily – first get up and find where she is!"

That seems to be the situation. When you are making love, is your woman really there? Is your man really there? Or are you just doing a ritual – something which has to be done, a duty to be fulfilled? If you want a harmonious relationship with your man, you will have to learn to be more meditative. Love alone is not enough. Love alone is blind; meditation gives it eyes. Meditation gives it understanding. And once your love is both love and meditation, you become fellow travelers. Then it is no longer an ordinary relationship between husband and wife. Then it becomes friendliness on the path towards discovering the mysteries of life.

Man alone, woman alone, will find the journey very tedious and very long, as they have found it in the past. Because seeing this continuous conflict, all the religions decided that those who wanted to seek should renounce the other – the monks should be celibate, the nuns should be celibate. But in five thousand years of history, how many monks and how many nuns have become realized souls? You cannot even give me names enough to count on ten fingers. And millions of monks and nuns of all religions – Buddhist, Hindu, Christian, Mohammedan... What has happened? The path is not so long. The goal is not that far away. But even if you want to go to your neighbor's house, you will need both your legs. Just jumping on one leg, how far can you go?

I am introducing a totally new vision: men and women together in deep friendship, in a loving, meditative relationship, as organic wholes, can reach the goal any moment they want. Because the goal is not outside you, it is the center of the cyclone; it is the innermost part of your being. But you can find it only when you are whole, and you cannot be whole without the other.

Man and woman are two parts of one whole.

So, rather than wasting time in fighting, try to understand each other. Try to put yourself in the place of the other – try to see as a man sees, try to see as a woman sees. And four eyes are always better than two eyes; you have a full view all four directions are available to you.

But one thing has to be remembered: that without meditation, love is destined to fail; there is no possibility of its being a success. You can pretend and you can deceive others, but you cannot deceive yourself. You know deep down that all the promises love had given to you have remained unfulfilled. Only with meditation does love start taking on new colors, new music, new songs, new dances – because meditation gives you the insight to understand the polar opposite, and in that very understanding the conflict disappears.

All the conflict in the world is because of misunderstanding. You say something; your wife understands something else. Your wife says something; you understand something else. I have seen couples who have lived together for thirty or forty years; still, they seem to be as immature as they were on their first day together. Still the same complaint: "She doesn't understand what I am saying." Forty years being together and you have not been able to figure out some way that your wife can understand exactly what you are saying, and you can understand exactly what she is saying.

But I think there is no possibility for it to happen except through meditation, because meditation gives you the qualities of silence, awareness, a patient listening, a capacity to put yourself in the other's position. It is possible with me; I am not concerned with the trivia of your life. You are here basically to listen and understand. You are here to grow spiritually. Naturally there is no question of conflict, and the harmony arises without any effort. You can love me with totality, because with me your relationship is of meditation. With any other man or with any other woman, if you want to live in harmony you will have to bring the same atmosphere and the same climate that you have brought here.

Things are not impossible, but we have not tried the right medicine. I would like you to be reminded that the word *medicine* comes from the same root as *meditation*. Medicine cures your body; meditation cures your soul. Medicine heals the material part of you; meditation heals the spiritual part of you. People are living together and their spirits are full of wounds; hence, small things hurt them so much.

Mulla Nasruddin was asking me, "What to do? Whatever I say I am misunderstood, and immediately there is trouble."

I said, "Try one thing: just sit silently, don't say anything."

The next day, I saw him in more despair than ever. I said, "What happened?"

He said, "I should not ask you for advice. Every day we used to fight and quarrel, but it was just verbal. Yesterday, because of your advice, I got beaten!"

I said, "What happened?"

He said, "I just sat there silent. She asked many questions, but I was determined to remain silent. She said, 'So you are not going to speak?' I remained silent. So she started hitting me with things! And she was very angry. She said, 'Things have gone from bad to worse. At least we used to talk to each other; now even we are not on speaking terms!'"

I said, "This is really bad."

He said, "You are saying *bad*? The whole neighborhood gathered, and they all started asking, 'What happened? Why aren't you speaking?' And somebody suggested: 'It seems he is possessed by some evil spirit.'

"I thought, my God, now they are going to take me to some idiot who will beat me and try to drive the evil spirit out. I said, 'Wait! I'm not possessed by any evil spirit, I'm simply not speaking because to say anything triggers a fight: I say something, then she has to say something, and then I have to say something, and nobody knows where it is going to end.' I was simply meditating silently, doing no harm to anybody – and suddenly the whole neighborhood was against me."

People are living without any understanding. Hence, whatsoever they do is going to end in disaster.

If you love a man, meditation will be the best present that you can give to him. If you love a woman, then the Kohinoor is nothing; meditation will be a far more precious gift – and it will make your life sheer joy. We are potentially capable of sheer joy, but we don't know how to manage it.

Alone, we are at the most, sad. Together, it becomes really hell. Even a man like Jean-Paul Sartre, a man of great intelligence, has to say that the other is hell, that to be alone is better; you cannot make it with the other. He became so pessimistic that he said, "It is impossible to make it with the other, the other is hell". Ordinarily, he is right. With meditation the other becomes your heaven. But Jean-Paul Sartre had no idea of meditation.

That is the misery of Western man. Western man is missing the flowering of life because he knows nothing about meditation, and Eastern man is missing because he knows nothing of love. And to me, just as man and woman are halves of one whole, so are love and meditation. Meditation is man; love is woman. In the meeting of meditation and love is the meeting of man and woman. And in that meeting, we create the transcendental human being – which is neither man nor woman.

Unless we create the transcendental man on the earth, there is not much hope, but I feel my people are capable of doing the apparently impossible.

Osho,

Even in my childhood I never rebelled when something wasn't authentic. I learned to wear a mask. I learned it so well that it is very difficult for me to see whether I'm authentic or phony.

Tomorrow I am going to take sannyas.

Is it alright with you to have a disciple who has so little authenticity and who hardly knows what love is?

The question is such: it is as if you are sick and you go to a physician and ask him, "Is it all right for you to accept a sick man as a patient, or do you accept only the healthy people?" My whole business is to accept all kinds of people – hypocrites with all kinds of masks – insincere, obedient against their own intelligence. But these are the people who need me, and these are the people I need too.

Bring all your sicknesses. Don't be worried, I have even initiated a few dead people in the hope that resurrection is possible!

Osho,

Sometimes life seems to be such a drag that I would rather like to die. Any advice?

There are many methods to die, but one thing: anybody who really wants to die never asks for advice. Living may be a drag, but death is very quick. All around you, there are so many ways... But you don't want to die. In fact, even the people who commit suicide don't want to commit suicide. They commit suicide because they expected too much from life and they could not get it. The failure was so great, that to live shamefully became difficult. They committed suicide not *against* life; they committed suicide because they could not manage to learn the art of life. They wanted life to be a great benediction, and it was a drag.

It seems to be a fallacy all over the world that just because you are born, you know how to live. This is not right. To be born is one thing. To know the art of living and of living fully is totally different. Birth is only an opportunity – you can make it or mar it. Birth is not equivalent to life. Almost everybody thinks that birth is equivalent to life, so it is bound to become a drag – just breathing, eating every day, going to sleep, waking up in the morning, going to the same office, the same files and the same routine. For idiots it is perfectly okay, but for anybody who has some intelligence it is bound to become a drag. Because he can see: what is the point? Why after all am I living? If tomorrow is again going to be just a repetition of today, as today has been a repetition of yesterday, then why go on living? What is the point of unnecessarily repeating the same circle, the same routine, the same happenings?

But the fallacy is in the fact that you have accepted a wrong concept, that birth is life. Birth is only an opportunity. Either you can learn to live a beautiful life or you can just drag yourself toward the graveyard. It is up to you. There are people for whom life is a drag, and there are people for whom even death is a dance.

I want to say to you that if you make your life an art, your death will be the culmination of the art – the highest peak, a beauty in itself.

There are millions who are in the same position with the same question. They don't know why they are living and they don't know if there is any point in dying either. Life is futile – how can death appear to be significant? So they are afraid of suicide also, because if life is such – just a dark hole – death is going to be even worse.

One day I saw Mulla Nasruddin with his gun, a rope, and a tin of kerosene oil. I said, "Where are you going, Mulla?"

He said, "Enough is enough. I was just coming to say good-bye to you. I am going to commit suicide."

I said, "But so many arrangements?"

He said, "You know me, I am a perfectionist. I don't take chances. I have made every arrangement."

I said, "Can I come just to watch, and just to wave when you are disappearing in smoke?"

He said, "You can come."

So I went with him and sat on a rock by the side of a river. He made the arrangements very efficiently. On a branch of a tree, which was hanging over the river, he tied the rope by which he was going to hang himself.

I said, "Mulla, that's enough."

He said, "I don't believe it. Unless I have done everything, no loopholes should be left."

He put his neck into the rope, poured the kerosene oil over himself.

I said, "Mulla, is it going to be real?"

He said, "What do you think?"

He lit a match, set fire to himself, and before jumping from the tree, he fired the gun – the last resort – at his head. But that's where everything went wrong – the gun missed the mark and cut the rope and he fell into the river. Naturally, the fire was finished, and he started swimming!

I said, "Mulla, what are you doing?"

He said, "What to do? I know how to swim."

I said, "This is strange. You arranged everything so well, but still there was a loophole, the swimming. You should not have started to swim. You should have remained there and died."

He said, "That's just it – dying is not so easy. When I saw the gun had misfired, when I saw the water had put the fire out, it became clear: God wants me to live. And moreover, I know how to swim! It is impossible when you know swimming not to swim. Next time, some other arrangement..."

Nobody wants to die. And it is true that life is a drag. But it is not *life* that is a drag, it is *you* – you have not learned the art of making life a joy, a thing of beauty, a piece of art. Unless a man is creative, he cannot find much joy in life.

So the first principle is: Be creative.

Don't bother whether you become a world-famous artist or not; that is not the significant thing. But create something: a beautiful song, a little music, a dance, a painting, a garden. And when the roses blossom... You cannot say that life is a drag with so many roses blossoming. A beautiful painting... You cannot say life is a drag, because this painting has been created for the first time in the world and for the last time. Nobody has done it before, and nobody will do it again; only you were capable of doing it.

Express your uniqueness in whatsoever you do. Express your individuality. Let existence be proud of you. Life will not be felt like a drag; it will become a fragrance. Not only will life be a joy and a dance – for a creative person, for a meditative person, even death will be transformed.

I have always loved a story about Bokuju, a Zen master...

He was ninety years old when he died. Three days before, he informed all his disciples: "If you want to come for the last good-bye, then come. In three days' time I am going to leave the world."

So thousands of his disciples came – and he was one of the most unique masters Zen has produced. On the third day, in the morning there was a great gathering in his garden, and he was lying under his most beautiful tree.

He suddenly asked, "Just tell me one thing: in what way should I die? – because I don't want to die like everybody else. Ninety-nine percent of people die in their beds." He said, "That is out of the question. Remove the bed from here!"

The bed is the most dangerous thing. Ninety-nine percent of people die there, and every night you go to bed without thinking of the danger. When the light is turned off, just put your mattress down on the floor. Then there is some chance of surviving – death may try to search for you on the bed and may not be able to find you.

Bokuju said, "Take this bed away from here, and suggest something, something unique, worthy of Bokuju."

The disciples thought what to suggest. Somebody said that, "You can die sitting in a lotus posture. Many masters have died in the lotus posture."

But Bokuju said, "That is not very unique, because many people have died in that posture."

Somebody said, "You can die standing."

He said, "That seems to be appealing."

But one man objected, he said, "That's not right, because I know of a Zen master who died standing. It will not be unique."

Bokuju said, "It is very difficult. Find out quickly because my time is running out, and I cannot delay any longer. So many idiots are here, and you cannot find just one unique way of dying for your beloved master?"

One man suggested, "Nobody has ever died standing on his head. You can do a headstand and die."

Bokuju said, "Perfectly right!"

He stood on his head and died.

Now the problem was... The disciples said, "What to do?" – because they know what has to be done when a person dies in his bed. But what to do with this fellow who has died standing on his head?

Somebody said, "His elder sister, who is also a great master, lives just close by. It is better to call her and not to interfere, because this is a strange thing. We will be condemned later on if we don't do the right thing, so it is better to call somebody who can take responsibility."

The sister came and she said, "Bokuju! From your very childhood you have been mischievous – and this is no time to be mischievous! Just lie down!"

And Bokuju laughed and said, "Okay sister – because I cannot disobey you. I was almost dead. I was just waiting to see what these people would do trying to work out what to do with me after death. But these idiots have brought *you* here! And you always were a killjoy. You've destroyed the whole fun! Now I will die in the ordinary, orthodox way." And he died.

And his sister did not even look back; she just went away. People said, "But he has died!"

She said, "It was time. He was delaying it. And it is not right to play jokes on existence. At least at the time of death one should be serious. Now he is dead, you do whatever you want to do. Even if he is not dead, finish him off – his time is up."

Make your life; find out why you are feeling bored. Change! It is such a small life. Take risks, be a gambler – what can you lose? We come with empty hands; we go with empty hands. There is nothing to lose. Just a little time to be playful, to sing a beautiful song, and the time is gone. Each moment is so precious.

If you are silent, if you are creative, if you are loving, if you are sensitive to beauty, if you are grateful to this vast universe... There are millions of stars, which are dead – and you are so small – yet you have the most precious thing in existence: life. And not only life, but the possibility of becoming a consciousness, of becoming enlightened, of coming to a space where death has never entered.

If Bokuju is not serious, the reason is because he knows there is no death, it is only changing houses, or at the most changing clothes. It is excitement – even death is a great excitement and ecstasy.

It is just your wrong approach. Drop it, and don't drop it slowly, slowly, piece by piece. Drop it totally, instantly. When you go out of this place, go dancing and singing. Let the whole world think you are insane, that is far better.

Osho,

In 1980 you gave me sannyas. I was not even looking for a master. Since then I have experienced the joy and fun of being one of your disciples.

But now I start feeling the pain: you are so vast – where is the way? Is there a way? Just to be true is so difficult.

And is that all?

You have asked three questions in one question First, you found me although you were not looking for a master. Let me make it clear to you that I was looking for a disciple, and that is far more important.

Your looking for a master is not so important because you are asleep and dreaming. So whenever I see some sleepwalker passing by, and see some possibility that he can be awakened, I just turn his way – and he is a sleepwalker so there is no problem. It does not matter where he is going. I give him sannyas, he takes sannyas – because in sleep it does not matter. I create a beautiful dream for him. I am not a hard taskmaster. First I create a beautiful dream, and then slowly, slowly I take you out of it. Now you are out of the dream, so the second problem arises: where is the path? In fact, it is my doing. While you were asleep I was talking about the path..."the path...the mystic path..." to wake you up. Now you are awake so you are asking, "Where is the path?"

There is no path. It was just a device to wake you up. You have not to go anywhere. You are exactly at the place where you have to reach. You are exactly that which you have to become. There is no path; there is no goal.

Your isness is your realization.

And thirdly: waking up, you see me vast like an ocean. While you were asleep, you were not aware of where I was leading you. Now you are fully awake, and you see the vast ocean. It is not me. It is the reality – and it is *your* reality. And the ocean that you see outside you will remain outside till your dewdrop disappears into it. And the dewdrop is slipping from the lotus leaf. Any moment it will be part of the ocean and you will know that no man is an island; we all belong to one reality, one consciousness, one continent. It is only in our sleep that we are separate. The moment we are awake we are one.

There will be a little fear. It is said that even before a river falls into the ocean, it trembles with fear. It looks back at the whole journey, the peaks of the mountains, the long winding path through the forests, through the people, and it sees in front of it such a vast ocean that entering into it is nothing but disappearing forever. But there is no other way. The river cannot go back. Neither can you go back. Going back is impossible in existence; you can only go forward. The river has to take the risk and go into the ocean. And only when it enters the ocean will the fear disappear because only then will the river know that it is not disappearing into the ocean; rather, it is becoming the ocean. It is a disappearance from one side and it is a tremendous resurrection on the other side.

So don't be worried. Things are happening perfectly right for you. You had not come in search of a master, but what to do? A master was in search of you. And now there is no going back. Even if you try to close your eyes, that sleep in which you were living cannot be recalled. And the vastness is not something to be afraid of. It is very friendly; it is very loving. Disappearing into it is almost like finding the womb and its warmth and its nourishment again.

Osho,
Do you have any problem which you have not solved yet?

I don't have any problem. I used to have problems, but I never solved them. My procedure is totally different. I *dissolve* the problem; I never solve it, because solving does not help. You solve a problem, and you will find that ten other problems have arisen out of your solution. I have been dissolving, I have been getting rid of – because no problem is significant. All problems are barriers between you and existence.

Now I have only mysteries – no problems, no questions. In that way I am a very poor man. No problem, no question; I am utterly silent. But silence has a richness that millions of problems cannot give to you. Silence has a richness that all the philosophies of the world and all the answers together cannot give you.

When I answer your questions, it is not that I have got an answer and I simply give it to you. I don't have any answer. I simply listen to your question and let my silence respond to it; hence, you can find many contradictions in my answers. But I am not responsible, because *I* have never answered. It is the silence that goes on responding at different moments in different times to different people in different ways. Just as you listen to the answer, I also listen to it. There is no speaker here. Here, there are only listeners.

Osho,

What is the last question we should ask you, Osho?

There is not even a first question, so the question about the last question does not arise. You should learn to be silent, to be at ease with me, to be in tune with me. In that silent harmony all is achieved: all the treasures that existence has been keeping safe for you, so that when you wake up you can claim your portion. And everybody's portion of the treasure is infinite. It is not that because it is a portion, it will be limited.

The upanishadic seers have said: "You can take out even the whole from the whole, yet the whole remains behind". Existence is such a mystery that it can give to each person infinite treasure, eternal life, unbounded beauty.

So don't be worried about the last question. There is not even a first question. Be innocent and silent, and just be open and receptive to my heartbeats. The moment your heartbeats are also dancing to the same tune, you have come home.

In fact, you have never gone anywhere. You have just forgotten that this is your home.

17 The Point of No Return

Osho,
Sri Aurobindo declared that there is something beyond that which Buddha calls enlightenment. His whole aspiration was dedicated towards opening a door for this new step in human evolution.
Osho, what could not happen with Aurobindo, is it happening with you?

Sri Aurobindo is a strange case. He knows everything about enlightenment, but he is not enlightened. He is one of the greatest scholars of this age, a genius; vast is his knowledge, but his knowing is nil. He knows about the scriptures, and he knows better than anybody else. His interpretation is profound, very logical, but heartless. It is dead; it is not coming out of his own realization.

This is one of the great problems for all seekers of truth: one can get lost in knowledge without knowing anything about the reality. He knows all the theories, all the philosophies, but he is just a blind man who knows everything about light but has not seen the light himself. And it is possible to remain in a deception for your whole life because you know so much, and people start worshipping you, people start believing you. And belief has its own psychology, if many people believe in you, you are bound to believe in yourself.

I have often told a small story about a great journalist who died and reached the doors of heaven.

The doors of heaven and hell are not far apart; they are just opposite each other. The distance is not much, and naturally one would like to enter heaven. So he knocked on the door. The doorkeeper opened a small window in the door and asked, "What do you want?"

He said, "I am a great journalist. I have just died, and I want to enter."

The doorkeeper said, "I am sorry but I have to refuse you because we have a quota; we can have only twelve journalists in heaven. That quota has been filled for centuries, for centuries no new journalist has entered. And anyway, even those twelve are utterly useless because nothing happens in heaven. They tried to publish a newspaper, but only one issue appeared because there are only saints here – no murder, no suicide, no crime, no politics, no struggle for power. No change ever happens; everything is eternally the same – from where can you get news?"

"And," the doorkeeper said, "you must have heard the definition of news: when a dog bites a man it is not news, but when a man bites a dog it is news. So nothing sensational happens here, no love affair. When people get bored, they read the first issue that was published centuries ago.

"You should go to hell. Every moment tremendous things happen there. All the active people of the world, all the creative people of the world are there: painters, musicians, poets, actors, dancers, thieves, murderers, rapists, psychoanalysts, philosophers; you will find every variety.

"Heaven is monotonous. Only dull, dead saints, skeletons... Their only quality is that they don't do anything. So just go to hell and enjoy. You will find everything that you may have missed on earth, because for centuries upon centuries, all the juicy people have collected there. In fact, I myself want to go, but once you get into heaven, you cannot escape. So I am stuck here. My suggestion is that you just go."

But journalists are stubborn people. He said, "I have a suggestion, and I think you must be compassionate enough to do it for me. Just give me twenty-four hours' entry. If I can convince one of the journalists inside to go to hell then you can put me in the quota; twelve journalists will remain twelve."

The gatekeeper said, "It is unheard of, there is no precedent. But I cannot say no to you. Go in, have a try. But remember, after twenty-four hours... I am taking a risk. After twenty-four hours, come back."

After twenty-four hours he came back. In those twenty-four hours he had created a rumor among all the journalists: "A big newspaper is going to be started in hell and there is great need for editors, sub-editors, story writers, all kinds of journalists. The salaries are great. So what are you doing *here*?"

After twenty-four hours when the journalist came to the gate, the gatekeeper said, "Go back. You cannot go out now."

The journalist said, "Why not?"

The gatekeeper said, "I have kept my word, and you have to keep your word. You were very convincing. All twelve journalists have gone. I tried hard to explain that 'This is just a rumor; don't spoil your heaven.' But they wouldn't listen."

The man himself had created the rumor, but he had started thinking perhaps there was something in it; otherwise twelve persons wouldn't go to hell for no reason.

He said, "Just open the door!" He was convinced by others being convinced.

And this happens to millions of people. When you see that seven hundred million people are convinced that Catholic Christianity is the only religion, it is difficult to say that those seven hundred million people can be wrong. The sheer number has such weight. That's why all the religions go on trying to increase their numbers. They have their methods to increase their numbers because the more you increase the numbers the more you convince those who are not in your fold that they are wrong and you are right. Your sheer majority is an argument; it validates anything you say.

Sri Aurobindo was a great intellectual, a very convincing, rational philosophical genius. He convinced many people, and those many people convinced him that he was enlightened. He knows nothing of enlightenment. It is true that there is something more in existence than the enlightenment Gautam the Buddha achieved. But it is Gautam the Buddha himself who, for the first time in the world, indicated the possibility of the beyond. Naturally, nobody else can say that there is something beyond – unless they reach that boundary. So when Sri Aurobindo says there is something more than the enlightenment of Gautam Buddha, he is hiding the fact that it was Gautam Buddha himself who was the first man in the whole of history to say that "This is not all; there is something beyond."

Buddha says – and you can see the sincerity of the man – "A man who has entered the path, *srotapanna,* who has entered the stream that leads to the ocean, is millions of times more respectable than anybody else, just because he has entered the path in search of the truth. He has not found, but just the urge, just the effort, the first step, and he has become millions of times more honorable than all your respectable generals, kings, emperors and world conquerors. "The person who has reached the point from which he will not turn back, *anagamin*, is millions of times more honorable than the *srotapanna*, than the one who has entered the stream. And the man who has become enlightened, who has become a buddha, is millions of times more honorable than the person who has reached the point of no return."

The point of no return is something worth understanding. Many people start the search and then drop out. It is arduous, it is moving into the unknown; nobody knows whether there is anything like enlightenment or if it is just a fiction created by a few people like Gautam Buddha. Perhaps they are not lying, perhaps they themselves are deceived – who knows? There is no guarantee.

So many start, but very few remain. Most of them return to the world sooner or later, finding that they are going into an unknown territory without a map, without any guide. They start feeling crazy because the whole world is going in a totally different direction, and they are left alone. Their whole strength was in the crowd. Alone, a thousand and one doubts arise. Alone, one starts feeling that millions of people cannot be wrong, "And I am alone, thinking that I am right – I must be getting crazy."

Anagamin is one who has come to a point from where he cannot return. He is not enlightened but he has seen, from far away, the possibility. He has not reached the peak; he is still in the dark valley. But he can see the sunlit peak; it is a reality, it is not a fiction. Now there is no force in the world, which can make him go back.

Buddha says, "But the one who has become enlightened is millions of times more honorable than the person who has reached the point of no return." And here is the sincerity of the man – he says: "The man who has transcended buddhahood, who has gone beyond enlightenment, is millions of times more honorable than anyone who is enlightened." He is not claiming that he has gone beyond; he is simply saying "I can see from my place that faraway star."

And he was the first to see that faraway star: beyond enlightenment.

Sri Aurobindo is not sincere. He never quotes this passage, which was his duty to quote. He tries to convince his readers and followers that he is working to open the door beyond enlightenment. He is not even courageous enough to declare himself, to say that he is enlightened. He never declared that. But only indirectly... He is assuming that you will understand that he is enlightened because he is trying to open the door beyond enlightenment. Naturally he must be enlightened, but he is not saying it. To declare it needs courage, not scholarship.

He gives a hint, as if he is enlightened and he is working for others so that they can also go beyond enlightenment. They have not even reached enlightenment. It is hilarious, the very idea that he is trying to open the door...his whole life's aspiration. All his aspirations were stupid.

They were stupid because others will need that door only if they have become enlightened. First help people to become enlightened, Rather than helping people to become enlightened, he was devoting his whole energy to opening the door beyond enlightenment. And it is not only on this point that he was talking nonsense; he was talking nonsense on many points. Another of his aspirations was physical immortality; he was working so that man can become physically immortal. Naturally you will think *he* has become physically immortal – these are natural assumptions. And his followers all over the world started spreading the great news, the good news, that Sri Aurobindo had become physically immortal: "Now he is trying to find the right techniques so that every human being can become physically immortal." And then one day he died!

One of my friends was living in Sri Aurobindo's ashram. I phoned him immediately and asked him, "What happened?"

But such is blindness. He said, "Here in the ashram everybody was shocked. But the mother of the ashram told us that he has simply gone into a long *samadhi*. He is not dead; it is part of his project to find immortality. He has found all, but just for the last missing link he has to go into deep samadhi, to dive deep into the ocean." And he told me that everybody believed it.

For three days they did not cremate his body or bury his body because they believed that he would be coming back. But in three days the body started stinking. Then they became afraid that if the news spread that the body was stinking...

The man was dead; he was not going to come back. After three days they put his body into a marble grave. Still they did not burn his body because he might come back at any moment. The really faithful ones still believe that one day he will come back. And the whole belief shifted towards the mother – she was the co-partner in the business of finding immortality for humanity. And it looked as if she *had* found it, because she lived for almost a century. It seemed probable; perhaps she had found it. And she was saying that she was going to live forever.

Now this is the beautiful thing about spirituality: I can say to you that I am going to live forever and tomorrow I can die – who are you going to argue with? And one day the mother died. Again the same thing: they waited for three days, and when the body started stinking, she was put into another marble grave next to Sri Aurobindo. And the faithful ones still sit beside the graves every day, waiting for them to return. Slowly, slowly, the number of faithful ones is lessening. The hope is turning into hopelessness, into despair. Perhaps they have not yet found the missing link together.

It is enough that man has an immortal soul, an immortal consciousness, an immortal life principle. But Sri Aurobindo was obsessed with the idea that he had to bring some original contribution to the spiritual progress of humanity. That the human soul is immortal, is as ancient an experience as humanity itself. Even the Vedas, five thousand years old, declare man as *amritasya putrah:* "you are sons of immortality." Something new, something original – and this was a great original idea, that your body can be immortal. One cannot conceive how intelligent people can get caught up in such absurd ideas.

Sri Aurobindo was a child, he became a young man, he became old. If the human body is immortal, then you will have to say at what age it is going to be immortal: as a child, as a young man, as an old man, or as a dead man? The last seems to be the only possibility. As a dead man, the human body is immortal. And certainly it is, because all the elements of the human body disperse into nature. Nothing is going to die; everything is going to merge. The earth into earth, the water into water, the air into air; all the elements will go to their sources. In that sense the human body has always been immortal. Not only the human body: buffaloes, donkeys, monkeys, *everybody* is immortal. It does not need a Sri Aurobindo to declare that his body is immortal.

Gautam Buddha is the rarest human being in that he recognizes that there is still something more, he has not reached the end of evolution. In Japan, they had a beautiful collection of paintings called *Ten Zen Bulls*." It is a series of paintings depicting the whole story of the search.

In the first, a man is looking here and there...his bull is lost. You see forest all around, ancient trees, and the puzzled man standing there looking, and he cannot see the bull.

In the second painting, he looks a little happier because he has seen the bull's footprints. It is the same painting, the same forest.

Just one thing he has discovered in this painting and that is, he has seen the bull's footprints, so he knows where he has gone.

In the third painting he moves and sees the backside of the bull – because it is standing by the side of a tree, and the man is behind him – so he looks... And just the backside is shown in the painting.

In the fourth he has reached the bull; he sees the whole bull.

In the fifth he has caught hold of the bull by the horns.

In the sixth he is riding on the bull. It is difficult; the bull is trying to throw him off.

By the eighth he is returning home, the bull is conquered.

In the ninth the bull is back in the stall and the man is playing on a flute.

In the tenth, there is no question of the bull at all. The man is seen in the marketplace with a bottle of wine, drunk.

Buddhists were very much embarrassed about the tenth painting. It does not seem to be Buddhist at all – and there is no connection, because nine seems to be perfect, there is no need for the tenth. So in the Middle Ages they dropped the tenth painting, and they started talking of the nine paintings. Only recently has the tenth painting been discovered again in the ancient scriptures with its description – because each painting has a description of what is happening. The bull is lost, your soul is lost; the bull represents your soul, your energy, your spirit. When the bull is found, you have become a realized soul. You are singing a song on the flute; that is the stage of enlightenment.

What about the tenth? That is the stage when you go beyond enlightenment; you become ordinary again. Now there is no split between this world and that, now there is no split between good and bad. Now all opposites have joined together into one single harmony; that's what is represented by the bottle of wine, a bottle of wine in the hands of a buddha.

Sri Aurobindo never talked about the Ten Bulls because that again would have destroyed his originality. The paintings of the Ten Bulls are at least fifteen centuries old.

The Buddhists in the Middle Ages were cowardly; they could not understand the tenth. But as far as I am concerned, I can see a natural growth from the ninth to the tenth, from enlightenment to beyond enlightenment.

Enlightenment makes you special. That means something of the ego in some subtle form still remains. Others are ignorant, you are a knower; others are going towards hell, your paradise is guaranteed. These are the last remnants of a dying ego. And when this ego also dies the buddha becomes an ordinary human being, not knowing at all that he is holier than thou, higher than thou, special in any sense – so ordinary that even a bottle of wine is acceptable. The whole of life is acceptable; the days and the nights, the flowers and the thorns, the saints and the sinners – all are acceptable, with no discrimination at all.

This ordinariness is really the greatest flowering of human reality.

Sri Aurobindo will be remembered as a great philosopher – *should* be remembered as a great philosopher, a man of tremendous insight into words, scriptures, immensely articulate in bringing meanings, interpretations to them, novel, original – but he was not a man of realization. And he was not sincere, he was not an authentic man. He had a great desire to prove himself, to prove that he was greater than Gautam Buddha. That was his ego.

To go beyond enlightenment is not to become greater than Gautam Buddha. To go beyond enlightenment is to become an ordinary human being: to forget all about enlightenment and all about great spiritual aspirations and to live simply, joyously, playfully. This ordinariness is the most extraordinary phenomenon in the world.

But you will not be able to recognize him. Up to Gautam Buddha you will be able to recognize, but as a person moves beyond Gautam Buddha, he will start slipping out of your hands. Those who have recognized him as an enlightened being may remain aware of who he is, but those who come new will not be able to recognize him at all, because he will be simply a very innocent, ordinary human being – just like a child collecting seashells on the beach, running after butterflies, gathering flowers. No division of body and soul, no division of matter and spirit, no division of this life and that – all that is forgotten; one has relaxed totally.

If Sri Aurobindo had known even the meaning of what it is to go beyond realization, beyond enlightenment, he would not have even thought about it. He was thinking that going beyond enlightenment is something greater than Gautam Buddha. He was continuously in an inner jealousy, and of course the jealousy was of Gautam Buddha. And he wanted to come up with some original ideas so that he could prove them, but he has not proved anything. I respect Sri Aurobindo as a scholar – but scholars are just scholars, a dollar a dozen.

Osho,

The other night you talked about the master and the mystic.

My question is about the mystic and the skeptic. Is it possible for a skeptic to become a mystic? So much of the esoteric and mystical seems to be a process of autosuggestion, imagination and wishful thinking. I sometimes feel very discouraged and want to give it all up as nonsense. Yet there is also an inner voice leading me on. The biggest relief for me seems to be in your continual encouragement to let go and trust.

Osho, do you see any possibility for a skeptic to get through this conglomeration of mind fabrications?

The skeptical mind is one of the most beautiful things in the world.

It has been condemned by the religions because they were not capable of answering skeptical questions. They wanted only believers, and the skeptical mind is just the opposite of the believer. I am all in favor of the skeptical mind.

Do not believe anything unless you have experienced it. Do not believe anything – go on questioning, however long it takes. Truth is not cheap. It is not available to the believer; it is available only to the skeptical.

Just remember one thing: don't be skeptical halfheartedly. Be a *total* skeptic. When I say be a total skeptic, I mean that your skeptical ideas should also be put to the same test as anybody else's beliefs. Skepticism, when it is total, burns itself out because you have to question and doubt your skepticism too. You cannot leave your skepticism without doubt; otherwise that is the standpoint of the believer.

If you can doubt the skeptic in you, then the mystic is not far away.

What is a mystic? – one who knows no answer, one who has asked every possible question and found that no question is answerable. Finding this, he has dropped questioning. Not that he has found the answer – he has simply found one thing, that there is no answer anywhere.

Life is a mystery, not a question. Not a puzzle to be solved, not a question to be answered, but a mystery to be lived, a mystery to be loved, a mystery to be danced.

A totally skeptical mind is bound to finally become a mystic; hence my doors are open for all. I accept the skeptic because I know how to turn him into a mystic. I invite the theist because I know how to destroy his theism. I invite the atheist because I know how to take away his atheism. My doors prevent nobody, because I am not giving you any belief. I am giving you only a methodology, a meditation to discover for yourself what in reality is the case.

I have found that there is no answer. All questions are futile, and all answers are more futile. Questions have been asked by foolish people, and great philosophies have arisen because of their questions. These philosophies are created by the cunning and the shrewd. But if you want to have a rapport with reality, you have to be neither a fool nor shrewd; you have to be innocent.

So whatever you bring – skepticism, atheism, theism, communism, fascism, any type of nonsense you can bring here – my medicine is the same. It does not matter what kind of nonsense your head is filled with when you come here. I will chop off your head without any distinction. What is in your head does not matter – my concern is chopping!

I am just a woodcutter.

Osho,

I cannot find the question, but my heart needs an answer. What is it?

It is a very profound inquiry. Anybody who is sincere will have the same inquiry. All questions are foolish, silly at the most. But still, there is some existential need for an answer. The question is not known.

I have told you about one of the most beautiful woman poets, Gertrude Stein. She was dying, and a small circle of friends had gathered around her. Just before her death she opened her eyes and asked, "What is the answer?"

They were all puzzled because this is not the way... First you have to ask the question. She is first asking what the answer is – answer to what? But you cannot be hard to a dying woman – and no ordinary woman, a really great poet. And even in this statement her greatness is absolutely present.

For a few seconds there was silence. Then one person gathered courage and said, "Stein, you have not asked the question. This is strange that you are asking what the answer is."

So the dying woman opened her eyes and said, "Okay. So tell me what the question is." And she died.

This is something truly mystic. There is no question, but there is an existential thirst which appears to the mind as a search for an answer. But there is no answer.

Existence is, and it is tremendously beautiful, psychedelically colorful. It is song and dance and celebration all over. But please don't ask any question or any answer. It is a mystery. Mystery means there is no way to solve it; whatever you do is going to fail. Rather, live it, drop solving. Perhaps through living you will come to an understanding. But that will not be the answer, it will be *more* than the answer; it will be an alive experience. You will have become part of the mystery itself.

Even the greatest philosophers have been behaving like children. They go on representing life as if it is a puzzle, a crossword puzzle. It is not a puzzle. It is simply an unanswerable but experience-able phenomenon. That's what I mean by *mysticism*.

Philosophers miss it completely because they try to find questions, and then answers. Questions are man-made. A rosebush never asks a question, a cloud never bothers about a question, a mountain never raises a question. It does not mean that they have the answer; it simply means they are beyond the question-answer game. And when I say *going beyond enlightenment* I am saying the same thing in other words – going beyond the question-answer game and just accepting reality as it is, whatsoever it is. Otherwise, there are troubles upon troubles. First you create the question, then you create the answer. Then the answer creates ten more questions; you create ten more answers and then each answer creates ten more questions. It is like a tree; it goes on growing and becoming bigger and bigger, and there is no end.

Just live life simply, without putting a question mark behind every experience. People may think you are crazy, but if *you* are crazy then the whole of existence is crazy – what to do? It is out of our hands. Why does the sun rise in the morning every day? Not even a single day is a holiday. Not even for a single day does it rise from the West – just for a change: "I am getting tired of rising from the East... No, things are simply going so smoothly; only man is in trouble.

The moment you also start living like a rosebush, rising like a sun, floating like a white cloud, you have come to a profound understanding of the mysterious, of the miraculous truth of existence.

Osho,

A woman friend of mine often uses the words *male ego* about me, which I feel is not true about me.

From the very beginning I have been open and vulnerable to feminine energy, which is teaching me to become a disciple every day. Moreover, I have felt that when she used this word there was some kind of hatred towards men.

Osho, can you explain what the male ego is, and what it means when a woman uses this expression about a man?

The ego is simply the ego; it is neither male nor female. But man has been very inhuman towards women for centuries, continuously. And the strange thing is that the man has been so cruel and inhuman towards women because he feels a deep inferiority complex in comparison to them. The greatest problem has been that the woman is capable of becoming a mother; she is capable of giving birth to life, and man is not. That was the beginning of the feeling of inferiority: that nature depends on woman, not on man.

Moreover, he has found that she is in many ways stronger than him. For example, for every one hundred and fifteen boys that are born, only one hundred girls are born, because fifteen boys will pop off by the time they become sexually mature, but the girls will remain; they have a certain stamina. Women fall sick less often than men. Women commit suicide less often than men – although they talk about suicide more, they simply talk. At the most they take sleeping pills, but always in such a small quantity that they never die. Men commit suicide in almost double the numbers. Women live five years longer than men.

Women are more patient, more tolerant than men. Men are very impatient and very intolerant. Women are less violent than men. Women don't commit murders; it is the man who commits murders, who wages crusades, who is always getting ready for war, who invents all kinds of deadly weapons, atomic bombs, nuclear weapons.

The woman is completely out of this whole game of death.

Hence it was no coincidence that man started feeling somehow inferior. And nobody wants to be inferior; the only way was to force the woman in artificial ways to become inferior. For example, not to allow her education, not to allow her economic freedom, not to allow her to move out of the house, but confine her to an imprisonment. It seems almost unbelievable what man has done to woman just to get rid of his inferiority. He has made the woman artificially inferior.

In China, for five thousand years it was thought that women had no soul. Of course all the writers were men; they proposed the idea that a woman is only a machine, a reproductive machine. And the idea gained so much influence that it even entered the justice system of China. If a man murdered his wife, he was not a criminal, because he had simply broken a chair, a table, at the most a television. But it was his property, and he had the right to destroy it. So in China, thousands of women were killed by their husbands, but the husbands could not be punished by the government or the courts, because the basic principle that the woman had a soul was denied.

In India for ten thousand years the woman was told that even to dream of some other man is a sin. The same was not said to the man. The woman had to live a very virtuous life while for the man there was freedom. Man created prostitutes for his freedom. And this possessiveness in India took on almost insane proportions. When a man died, his wife had to die with him. She had to jump alive onto the funeral pyre, and for ten thousand years that continued. If some woman was afraid – anybody would be afraid to jump alive into a funeral pyre – then she was condemned as immoral. The husband's wish was that she should die with him because he could not trust her: when he has gone, she may start having some love affair with somebody else, and this cannot be tolerated. But the strange thing is that the same rule was not applicable to men: that when the wife dies the husband should jump into the funeral pyre. No, man was a higher quality of being.

The way they used to do it brings tears, because to burn a woman alive is not an easy task. First they would make the funeral pyre, put the dead body of the husband on it, and force the woman to lie down next to the dead body. Then they would put more wood on top of both of them and pour refined butter all over the funeral pyre, so that the fire would get going fast, strong – and not only fast and strong, but it would create so much smoke that nobody could see what was happening there – because sometimes the woman would try to jump out of the funeral pyre.

There were priests standing around the funeral pyre with burning torches in their hands. If the woman tried to jump out, they would force her, with the burning torches, back into the funeral pyre. Hence so much smoke was needed, so nobody could see what the priest was doing. The woman was bound to cry and scream. Her screams should not be heard, so there was an arrangement: behind the priests, there was another row of thousands of people playing music, dancing, singing, shouting as loudly as possible just to drown out the screams of the woman, coming from the funeral pyre. And they were celebrating, because one woman had proved her love, her trust, by committing suicide.

She was forced; she did not come to do it willingly, she was brought there. And the same situation has happened all over the world. In different ways, they have been cutting woman's wings, her abilities, her talents, her genius.

It is not only a question for you. When your woman is telling you that you have a male ego, she is simply representing all women, and you are nothing but a representative of all men. Your forefathers have done so much harm that there is no way to come to a balance. So when your woman says that this is male ego, try to understand – perhaps she is right. Most probably she is right, because the male has accepted himself as superior for so long that he does not feel that it is his ego. It is the woman who feels it.

Don't deny her feeling. Be grateful to her, and ask her where she feels the ego so that you can drop it. Take her help. You are simply denying it, you don't feel that you have any male ego. But it is simply a traditional heritage.

Every small boy has a male ego – just a small boy. If he starts crying you immediately say, "Why are you crying like a girl? A girl is allowed to cry because she is subhuman. You are going to be a big male chauvinist; you are not supposed to cry or weep." And small boys start stopping their tears. It is very rare to find men who are as ready to cry and allow tears to flow as women are.

Remember, you both have the same size tear glands in your eyes, so nature does not make any difference. Listen to the woman. You have suppressed the woman and oppressed the woman so much, it is time that she should be listened to and things should be corrected. At least in your personal life do as much as you can to allow the woman as much freedom as possible – the same freedom that you allow yourself. Help her to stand up so that she can blossom again.

We will have a more beautiful world if all women – and women are half of the world – are allowed to grow their talents, their genius. It is not a question at all. Nobody is higher; nobody is lower. Women are women, men are men; they have differences, but differences don't make anybody higher or lower. Their differences create their attraction. Just think of a world where there are only men. It will be so ugly: everywhere Morarji Desai, Morarji Desai – all drinking their urine, nothing else to do.

Life is rich because there are differences: different attitudes, different opinions. Nobody is superior; nobody is inferior. People are simply different. Accept this, and help your woman to be free from ten thousand years of repression. Be a friend to her. Much harm has been done; she has been wounded so much that if you can do some healing with your love, you will be contributing to the whole world, to the whole world consciousness.

Don't feel bad if your woman says, "This is male ego." It is there in a subtle form, unrecognizable because it has been there for so long; you have forgotten that this is ego. Take her help so that you can recognize it and destroy it.

18 Meditation: The Courage to Be Silent and Alone

Osho,
I am always afraid of being alone, because when I am alone I start to wonder who I am. It feels that if I inquire deeper, I will find out that I am not the person who I have believed I was for the past twenty-six years, but a being, present at the moment of birth and maybe also the moment before.
For some reason, this scares me completely. It feels like a kind of insanity, and makes me lose myself in outside things in order to feel safer.
Osho, who am I, and why the fear?

It is not only your fear, it is *everybody's* fear – because nobody is what he was supposed to be by existence. Society, culture, religion, education have all been conspiring against innocent children. They have all the power – the child is helpless and dependent. So whatsoever they want to make out of him, they manage to do it. They don't allow any child to grow to his natural destiny. Their every effort is to make human beings into utilities.

Who knows, if a child is left on his own to grow, whether he will be of any use to the vested interests or not? The society is not prepared to take the risk. It grabs the child and starts molding him into something that is needed by the society. In a certain sense, it kills the soul of the child and gives him a false identity, so that he never misses his soul, his being. The false identity is a substitute. But that substitute is useful only in the same crowd which has given it to you. The moment you are alone, the false starts falling apart and the repressed real starts expressing itself; hence the fear of being lonely.

Nobody wants to be lonely. Everybody wants to belong to a crowd – not only one crowd but many crowds. A person belongs to a religious crowd, a political party, a rotary club, and there are many other small groups to belong to. One wants to be supported twenty-four hours a day because the false, without support, cannot stand. The moment one is alone, one starts feeling a strange craziness.

That's what you have been asking about – because for twenty-six years you believed yourself to be somebody, and then suddenly in a moment of loneliness you start feeling you are not that. It creates fear: then who are you? And twenty-six years of suppression... It will take some time for the real to express itself. The gap between the two has been called by the mystics "the dark night of the soul" – a very appropriate expression. You are no longer the false, and you are not yet the real. You are in a limbo, you don't know who you are.

Particularly in the West the problem is even more complicated because they have not developed any methodology to discover the real as soon as possible, so that the dark night of the soul can be shortened. The West knows nothing as far as meditation is concerned. And meditation is only a name for being alone, silent, waiting for the real to assert itself. It is not an act; it is a silent relaxation – because whatever you do will come out of your false personality. All your doing for twenty-six years has come out of it; it is an old habit and habits die hard.

There was one great mystic in India, Eknath. He was going for a holy pilgrimage with all his disciples – it was almost a three to six months' journey. One man came to him, fell at his feet and said, "I know I am not worthy. You know it too, everybody knows me. But I know your compassion is greater than my unworthiness. Please accept me also as one of the members of the group that is going on the holy pilgrimage."

Eknath said, "You are a thief – and not an ordinary thief, but a master thief. You have never been caught, and everybody knows that you are a thief. I certainly feel like taking you with me, but I also have to think about those fifty people who are going with me. You will have to give me a promise – and I am not asking for more, just for these three to six months' time while we are on the pilgrimage – you will not steal. After that, it is up to you. Once we are back home, you are free from the promise."

The man said, "I am absolutely ready to promise, and I am tremendously grateful for your compassion."

The other fifty people were suspicious. To trust in a thief... But they could not say anything to Eknath. He was the master. The pilgrimage started, and from the very first night there was trouble. The next morning there was chaos – somebody's coat was missing, somebody's shirt was missing, somebody's money had gone.

And everybody was shouting, "Where is my money?" And they were all telling Eknath, "We were suspicious from the very beginning that you were taking this man with you. A lifelong habit..."

But then they started looking, and they found that things were not stolen. Somebody's money was missing, but it was found in somebody else's bag. Somebody else's coat was missing, but it was found in somebody else's luggage. Everything was found, but it was an unnecessary trouble – every morning! And nobody could conceive... What can be the meaning of it? And now certainly it is not the thief, because nothing is stolen.

The third night, Eknath remained awake to see what was going on. In the middle of the night, the thief – just out of habit – woke up, started taking things from one place to another place. Eknath stopped him and said, "What are you doing? Have you forgotten your promise?"

He said, "No, I have not forgotten my promise. I am not stealing anything, but I have not promised that I will not change things from one place to another place. After six months I have to be a thief again; this is just practice. And you must understand, it is a lifelong habit; you cannot drop it just like that. Just give me time. You should understand my problem also. For three days I have not stolen a single thing – it is just like fasting! This is just a substitute; I am keeping myself busy. This is my business time, in the middle of the night, so it is very hard for me just to lie down on the bed awake. And so many idiots are sleeping, and I am not doing any harm to anybody. In the morning they will find their things."

Eknath said, "You are a strange man. You see that every morning there is such chaos, and one or two hours unnecessarily are wasted in finding things: where you have put them, whose thing has gone into whose luggage. Everybody has to open everything and ask everybody, 'To whom does this belong?'"

The thief said, "This much concession you have to give to me."

Twenty-six years of a false personality imposed by people who you loved, who you respected, and they were not intentionally doing anything bad to you. Their intentions were good, just their awareness was nil. They were not conscious people – your parents, your teachers, your priests, your politicians – they were not conscious people, they were unconscious. And even a good intention in the hands of an unconscious person turns out to be poisonous.

So whenever you are alone...a deep fear, because suddenly the false starts disappearing. And the real will take a little time. You lost it twenty-six years ago. You will have to give some consideration to the fact that the twenty-six years' gap has to be bridged.

In fear that "I am losing myself, my senses, my sanity, my mind – everything" because the self that has been given to you by others consists of all these things, it looks like you will go insane. You immediately start doing something just to keep yourself engaged. If there are no people, at least there is some action. So the false remains engaged and does not start disappearing. Hence people find it the most difficult on holidays. For five days they work, hoping that on the weekend they are going to relax. But the weekend is the worst time in the whole world – more accidents happen on the weekend, more people commit suicide, more murders, more stealing, more rape. Strange! And these people were engaged for five days and there was no problem. But the weekend suddenly gives them a choice, either to be engaged in something or to relax – but relaxing is fearsome; the false personality disappears.

Keep engaged, do anything stupid. People are running towards the beaches, bumper to bumper, miles-long traffic. And if you ask them where they are going, they are getting away from the crowd – and the whole crowd is going with them. They are going to find a solitary, silent space – all of them! In fact, if they had remained home it would have been more solitary and silent, because all the idiots have gone in search of a solitary place. And they are rushing like mad, because two days will be finished soon; they have to reach. Don't ask where!

And on the beaches, you see they are so crowded, not even marketplaces are so crowded. And strangely enough, people are feeling very much at ease, taking a sunbath. Ten thousand people on a small beach taking a sunbath, relaxing! The same person on the same beach alone will not be able to relax. But he knows thousands of other people are relaxing all around him. The same people were in the offices, the same people were in the streets, the same people were in the marketplace; now the same people are on the beach. The crowd is essential for the false self to exist. The moment it is lonely you start freaking out.

This is where one should understand a little bit of meditation. Don't be worried, because that which can disappear is worth disappearing. It is meaningless to cling to it – it is not yours, it is not you. You are the one when the false has gone and the fresh, the innocent, the unpolluted being arises in its place. Nobody else can answer your question "Who am I?" – but you will know it. All meditative techniques are a help to destroy the false. They don't give you the real – the real cannot be given. That which can be given cannot be real. The real you have got already; just the false has to be taken away.

It can be said in a different way: the master takes away things from you, which you don't really have, and he gives you that which you really have.

Meditation is just courage to be silent and alone. Slowly, slowly, you start feeling a new quality to yourself, a new aliveness, a new beauty, a new intelligence, which is not borrowed from anybody, which is growing within you. It has roots in your existence. And if you are not a coward, it will come to fruition, to flowering.

Only the brave, the courageous, the people who have guts, can be religious. Not the churchgoers – they are the cowards. Not the Hindus, not the Mohammedans, not the Christians – they are against searching. The same crowd, they are trying to make their false identity more consolidated.

You were born. You have come into the world with life, with consciousness, with tremendous sensitivity. Just look at a small child, look at his eyes, the freshness. All that has been covered by a false personality.

There is no need to be afraid. You can lose only that which *has* to be lost. And it is good to lose it soon, because the longer it stays, the stronger it becomes. And one does not know anything about tomorrow. Don't die before realizing your authentic being.

Only those few people who have lived with authentic being and who have died with authentic being are fortunate, because they know that life is eternal, and death is a fiction.

Osho,

Is sitting silently, doing nothing, watching the grass grow – and maybe falling asleep – really enough?

I once heard you say about Freud that he himself was probably not able to create. Or I heard you say that we create our own lives, our own hells and miseries, and that we are responsible.

If sitting silently really is enough, where do the words *effort* or *discipline* come in? Then, if we are doing something, what are we *doing*? Can we do anything at all, or am I dreaming that I am doing something?

Somewhere I am so tired of it. But then also am I going to end up in a state of lethargy and indifference, in which I cannot see any love or beauty?

The people who have been exploiting humanity have created great philosophies, theologies, disciplines. Without the support of all this philosophical, theological, religious framework, it would be impossible to create the false personality.

The word *discipline* comes from these people, and the word *effort* also comes from these people. They have created such a world emphasizing work, effort, endeavor, struggle, achievement; that they have turned almost everybody into a workaholic – which is worse than an alcoholic, because the alcoholic at least feels that he is doing something wrong. The workaholic feels he is doing the right thing, and those who are not workaholics are lazy people, worthless; they don't even have any right to exist, because they are a burden.

They have destroyed beautiful words, given them new connotations, new meanings. For example, *discipline*. Discipline does not mean what you have heard that it means. The word *discipline* comes from the same root as *disciple*. Its root meaning is: capacity to learn, learning to be more sensitive, to be more aware, to be more sincere, to be more authentic, to be more creative. Life is a beautiful journey if it is a process of constant learning, exploration. Then it is excitement every moment, because every moment you are opening a new door, every moment you are coming in contact with a new mystery.

The word *disciple* means one who learns, and *discipline* means the process of learning. But the word has been prostituted. Discipline means obedience. They have turned the whole world into a camp of boy scouts. High above there is somebody who knows – you need not learn, you have simply to obey. They have turned the meaning of discipline into its very opposite. Learning automatically consists of doubting, of questioning, of being skeptical, of being curious, certainly not of being a believer, because a believer never learns. But they have used the word for thousands of years in this way. And it is not only one word that they have prostituted; they have prostituted many words. Beautiful words have become so ugly in the hands of the vested interests that you cannot even imagine the original meaning of the word...thousands of years of misuse.

They want everybody to be disciplined the way people are

disciplined in the army. You are ordered; you have to do it without asking why. This is not the way of learning. And even from the very beginning they have imposed stories on the minds of people, that the first sin committed was disobedience. Adam and Eve were expelled from the Garden of Eden because they disobeyed. I have tried in thousands of ways, but I don't see that they have committed any sin or any crime. They were simply exploring. You are in a garden and you start exploring the fruits and flowers and what is edible and what is not edible.

And God is responsible, because he prohibited them from two trees. He indicated the trees: "You should not approach these two trees. One is the tree of wisdom, and the other is the tree of eternal life." Just think, if you were Adam and Eve was not God himself tempting you to go to those two trees? And those two trees were of wisdom and of eternal life. Why should God be against them? If he was really a father, one who loves you, he might have pointed to them, saying, "This is a poisonous tree, don't eat from it" or, "This is the tree of death; if you eat anything, you will die." But these two trees are perfectly fine – eat as much as you can, because to be wise and to have eternal life is absolutely right.

Every father would wish his children to have wisdom and eternal life. This father seems to be absolutely loveless. Not only loveless, but as the Devil said to Eve, "He has prevented you from these two trees. Do you know the reason? The reason is that if you eat from these two trees you will be equal to him, and he is jealous. He does not want you to become divine. He does not want you to become gods, full of wisdom and eternal life."

I cannot see that the Devil's argument has any flaw in it. It is absolutely right. In fact, he is the first benefactor of humanity. Without him, perhaps there would have been no humanity – no Gautam Buddha, no Kabir, no Christ, no Zarathustra, no Lao Tzu but just buffaloes, donkeys and Yankees, all eating grass, chewing grass contentedly. And God would have been very happy, that his children are very obedient. But this obedience is poison, pure poison. The Devil must be counted as the first revolutionary of the world, and the first man to think in terms of evolution, of wisdom, of eternal life.

And God said – so the priests have been saying, the Jewish rabbis, Christian priests, Mohammedan *maulvis*, ayatollas, they all have been saying for centuries – that it was the original sin. Again, another prostitution of a beautiful word: the word *sin* in its roots means forgetfulness. It has nothing to do with sin as we have come to understand it. To forget yourself is the only sin. And to remember yourself is the only virtue. It has nothing to do with obedience, nothing to do with discipline. But the people who want to exploit – their very effort is that of a parasite, taking every drop of blood out of you – they say, "Work. Work hard, be disciplined, obey the orders; there is no need to question because the orders are coming from a higher intelligence than you have." They are in such a mind that they don't even want you to sleep.

In the Soviet Union, they are now developing a whole educational system. Every child will be educated during the day in school – but why waste his whole night? People, after a while – twenty-five years – have to come out of the university and work in the world. But they work only five hours, six hours, and their whole night is sheer wastage; it can be used. Now they are developing methods and means to use it.

For example, it can be used for teaching. The child's ears are plugged with a very subtle mechanism controlled by a central system in the town, and what they call subliminal education... It does not disturb your sleep. Very slowly, so quietly that it cannot even be called whispering, because even whispering may disturb your sleep... Its range is lower than a whisper. And the strangest thing is – which was known long before about women, but it was not known that it could be used in such a way...

It has been known for centuries about women, that if you want them to hear what you are saying, then whisper. If you just start whispering with someone, any woman around is going to hear exactly what you are saying. If you are talking loudly, nobody cares. Whispering means that you are trying to hide, something is secretive. The woman becomes alert with her more sensitive being, and she catches everything that you are saying. So if you want to say anything to any woman, just whisper it to somebody else and she will get the message absolutely correctly – and no argument!

Subliminal education is a lower range whispering. They have found that it does not disturb sleep; it does not even disturb dreams. Dreams are there; sleep is lower than dreams, and subliminal whispering is lower than sleep – so it simply goes underground. For eight hours continuously in the night you can teach whatever you want to teach, and the most wonderful thing about it is that the child will remember everything – there is no need for him to memorize it, there is no need for him to do homework for it. It has simply entered into his memory system from an underground source. Now they have captured your twenty-four hours. Even freedom to dream may be taken away one day! It is possible that the government could decide for you, what to dream and what not to dream. Dreams could be projected just like projecting pictures on a screen, and you would not be able to tell the difference, whether you are dreaming or the government agency is projecting some idea. Subliminal teaching is really one of the most dangerous things discovered by the psychologists. It has been tried in many countries and found to work immensely well.

For example, you go into a movie, you see advertisements – they work, but they need constant repetition. A certain brand of cigarette... You have to read it in the newspaper, you have to see it on television, you have to hear it on the radio, you have to see it on the street on the billboards, you have to see it in the movie house, it has to be repeated continually. A certain brand, you don't take any note of it. You simply read it and you forget about it, but it is going to make a mark inside you. And when you go to purchase cigarettes, suddenly you will find yourself asking for that brand. But it is a long process. Up to now, advertising has been a lengthy process. With subliminal teaching, it becomes very shortcut and very dangerous.

They have tried in a few movies, experimentally, between two frames. You are watching the movie and you will not be aware that something has happened; you will go on seeing the movie. The story is going on and in just a flash – so short that you will not be able to detect with your eyes that something has passed on the screen –

you feel very thirsty and you need a Coca Cola. You have not read *Coca Cola*, but even though you have not read it, your memory has simply got the idea. And they found that on that night, in that movie house the sales of Coca Cola rose by seventy percent. The people who ask for Coca Cola don't know why they are asking for Coca Cola – they feel thirsty. They are not really *feeling* thirsty, they don't *need* Coca Cola, but a subliminal impact... This is dangerous. It is taking away your freedom. You are not even free to choose, you are simply being ordered, and in such a way that you are not even aware that you have been ordered to purchase Coca Cola.

Political parties are going to use it: "Vote for Ronald Reagan." There is no need to destroy all the walls and write everywhere "Vote for Ronald Reagan" – just subliminal, on television, in the movies.

And in the Soviet Union, the educationalists are thinking that everybody's night can be used for further training, refresher courses. For example, a doctor comes out of the university... But medical science goes on growing, and the doctor is always lagging far behind. He uses medicines which are no longer valid; science has gone farther ahead, has found better medicines. But the doctor has no opportunity to read all that literature – his night can be used. During the day he can look at the patients; at night he can be given the latest information. But that means you have made the man a robot, twenty-four hours a day geared to work, and geared to do whatever kind of work you want. It is not his free will. These people have brought these beautiful words like *discipline*, *work*, *obedience*, to such a distasteful state that it is better for a few days to abandon them completely.

Work is beautiful if it comes out of your love, if it comes out of your creativity. Then work has some spiritual quality. Discipline is good if it comes out of your learning, your disciplehood, your dedication, your devotion, then it is something that is growing in you like a beautiful flame, directing your life in its light. If obedience comes out of trust – not that somebody is more powerful and if you don't listen you will be punished... Even God could not forgive just one act of disobedience. The poor fellows Adam and Eve had eaten one apple!

For five years continuously I lived on apples. My mother used to say, "You should think about it – just one apple and Adam and Eve were turned out of the Garden of Eden. And you are simply living on apples!" For five years I didn't eat anything else.

I said, "That's what I want to see: where to... Now at the most he can drive me *into* the Garden of Eden. There are only two places: the Garden of Eden and the world. There is no other world he can drive me to." Naturally God remained silent: "What to do now? He is committing sin from morning to night, sin upon sin" – because that was my whole food.

God could not forgive a small thing. No, it is not the question that they had committed a great sin. The question is that God's ego is hurt; it is revenge. With great vengeance... It is unbelievable that even now you are suffering because of the sin committed by Adam and Eve. We don't know these people – when they existed, whether they existed or not; we have no part in their act – yet still we are suffering.

Every human child is going to suffer such vengeance? – it doesn't seem to be divine. God seems to be more evil than the Devil. The Devil seems to be friendlier, more understanding. The people who brought these words – *work, discipline, obedience* – are the priests of this God, they represent him. They have destroyed the beauty of simple words.

Obedience can also be of tremendous beauty. But it should come out of your commitment, not out of an order from somebody. It should come out of your heart. You love and you respect and you are dedicated to someone so deeply that your heart always says yes; it has forgotten how to say no. Even if you want to say no, you have forgotten the word. Then, obedience is religious, spiritual.

Osho,

In nine years of being with you, I feel that I have done all I can as far as intelligence goes, to be with you. And yet now I feel in more chaos and confusion, and more ignorant than ever. I even feel on the point of giving up.

Is there something I should be doing? Is there some way to be more intelligent and more wakeful? – because I am sure that I have already missed a thousand times.

It will be great if you can give up. That is the trouble. I have been telling you to give up. From the very beginning – don't start! But you don't listen.

Nine years of great work, hard work, and still you are asking, "Should I bring more intelligence and more work?" And you think you have been missing the train because you are not working hard enough. Just the opposite is the case. You are missing the train because you are working too hard! You are so involved in your work that you don't see that the train has come and passed. By the time you see other passengers getting out on the road you become aware that the train has come and passed.

Simply give up and rest on the platform. So whenever the train comes... What is the need to miss the train? But you cannot rest, you cannot relax, you cannot let go. You have made it a project. You are aggressive, goal oriented, always trying to achieve something.

And here you are with a man who is saying to you that all that you want to achieve is already within you – just relax, because only in relaxation will you realize what is hidden in you. But you are running so fast. You don't stop, you are putting your whole intelligence – nine years... You could have made it the very first day you had come to me. And you can make it right now – because the train is always standing at the platform. It never leaves because there is nowhere to go.

Osho,

Before becoming your sannyasin, I was desperately seeking spiritual truth. Despite what I felt to be many genuine spiritual experiences, I remained discontented and desperate.

After sannyas I began to live with your people, work in your communes and most of all, feel your beauty and peace grow in my heart. In this time, my burning desires for spiritual experience and the fruits of those experiences have been slowly disappearing.

Nowadays I simply enjoy everyday life, and everything that goes with it – a tasty meal, a walk in the countryside, a good laugh with a loved one, and so on.

Beloved Master, am I getting lazy on the way to enlightenment?

Can you please talk on the difference between falling asleep and letting go?

You are doing perfectly well. Just forget all about enlightenment. Enjoy simple things with total intensity. Just a cup of tea can be a deep meditation. If you can enjoy it, the aroma of it, slowly sipping it, the taste of it... Who cares about God?

You don't know that God is continuously feeling jealous of you when he sees you drinking a cup of tea and the poor fellow cannot have it. Instant coffee... These things are not available in the Garden of Eden. And since Adam and Eve left, there is no human company at all – just living with animals, who don't know how to make tea. God is very jealous of you and very repentant that he drove Adam and Eve out of the Garden of Eden, but now nothing can be done about it. The sons and daughters of Adam and Eve are living far more beautifully, far more richly.

Enlightenment happens when you have forgotten all about it.

Don't even look out of the corner of your eye: just in case enlightenment is coming and you will miss it. Forget all about it. You just enjoy your simple life. And everything is so beautiful, why create unnecessary anxiety and anguish for yourself? Strange problems of spirituality... Those things are not something you can do anything about.

If you can make your ordinary life a thing of beauty and art, all that you had always desired will start happening of its own accord.

There is a beautiful story:

There is a temple in this state of Maharashtra. It is a temple of Krishna, and a strange story is connected with the temple because the statue of Krishna – in Maharashtra he is called Bitthal – is standing on a brick. Strange, because nowhere in any temple is any god standing on a brick.

The story is that one beautiful man, enjoying life, every bit in its totality, was so contented and so fulfilled that Krishna decided to appear before him. Ordinarily there are people who are singing and dancing their whole life, "Hare Krishna, Hare Rama" and neither Rama appears nor Krishna appears – nobody appears. And this man was not bothering about Krishna or Rama or anybody. He was simply living his life, but living it the way it should be lived: – with love, with heart, with beauty, with music, with poetry. His life was in itself a blessing, and Krishna had to decide, "This man needs a visit from me."

You see the story: the man was not at all thinking of Krishna, but Krishna, on his own part, felt that this man deserved a visit. He went in the middle of the night, so as not to create any trouble in the whole town. He found the door open and he went in.

The man's mother was very sick, and he was massaging her feet. Krishna came behind him and said, "I am Krishna and I have come to give you an audience, a *darshan*."

The man said, "This is not the right time; I am massaging my mother's feet."

Meanwhile, just by his side there was was a brick; he pushed the brick back – he did not even look back to see who this Krishna is – he pushed the brick and told him to stand on it, and that when he is finished with his work he will see him. But he was so much absorbed in massaging his mother's feet – she was was almost dying – that the whole night passed, and Krishna remained standing there.

He said, "This is a strange stupidity. People are singing their whole life, 'Hare Krishna, Hare Rama' and I never go there. And I have come here and this fool has not even looked back, has not even said to me, 'Sit down' but tells me to stand on the brick!"

And then it was getting light, the sun was rising, and Krishna became afraid, because people would be coming in. The road was just by the side of the house, and the door was open, and if they saw him standing there, soon there would be trouble, great crowds would come. So he disappeared, leaving just a stone statue of himself on the brick.

When the mother went to sleep, the man turned and said, "Who is the fellow who was disturbing me in the night?" And he found just a statue of Krishna.

The whole village gathered – what had happened was a miracle.

He told the whole story. They said, "You are a strange fellow. Krishna himself came, and you are such a fool! You could have at least told him to sit down, offered him something to eat, something to drink. He was a guest."

The man said, "At that time there was nothing by my side except this brick. And whenever I am doing something, I do it with totality. I don't want any interference. If he was so interested in being seen, he can come again, there is no hurry."

That statue remains in the temple of Bitthal, still standing on a brick. But the man was really a great man, not bothering about rewards or anything, absorbed so fully in every action that the action itself becomes the reward. And even if God comes, the reward that is coming out of the totality of action is bigger than God. Nobody has interpreted the story the way I am interpreting it, but you can see that any other interpretation is nonsense.

So just forget about spirituality, enlightenment, God – they will take care of themselves. That is their business. They are sitting there without customers. You need not worry; do the best you can do with life – that is your test, that is your worship, that is your religion. And everything else will follow on its own accord.

Osho,

If the master is the one who chooses the disciple and drops him – though it may appear to the disciple that he has chosen the master, and in the course of time, has dropped him – beloved Osho, why did you have to tell us?

Now I have the feeling and fear that you might drop me at any time. Beloved, please don't do that to me. It hurts very much to think of it because if a man like you cannot help me, then who will? I have always been let down, and it hurts. And to think of you letting me down is too much.

Osho, please promise that you won't let me down, even if I am of no use to you. I know you won't, but still that fear is there. Please be with me always, will you?

It is a tricky question. I can promise I will not drop you. The only problem is that if *you* want to drop *me*, then you will find it very difficult to drop; I won't let you drop! So now this will be your fear: I will fulfill my promise in any case, whether you want it or not. So if this dispels your fear, perfectly good. It is not a problem for me, I can promise.

I just don't want to interfere with anybody's freedom. I want to keep the door open; if you want to go out, I don't want to close it. But if that is what you want, the door is closed and locked! Now don't come next time saying that you are now fearing that if you want to get out, now there is no way. A promise is a promise!

Osho,

My beautiful master, first I wanted to run away; now I never want to leave you. What happened?

I changed my mind.

19 The Future Belongs to the Creative Man

Osho,
I am a two-year-old child in sannyas at the age of sixty!
I consider myself blessed to have come into the fold of your grace.
Was this destined to be so? Then why was it so late in life? Can the child in me become mature in what remains of my life? How? Kindly help.

The question you have asked has many implications. It is many questions in one.

First, you say that at the age of sixty you are a two-year-old child as far as sannyas is concerned. This reminds me of an ancient tradition in the East. We used to count life from the day a man was initiated into sannyas, not from the day he was born. Because birth does not necessarily turn into life, more often it only turns into vegetation.

There are cabbages and there are cauliflowers, but the difference is not much. The experts say that cauliflowers are cabbages with university degrees. But most people simply vegetate; they do not live, they do not come into contact with the living waters of life. They breathe, they grow old, but they never grow up. Between their birth and their death is a horizontal line. There are no peaks of delight, no sunlit peaks of ecstasy. There are no depths of love, of peace, of silence. There is just a horizontal, flat routine from the cradle to the grave; nothing happens. They come and they go.

It is said that most people realize that they were alive only when they die – because life was so flat, so colorless. It was not a dance, it was not beauty, it was not a blessing; there was no gratitude in the heart: "Existence has chosen me, and not anybody else in my place, that without me existence will be a little less. There is nobody else who can replace me; I am occupying a unique position and I never asked for it, I never deserved it. It is a sheer gift out of the abundance of existence."

It happened that Gautam Buddha was having a meeting with one of the most intelligent emperors of those days. Just in the middle of their dialogue an old sannyasin – must have been seventy-five years old – came to touch the feet of Buddha. He asked the emperor to forgive him because he was interfering in their conversation, but it was out of necessity. No Buddhist monk can travel in the night; they can move between sunrise and sunset, but at night they have to remain in one place.

"I have been ordered to go to the nearest village, and I cannot go without touching the feet of my master. The sun is going down every moment, and your dialogue seems to go on and on – so please just forgive me."

Gautam Buddha asked the sannyasin, "How old are you?"

The emperor was very much puzzled; what was the need? – just bless him and let him go.

And the old sannyasin said, "Forgive me, I have come very late. My age is only four years."

The emperor was even more puzzled, and he could not contain himself. He said, "This is too much! This man might be seventy-five, might be eighty, might be seventy, but not four years of age. Absolutely not!"

Gautam Buddha said, "Perhaps you do not know about the way we count age. This man became a sannyasin four years ago. Hence, the real brahmin, the one who has known the divine, the *brahma* is called *dwij*, twice born. The first birth is only an opportunity for the second birth. If the second birth does not happen your first birth is meaningless.

And to the sannyasin Buddha said, "Don't be worried. We have an ancient proverb." He quoted it: "The man who gets lost in the morning, if he comes back home by the evening he should not be called lost. Four years are plenty. Even one minute of awareness is equal to eternity."

So the first thing: don't be worried about the fifty-eight years that have passed in sleep. Whether they existed or not does not matter; they were like signatures made on water – you go on making them, and they go on disappearing.

These two years you have been a sannyasin are immensely significant. And the significance does not require time, it requires depth. You can have the whole eternity superficially. And you can have one single moment of abysmal depth or of the height of Everest and you are fulfilled.

So the first thing I want to say to you: don't be worried about the fifty-eight years that were lost wandering in the desert. Be grateful for the two years that you have entered into the garden of existence. Now it is up to you to make each moment a deep contentment, a profound silence, a joyful dance, an eternity of rejoicing, a fragrance that is not of this world, that is not of time and space but belongs to the beyond.

And as I see it, you are growing on the right path with a sincere heart. I have been listening to your songs; they have a sweet pain, a heartfelt thankfulness, sweet because nothing can be sweeter than to come in contact with the immortal, timeless, deathless source of life.

To be in touch with a master is, in an indirect way, to be in touch with the godliness of existence.

There is sweetness in your songs, and there is a certain pain too. Pain because whatever you want to express, words are impotent to express it. What you want to sing, your heart is overflowing with it, but the language is not capable of translating it.

Your musical instruments, howsoever refined, are not able to bring the music of silence into the world of sound. They are two diametrically opposite dimensions. But your pain does not destroy the beauty of your sweetness; it makes it even more beautiful, gives it depth. It shows your experience and, at the same time, the inability to express it. That which can be expressed is mundane. That which cannot be expressed is sacred.

And every artist: musician or poet, painter or dancer, all have been trying in different ways for millions of years to give expression to the inexpressible – even if they can give an indirect hint, just a finger pointing to the moon, that is success enough. And you are successful.

Sing without any hesitation, without being worried that you will be thought crazy. Unless a singer is thought by the world to be insane, he is not a singer at all; if a dancer is not forced into a madhouse, the world has not given him the certificate. All geniuses are bound to be thought of in this way by the world: "Something has gone wrong with these poor people."

Vincent Van Gogh, one of the Dutch painters, could not sell a single painting in his whole life. Now only two hundred paintings have survived out of thousands that he painted, because nobody took care of them. He was simply distributing them to friends; nobody would purchase them. People were afraid even to hang his paintings in their sitting rooms because whoever saw them would think that they were crazy: what kind of painting are you hanging here? People were taking them – not to hurt him – thanking him, and throwing his paintings into their basements so nobody would see them.

Now each of his paintings is worth a million dollars. What happened in one hundred years?

The man himself was forced into a mad asylum when he was only thirty-two. And he was forced because of his painting; he was not harmful, he was not violent, he was not doing anything to anybody. But anybody who looked at his paintings was absolutely certain that this man was mad and unreliable. He should be put in a madhouse. If he could paint these things, he might do *anything*."

For example, he always painted stars as spirals. Even other painters told him, "Stars are not spirals!"

He said, "I also see the stars. I see that they are not spirals, but the moment I start painting them something in me says so strongly that they *are* spirals. The distance is so vast; that's why your eyes cannot see exactly what their shape is. And the voice is so strong. I am simply unable to do anything else but what my inner being says to do."

And now physicists have discovered that stars *are* spirals. It has gone like a shock throughout the world of painters, that only one painter in the whole history of man had some inner contact and communication with the stars – and that was a man who was thought to be mad. And because he was thought to be mad, nobody was ready to give him any service. Every week, his brother used to give him enough money to last for seven days. And he was fasting three days in a week and eating four days, because that was the only way to purchase canvas and colors and brushes to paint with. Painting was more important than life.

He committed suicide at the age of thirty-three. Just after his release from the madhouse, he painted only one painting, which they had prevented him from painting in the madhouse. He wanted to paint the sun. It took him one year. He lost his eyes... The burning sun, the hot sun, and the whole day long he would be watching all the colors, from the morning till the evening, from the sunrise to the sunset. He wanted the painting to contain everything about the sun, the whole biography of the sun.

Everybody who was sympathetic to him told him, "This is too much. Just studying it one day is enough; it is the same sun."

Van Gogh said, "You don't know. It is never the same. You have never looked at it. I have never seen the same sunrise twice, never seen the same sunset again. And I want my painting to be a biography."

One year, the whole day watching the sun. He lost his eyes, but he painted. And when the painting was complete, he wrote a small letter to his brother: "I am not committing suicide out of any despair – because I am one of the most successful men in the world. I have done whatever I wanted to do in spite of the whole world condemning me. And this was my last wish, to paint the whole biography of the sun in one painting. It is completed today. I am immensely joyful, and now there is no need to live. I was living to paint; painting was my life, not breathing." And he shot himself dead.

You cannot categorize him with ordinary suicides. It is not a suicide out of despair, out of sadness, out of failure – no. Out of immense success, out of total fulfillment; seeing that now, why unnecessarily go on living and waiting for death? "I have done the work that I wanted to do."

Every creative artist has to understand this: the moment people start thinking about him that he is a little bit off center, that something is loose in his head, he should rejoice that he has crossed the boundary of the mundane and the mediocre. Now he has grown the wings which others don't have. And I can see in you the possibility, the potential. Meditate, and let music become your meditation. Sing and let singing become your life, your very breathing, your very heartbeat.

A very stupid idea has prevailed in the world, that only saints are religious. In fact, almost 99.9 percent of saints are not religious. The real religious people will be found in creative dimensions – dancers, poets, painters, singers, musicians, sculptors. The future belongs to the creative man.

The past belonged to the uncreative saints. They have not created anything; their only quality was self-torture. They were really all masochists. In a better world they would have been treated, not worshipped. They were not saints, they were psychologically sick. But because the uncreative was on the heights, was dominant, creative people suffered very much. They were thought to be sick. The future is going to be totally different. Now nobody can be a saint just because he is capable of torturing himself. He may be good in a circus...

There is a beautiful story by Turgenev:

In a circus there was a man whose sole qualification was that he could fast continuously for forty days, fifty days – and that was the longest time the circus would remain in one town. So for the whole time the circus was in the town, he would be on a fast. Doctors were checking, people were watching, but he would not eat.

The circus moved from one town to another town, and then it came to the capital, where it remained longer than forty days. And what is there in a man who is fasting? You can go to see him one time – after that there is nothing intriguing, nothing interesting about it. So after a few days people forgot all about him. There were many stalls, but because nobody was coming to visit his stall, it was placed at the end. Finally, people completely forgot about him. Even the circus management forgot about him, because there was no need. And after forty days, he continued his fasting, because he had forgotten to count the days. He knew only that when the circus moved from one town to another town, on the way they would give him food.

He was dying. And then somebody remembered: what happened to the great fasting man? The manager rushed. The man was almost dead; it had been ninety days. Ninety days is the limit for how long a man can fast if he is healthy.

They asked him, "Are you mad or something? After forty days you should have reported, you should have called somebody."

He said, "There were two reasons: one, I have never counted the days; second, I slowly became aware that the time seemed to be longer this time, but fasting has become a habit. Now, eating is troublesome. So whenever you change towns, it is very hard for me. Forty days I am hungry. For seven days while you are changing towns, for me to put the whole mechanism back into eating and digesting is such a torture. I felt relieved that the time had become longer."

And with hunger there are a few points to remember. If you fast, you will feel hunger for only three days. After the third day, hunger will start disappearing because the body has an emergency arrangement; for three days it waits for food, it cannot wait longer. After the third day it starts eating itself. That's why you start losing weight. Have you ever wondered where that weight disappears to? Fasting is a kind of cannibalism: eating yourself. The worst kind of cannibalism – eating somebody else one can understand, but eating yourself…

But these were your saints. Their qualities were all in the service of death, not in the service of life. I want my sannyasins to be saints with a new quality: the quality that serves life, the quality that nourishes life, affirms life, that makes life a little more beautiful, brings a few more flowers to it.

Meditation in the past has been life negative: renounce life and everything that makes life worth living. To me, meditation is just the opposite of what it has been up to now. Meditation is a silent heart, a peaceful mind which can make life more lovable, more livable, which can make life richer in every dimension.

I don't want you to renounce anything. I want you to rejoice in everything, whatever you are doing. You are a musician. Let music be your meditation. This is your religion – not Mohammedanism, not Hinduism, not Christianity. Music is your religion. If you are a dancer, then dancing is your religion.

Osho,

Why does everyone want to pretend to be what they are not? What is the psychology behind it?

Everybody is condemned from his very childhood. Whatever he does on his own accord, out of his own liking, is not acceptable. The people, the crowd in which a child has to grow, has its own ideas, ideals. The child has to fit with those ideas and ideals. The child is helpless. Have you ever thought about it? The human child is the most helpless child in the whole animal kingdom. All the animals can survive without the support of the parents and the crowd, but the human child cannot survive, he will die immediately. He is the most helpless creature in the world, so vulnerable to death, so delicate.

Naturally those who are in power are able to mold the child in the way they want. So everybody has become what he is, against himself. That is the psychology behind the fact that everybody wants to pretend to be what he is not. Everybody is in a schizophrenic state. He has never been allowed to be himself; he has been forced to be somebody else that his nature does not allow him to be happy with.

So as one grows and stands on his own legs, one starts pretending many things, which he would have liked in reality to be part of his being. But in this insane world, he has been distracted. He has been made into somebody else; he is not that. He knows it. Everybody knows it: that he has been forced to become a doctor, to become an engineer; he has been forced to become a politician, to become a criminal, to become a beggar.

There are all kinds of forces around. In Mumbai there are people whose whole business is to steal children and make them crippled, blind, lame, and force them to beg, and each evening to bring all the money that they have gathered. Yes, food will be given to them, shelter will be given to them. They are being used like commodities; they are not human beings. This is an extreme example, but the same has happened with everybody to a lesser or greater extent. Nobody is at ease with himself.

I have heard about a great surgeon who was retiring. He was very famous. He had many students and many colleagues. They all gathered, and they were dancing and singing and drinking, but he was sad, standing in a dark corner. One friend came up to him and asked, "What is the matter with you? We are celebrating and you are standing here so sad. Don't you want to retire? You are seventy-five; you should have retired fifteen years ago. But because you are such a great surgeon, even at seventy-five nobody can compete with you, nobody comes even close to you. Now, retire and relax!"

He said, "That's what I was thinking. I am feeling sad because my parents forced me to become a surgeon. I wanted to be a singer, and I would have loved it. Even if I was just a street singer, at least I would have been myself. Now I am a world-famous surgeon, but I am not myself. When people praise me as a surgeon, I listen as if they are praising somebody else. I have been given awards, doctorates, but nothing rings a bell of joy in my heart – because this is not me. This being a surgeon has killed me, destroyed me. I wanted to be just a flute player, even if I had to be a beggar on the streets. But I would have been happy."

In this world, there is only one happiness and that is to be yourself. And because nobody is himself, everybody is trying somehow to hide: masks, pretensions, hypocrisies. They are ashamed of what they are.

We have made the world a marketplace, not a beautiful garden where everybody is allowed to bring his own flowers. We are forcing marigolds to bring roses. Now from where can marigolds bring roses? Those roses will be plastic roses, and in its heart of hearts the marigold will be crying, and with tears feeling ashamed that: "We have not been courageous enough to rebel against the crowd. They have forced plastic flowers on us, and we have our own real flowers for which our juices are flowing, but we cannot show our real flowers."

You are being taught everything, but you are not being taught to be yourself. This is the ugliest form of society possible, because it makes everybody miserable.

I have heard of another great man, a great professor of literature who was being retired from the university. All the university professors had gathered, all his friends had gathered, and they were rejoicing. But suddenly they became aware that he was missing. One of his friends, an attorney, went out... Perhaps he in was the garden. But what was he doing there? He was sitting under a tree.

The attorney was his closest friend, a boyhood friend. The attorney said, "What are you doing here?"

He said, "What am I doing here? Remember fifty years ago? I had come to tell you that I wanted to kill my wife. And you said, 'Don't do any such thing, otherwise: fifty years in jail.' I am thinking that if I had not listened to you, today I would have been out of jail, free." He said, "I am feeling so angry that a desire comes to me: why should I not at least kill *you*! Now I am seventy-five. Even if they put me in jail for fifty years they cannot keep me there for fifty years. Within five, seven years I will be dead. But you were not a friend; you proved to be my greatest enemy."

To be what you don't want to be, to be with someone you don't want to be with, to do something you don't want to do is the basis of all your miseries. And on the one hand society has managed to make everybody miserable, and on the other hand the same society expects that you should not show your misery – at least not in public, not in the open. It is your private business. They have created it; it really is public business, not private business. The same crowd that has created all the reasons for your misery finally says to you, "Your misery is your own, but when you come out, come out smiling. Don't show your miserable face to others." This they call etiquette, manners, culture. Basically, it is hypocrisy.

And unless a person decides that: "Whatever the cost, I want just to be myself. Condemned, unaccepted, losing respectability, everything is okay but I cannot pretend anymore to be somebody else." This decision and this declaration – this declaration of freedom, freedom from the weight of the crowd – gives birth to your natural being, to your individuality. Then you don't need any mask. Then you can be simply yourself, just as you are.

And the moment you can be just as you are, there is tremendous peace that passeth understanding.

Osho,

Could you please explain the difference between trusting existence and fatalism?

The difference between trust and fate is very subtle. On the surface it seems they mean exactly the same thing, but in reality they are diametrically opposite experiences.

Fate is a consolation. You are poor, and you see others getting richer and richer – some consolation is needed. You do everything and you do it honestly, truthfully, morally. You never use wrong means; still you are a failure. And you see others being dishonest, cunning, insincere, immoral, criminal, using all kinds of wrong means and succeeding, becoming richer, attaining power, prestige. How to explain it? It is not new. Since the very beginning man has been puzzled by it. And he had to create some idea as a consolation. Fate, kismet, destiny, God – everything is written in the lines of your hand, in the lines of your forehead; everything is predetermined in your birth chart, you cannot do anything against it. The forces that have determined your life are too big. You are going to fail; it is better to accept your failure as destiny. It hurts less to say it is fate; it gives consolation. It is not your doing, it is not your failure – what can you do against the stars? You cannot determine your birth time and the day and the year.

You come into the world just like an actor comes onto the stage fully prepared. He cannot change anything. But once in a while actors *can* change things, because a drama is a drama.

I have heard that in a village... All over India, every year at this time every village is playing the drama of the life of Rama, the Hindu god. And in the beginning it is just like any film story: a triangle – two lovers, one woman. Sita is the woman, and Rama and Ravana are the two lovers. Rama is a young man. Ravana is very strong.

In those days, the daughters of kings had the right to choose any device for selecting their husbands. Sita had asked...because in their family they had the bow that had belonged to the god, Shiva. It was such a big strong bow that even to pick it up needed a great wrestler; it was not easy for one person to raise it. As a device, Sita chose that anybody who could raise the bow, and not only raise it but break it with his hands alone – it was a steel bow – that man she would choose as her husband.

Hundreds of kings, great wrestlers, archers... Rama was also present there. But nobody thought he would be of any use; he was too young. Everybody was worried that Ravana – who was a huge, dangerous man, had ten heads – was going to win. And everybody was worried – Sita's father was worried, everybody concerned was worried – that Sita would fall into the hands of this idiot. Somehow she had to be saved.

So just as the others were coming forward – and they could not even move the bow, raising it was out of question; they were becoming laughingstocks... Before Ravana stood up, a man came running... It was a device to send Ravana back to his kingdom. He was the king of Sri Lanka. And the man said, "What are you doing here? Sri Lanka is on fire. Your whole kingdom is burning."

Ravana forgot all about getting married to Sita. He rushed off to see what was happening in the kingdom first. It was a false strategy; there was no problem, Sri Lanka was perfectly okay. But by the time he came back, Rama had broken the bow, married Sita, and gone.

This was a conspiracy, and Ravana could not forgive it. He was continually in search of Sita, to steal her. Finally he stole her, and for three years he kept her imprisoned. That's how the whole story goes. In every village it is enacted every year.

In this particular village, the man who played the part of Ravana was really in love with the girl who was playing the part of Sita. But they belonged to different castes; marriage was not possible.

Every year it was happening: the moment this man would stand up, the other man would come out shouting: "Sri Lanka is on fire!"

This time he was determined – because outside the drama they wouldn't allow the marriage. They were not of the same caste and in India you cannot marry in another caste. And the man who played Ravana was in a lower caste; the girl was a brahmin. This time he thought, something has to be done.

The man came running and he said, "Sri Lanka is on fire!"

Ravana said, "Let it be. This year I am not coming!" Everybody laughed; nobody could believe it.

The prompter was behind the curtain: "What are you saying?"

And he said, "This year I am going to marry Sita!" And he went up... And it was just an ordinary bow, everybody had just pretended that it was so heavy that nobody could pick it up; it was just ordinary bamboo. He took it up, showed it to the audience, broke it, threw the pieces into the audience and told Sita's father, "Bring your daughter! Enough is enough, and the story is finished!"

Even people who had fallen asleep woke up – "What is happening? Something new!" The director didn't know what to do. For a moment there was silence.

And Ravana was shouting, "Where is Sita? Now fulfill the promise!"

And nobody could say to him, "You are not following the part that has been given to you" – because that would not be right to say in front of the public.

But the king, Sita's father, was a very wise man. He said to his servants, "You idiots, this is not Shiva's bow; this is the bow my children play with. Take it away. Bring the real bow."

So the servants took away the broken parts. The curtain was pulled down, and they all jumped on Ravana and said, "You idiot, you are going to destroy the whole story."

He said, "This time I am determined."

So the police had to be called, and Ravana was sent to the police station: "Take him, because he is destroying our whole drama."

In a drama it is possible that you can change things. But in life you don't know exactly what is written in your fate, so whatever happens has to be accepted: "This must be written in my fate." The belief in fate is simply a consolation because we cannot accept our failure as failure. And we cannot accept our failure for another reason – because it has implications for all our moral values: "We were honest, we were moral, we followed right means, we were truthful, and yet we failed; and the other person was dishonest, cunning, insincere, immoral, criminal, and yet he succeeded."

Now, the whole moral system teaches that truth is going to win, that morality is going to win, that honesty is going to win. But in life we see that all the honest people are losing and immoral people are gaining. The cunning, the clever become powerful. The simple and the innocent are crushed. Our whole value system is at stake. So it was necessary for the priests and the prophets to find a way in which your failure would not be your failure. "You cannot do anything, it is written in your fate. Your failure is not the failure of your sincerity, morality, honesty. And the other person's success is not the success of wrong means, dishonesty, cunningness; it is his fate. And as far as fate is concerned, nothing can change it – neither honesty nor dishonesty. Yes, because you have been honest you will have a better fate in your future life. Because he has been dishonest, he will have a bitter fate in his future life."

So this was a beautiful consolation, and a beautiful, rational defense for our moral system. But it is all bogus. The truth is the man has succeeded because of dishonesty, not because of his fate. He has succeeded because of his immorality; he has succeeded because he does not care what kind of means he is using.

Existence gives you birth as a *tabula rasa*. No fate is written; there is no destiny such that whatever you do, it has to happen. Existence is freedom. Fate is slavery. Freedom means it is up to you to decide what is going to happen. Fate is a bogus hypothesis.

But trust is a totally different thing. Trust is not fate. Trust simply means that: "Whatever happens, I am part of existence and existence cannot be intentionally inimical to me. If sometimes it feels that it is, it must be my misunderstanding."

I have always loved to remember a Sufi master, Junnaid. He was the master of al-Hillaj Mansoor. He had a habit: after each prayer – and Mohammedans pray five times a day – after each prayer he would say to the sky, "Your compassion is great. How beautifully you take care of us, and we don't deserve it. I don't even have words to show my gratefulness, but I hope you will understand the unexpressed gratitude of my heart."

They were on a pilgrimage, and it happened that for three days they passed through villages where orthodox Mohammedans would not allow them even to stay in the villages; there was no question of giving them food or water. For three days without food, without water, without sleep, tired, utterly frustrated... The disciples could not believe that this man Junnaid, their master, still goes on saying the same things. Before, it was okay – but *still* he goes on saying, "You are great, you are compassionate, and I don't have words to express my gratitude."

On the third evening when he had finished his prayer, his disciples said, "Now it is time for an explanation. For three days we have been hungry, we have not had water, we are thirsty; we have not slept, we have been insulted continually, no place has been given to us, no shelter. At least today you should not say, 'You are great, you are compassionate.' For what are you showing your gratitude?"

Junnaid laughed. He said, "My trust in existence is unconditional. It is not that I am grateful because existence provides this and that and that. I am – that's enough. Existence accepts me – that's enough. And I don't deserve to be; I have not earned it. Moreover, these three days have been of tremendous beauty because I had an opportunity to watch whether anger would arise in me, and it didn't arise; whether I would start to feel that God had forsaken me, and the idea did not arise. There has been no difference in my attitude towards existence. My gratitude has not changed, and it has filled me with more gratitude than ever. It was a fire test, and I have come out of it unburned. What more do you want? I will trust existence in my life and I will trust existence in my death. It is my love affair.

"It is not a question that somebody is rich and somebody is poor, that somebody is successful and somebody is not. It has nothing to do with anybody. It is my personal, intimate contact with reality. And there is great harmony. I am completely at ease and at home."

Trust is the outcome of deep meditation. Fate is the outcome of your failures, and a mind consolation. They are totally different.

Osho,

Why do I like so much to criticize people and complain against life?

Everybody likes it. To criticize people, to complain against people, gives you a good feeling. Criticizing others, you feel you are higher; complaining about others, you feel you are better. It is very ego fulfilling. And I am saying almost everybody does it. A few people do it out loud, a few people do it just within themselves, but the enjoyment is the same.

Only rarely are there people who don't criticize, who don't complain; those are the people who have dropped their egos. Then there is no point, why should you bother about it? It is none of your business; it no longer pays you. The ego was helped, nourished.

Hence my emphasis is: drop the ego. With the dropping of the ego, you will find almost a whole world disappearing. The whole world that was knit around the ego falls away completely, and you start seeing people in a new light. Perhaps the same person that you might have criticized in the same situation, instead of criticizing him you feel a great compassion for him, a great love, a deep desire to help. The same person and the same situation you would have complained against, now your eyes are different and you see things differently, perhaps you will see that in his place in this situation you would have behaved in the same way; there is nothing to complain about.

Your outlook will become more human, more friendly: a deep acceptance of people as they are.

You know only some part of them; you don't know their whole

life. And it is not good to decide from a small fragment about the whole person. That small fragment may be absolutely fitting and right in the whole context. But the situation is this: it is very easy to criticize. It does not need much intelligence.

I have often told a story of Turgenev's, *The Fool*. In a village, a young man is very disturbed because the whole village thinks he is an idiot. A wise man is passing through the village and the young man goes to him and says, "Help me! For twenty-four hours a day I am criticized; whatever I do I am criticized. If I don't do anything I am criticized. If I speak I am criticized, if I don't speak I am criticized. I don't know any way out."

The wise man said, "Don't be worried." He whispered the secret in his ear, and told him, "After one month I will come back. Meet me then and tell me how things are going."

The young man went to the marketplace and started working on the formula given by the wise man.

Somebody said, "What a beautiful sunset!"

And he said, "What is beautiful in it? Prove what is beautiful in it!"

The man who had said it was a beautiful sunset was shocked. It *was* a beautiful sunset, but what was the proof? Is there any evidence? Do you know what beauty is? Everybody knows, but nobody can prove it.

The man remained silent. Everybody started laughing.

And everybody said, "Strange, we used to think this man was an idiot. He is a great intellectual."

This was the formula given by the old man: criticize everything, just roam about the village watching and when anybody says anything, does anything, criticize it. And particularly criticize things which are taken for granted and nobody questions. Somebody uses the word *God* – immediately catch hold of him: "Where is God? What nonsense are you talking about?" Somebody talks about love – catch hold of him: "What is love? Where is love? Put it here in front of everybody!"

Somebody would say, "Love is in the heart."

And he would say, "No, there is nothing in the heart. You can go and ask any surgeon – in the heart there is nothing like love. There is only a blood-circulating system, which just pumps blood and purifies it. What does it have to do with love?"

After one month the old man came back. By that time the idiot had become a wise man. He touched the old man's feet and he said, "You are great! That trick worked; now the whole village thinks I am a wise man."

The old man said, "Just remember one thing: don't assert anything from your side, so nobody can criticize *you*. Let *them* assert things; you just criticize and complain. And always be aggressive; never be defensive. Don't take a defensive attitude. Attack, be aggressive, criticize each and everybody, and they will all worship you."

And the idiot became the wise man.

It does not need much intelligence to criticize or to complain. And cheaply you become wise; cheaply you become very intelligent.

One of my professors... He used to teach me logic. Within a few days I found out that even if I mentioned the name of a book which did not exist, a fictitious writer, he would immediately criticize it: "I have read that book, and there is nothing in it."

I went to the vice-chancellor and I told him the whole thing. I said, "This is sheer dishonesty, because first he criticized those who have *really* written books. And seeing his attitude – that he criticizes everybody, I suspected that he had not read them, but was just trying to show that he is so well-read, so wise, so intelligent. So I tried a few fictitious names and he criticized them also. He said: 'There is nothing in those books. Those writers know nothing.'" And I said, "Those writers don't exist. Those books don't exist!"

The vice-chancellor said, "This is strange. I used to think that man was a responsible man."

I said, "Call him in sometime, and I will drop in casually, by the way." I wrote down three or four names of books which don't exist, have never existed and will never exist, with writers who are just fictitious. I gave those names to the vice-chancellor and I told him, "I will come when he is here and we will talk, and just by the way you bring up these names and see what his reaction is."

And he brought up those names and the professor immediately said, "Don't waste time. Those are all ordinary, mediocre writers, and the books they have written have nothing original in them."

The vice-chancellor could not believe his eyes. He said, "Do you know that these four books do not exist at all? Neither have these four men ever existed. Why are you criticizing them?"

And before the vice-chancellor, he became afraid. He said, "Never existed? How did I get the idea that..."

I said, "Don't try to befool anybody, because I have been asking you about other books which have not existed. This was only proof. I wanted to show the vice-chancellor that a professor should at least be sincere enough to acknowledge that he has not read a particular book."

I said to the vice-chancellor, "What kind of respect does this man want from us? My feeling is that he has not read anything; he has simply read Turgenev's story, *The Fool*."

I had brought the book, and I read the story to the vice-chancellor. And I said, "This man is the idiot from this story. You should make him alert that if it happens again in the class, we are going to boycott him completely. Either he will have to find the book and prove...he never even goes to the library!"

I had looked into all the records before I went to the vice-chancellor. The professor had never been to the library. Under his name – and he had been in the university for ten years – not a single book was issued. And this man was ready to criticize anybody.

I said, "A wise man, an intelligent man is always humble."

Your question about why we are so ready to criticize, to complain is very simple. The psychology behind it is that this is the simplest way, the cheapest way to prove that you are somebody special, that you know more. But in fact you are simply proving that you are the idiot of Turgenev and nobody else.

Be humble in the world of wisdom. Before criticizing anybody, look into the fact from all directions, from all angles, from all possible viewpoints, and you will be surprised: there is very little that can be criticized or complained about. And if you pay that much attention, then whatever you criticize will be accepted, and accepted with gratitude because it is not to fulfill your ego; it is just to help the other person on the path. But you have to do so much work.

One of my professors had written his doctoral thesis on Shankara and Bradley. I told him, "I have read the thesis, and now I am studying everything possible about Shankara and Bradley before I say anything about your thesis."

He said, "You are strange, because I have given my thesis to many professors and they have all given their opinions."

I said, "I cannot give you my opinion in such a cheap way. I will look at all the sources you have looked into; I will look into other sources that you have not looked into." And it took me almost six months to study Shankara and Bradley.

When I gave my opinion to him he said, "My God, it is good that you were not one of my examiners; otherwise, I would never have been able to get the doctorate. I worked on it for six years, and in six months you have gone through all the sources that I have referred to. You have even gone to other sources which I have not even heard of."

I said, "Your treatise is juvenile, it is written by an amateur. Shankara and Bradley are very mature philosophers of the East and West. You have not paid enough respect to these two geniuses. You have done a clerical job. You have looked at a few books of Shankara, a few books of Bradley, taken a few pieces from here, from there, and your thesis was ready. Your thesis does not contribute a single original point. And unless a thesis contributes an original point, it does not deserve a doctorate; it is at the most a beautiful essay. You can publish it as a book, but not for a doctorate."

But he was a humble man; he accepted it. He said, "You are right. I myself was feeling that I had not done them justice. Six years were not enough to cover Bradley's whole life and Shankara's whole life. These two are the very highest peaks of genius; six years are not enough. But nobody pointed it out to me, not even my examiners. The examiners will not point it out because to do that they would have had to read it, they would have had to go through the whole thing. Who bothers? In fact, perhaps some of their students gave me the marks and the examiners have not even looked at the thesis."

Nobody is interested in praising anybody, in finding those qualities which everybody has. Nobody is ready to help those qualities grow. Everybody is afraid: if all are growing, what about him? His whole concern is that his ego should go on becoming bigger, and the easier way is to criticize everybody, to complain against everything: be negative, make negativity your very approach. And for this you don't need intelligence; any idiot can do it. But to be really critical, one has to be very compassionate, very loving. And one has to be ready to devote time and energy and intelligence. Then it is not criticism, then it is not inimical, it is not antagonistic; it is a friendly suggestion, a sympathetic approach.

Everyone here should learn to be sympathetic. Your meditation should help you not to criticize but to appreciate. And if you are intelligent enough, you can appreciate in such a way that whatever you wanted to criticize will be understood without being said.

Osho,

The buddha in me condemns the zorba, and the zorba envies the buddha. How can these two beloveds within me become friends?

Just let them fight one day more. Tomorrow we will settle it!

20 Let Go: The Cure for the Disease of Becoming

I first have to reply to the question that I received before. The question was important. I never postpone a question because one never knows what is going to happen tomorrow. I may be here to answer it or not. You may be here to listen to it or not. But I had to postpone, because the question was important, and the time was already 9:30. I never want to do an imperfect job, so I took the risk. I hoped for the best – that tomorrow we would be meeting – and by chance it has come true.

The questioner said that the buddha and the zorba are in constant conflict within his personality.

My whole philosophy is to bring a harmonious unity between the zorba and the buddha within every human being. But the questioner is asking only from the mind. In reality, in actual experience, zorba and buddha can never be in conflict. This has to be underlined – because in reality the zorba is completely asleep; he does not know anything about the buddha, and you cannot fight with something you know nothing about. The zorba is not even suspicious that there is anything more in life than to eat, drink and be merry. That is his whole philosophy of life, there is nothing beyond it. How can he be in conflict with the buddha? Both have to be present simultaneously to be in conflict. This is very simple arithmetic.

If the buddha has arisen in you, if that awakening has happened in you, zorba disappears. It is just like you were asleep, and now you are awake. When you are awake, sleep is no more. Zorba is the name of your spiritual sleep. They cannot co-exist. The moment you are conscious, alert, aware, the darkness of the unconscious disappears. Either there is zorba, and buddha is dormant... Buddha is just a seed as far as zorba is concerned, it is non-existential. When buddha has blossomed, zorba disappears, just as darkness disappears when you bring the light in. You cannot have light and darkness together.

I have always loved an ancient story...

God made the world, and from that very day the sun went running after darkness. And darkness could not understand: it has not harmed the sun, it has not even talked with the sun; it has not even met the sun, yet the sun is continuously harassing her.

After millions of years of harassment, she finally got tired and went to God and said, "It is ungrateful to complain, but there is a limit to everything. I have been harassed for millions of years, and I cannot conceive of any fault on my part. The sun goes on expelling me from everywhere. It is even difficult to take a rest without anxiety – the sun may be coming, the sunrise may be close. I have not slept for millions of years – the anguish would not allow it. The sun has been almost a continuous torture, and without any reason. I simply want to know: what have I done wrong?"

God said, "You should have come earlier. There was no need to wait so long. This is very ungentlemanly on the part of the sun. The sun should be called immediately."

The sun was called. He asked the messenger, "What is the problem? – because I have never done anything wrong. I simply go on doing the same routine every day. Since God made me, I have not done anything else."

But the messenger said, "God is very angry. You have been hurting, harassing a poor woman – darkness."

He said, "My God! I have never heard of her. I have never met her. I am not interested in women at all – I am a born celibate. I am coming, I want to see who this woman is."

And as the sun came to the house of God, darkness disappeared.

God said, "Where has that woman gone?" They searched everywhere; darkness was not found.

Millions of years passed again, and one day the woman appeared and she said, "You have not done anything; it is still continuing, the same torture."

God said, "You are strange. When the sun was here, where did you go?"

She said, "You are behaving like a simpleton. If the sun is here, I cannot be here; if I am here, the sun cannot be here. We cannot stand each other. You will have to hear our story separately and then decide."

God said, "That is not my way. You both have to be present here so I can be certain that nobody is lying."

The woman said, "Then it is better I take my complaint back."

Since then, the woman has not appeared again. Once in a while the sun comes to inquire, "What happened to the woman – because I want to clear it up, it has become a worry on my head that somebody is being hurt by me, perhaps unknowingly."

God said, "You need not be worried. The problem is such that it cannot be solved. I cannot give any decision unless you are both present in my court together and I have listened to both sides in the presence of each other. But by the very nature of things, you cannot both be present. That woman is your absence. So of course you cannot be present and absent simultaneously. Drop your worry. You are doing perfectly fine, and that woman is not going to report against you again. The file in your case is closed."

Exactly the same is the case with zorba and buddha. The moment buddha arrives with all his light and beauty, with all his awareness, with all his joy, zorba disappears, dissolves. Conflict is impossible. Conflict is possible only in your mind.

You have been listening to me so you have made a concept of zorba and a concept of buddha; you have neither lived zorba nor have you lived buddha. These are only words in your mind. Then conflict is very easy; then you can go on arguing within your mind: "How can zorba and buddha become one? They are antagonistic, they are enemies; harmony is not possible." Yes, in the mind it is not possible.

That's why I am telling you constantly to go beyond mind, where it is possible – not only possible, it is already happening – beyond mind, zorba *is* the buddha; there is no dividing line. All that is beautiful in zorba becomes even more beautiful when buddha arrives, everything becomes a thousandfold more glorified. And all that is wrong and ugly in zorba disappears like darkness. That which can be absorbed is absorbed, and that which is not worth absorbing is dissolved. But don't make it a mental problem. My approach is not of the mind; it is of meditation. It is an existential approach.

Zorba loves singing, playing on his musical instruments, dancing. Buddha will make it perfect, absolute. Even silence will become a song, even stones will become sermons, and whatever you touch will become a musical instrument because your hands will now have the magic of the whole existence, they will have the grace, the beauty, the poetry.

Your life will not be a struggle between zorba and buddha, but a love affair – so deep that two lovers disappear into each other, never to separate again. The union, the harmony, the accordance is going to be eternal.

But avoid the mind. Mind knows only conflict. Even where there is no conflict, mind creates it; even where there is no problem, mind creates it. Mind cannot exist without problems; problems are its nourishment. Conflict, fight, disharmony – and the mind is perfectly at ease and at home. Silence, harmony – and the mind starts becoming afraid, because harmony, silence and peace are nothing but death to the mind.

So just shift your problem from the mind. Start living. And with me, it is easy; it has never ever in history been so easy, because I am not telling you to disown zorba, I am telling you to live zorba to its utmost. There is nothing to be afraid of. Only add one more thing, and that is meditation.

Meditation is the bridge between zorba and buddha. Once the bridge is complete and the buddha descends, there will be a tremendous change in your zorba: all that is ugly will have gone, and all that is beautiful will be beautified tremendously.

The zorba is not going to lose anything. Without buddha, zorba is just a mundane existence. Without zorba, the buddha has no roots – only flowers. But how long can flowers live without roots? Roots are ugly; that's why they remain hiding underneath the ground – but they are the source of life and juice. Those beautiful flowers cannot exist without those ugly roots underneath the ground; those roots are continuously nourishing them, giving their life to the flowers. And this miracle is happening everywhere. But we are so blind that we cannot see.

When you see a roseflower, you don't see that in the roseflower is hidden the whole philosophy of life – the leaves are not red, nor are the thorns red nor are the roots red. Yet out of this green foliage comes a beautiful red rose. It is nourished by everything: by the roots, by the leaves, because the leaves are breathing constantly; otherwise, the rose would die. Branches are constantly doing a miracle bringing juice and water from the depths of the earth upwards, against gravitation. And there is no pumping system.

In the beginning scientists were puzzled at how trees one hundred and fifty feet high managed to keep their leaves green – lush green, at a hundred and fifty feet high. Water goes against gravitation with no apparent mechanism. Miracles are everywhere; one just needs a sensitive heart, a perceptive eye, and you will see matter and spirit dancing together everywhere.

Zorba and buddha are never separate. There is just one possibility: buddha can be asleep; then zorba has to live a mundane life. Or, under the stupid influence of the past, you can disown your body, become destructive of your body and try to achieve the impossible: living like a buddha without having anything to do with zorba.

Thousands of saints have done that, but you will not find in their life roses flowering; you will not find in their life the lush greenery of existence; you will not find in their life songs and dances. They are almost the living dead. I am fighting against that whole past. I want you to be a zorba and a buddha together; then whatever is ugly in zorba will disappear on its own accord – you are not to renounce it. And whatever is beautiful will be absorbed in the new consciousness, in the new awakening. But don't make it a mind problem.

Osho,

Before meeting you and taking sannyas in 1980, I used to achieve whatsoever targets and goals I made. But since then I have been relaxing at the platform, waiting for the whistle of the incoming train. Relaxing and waiting has increased to such an extent that sometimes during your discourses the sound of my own snoring makes me get up, feeling as if the train has arrived – but the train never arrives.

Beloved master, what next?

Learn to snore totally! This is not right, that your own snoring wakes you up. Be a real authentic snorer, so that it wakes up everybody but you. Snoring is an art. And as far as the platform is concerned, you are not on the platform. You are sleeping on the train, so no need to worry. The train is taking you; that's why you don't hear the whistles of oncoming trains. Snore fully, sleep well; the train is going fast.

This is one of the problems for those who in their life have been achievers – whatever they wanted, they achieved; whatever the target, whatever the goal, they managed it. But enlightenment is not a goal. And godliness is not an achievement.

Godliness is your very reality. All that you need is to relax completely. That's why I am saying snore perfectly. This getting up again and again and watching whether the train is coming in or not, unnecessarily disturbs your sleep, disturbs your relaxation. My sannyasins are not goal oriented.

My whole approach is that of let-go; it is not of effort. You just relax and enjoy. Even in the discourse sleeping is not prohibited, nor is snoring prohibited. Just snore a little musically so everybody can enjoy it. You do not have to do anything; so don't ask what next. You just have to relax so totally that you can feel your being in its ultimate glory, its blissfulness and benediction.

I am telling you that you are already where you want to be; you are already that which you are thinking to become. Becoming is a disease. You are a being. You are not to become anything, but because in your whole life you have been a hard worker, achieving everything that you wanted, it is just the old habit that makes meditation also an effort, enlightenment also a goal, godliness also somewhere else.

In this wide world, why do so many people go on missing? And why do only so few people realize the truth, the beauty, the bliss? The reason is simple: everybody is thinking in terms of goals. And those who are thinking in terms of goals are going to fail, because it is not a goal. It is already within you. So the more you run to get it, the farther you go away from it.

Coming to oneself is not a journey; it is just renouncing all effort, all goals, all becoming. Just start enjoying wherever you are whatever you are. This is the simplest thing but it appears very difficult because we have been trained for goals. There is nothing that you have to do. All that is needed is for you to sit silently doing nothing; the spring comes, and the grass grows by itself.

Naturally, the grass never gives any whistles, it simply grows; it is not a railway station. And the grass *is* growing. But if you see it every day, you will not feel that it is growing. You are all growing. You will realize it only when the growth has come to such an explosion that you cannot conceive that it is possible without growth. You are growing every day: from a child you become young, from being young you become old. But you cannot find the point at which you started becoming young, at what point you started becoming old, because you are so close to your growth and it happens slowly every day.

Being close to me, you are not aware of the fact that you are no longer part of the world in which you are living. Superficially you are living in the same world, but deep down you have entered a different world with me – a world of no effort, a world of non-doing, a world of no goal, a world of *isness*, of here, of now.

Osho,

Why do I feel that I have failed? Is it because I still hanker to be perfect, superhuman, special? Osho, please don't spare me anything!

The answer that I just gave is also the answer for you. Only people who want to be somewhere, somebody, have to suffer the sadness of failure. But a person who never wants to be anybody, never wants to be anywhere else, cannot suffer the sadness of failure. He is always successful, just like me!

From my very childhood, my parents, my well-wishers, my neighbors, my teachers, everybody was saying that, "You are going to be utterly worthless, a good-for-nothing."

I said, "If that is my destiny, I am perfectly happy. Why should I try to be somebody else? Utterly useless? – that's perfectly good! Good for nothing? – I don't see anything wrong in it."

And they would say, "Can't you ever talk reasonably?"

I said, "It *is* just a question of reason. Whatever is going to happen, I am going to be successful, because I have not made a criterion that this has to happen, only then will I be successful. Just vice-versa: I *am* successful. Whatever happens, that does not matter; my successfulness is certain."

One of my professors was very concerned. He loved me so much that he said, "You could top the university with your left hand, but your behavior is such that even if you manage to get a third class, that would be a miracle, because I never see you reading any textbook."

He used to come to the hostel to check. He never found a textbook in my room. I had never purchased one.

"When the professors are lecturing, you are sleeping. And the professors don't disturb you because when you are awake, you are arguing. It is better that you remain asleep so there is no disturbance."

He was so worried: I may go to the examination hall – but I may not go. Just before my post-graduate final examination, he came in the evening and said, "Give me a promise."

I said, "I can give you a promise, but I lie. So, it is not of much use."

He said, "You lie?"

I said, "Yes, I lie; whatever suits the purpose, I do it. You want a promise? – I'll give you a promise. If somebody else comes and asks for a promise, I'll give him a promise also."

He said, "That means you will torture me. Tomorrow morning, be ready at seven; I will pick you up and leave you at the examination hall every day."

And it was really a torture for him, because he was a drunkard, but a really good man. He never used to get up before one o'clock. To get up at six o'clock and get ready, and... And he had perhaps the oldest model car; it would take hours to start it. The whole neighborhood would be pushing it. Somehow he would manage once it had started.

But he would reach there exactly at seven. All these difficulties... And he would find me sleeping, and he would wake me and say, "This is too much. I never get up before one, now I am getting up at six. And you know my car; she is lazier than me. To start it in the cold at six o'clock is so difficult – the whole neighborhood has to help. And you are sleeping."

I said, "When you told me that you would be coming, I trusted." I said, "Then why bother to get up early? When you come, I will get out of bed and sit in your car."

He said, "You are not going to take a bath or anything?"

I said, "Everything after the examination."

"Any preparation?"

I said, "Who bothers about preparation?"

On the way to the examination hall, he would try to tell me, "Listen, remember a few things: this is your roll number. Don't forget." He would force me to write the roll number on my hand, so that I wouldn't forget it. I would write the roll number on my hand, and he would say, "Write your name; otherwise you will wonder what this is, whose roll number it is."

I said, "You should trust me just a little bit."

He said, "I don't trust you. First do this examination. You have to top the university."

I said, "Whatever happens, I am happy."

And he would tell the superintendent, "Don't let him out of the hall for three hours." Three hours was the time – because he was worried that once he was gone, I may go back to my bed. And the superintendent came to me and said, "Remember, there is no hurry for you to finish the paper. Take your time. You cannot get out of here for three hours. Your professor has ordered me, and I respect that old man."

I said, "This is strange."

I would finish the paper in two hours or one and a half hours, and I would ask the superintendent, "You can see I have finished the paper. Now don't bother me, because I have not even taken a bath yet. I have to go and wash my mouth, take a bath and change my clothes. I have come directly from bed."

He said, "Directly from bed? But who forced you?"

I said, "The same professor who forced you." And I said, "I will not report against you. Nobody is going to report it; everybody is so engaged in writing."

He said, "If this is the situation, you can go. But have you answered all the questions?"

"I...you can see!" He knew that I had answered, but he would look. He would say, "This is strange. In a post-graduate examination, your answer to the question is just one page, half a page. Do you hope to pass?

I said, "I never hope anything. This much I enjoyed; more than that... I never do anything that I don't enjoy."

And by chance it happened that one of the retired professors, Professor Ranade of Allahabad University – he was a world-famous authority – got my examination papers, my answers. So my professor was going completely mad.

He said, "First I did not think that you would even get a third class degree, although you deserve to top the university. But now you are in a very dangerous man's hands; it is known for years, he has not given a first class to anybody in his whole life. He is retired now, but he still gets the examination papers. And by chance he is going to examine your papers. You are finished."

I said, "Don't be worried. That makes me happy; I will be staying one more year with you."

He said, "Don't talk nonsense."

I said, "I am not talking nonsense. You will have another chance to take me to the examination hall, to torture me. You should be happy."

But this is what I call... Strange things happen: Ranade gave me ninety-nine percent marks, with a special note saying that, "I wanted to give a hundred percent but that might look a little prejudiced. The reason I am giving him ninety-nine percent – and for the first time in my whole life a first class – is because I always wanted the answers to be to the point. And I have never seen a man who would answer a whole question in just one paragraph. I loved the boy!"

He had written the note to the vice-chancellor saying, "Tell the boy from me, show him my note" – he was very old, seventy-five years – "that he is the first in my whole life to whom I am giving a first class."

I topped the university. My professor, who had been so anxious, now could not believe it. When the results came, he asked me, "What is the matter? There must be some mistake. You...and topping the university? Just go to the vice-chancellor's office, find out – there is some mistake in the newspaper."

I said, "Don't bother. If there is some mistake, that is perfectly good."

But he himself was so anxious that I had to push his car, start his car, and take him to the vice-chancellor's office. Till he saw the note, he did not believe it.

And coming out of the office he looked me up and down, and he said, "This is the strangest thing that I have seen in my life, that you have been getting out of bed – no preparation, nothing – and now you are the gold medalist. For the first time," he said, "I have started believing in God – because you could not have managed it. God must be behind you."

I said, "That is absolutely clear. That's why I was so relaxed. You were unnecessarily worried. God is just exactly behind me the way I am behind your car to start it. He starts me, and once I am started everything goes well."

There is no failure in life. It all depends how you take things. If you desire too much, you want to reach too high, and you cannot, then there is frustration and failure. But if you do not desire anything and you are perfectly happy wherever you are, life is a moment-to-moment victory.

Osho,

Why is the mind running like crazy when the heart wants to say something?

Mind is always afraid only of one thing, and that is your heart – because mind is basically meant to be a servant but has managed to become the master. And the heart, which was going to be the master, has not even bothered to interfere, and has allowed the mind to remain the master. But the mind is aware that if at any moment the heart wants it, his mastery will be gone. So whenever the heart wants to say something, a fear arises in the mind.

Mind is very much afraid of love. Mind is very much afraid of trust. Mind is very much afraid of anything that has to do with the heart. The heart is naturally the master, because the mind's mastery is not part of nature. But this is the problem: because the heart feels its mastery so definitely, with such a certainty, it never asserts itself, there is no need. It is an intrinsic knowing in the heart that the mind can be pushed aside at any moment. And the mind knows perfectly well that he is just a servant. Because the master is so gentlemanly, he has allowed even the servant to pretend to be the master. But a servant is a servant.

So whenever your heart wants to say something, the mind starts feeling shaky – it wants the heart to remain completely dead, it wants man to become completely heartless. And it has succeeded all over the world in making people heartless.

But once in a while a few people escape from the slavery of the mind and start asserting the rights of their heart. This is the greatest revolution there is, the revolution of the heart against the mind.

I call it the essential sannyas.

Osho,

Always when I walk across to your house I would like to dance and sing, but then tears come into my eyes and strong feelings overwhelm me and I would like to shout to everybody, "Wake up! Here is Osho. He is available for everybody!" I am so grateful for all I have got from you, and sometimes it is so difficult to keep all this to myself – but I won't go on a missionary trip.

What can I do?

To have a mission and to be a missionary are two different things. The missionary is functioning from the mind. And to have a mission is the overflowing experience of the heart. The distinction is difficult, but not impossible. The missionary is trying to convince people about something of which he himself is not convinced – because the things that he wants people to be convinced of are not things that he has experienced. A missionary is simply a computer transferring knowledge from one generation to another generation.

But to have a mission is a totally different thing. Jesus is not a missionary; Pope the polack is. Jesus has a mission. Gautam Buddha has a mission. To have a mission means you have experienced something, and it is against human compassion and love not to share it. It is not a question of converting anybody; it is a question of sharing. So there is no harm. If it is your experience, shout it from the housetops. If it is coming from your heart, then don't prevent it – because the more you spread it, the deeper will go its roots. It is just like a tree; the tree goes on spreading its branches far and wide in the sky, and underneath the earth the roots go on spreading.

If you have an experience that you feel is capable of quenching the thirst of many, then take every risk – shout it, sing it, dance it, do whatever you can do. Even if the whole world thinks you are insane don't be worried. The more you share your experience, the deeper it will go into your own heart, and the stronger it will become; your individuality will become a tremendous force.

Never become a missionary. A missionary is a servant, a poor servant – just like any other servant. He gets a certain salary to spread the message of the bible. He is not a bit concerned about the message; his whole concern is about his salary. If somebody else is ready to give him double his salary, he would be ready to speak against the bible.

I have heard that in a church a bishop was very much worried because one of the eldest and the richest members of the church used to sleep. But it was not a place like this, where even snoring is allowed – as long as you are a little musical. And the old man used to snore. The bishop was very disturbed as the man was always sitting right in front of him.

Finally, the bishop found a way – because the old man would always come with a small boy, his great grandson. The bishop caught hold of the great grandson one day, took him to a corner and told him, "Can you do one thing for me? I will give you fifty cents every Sunday." The boy said, "Done. What do you want?"

He said, "You don't have to do much. Whenever your old man starts snoring, just nudge him, wake him. His sleeping is not a problem; the problem is that when he snores, he wakes up the whole congregation. And I don't have many sermons – only three. So I don't want people to be awake, otherwise they will start getting bored."

The boy said, "Advance me."

The bishop said, "Advance? You are something! Don't you believe me?"

The boy said, "Business is business. It is not a question of belief; it is not religion. Just give me fifty cents and then you will see my performance next Sunday."

And the boy performed well. He did not allow the old man to sleep at all. Whenever he snored the boy would start hitting him. He looked many times at the boy: "What has happened to you?"

But the boy would not look at him; he would listen to the sermon so religiously, unconcerned with what was happening.

Outside, the old man said, "You rascal, why were you...? The whole night I cannot sleep because of my old age and this is the only time in the week that I have a good sleep, and you disturb me. What happened? What went wrong in your mind? And you looked so religious, listening as if you understood what was being said."

He said, "It is not a question of religion. I get fifty cents for my performance. The bishop gave me an advance for today. And I am going to the bishop to get an advance for next Sunday."

The old man said, "Wait. I will give you a dollar – but don't disturb me!"

He said, "Perfectly okay. Advance me."

Next Sunday, the bishop was very puzzled. Many times he inquired of the boy, but the boy looked everywhere else, but never at the bishop. "What happened to the boy? Perhaps I have not given him the advance after all so he is not bothering."

He tried somehow hoping that nobody would understand what he was trying to do, he made gestures. But the boy said, "What is the matter?"

After the meeting he got hold of the boy saying, "What is the matter? Can't you even trust me for fifty cents? Here is fifty cents."

He said, "It is not a question of your fifty cents. My old man is giving me a dollar not to disturb him. Now, if you want... It is up to you."

The bishop said, "I am a poor man. If I go on giving to you in this way, and your old man goes on doubling it... He is a rich man."

The boy said, "Business is business. If you cannot go beyond a dollar, then not only will my grandfather snore, I am going to snore too; and then you will see real chaos. Then not only will you have to pay for my old man, you will have to pay for me – separately: fifty cents for me, and a dollar and a half for the old man – only two dollars. But it will change every Sunday; it all depends on how business goes."

A missionary is a poor servant. Christianity pays him; he believes in Christianity. If somebody else pays him more, he is ready for it. But a man of mission is a totally different thing – you cannot change him. You can crucify him, but you cannot change him.

Osho,

Your first silent message to me was: "Don't be so serious, enjoy, celebrate!"

After three years I finally got it! Why did it take me so long to wake up? Am I really waking up?

Do you think three years is so long? What is your criterion. Time is eternal. Three years are not even equal to three seconds.

If you can understand the message to celebrate, to rejoice, even in three lives it is early; it is not late. You are fortunate that you got it in three years. How much time you take depends on you. You could have got it the very moment I gave it to you. You took three years – postponing for tomorrow because so many other things have to be done, postponing for other reasons. Because, celebrating when the whole world is in misery, you will look insane. "What are you doing? The world is facing a nuclear disaster and you are celebrating?" You have found many reasons to remain miserable, to remain sad, to remain serious; but you managed to come out of them in three years.

If you ask me, you have come home quite early. It is not a long time. In fact, whenever you understand it, it is always early, because thousands of times, for thousands of lives you have heard it and you did not get it. You went on postponing, you went on forgetting.

I was referring in a talk to a beautiful book, *Waiting For Godot*. The author certainly means waiting for God; but not to hurt anybody, he manages to create a fictitious name *Godot*. But reading the whole story – and it is a small piece – two persons are sitting underneath a tree, and they are saying, "He has not come, this is the time; he should have reached here by now." They are getting worried and they are talking, and... And nobody says who this Godot is. Or when this Godot promised to come, or who has ever met him – nobody touches any sensitive points. It is taken for granted that Godot is coming. It is good when you have nothing to do, at least to wait – something is going to happen.

I thought perhaps Godot may be the German word for God, so I asked my oldest German sannyasin Haridas, "Haridas, is Godot a German word for God?"

Haridas said, "No."

I said, "What is German for God?"

He said, "The German word is *Gott*!"

And I said, "That is really German! *Gott*!"

There is no question of getting it; in three years you *gott* it!

21 The Watermelon and the Knife

Osho,
I'm so glad and happy to be with you. My beloved master, I'm so grateful to you because you are still available to all of us who want to drink from your never-ending source. It's such a blessing to be showered from your love and compassion that I'll never find the words to say thank you for everything you have given to us.
Soon I'll be back in that crazy world out there, where you will be present only in my heart. Sometimes I wonder if it's still worth it to work outside to spread your teachings; I wonder if you still have a design, a hope to do something about this crazy world, or if you just wish to stay with your sannyasins.
Can you say something about this?

The question has many questions in it. First, real gratitude can never find words to express itself. The gratitude that can find words to express itself is just a formality, because anything heartfelt immediately goes beyond words, concepts, language. You can live it, it can shine from your eyes; it can come as a fragrance from your whole being. It can be the music of your silence, but you cannot say it. The moment you say it, something essential immediately dies. Words can only carry corpses, not living experiences. So it is understandable that you find it difficult to express your thankfulness. It is not your difficulty; it is the difficulty of the experience of thankfulness itself. And blessed are those who have such experiences, which are beyond words. Cursed are those who know nothing except words and language.

Secondly, you are saying that soon you will be going away from me and I will be only in your heart. If I am in your heart, there is no way to go away from me. You can go away from my physical presence, but my physical presence is no longer significant if you are already feeling my presence in your heart. You have become aware of my spiritual presence. The physical presence is only a triggering point – if it can lead you to the spiritual presence, its work is done. Now I will be beating in your heart wherever you are, it does not matter whether you are here or on a faraway planet.

Love is the only phenomenon which destroys space, distance, time.

The chemistry of love has not been understood yet. Physicists are concerned about space and time, and they have not yet come to understand the point that there is something more in existence, where time and space both disappear. Love is a phenomenon which knows no time, space, distance. Perhaps science will never be able to understand it. Perhaps it is beyond the scope of science. But it is not beyond the scope of poetry, of religion. It is not beyond the scope of meditation. It is not beyond the scope of every individual who is ready to dissolve himself into love. Science then remains a faraway echo, and love becomes the only reality.

People like Shankara, Bosanquet, Bradley, were not talking nonsense when they said that the world is an illusion. The world consists of time and space – but these people tried to argue that the world is an illusion. They made a philosophical system propounding the illusoriness of the world. Their very effort confutes them – if the world is illusory, then what is the need to prove that it is illusory? If something is not, it is not. But if Shankara had to go out of this room, he would go through the door, not through the wall. The wall is real.

If Bradley had to take his lunch, he would not eat stones. Because what difference can there be, when bread is illusory, and stones are also illusory? Both are illusions.

These people were trying to prove something which they had not experienced in their own being. It was not the experience of love; it was mere logic. Hence, hundreds of philosophers have been trying to convince the world that all is illusory, but nobody is convinced. Even they themselves are not convinced.

I am reminded of a story:

One Buddhist philosopher was brought to the court of a king. People said that he was one of the greatest logicians they had ever heard about. And he propounded the theory that everything is illusory, all is made of the same stuff that dreams are made of.

But the king was a very pragmatic, practical man. He said, "Wait. Announce that all people should go into their houses and close their doors, shops should be closed, because our mad elephant is going to come out on the road." And this Buddhist philosopher was left standing on the road, and he was crying and weeping and shouting, "Save me! Nothing is illusory – at least this elephant is not illusory." And the elephant was really mad.

Seeing his condition...the elephant was stopped from attacking him. The philosopher was brought back to the court and asked, "Now what do you say about your philosophy?"

He said, "Everything is illusory."

The king said, "And the elephant?"

He said, "The elephant is illusory, the philosopher who was crying and weeping is illusory, and the king who has saved him is illusory – everything is illusory. But please don't put me out there again – because it is a philosophy. I am ready to argue, but you cannot argue with a mad elephant. If you have any philosophers, bring them and I will prove that everything is illusory."

These philosophers were saying something which has a piece of truth in it. But they were trying to *prove* it. That's where they went wrong. Love cannot be proved. It can be only be experienced. And in love, all that consists of space and time appears to be made of the same stuff as dreams are made of. It is not an argument, not a philosophy.

You can sit close to a person, your bodies are touching and yet you can be hundreds of miles away from each other. You can be hundreds of miles distant from each other, and yet love can bring you so close that you can melt into each other. So remember, if you feel me in your heart, then I am coming with you. Wherever you go, I am coming with you – and without a ticket, because they have not yet found a way to know whether a person is traveling with someone hiding in his heart.

Thirdly: the world is certainly crazy. And it is not that it has suddenly become crazy – it has always been so. I am not a pessimist; neither am I an optimist. I am simply a realist. I know that it is impossible to change this whole crazy world. Even if I can change my people, my sannyasins, that is hoping too much.

So I don't want you to become a missionary, making efforts to change the crazy people. Change yourself, and help the fellow travelers, the sannyasins who are on the same path, in the same search – encourage them, help them in every possible way. There are moments of darkness, there are moments of discouragement, there are moments one feels perhaps he should not have chosen this path because it goes against the whole crazy world. To be sane in this insane world you are bound to be against it. So help those few people who are moving towards sanity, and never ask for the impossible. This is possible: to change a few thousand sannyasins around the world. And perhaps if a few thousand sannyasins are changed, that may create a certain magnetism, a certain gravitation, such that many more millions of people may be pulled into it.

But you should begin with yourself. If you can change yourself, that is much, and if you can help those who are on the path, it is enough for your compassion and for your love. In the crazy world there are also many people who don't want to be the way they are, they want to be transformed. And if you find someone who has a deep longing to be transformed, help him. But never impose yourself on anybody, because if somebody wants to remain insane that is his birthright. Don't disturb him; he is already disturbed too much. Just leave him alone, and let him live his insanity. Bless him that: "Live it totally." Perhaps by living insanity totally he may come out of it.

The problem with insane people is that they are always living it partially, they are always repressing, they are always not doing what they want to do. If they are allowed total freedom, perhaps they may come out of their insanity. At least my people should give everybody freedom to be himself, without any judgment, without any condemnation, without calling him insane, without calling him a sinner, without sending him to hell. Just accept. A loving person accepts the other, as he is, without demanding any change.

Osho,

Once I was happily waiting to greet you on your way to Sanai Grove. I was joyfully dancing and singing.

When you came closer, my body started moving with the movement of your hands; such weightlessness and joy exploding more and more beyond boundaries into vastness, and then falling into a deep, silent abyss inside myself.

Afterwards I felt grateful and so relieved; I had been looking for this experience by being with men, and it had happened through being with you.

Is such great bliss or ecstasy or orgasm – I don't know what to call it – only possible with a master, or also with a man?

The experience of ultimate blissfulness, ecstasy or orgasm has nothing to do with the other. It happens within you; the other is only an excuse. It can be the master; it can be anybody else.

With the master it is easier, because with the master you don't have any expectations. With any other man you have expectations. With any other man you want to dominate; with any other man your relationship is not a relaxed phenomenon. It has nothing to do with the man; it is your attitude, your approach that is decisive. If your relationship with the master is full of expectations, then this experience cannot happen. The experience can happen even with a tree, or even with the stars, or even just sitting alone in your room. It has nothing to do with anybody else. You have to understand it clearly: it is an explosion of joy within *you*.

But sitting alone in your room is the most difficult, because you don't have any excuse. You cannot even smile because you will think, "Am I going crazy? There is nobody and I am smiling."

I was waiting at a railway station. The train was due to come late in the night, and there were few other people. One man relaxing in an easy chair was attracting everybody's attention because sometimes he would make gestures as if he was throwing something away, and sometimes he would smile and sometimes he would laugh, and the laughter would be so much that he would have to hold his belly, because the whole body was laughing.

I was just sitting by his side. I didn't want to disturb anybody – he was enjoying so much – but it was difficult to resist the temptation to know what was happening to the man. I asked him, "It is interference on my part, I am sorry, but I cannot resist anymore, and we have to sit here for a few hours more. What is going on? Sometimes you throw things away just by a gesture of your hand. And you make such faces, and sometimes you smile, and sometimes you have such a belly laughter that you have to hold your belly – and you are alone."

The man said, "I don't tell the secret to anybody. But you have been sitting by my side for three hours, and I can understand how difficult it must have been for you to resist the temptation of asking. I will tell you the secret. Just come close."

So I went close. I pulled my chair close to him. And he said, "It is nothing special. I am just telling jokes to myself."

I said, "Jokes?"

He said, "Yes, I am telling jokes, but sometimes old jokes that I have told many times start, so I throw them away. And sometimes the jokes are so juicy that I cannot contain myself from laughing loudly, but people are sleeping, and there are so many people, so I have to hold myself and my laughter. A few jokes are such they don't create laughter, but just a very gentle smile."

I said, "You are a great man. You have found a great secret."

He said, "What do you mean by finding a great secret?"

I said, "If everybody knew this secret, the world would be much nicer, less miserable; there would be more laughter, more joy. There is no need to wait for somebody else to tell you a joke. This is perfectly good – you tell a joke to yourself, and if you don't like it you can simply throw it away. With somebody else telling a joke, if you don't like it you still have to smile, you have to be a hypocrite. Deep down you are saying, 'Rotten!' but on the surface you are smiling and saying what a great joke it is. And you have found a tremendous freedom. You can choose your own jokes, and you can enjoy any juicy joke as many times as you want – you can start telling it again."

The scientists have discovered that all that happens to you happens in the centers of your brain. Excuses may be outside, but the real happening is in the seven hundred centers in the brain.

One of the most important men of this century was Delgado. For his whole life he worked on animals and how their brains function. And he was surprised to find that what you call sexual orgasm – which the ordinary man finds to be the ultimate in pleasure – can be managed without anybody, you can do it alone. It has nothing to do with anybody else. You can keep just a small remote controller in your pocket...because there is one center that controls your sexual pleasure.

Delgado was working on white mice. He had opened the brain of one mouse, and planted an electrode at the sex center in the brain. According to his findings, sex has nothing to do with your genitals. Sex is centered in the head – the genitals are only branches spreading out, connected to the center.

He fixed the electrode to a remote controller, and as he would push the button the poor mouse would go into a thrilling experience, ecstasy, orgasm. Delgado could not believe it; it had nothing to do with the genitals, it was direct. Then he made a small machine with buttons on it, and trained the mouse to push the button if he wanted a mild orgasm, or if he wanted a very strong one, or if he wanted the strongest.

And you will be surprised – even mice are not so stupid – when there is a choice, who will go for the mild orgasm? He had just to push the button and his whole body would go into a thrill. By his side was put his food, water, everything that he liked – but he was not interested in anything. In one hour he had six hundred strong orgasms – and of course he died, because you cannot survive that much, there is a limit to everything. Six hundred orgasms in one hour, ten orgasms per minute... And he forgot about drinking or food.

Delgado says that whenever we think that our pleasure, our pain, our misery, our joy is dependent on somebody outside, we are wrong. Outside are only excuses. And this is the teaching of all the ancient mystics: that your bliss is within you, the kingdom of god is within you. There are different ways of saying it. Delgado speaks in scientific terminology. Jesus speaks in a religious way.

You are saying that here with me, you feel ecstatic, orgasmic experiences. I want you to remember, I may be the excuse, but the whole doing is yours. You are absolutely independent. And it is better to remember it; then it can happen with any man, any tree, any beautiful sunset, any starry night, or just sitting silently doing nothing in the darkness of your room. You just have to find out what happens in you.

You are focused on the outside; that's why you go on missing what is happening inside. You think it is happening because of the master, so you are focused on the master. Then you become attached to the master – that becomes your slavery. When something like this happens, close your eyes and see what is happening within you, and soon you will find small clues: how it happens, in what situations. You were silent, you were relaxed, you were not thinking. Your mind was empty, and it came like a flood. Then try it alone.

It is not happening with any other man because with any other man you are not silent. With any other man you are constantly quarreling, fighting, nagging. It is very difficult to find a woman who is not bitchy, and being bitchy do you think you will have ecstasy? You are bitchy, but the man will be the target. You think that he is the cause: why did he come late, where has he been?

One day Mulla Nasruddin's wife was crying. As I entered their house, she started crying even more loudly. I said, "What is the matter?"

She said, "Now things have gone beyond control. This man" – and she pointed towards Mulla Nasruddin, her husband – "has been having affairs with women. There is no doubt about it, because many times I have found hairs on his coat, which are not his hairs – he is bald. The color is different."

I said, "Have you found any today?"

She said, "Not today – that's why I am crying, because today I looked minutely and found that there was no hair. It means he has started having affairs with bald women. This is too much; I cannot tolerate this. With women who have hair it is okay, but with women who are bald..."

It is you who are finding things which can make you joyous, which can make you miserable. It was not happening with the man for a simple reason: first, you were always quarreling, always demanding. And these experiences are not such that they can be produced on demand: "Bring one ecstasy just now." Nobody can do that except Delgado. But for that you will have to go through a small operation. In your skull he will make a small hole and put in an electrode. And he can give you a remote control – just a small size, you can keep it in your pocket. And there will be no need to ask anybody; you can give yourself as many orgasms as you want.

But the danger is the same: what happened to the poor white mouse is going to happen to you, because the experience is so beautiful that you will not want to lose a single moment for anything else. Perhaps... The mouse is a small thing, died in one hour; you may take twenty-four hours. But more than that, you cannot hope to survive. Man can survive in misery for seventy-five years, but in ecstasy... Seventy-five years in ecstasy? Impossible! Your organism is not made of steel. It will have a breakdown.

I can provide you an atmosphere in which it is easier to move into such spaces. If you are intelligent, you will start looking inside yourself for why these spaces are happening. And you will start on your own, alone, so that you can have those experiences without me. If you are unintelligent, then you will start clinging to me, and that's how so many people in the world are being exploited. If you go to someone and say, "It is because of you, master, you are the lord of my heart," you are giving that man a chance to exploit you and others. Out of all the so-called spiritual teachers, masters, prophets, saviors, ninety-nine percent are simply frauds. But you are responsible. You have made them frauds.

I don't want anybody to cling to me, to be attached to me in any way. My whole effort is to give you total freedom, and methods so that whatever you want, you can create it within yourself. Not even God is needed; nothing is needed.

You are enough unto yourself.

This is the great blessing of existence to every human being. You are made with such perfection – but you never explore it, it remains dormant. Just become an explorer of your own interiority, of your own subjectivity, and you will find thousands of ecstasies, immense blessings, unimagined, undreamt of. You are a paradise, but have you forgotten yourself. You are looking everywhere except within you, and that is the only place where you are going to find the treasure, the truth, the beauty.

Osho,

In this phase of your work, are you giving the final touch to the painting of your whole life, for the transformation of the new human being?

My work is not like a painter's work. It is not that I can complete the painting; it is one long painting. And I will be giving touches to the painting even when I am breathing my last – still, the painting will be incomplete. In life, only mad people ask for perfection. The perfectionist is another name for someone who is getting ready to become mad.

I was a guest in a maharaja's palace, and the maharaja was showing me around – it was a beautiful palace. At a certain place he stopped and said, "Do you see?" There was a wall, incomplete. I said, "Why have you left it incomplete?"

He said, "The palace was made by my grandfather, and this is the tradition in our family that nothing should be made perfect. Some imperfection should be left so that the coming generation remembers that life does not allow perfection."

Imperfection is not something bad. Imperfection is the root of all growth; perfection can only be death. Once something is perfect it is dead.

The painting that I have started will remain imperfect, although I will go on trying to make it perfect, but it is the very nature of existence that it cannot be perfect. And it is not *my* painting.

Those who are with me – it is as much their painting too. When I have gone, you have to continue to paint it. The painting has to go on growing new flowers, new foliage. Don't let it be dead at any point. In other words, don't let it become perfect. Make every effort to make it perfect, but don't let it become perfect. Then there is tremendous beauty, and always flowing and growing, and there comes no full stop.

In life we are always in the middle. You don't know the beginning of life, you don't know the end of life. We are always in the middle and everybody has always been in the middle. It is a process, an ongoing process, a river that goes on flowing. That's the beauty of it, that's the glory of it. And not only with the painting, with everything – remember it. Accept that imperfection is the rule, that something becomes perfect only when its death has come. To ask for perfection is to ask for death. Death is the full stop. In life you can use commas, semi-colons, but never a full stop.

In one of the poems of Rabindranath Tagore... The critics all over the world criticized it because it suddenly begins and it suddenly ends; there is no beginning and no end. It seems as if it is a middle portion – something in the beginning is missing, something in the end is missing.

And Rabindranath was asked, "You have been criticized but why are you silent?"

He said, "Those people don't understand life. Life is always in the middle, and my poetry represents life. Out of nowhere it begins, and suddenly it disappears and evaporates without giving you the feeling of completion."

But the mind is a perfectionist. Hence the mind always feels uneasy with the heart, with love, with life, with meditation, with beauty. With everything that grows, mind is always feeling uneasy. It is perfectly at ease with machines; they are complete. Machines are perfect.

To me, imperfection is not something to be condemned; it is

something to be rejoiced in, something to be appreciated, because it is the principle of life itself.

Osho,
A strange thing happened when I last saw you in discourse: looking at you, I felt as if I could not see you; I had to close my eyes to be centered again. And even then I cannot say I found you.

Also, during the day when I go inside there is so much love and gentleness in being with myself. It is almost like where I used to find you before there is just a vast, loving space and it feels like me. You are somehow distant and cool. This puzzles me.

Is something going wrong? – although I feel rich, and you are my most beloved master.

There is no need to be puzzled. Nothing has gone wrong. Everything is as it should be. The more you love me, the closer you come to me, the more you will find I am disappearing. At a certain point, you will find that where I used to be there is only love, a fragrance, a presence. And the strangest thing is that it will feel as if it is *your* center, it is you. This is one way of coming close to the master.

People are different. Somebody may have just the opposite thing: as he comes closer to me, *he* starts disappearing. And as he comes very close, he finds he is no longer. But it does not matter. The basic thing is that two are not allowed to enter into the door of heaven. The two should become one. Now who disappears and who remains is just a question of language, absolutely immaterial.

And you are feeling love, you are feeling blissful, you are feeling rich, so certainly everything is going right. When things are going right, they give you indications. When things are going wrong, you are miserable, you are in despair, you are in anguish. There is no need to inquire, you can simply see your own state, and you can find out whether things are going right or wrong. If you are feeling loving, richer, fuller, contented, then everything is going right. You are blessed. And whether the master disappears in the disciple or the disciple disappears in the master is only a question of from where you are seeing it.

My grandfather used to say... He was not educated; he was not a thinker. He was a very practical man. But once in a while he used to say things, just out of his practical life experiences, which had a tremendous validity. He was a cloth merchant. I used to sit by his side once in a while when he was dealing with customers – his way of dealing with the customers was strange. But they loved him; if he was not there they would ask "Where is he? When will he be here? – then we will come."

The first thing he would ask the customer was, "Do you want to be cheated? It is up to you. Do you want to pay the right price, or do you want to pay more? You can decide; just tell me. If you want to pay more, then haggling is going to happen. And remember one thing."

In my village there was a beautiful river, and very sweet watermelons used to grow by the side of the river. Moving around the world, I have never come across such sweet watermelons in my whole life. The watermelons were so sweet that the name of the river became *sakkar*, sugar.

So he used to say to customers, "Listen, whether the watermelon falls on the knife or the knife falls on the watermelon, in each case the watermelon is cut. You are the watermelon; I am the knife. So what do you decide – haggling or no haggling? In haggling you will pay more. I know the exact price. I cannot go below that, above that I can say yes at any moment. But if you don't want to be cheated, I will tell you the right price exactly. Just remember the watermelon and the knife."

So whether the disciple disappears in the master or the master disappears in the disciple, it does not matter, it is just the watermelon gone.

And you are the watermelon and I am the knife. So enjoy, and feel rich. Everything is going right.

Osho,

When I sit in your lecture I feel your silence and feel I become part of it. This is a wordless process in melting more and more into silence.

At the same time, there are words from you. I hear them, and suddenly a connection happens from the silence to the words, and I feel golden, golden gratefulness about your beloved, wonderful words. The silence and the words are one.

Please can you say something about this process – if it is really possible that words can say the wordless.

Yes, the word can say the wordless but only to the chosen few, only to those who are absolutely silent. The word coming out of silence carries around it the wordless silence. Now the question is at the receiving end. If it is received by a mind full of words and chattering, then the silence and the wordlessness is destroyed; you only hear the word. But if you are silent, you hear the word and you also hear the wordless; you hear the sound, and you also experience the soundlessness.

In Mahavira's life a strange thing is reported. It is very difficult to say that it can be factual, historical. Particularly in the outside world, it will look absolutely absurd and irrational. But here, I can tell you the story. And I can tell you that it may have happened – because it is happening here, so there is no reason why it could not have happened in Mahavira's time. Time is irrelevant, but it can be told only to those chosen few people who have experienced something similar.

It is said that Mahavira never spoke, although there are scriptures. But Mahavira never spoke, he just remained silent. He had eleven disciples who were deep in silence, and there was something transferred from Mahavira in silence to the disciples. And these eleven disciples have written the scriptures; they told the people what Mahavira was saying.

So whenever it is said that Mahavira said this, remember, what he said is not a direct statement. Mahavira never spoke; he was silent. But something transpired between him and his chosen group of disciples, and those disciples became his spokesmen. They went around spreading his message.

What is the guarantee that they heard the right thing? What is the guarantee that they did not imagine that they were hearing? What is the guarantee that they are not saying things of their own?

There is a guarantee, and the guarantee is that all the eleven heard the same thing.

All the eleven had to immediately write down what they heard, and because all eleven could not have imagined the same thing, it becomes an absolute guarantee: they *have* heard, silence has spoken to them. From silence to silence there has been a communion. The followers of Mahavira cannot prove this.

I have asked many Jaina monks, "Can you prove this?"

And they said, "Those were the days of truth, and this is the age of darkness. Now it cannot be proved; neither can it be experienced."

To them it is simply a belief, and most often they don't mention it because it is embarrassing. If somebody raises a question, they don't have the right answer.

But in this mystery school it is happening, so there is no question of the story about Mahavira being a fiction. As my sannyasins are growing in silence, moving deeper into meditation – as their masks are falling down, as they are becoming more and more innocently connected with me – first it will happen that they will hear my words, and along with my words, the wordless message.

And at the second step, there will be no need for me even to use the word. I can simply sit here, and you can hear the wordless message. And before I leave this body, I want it to become an existential experience not only to eleven people but to thousands of people. Only that can give credibility to Mahavira's story. In twenty-five centuries Mahavira's disciples have failed, they have not been able to bring any rationality, because it is not a question of reason, it is a question of meditation. And you will be surprised that Mahavira's whole life is a life of meditation, and in Jainism meditation is simply forgotten. The whole religion has become a ritual.

So it is true: you can hear the wordless side by side with my words. And soon you will be able to hear the wordless even without the words. And that day will be a day of great celebration – when I can speak to you without speaking. A silent meeting, a communion with no noise, a music with no sounds, nothing is said but everything is heard, understood, immediately experienced.

Osho,

German youngsters seem to contradict Nietzsche! I have read: "God is not dead, it's just that he can't find a space to park his car." What do you think?

The German young people are not wrong, neither are they right; they just don't know the whole thing. Frederick Nietzsche is also in the same position – neither right nor wrong – because he also does not know the whole thing. He says, "God is dead." That is true in a way, but the fact is God committed suicide. And why did he commit suicide? – because he could not find a parking place for his old, ancient Ford. So they are both right.

It is that same old Ford – the bible describes it – that God used when he drove Adam and Eve out of the Garden of Eden. Drove in what? It was an ancient Ford model-T. And it must be somewhere in Mumbai, because I have been all around the world. You cannot find such ancient models as you can find in Mumbai. And the Indian government is very protective of ancient models; it does not allow new cars to come in, and it does not allow the old cars to go out. Mumbai is a great museum for old cars. If you search, you may find the first car in which God drove Adam and Eve. Where did he drive them? – to Victoria Station!

22 The Forgotten Language of the Heart

Osho,
I am afraid to meet you. Trembling, shocked, alone – it means death.

The meeting with the master has always been a kind of death: death to all that you have been, death to your past, death to your ego, death to your personality. But it is not only death, it is also resurrection, the birth of the new, the birth of the fresh and the innocent, a new sunrise on the horizon, a new unfolding of your being. But naturally, first you have to meet the death; you have to pass through it. Resurrection can only be afterwards.

Death is what you pay for your resurrection; hence, your question is significant.

You are feeling afraid coming closer to me. This is not new. This has nothing to do with you or me. This is as old as man. The most ancient scriptures in the world are the Vedas. They describe the master as death – but a death which opens the door to the divine, certainly a death which happens only to the blessed ones. It is no ordinary death, it is not the death of your body; it is the death that transforms you. Everything remains the same – the body, the world – yet nothing remains the same because your vision, your perspective, your way of looking has gone through such a deep mutation that although superficially everything is the same, in depth everything has changed. You have entered a new dimension of life: the dimension of eternity, the dimension of ecstasy, the dimension which is beyond time and space.

But this much courage is needed: you will have to come close to the master, you will have to go through this fire which burns only that which is false in you. Out of it, you come as twenty-four karat gold. The function of a mystic school is to encourage you: "You need not be worried. We have passed through the test; the fire is cool and the death is a blessing."

But if you don't have any guts, then perhaps the time is not ripe for you, perhaps in some other life with some other master the death will happen. But why postpone? What is possible right now should not be postponed for tomorrow. Why remain in misery even for one day, even for one minute, even for one second?

The death of the ego, the death of your personality, the death of all that you have been thinking about yourself, immediately opens a door. New flowers start blossoming, new songs start stirring in your heart, new dances. You don't walk anymore, you simply dance; you fly. The ecstasy is such, the blissfulness is such...gather just a little bit of courage.

Osho,

You always said to us that we should rejoice in being alive, but deep in myself I found a very strong will to die – not that I want to commit suicide, but to die naturally.

Somehow I know that by dying I might find that which I really enjoy, which is silence. I can say that I am utterly bored and fed up with this ugly world. There is nothing that makes me feel attracted to do anything other than being with you.

Osho, what's wrong with me?

Nothing is wrong with you. Everything is wrong with the world. It is only the retarded people who don't feel bored. You are intelligent. You can see that there is nothing meaningful. Life is a drag, a repetition. There seems to be no adventure in it, no challenge;

there seems to be no hope. Tomorrow will be again the same as yesterday.

It is the prerogative only of human beings to get bored; no other animal gets bored in existence. Have you seen any animal in existence being bored? Boredom is a high quality of intelligence. It means you are perceptive; you can see that there is nothing but – finally – death. Empty handed you have come and one day empty handed you will leave, and all that happens in between birth and death is simply tedious. So I cannot say there is anything wrong with you.

Every intelligent person thinks that perhaps what is not available in life may be available in death. Psychologists have found that almost every intelligent person at least once in his life thinks of committing suicide – he may not commit it, but the idea comes. Particularly in this century, the greatest philosophers: Jean-Paul Sartre, Jaspers, Martin Heidegger, Soren Kierkegaard, Marcel... Almost all the topmost thinkers of the contemporary world are agreed on one thing – they don't agree on many things, but on one thing they are all in absolute agreement – that life is meaningless. And if this is so, then the question naturally arises, why go on living? If there is no meaning, no significance, then what is the need to be dragged from the cradle to the grave unnecessarily? This is the only contemporary philosophy: existentialism.

There have been many philosophies born in different ages, but in this age there has been only one philosophy and that is existentialism. And its basic ground is so strange that one feels that all these people are mad. If they are not mad, then we are mad – there is no other alternative.

The whole philosophical movement called existentialism talks about life as meaningless, accidental, there is no purpose behind it; it is full of anxiety and anguish – which are incurable. It is a nightmare. This is such a contrast.

Gautam Buddha, Lao Tzu, Nagarjuna and Bodhidharma – they talk of blissfulness, of tremendous possibilities of ecstasy, of growing into new dimensions of being. What has happened? Why this diametrical opposition?

And Jean-Paul Sartre or Jaspers or Martin Heidegger are not

unintelligent people; they are as intelligent as any Gautam Buddha. One thing is missing: they have depended only on reason. They are very rational people; they have completely forgotten the heart. They live in the mind and the mind is a desert. Nothing grows there – no flowers, not even an oasis. Modern man slowly, slowly has forgotten the language of the heart. The possibilities that open only through the heart have been completely forgotten. Only one thing has remained, and that is your reason, your rationality.

And the trouble is, all that is beautiful belongs to the heart, all that is meaningful belongs to the heart, all that is significant is a fragrance of the heart.

Reason is perfectly good as far as objects, dead objects are concerned; for scientific research it is the best instrument. For things, reason is the right method of discovery. But the moment the question arises about anything living, reason is impotent. And if you ask reason a question concerning life, love, peace, joy, blissfulness, it simply negates, as if these things don't exist. It is almost like a blind man. If you talk about light to the blind man, he is going to say that there is no light. Because to see light... Your hands cannot do anything to see light, your ears cannot hear it, you cannot taste it, you cannot smell it. All your senses are perfect, but only eyes have the capacity to see light and colors and rainbows. Reason has a limitation. It is a perfect tool for dead things. And this is one of the mistakes of this whole century: we have been asking blind people about light, or asking the deaf about music.

Asking reason about love, meaning, significance, ecstasy, is futile. Reason will simply say these things don't exist – because reason has never come in contact with any of these things. Reason is not intentionally denying you anything, it is just not its capacity; you are stretching it beyond its capacity.

It is good that at least in your life one thing is still significant: your love for me. But you cannot give any reason for it. Or can you? Is it something rational? Is there some arithmetic behind it, some scientific evaluation? Can your mind support it? It is not from the mind that you are related to me; it is that a part of your heart is still alive with me, is still dancing, is still singing. And that is the great hope: your heart is not dead; you have not completely denied it. This small loophole is enough. If I can enter through it, I can bring the whole of paradise behind me – don't be worried.

And you are such a nice man that you are not thinking of committing suicide. So there is time, you are waiting for a natural death. Don't be worried. Before natural death, I will give you the taste of natural life. And once you are drunk with natural life, death disappears; you become part of an eternal flow of life, which knows no end. Every moment is a new discovery, every moment a new peak. Every moment you think, "What can be more than this?" – yet the next moment something more becomes possible. This is an unending process. Just let me in. And the way to help me is to meditate. Sit silently...

Life is boring, so there is no harm in sitting with closed eyes, because there is nothing to see. Sit silently, peacefully. You have looked outside and you have found nothing but meaninglessness. Now give a chance to your inner world, look inwards.

And I promise you that the same eyes which have not found anything outside will find inside *everything*, a constant hallelujah.

Osho,

What is happening to me? I am opening more and more, and I have the feeling that the shadows in my body are gradually disappearing. When I close my eyes I can see more light in the body. It is so beautiful, and I feel so much for you – more than I ever felt before.

Osho, can this be? Is this me? Why do these doubts still arise? Would you please comment?

Whatever is happening is the deepest longing of every seeker. You are here only for this kind of happening. It is the beginning. In the beginning it is very natural; the mind will create doubts. There is no need to be angry with the mind; the mind cannot understand it, it is beyond the scope of the mind. And naturally the mind wants you to remain rational, reasonable, sane.

The mind creates doubts for the simple reason that it wants to protect you. It is not against you, it is trying to protect you so that you don't get into some crazy space. But it is only in the beginning that the mind creates doubts. And this is the time when the master and the school of the master helps you not to be bothered with what your mind is saying, but to explore the new that is arising.

You are feeling light. All shadows are disappearing, and a luminous body is arising within you, a body of light. The mind can accept a skeleton; it cannot accept a body of light. The mind is very primitive; it still believes in matter. Physicists have come to the conclusion that there is no matter at all; only energy exists. But the energy particles are moving so fast that they create the illusion of solidness.

It is just like a fan moving fast. You cannot see the three wings separately, it becomes a circle. If it moved with the speed of light, the way electrons move in a pillar, then you could sit on the fan and you would not fall, and you would not feel that something is changing beneath you and there are gaps. Because before you could feel the gap, the other wing of the fan would have come in and you would not feel anything, the fastness of speed would make it a solid thing. All that looks solid only looks solid. But mind is very primitive.

The heart is neither primitive nor contemporary. The heart is eternal; it knows no divisions of time. So the heart can see the body of light without any doubt. In fact, that body is truer than the solid body that we see, because the body of light means the body of electrons, pure electricity.

It happened after the Second World War: a soldier came back home. He had been away from home for five years, and naturally he was in a hurry to meet his wife. As he hugged his wife he got a shock – such an electric shock, he fell flat on the ground. He said, "My God, what has happened?"

For five years the wife had been waiting and waiting and waiting with such intensity, her electric forces had been accumulating.

Doctors were called. They could not even take her hand to check her pulse – immediate shocks. Then the electrician was called, hoping that something... Now it was no longer physical; something electrical had gone wrong. The electrician was very much afraid. He said, "First take this bulb in your hand." He gave the woman a five-candle bulb to put in her hand, and the bulb lit up.

That was the first happening of its type. The whole woman was throbbing with electricity. Because of her, research started into human electricity, and now it is an established fact that every human body has electricity.

If your eyes are very perceptive, you can see the electric aura around the body. As you have seen around the photos of Nanak, Kabir, Krishna, Rama, Buddha – those circles around the faces are not fictions, they are not the imaginations of the painters; they have been seen by disciples, by meditators.

And now in the Soviet Union, there is a photographer who even takes photographs... He has developed very sensitive plates. His name is Kirlian, and because of his name, his photography has become known as Kirlian photography. He has become world famous. If he takes your photo, it will not just be you but also surrounding your whole body will be an aura of light. And strangely enough, if somebody's hand has been cut off in an accident and Kirlian takes a photograph, the hand is not there in the photograph but the aura of the hand is still there. The electrical body is still intact – nothing has been disturbed, only the physical part has dropped. One of your fingers has been cut off for some reason, some accident; but in the photograph four fingers will show a darker photo of the physical finger with a lighter shade around it, and one finger will be simply the lighter electric shade. But the shade will still be there.

And this is not only with the human body. A roseflower... You can pluck a petal and Kirlian can say which petal has been taken out – his photograph will show the missing petal's electric aura.

So what is happening to you is that as you become silent, you start becoming aware of your inner being, which is surrounded by light. The ancients have called it the astral body, the body of light, the body made of starlight – that is what *astral* means. Just remember that it is not in the area of mind, and tell the mind, "This is none of your business. Do your thing."

And there are many more things. Existence is not limited to the mind; it is far bigger, far more mysterious. You have all the possibilities that any mystic has ever experienced anywhere in the world, but you will have to silence your mind; otherwise those doubts can go on disturbing you.

That's why my insistence is: before entering the mysterious world, first silence the mind. Discipline the mind for silence, for no-thinking, so that when you enter the mysterious world the mind does not come in the way, does not raise awkward questions which you cannot answer, and which even if you answer, the mind cannot understand.

Mind has a limited scope. It is a bio-computer. It is not your whole being. The heart is far bigger. And beyond the heart is your being, which is bigger than the heart. And beyond your being is the universal being – which is infinite. To enter into these mysteries you will need a silent mind that does not disturb you.

Osho,

Lao Tzu described buddha nature to be more like a woman than a man – which makes the story of meeting the buddha on the path and killing him highly suspect.

In other words, suppose I meet her on the path? Osho, this surely spells trouble. Any suggestions?

Milarepa, as far as *you* are concerned, if a buddha – as a woman – meets you on the way, your job is easier. You are a great ladykiller. So kill her lovingly – what is the problem in it? Lao Tzu has made things very easy for you.

It is true that all great qualities are feminine – love, compassion, sympathy, kindness. All these qualities have a flavor of the feminine.

There are male qualities, qualities of the warrior, courage. They are hard qualities; one has to be like steel. This is because man's qualities have developed through war, and female qualities have developed at home, in the garden of love, with the husband and children – she has lived in a totally different world. Man has lived continuously fighting. In three thousand years there have been five thousand wars on the earth – as if killing is man's only profession.

Just the other day, Nirvano showed me a photograph of Ronald Reagan kissing his wife. The way he is kissing her, it looks as if he will kill the woman! That photograph should be enlarged and hung everywhere all over the world – because he looks exactly like a chimpanzee. Even kissing has some violence in it – perhaps it is nuclear kissing.

The world has lived in two parts. Man has made his own world while the woman has lived in a shadow – she has created her own world in the shadow. It is very unfortunate because a man or a woman, to be complete, to be whole, must have all the qualities together. Both men and women should be as soft as a rose petal and as hard as a sword, both together. So whatever the opportunity and whenever the situation demands it... If the situation needs you to be a sword, you are ready; if the situation needs you to be just a rose petal, you are ready. This flexibility between the rose petal and the sword will make your life richer.

And it is not only between two qualities; it is between all the qualities. Man and woman are two parts of one whole; their world should also be one whole, and they should share all the qualities without any distinction. No quality should be stamped as feminine or masculine. When you make somebody masculine that person loses great things in his life. He becomes juiceless, he becomes stale, he becomes hard, almost dead. And the woman who completely forgets how to be hard, how to be a rebel is bound to become a slave, because she has only soft qualities. Now roses cannot fight with swords, they will be crushed and killed and destroyed.

A total human being has not been born yet. There have been men and there have been women, but there have not been human beings. My whole approach, Milarepa, is to bring the whole man to the earth, with all the beautiful qualities of woman and with all the courageous, rebellious, adventurous qualities of man. And they should all be part of one whole.

But from the very beginning we start telling children... A small boy, if he wants to play with toys like girls, we immediately stop him: "Be ashamed of yourself; you are a boy, you are a man, don't be girlish." And if a girl tries to climb a tree we stop her immediately: "This is not ladylike, climbing a tree, this is for the boys, rough. Just come down!"

From the very beginning we start dividing man and woman into parts. Both suffer – because climbing a tree has a joy of its own, no woman should miss it. To be on top of a tree when the wind is strong, in the sun, with the birds singing... If you have not been to that point, you have missed something – and just because you are a woman. Strange!

To be adventurous – to climb the mountains, to swim the oceans – should not be prevented just because you are a woman, because that thrill is something spiritual. A man should not be prevented when he wants to cry. He *has been* prevented, he cannot bring tears – tears are only for women: "You are a man; behave like a man." And tears are such a beautiful experience. In deep sadness or in great joy, whenever something is overflowing, tears give expression to it. And if tears are repressed, at the same time what they were going to express – the deep sadness or the great joy – is also repressed. And remember perfectly well that nature has not made any difference. It has given man and women the same tear glands, of equal size. But if you are a man and you are crying, then everybody condemns you, as if: "You are behaving like a woman."

You should say, "What can I do? Nature itself has given me tear glands. Nature is behaving like a woman. It is not my responsibility; I am simply enjoying my nature. Tears are my right." All qualities should be available to everybody.

There are men who become incapable of love because they are trained for certain qualities: "You have to be hard. You have to be competitive. You are not to show emotions. You must not be sentimental." Now how do you expect a man who is not emotional, not sentimental, who is not allowed to feel, how can you expect him to love? And when he misses love, his life becomes miserable. And the same is happening on both sides.

I would like all distinctions to disappear. Everybody should be allowed everything that is naturally possible to the person whether he is a man or a woman.

And we would have a richer world consisting of richer people.

Osho,
May I ask you a Tibetan question? Lord Buddha's third body

has now disappeared into you. Is it not called the mental body? Does it mean that the whole mental heritage of Buddha, all his teachings of meditation and initiation – his whole system – has dissolved into you? Does it also mean that you free this earthly globe from all systems, by swallowing them into your love and friendliness?

Please tell a joke. Jayesh is going mad!

First, Jayesh, the third body does not mean the mental body. The first body is the physical body. The second body is the mental body. The third body is the astral body. One becomes enlightened when one transcends the mental body. The astral body consists only of pure light, just a flame with no smoke around it.

Secondly, you are right: I am ready to take all the poison in the world that is driving people crazy and to drink it – because that poison cannot make *me* crazy. I can relieve people of their poisons: their theologies, their religions, their political ideologies. These are all poisons, and since the beginning they have been driving mankind into constant madness. Christians killing Mohammedans, Mohammedans killing Hindus, Hindus killing Buddhists, it goes on and on, atheists killing theists, theists killing atheists. It seems we don't want anybody in this world to be free – at least free to think.

In the Soviet Union, my sannyasins are being persecuted, they are being continually harassed by the government. They have done no harm. Just their being related to something which is not communism, is enough to freak the communists out: Communism should be the only religion in the Soviet Union.

Communists don't understand anything of what I am saying; they don't understand that my atheism is far more refined than their Karl Marx or their Engels or their Lenin; than any of their atheism is. They don't understand that I am for an authentic communism in the world. And in the Soviet Union there is no communism.

Yes, the capitalists are no longer there and now poverty has been distributed equally. I am not in favor of poverty. I want richness to be distributed equally – not poverty. And the basic idea in communism was to create a classless society – which has not happened. There are no more capitalists, but the people who are in power have become the new class, the power elite. Capitalists have never been as powerful anywhere in the world as the power elite are in the Soviet Union. And it is now sixty years, seventy years after the revolution. The same group of people is running the country; no new blood can enter the power class. And they want to overrule the whole world.

And America's intention is the same: to destroy freedom, to destroy individuality and to create an indirect imperialism all over the world. They have almost succeeded.

I would like to take all these ideologies away and make people free of their cages, give them their wings again, give them their sky back. So you are right. That has been my effort my whole life. And to my last breath I will continue to do the same: to free people from Hinduism, from Mohammedanism, from Christianity, from Judaism, from communism, from fascism, from nationalities, from distinctions and discriminations of man and woman, black and white.

How much insanity have we been carrying on our shoulders? Because of that burden we cannot grow. I would like everybody to be unburdened completely. I understand Jayesh. He is saying that he is going mad...because for almost three months he has been away from me. His has been a strange story.

He was a successful businessman; then he got tired. He heard about me, read about me and came from Canada to be with me in the commune in America with great expectations that: "Now I will be sitting and meditating."

And the next day he was arrested with me, and we were behind bars.

He told me, "Osho, this is too much. I came to meditate, but in a way I am fortunate that from the very beginning I am with you. Although it is jail, it does not matter."

And then he was with me all around the world, being deported from this country to that country.

For three months he has been away, working for me. Certainly he must be going mad because he has been trying to find headquarters for me. He works to the last – everything is complete – and then at the very end American pressure comes in. Because the American spies are continually surrounding him. The American ambassador is continually watching every move.

At the last moment, as they are going to sign an agreement that I can have a commune in their country, the phone rings and the American president himself is on the phone. And such blackmail! He threatens that: "If you allow Osho to remain in your country more than thirty-six hours then you will have to return all the loans that you have taken in the past" – which means billions of dollars. "And if you cannot return them, then your interest rate will be doubled. Secondly, whatever loan agreements there are for the future" – which are again for billions of dollars – "are canceled immediately. You can choose, you are free; you can choose Osho or you can choose American loans."

Naturally no country is in a position... They have to drop the whole idea.

Jayesh has been working, working, working for almost the whole year. It takes a month or two months to negotiate with the politicians and everybody, and when the final decision is about to be taken then immediately American pressure comes in. And it is not pressure, it is simply blackmail; it is threatening them that "We will kill you."

And certainly a country *will* be killed – it cannot pay the loans, and it has all its future programs based on the loans that America is going to give. All those programs: bridges will remain half built, hospitals will remain half built, and there will be such a great unemployment that the whole economy will flop. This is economic imperialism: on the surface politically you are free, but deep inside you are not free, nobody is free.

Naturally he needs a joke after three months, just to give him a laugh.

Jayesh, I have heard that a certain man, Reagy – no relation to Ronald Reagan – worked in a circus, and he was the elephant trainer. He trained the elephant so that on his order, the elephant would raise one of his legs up. Then he trained him to raise up two legs and then he trained him to raise up three legs. And he was such a perfectionist that he was trying to train the poor elephant to raise all four legs up, until he realized it seemed difficult, that it was impossible, it could not happen.

So he had a great idea: he declared in the newspapers that, "Anybody who can come and make my elephant raise all four of his legs simultaneously, I will give him a ten-thousand-dollar reward. Entry fee is one hundred dollars."

Many people came and lost their one hundred dollars. How can the elephant raise. They tried persuasion, hypnosis, meditation – nothing worked.

And Reagy was very happy; he was collecting money.

And then one day a blue convertible car came in, and a small man came out. And he said to Reagy, "Are you the man who is going to give me ten thousand dollars if I can make your elephant raise all four legs simultaneously?"

He said, "Yes. But before that you will have to give me one hundred dollars as an entry fee."

He gave him one hundred dollars, went back. From the back of the car he pulled out a steel rod.

Reagy could not imagine what he was going to do. People had come who had tried yoga who had tried all kinds of things. "What is he going to do?" He waited.

First the man went in front of the elephant and looked into its eyes. Then he went to the back of the elephant and gave it a good hit in the balls. The elephant jumped with all four of its legs.

Reagy was in tears. He had accumulated only eight thousand dollars! And this man cheated! He had to give him two thousand dollars from his own pocket. The man took ten thousand dollars away.

Then Reagy saw how to get those ten thousand dollars back.

Elephants are known to move their heads up and down, but they are not known to move their heads from side to side.

So he declared in another advertisement: "I will give ten thousand dollars to anybody who can make my elephant move his head from side to side."

Again people started coming for a hundred dollar entry fee. Again Reagy was very happy: people were coming – yogis, Taoists, Zen masters, all sorts of magicians – but nobody could manage it, he would only move his head up and down and they would lose their hundred dollars.

Then suddenly one day that blue convertible car came back again and out came the small man. And Reagy started to tremble that: "This man... Now let's see what he does."

He said, "Are you the man who is going to give ten thousand dollars if I can move your elephant's head from side to side?"

He said, "Yes, but first...one hundred dollars!"

The man gave one hundred dollars. Then he went behind the car and took out the rod.

Reagy said, "This idiot...with that rod again? How can he make his head move from side to side?

And the man came to the front of the elephant carrying the rod, he looked into his eyes and said, "Do you recognize me?"

And the elephant said, "Yes."

The man said, "Do you want the experience once more?"

And the elephant said, "No."

And he asked for another ten thousand dollars!

23 Ten Non-Commandments

Osho,
Today, after a year, I am coming to see you, to be with you. And since I awoke this morning I have been aware that my heart is beating harder and quicker than usual, and that there is a hollow, stage fright feeling in my belly. Tears are close to my eyes, but there is no sadness. On one hand I can see it as fear, nervousness. On another it is excitement, anticipation, and on yet another it is energy, pure and simple – life, pulsation.
Beloved friend, it certainly doesn't feel to be a problem, but could you speak about the phenomenon of the disciple coming closer to the physical body of the master?

There are very few moments in man's life more magical than the feeling of love and trust from a disciple towards the master. It is a relationship not of this world, because it is a ladder to the beyond.

Coming closer to the master certainly gives a new pulsation to the life energy, to your receptivity, to your openness. It gives you a dance; your heart starts singing a song. It is a moment of rejoicing. It is the same moment as when a river comes to the ocean, dancing, to disappear into the ocean – but the disappearance is only from the side of those who are standing on the bank. To the river itself, it is becoming bigger, vaster, oceanic.

Coming closer to the master is a way of becoming a master – and what can be more rejoicing, more joyful?

There are many kinds of love, but the love that exists between the master and the disciple is the purest, unpolluted by any expectations, by any demands, by any conditions. The master accepts you as you are, with no desire to make something else of you. You love the master because he gives you, for the first time in your life, in all your relationships, freedom to be yourself, without fear, without guilt. Your experience is natural.

It has happened to every disciple, it is a cosmic experience. But it cannot happen if you are only a student. If you have come here only to learn, to accumulate knowledge, then this kind of miracle is not possible. If you have come here to expand your consciousness, to make your being more integral; then you have not come to increase your knowledge but to be reborn. You have come to become a child again; you have come to get back the purity, the fragrance, the beauty of your innocence.

I am not a teacher, and this is not a place where knowledge is important. I am just a presence to inspire in you that which is dormant, to allow you to recognize yourself. I am not here to impose any religion on you. I am here to make you completely weightless – without religion, without ideology – just a profound silence, a serenity, a depth, a height that goes to the stars.

This is a place of a master, and the function of this place is magic – not ordinary magic, but magic that creates Gautam Buddhas. And naturally, when you are coming out of your darkness towards the light of becoming a Gautam Buddha, it is impossible not to be thrilled, not to be ecstatic, not to be in a dance.

If you are alive, stars will be born out of you, flowers will be blossoming in you. But if you are dead, as most of the people on the earth are, then nothing will happen to you. Nothing happens to the dead.

There is a beautiful story in Mahavira's life: Mahavira went to Vasali, one of the great cities in those days. In Vasali there was a great thief. He had only one young son whom he was training in his art. He said to him, "Listen, you are free to do everything, but don't go close to that man Mahavira. I am a master thief, but I also avoid him, because that man is dangerous. Something magical surrounds him, and once you are caught in it there is no way out. So remember, go everywhere else, but avoid the campus where Mahavira is staying."

The son was very obedient. He avoided Mahavira's campus for many days, but the temptation was natural: here is a man who his father fears so much that just to be close to him seems to be dangerous. It is worth testing. So one day he went just a little closer to the campus – not inside the grove where Mahavira was staying with his ten thousand disciples, but outside the grove. And he heard only one sentence. Mahavira was saying that in paradise, the angels and the female angels are tremendously beautiful, but just one thing is wrong: their feet are pointing in the opposite direction. The angels are going one way, but their feet are going in the opposite direction.

Being afraid that his father might come to know, the boy escaped. But he thought, "There was no danger there, and Mahavira was just telling a fictitious story." But that same night he and his father were both caught stealing. It was impossible to get any information from the father; hence, the king said, "Don't bother about the father, concentrate on the son. There is a possibility that we may be able to find out all the information that we need."

And the strategy was that he was given intoxicating drugs, so he slept for hours, completely unconscious. He was taken to the most beautiful room in the palace, and all the beautiful girls were serving him, bringing food, drinks. As he came back to consciousness, he thought, "My God, I am dead. I am in paradise. This is the paradise that fellow Mahavira was describing, and the girls are really beautiful. Everything is great."

But then he looked at their feet, and immediately he understood that there was some conspiracy: "This is not paradise, because their feet are just like our feet."

The women tried in every way to persuade him, "You are dead and you are in paradise." And they were saying, "This is just the reception. Before you enter the permanent paradise, you have to tell everything about your life. This is the rule. Everything will be written, recorded, and then you will enter permanent paradise."

They wanted him to confess all the sins that he and his father had been committing, all the thefts, murders, and things for which they had never been caught. But now he would simply smile.

He said, "Forget all about it; I have heard from Mahavira himself. Your feet have given me the clue that this is the palace of the king. And this is a strategy. Tell your king to try to befool somebody else. I am a disciple of Mahavira."

They said, "Strange. When did you become a disciple of Mahavira?"

He said, "Just passing by I heard one sentence, and that one sentence has saved me today."

And because there was no proof, finally they had to be released.

He told his father, "I am not going to listen to you at all. If I had not disobeyed you and had not listened to Mahavira, we would both be hanging on the gallows; just one sentence – and that too, a small part of a story – has saved me. I am going to the man. His magic has caught me."

He became a great disciple of Mahavira.

He said, "You have saved me. Now give me a new life, because I don't want just to be saved and continue to be a thief and a murderer. It was good that I was caught, a discontinuity has happened. You start my life from scratch; accept me as a child."

Coming to the master is coming in search of your innocence, in search of your lost childhood, in search of your originality, in search of your individuality, in search of freedom.

Osho,

One day – it was Friday, when orthodox Jews are preparing for the sabbath – a man who didn't like Jews met an orthodox rabbi on the street. In an attempt to torment him, he asked him to express the entire philosophy of Judaism while he stood on one foot.

The rabbi stood on one foot and said, "Do unto others as you would have them do unto you. That is the law – the rest is commentary."

If I were to be met by a tormentor and asked to stand on one foot and explain in one sentence what your teaching is, would I be correct in saying that it is freedom from suppression?

It will not be so easy. First, you don't know the name of the rabbi. His name was Hillel. He is the most famous Jewish philosopher, and he certainly condensed the whole philosophy of Judaism into a single sentence.

The incident is true. He was asked to stand on one foot and answer in the shortest way what the essence of Judaism is. And what he said is beautiful, but not without flaw. He said: Do unto others what you would like to be done to you by them. This is the essence of Judaism; the rest is commentary. All great scriptures of the Jews, the Torah, the Talmud, are all just commentaries on the single, small, seedlike statement: Do unto others what you would like to be done to you by them.

As far as Judaism is concerned, no Jewish thinker has raised any suspicion about it. Neither has any non-Jewish philosopher raised any question about it. But I am more concerned with human reality than just with philosophical arguments. And looking at human reality, the statement is not correct, because my taste and your taste may be different.

To do unto others what you would like to be done to you by them can be right only if everybody's taste is the same. And that is not the case. For example, somebody is a masochist; he likes to be beaten, he likes to be tortured. Now what should he do with you, torture you? According to the principle, he should beat you, he should torture you, because that's what he wants you to do to him.

Perhaps Hillel or the Jewish philosophers were not aware that there are people who love to be tortured and there are people who love to torture. It is the latest contemporary psychological insight that there are sadists who like to torture, and there are masochists who like to be tortured; hence, it is said that the best couple in the world would be if by chance a sadist and a masochist get married. Then they are living in paradise, because one wants to be tortured and the other wants to torture. Both are enjoying.

But it is very difficult. No astrologer thinks about it, no parents think about it. In fact, whether somebody is a sadist or a masochist is not considered at all when people are thinking about marriage. Before you fall in love, remember the first basic inquiry: if you are a sadist, then find a masochist; if you are a masochist, find a sadist. The best places to find such people are the offices of psychoanalysts. Just sit outside there; you will find all kinds of people. But this statement will not be applicable.

And you want to know if somebody asks you about my philosophical standpoint... It is not going to be that easy, because I see man as a multi-dimensional being. You will be able to state it standing on one foot, there is no need for sentences, but you will have to state ten non-commandments.

The first: freedom.

The second: uniqueness of individuality.

The third: love.

The fourth: meditation.

The fifth: non-seriousness.

The sixth: playfulness.

The seventh: creativity.

The eighth: sensitivity.

The ninth: gratefulness.

The tenth: a feeling of the mysterious.

These ten non-commandments constitute my basic attitude towards reality, towards man's freedom from all kinds of spiritual slavery.

Osho,

At Rajneeshpuram in 1983 something from the beyond entered into me. Since then I have not been the same person anymore. My old goals and desires have faded away. Things which were meaningful to me before, have lost their importance.

But when I talk to people about meditation, silence, and what keeps us away from it, a great new energy and clearness starts rising in me. Every cell of my body becomes alive. I myself become a listener to what is said through me, and I feel grateful and very loving towards the people with whom I can share.

Beloved master, have I become a flute, an instrument for the beyond? Or is my ego playing a horrible joke on me? Please comment.

It certainly has changed your life. You have become a flute to the divine – because if it was a projection of the ego, the ego would not have allowed you to ask the question. And the ego never becomes a vehicle, a medium, a flute. It is not a hollow bamboo. The ego is very solid, does not allow itself to be used by higher forces. It can exist only in the very mundane world. To allow the higher forces means you are entering into the sacred, going beyond the mundane. The ego cannot go outside the mundane world. And its very fabric is to praise itself, to brag about itself even when it is not valid.

For example, poetry descends in you but the ego grabs it and proclaims to the whole world, "I have written it." No great poetry has been written by any ego; nothing great can come out of it. The great comes only when the ego gives way, when it is not obstructing, when it is absent, on leave.

It is said about Rabindranath that whenever he wrote, he would close his door and inform the house that unless he opens the door, nobody is allowed even to knock on it. It was a big family. Rabindranath's grandfather was given the title of raja by the British government, although he was not a king – but he was so rich and he had so much land that he could have purchased a few maharajas. His family was very big; almost one hundred members were living in the palace.

And it was a very strange family. Rabindranath has written in his memoirs, "We have seen strangers coming into the family as guests and then never leaving. And my grandfather was such that he would say, 'It does not matter. He must be some distant relative. Perhaps we have forgotten, he has forgotten, but destiny has brought us together. Let him live here.'"

So the family went on growing. Anybody could come and say, "I am related to you, a far off, distant relation." And he was received not only as a guest, but once he entered the house it was against the culture to ask him, "When are you going to leave?" It was not asked.

It is not the culture of Mumbai. In Mumbai, the first thing people ask is, "When are you going to leave?" You have not even settled in the chair, your luggage is still in the taxi, and they are asking when you are going to leave – because tickets have to be advance-booked.

Those were different days, and a different kind of people. So nobody ever asked when you were going to leave. And why should one leave? Living in the palace of a king, living like kings, every need was fulfilled.

So a man used to go with a bell, all over the palace, announcing that nobody is to disturb Rabindranath. And all his brothers, his mother, father, grandfather, they were all concerned while he was inside his room – sometimes it would be three days, four days, and he had not eaten, he had not come out.

They asked him, "What is the matter? You can come out, you can eat, you can go back again. Nobody is going to prevent you, nobody is even going to ask you any question."

Rabindranath said, "It is not a problem for me to come out. The problem is that when something is descending in me, if I leave the room just to take a shower or just to drink a cup of tea, the process stops. And it is not in my hands to start it again. Then I don't know when it will start again; it is something falling upon me, falling through me. I am just a passage. I don't want anybody to disturb me because I don't want to disturb the process." Every great poet, painter, singer, dancer has been aware of the fact that he has been great only in the moments when he has not been. It is not a contradiction.

The greatest dancer of this age was Nijinsky. He went mad because he was born in the West; in the East, he would have become a Gautam Buddha. In the West there was no background to explain what was happening to him, and it was a weird experience. While dancing – once in a while when he would forget himself completely, would become so much absorbed in the dance that there was only the dance and no dancer – he would jump so high that it was against gravitation. No scientist had any explanation. Man cannot jump that high, it is simply not possible.

And that was not the whole story. When he came back down... When anything is falling, the gravitation of the earth pulls it forcibly.

But when Nijinsky came back down, he would come so slowly – just like a dead leaf falling from the tree, moving slowly, or like a feather. That was even more difficult to explain.

And when people asked him, "What do you do?" he said, "Whenever I try to do it, it never happens. Finally I give up, and then one day suddenly it happens – but it happens only when I am not, when I am not the doer. It is something of the beyond."

So don't be worried, if you are feeling silent, peaceful, loving. These are not the ways of the ego. The ego cannot feel silent, the ego cannot feel peaceful, the ego cannot feel loving. Your meditation has ripened. You have come to a maturity. Rejoice, and be grateful.

Existence is very compassionate. If we are ready to open our hearts without holding anything back, then immense treasures become available to us.

In the beginning such doubts may arise: "Perhaps it is ego." Don't give a place to such doubts. Remember, ego can create misery, ego can create anguish, ego can create hate, ego can create jealousy. Ego can never become a vehicle for the divine; it can never become the passage for the beyond.

Osho,
Why do I always compromise?

One compromises because one is not certain about one's truth, one is not certain about one's own experience. The moment you have experienced something, it is impossible to compromise. There is no possibility at all. You compromise only because your idea is only a mind thing, a borrowed thought. You don't know whether it is right or wrong, so even if half proves to be right, it is not a bad bargain.

There is an ancient story in Egypt. Two women came to the court of the king with a small child. They contended, both of them, that: "The child belongs to me, he is my child." And each woman was persistent: "The child is mine."

The king had to decide, and it was very difficult – how to decide? The husbands of both women had died in war, in the service of the king.

Finally he asked his master, an old wise man. The master came and he said, "It is very simple. Bring the child."

The child was brought to the master, who asked the king to cut him in two, and give half to each woman. "What is the problem? They both say the child is theirs. There being no other evidence, no witness, justice demands that the child should be divided into two."

The king was shocked. He said, "What are you saying?"

But before the king could say anything more, the master drew the king's sword out of its sheath. And one woman ran forward and said, "No! Give the child to the other; he is not mine."

The master gave the child to the woman who had run forward and said he was not hers. The king said, "What is happening? I don't understand. The woman is saying the child is not hers."

The master said, "Only the mother couldn't stand to see the child cut in two. The other woman is withstanding it perfectly well, without any difficulty – if the child is cut in two, there is no harm; it is not her child. She is ready to compromise, even if half a dead child is given to her. But the other woman is not ready to compromise – either the whole child or no child."

When you have a truth, you are almost like a mother – you have given birth to an experience. Either you would like to have it totally, or you would not like to have it at all. But you cannot be ready to cut it in two, because any living experience cut in two becomes dead. All compromises are dead. Nobody in the whole history of man who has known anything about truth, has ever compromised. Rather, he has been ready to die for it.

It happened with al-Hillaj Mansoor. His master Junnaid loved him very much – he was a man worthy to be loved – and he tried to persuade him for years, "In your room you can shout Ana'l haq – I am God – but don't do that in the streets. You know that the people are fanatic, I also know the fact."

But al-Hillaj said, "You only know the fact. I have experienced it. You have compromised with the society; you are a respected teacher. I don't want any respectability, but I will not hide my truth. Truth is like fire; you cannot hide it. I have to shout it from the housetops."

And in a Mohammedan country – where fanaticism is the rule,

not the exception – he was immediately captured, and brought before the caliph because: "This is against our religion; there is only one God, and he is in the heavens. You are just a mortal being. Even Mohammed has not said, 'I am God.' He simply says, 'I am the messenger of God.' And you are saying that you are God. Are you mad? Either stop it, or death is the only punishment for it."

Al-Hillaj said, "Death is accepted, but I cannot compromise on this point. It is my experience: I am God. And I say you are also God – but your God is asleep and my God is awake."

Junnaid again came into the jail to persuade him, "This is foolish. You are such a beautiful young man, with a great future. You can become a great teacher. I know that what you are saying is right, but can't you compromise?"

Al-Hillaj said, "With all honor I want to say to you, you don't know. That's why you have compromised. You have heard; I have seen. You have read; I have been. Death does not matter, but compromise is simply out of the question."

And the day he was crucified, thousands of people came to throw stones, to condemn him. Junnaid also came; he loved him, al-Hillaj was his student, and Junnaid knew that he had immense possibilities of growth. And he had understood perfectly well that he himself was only knowledgeable, and al-Hillaj had experienced. But this is how compromise works.

Everybody was throwing stones – not to throw a stone was to risk that people might think, "This man is in favor of al-Hillaj." So he brought a roseflower so that when so many people in the crowd were throwing stones he could throw the roseflower; people would see that he had thrown something, but who knew that he had thrown the roseflower?

The mind of compromise...nobody would suspect that he had not thrown a stone. So he was compromising on two grounds: one with the people, that he had thrown a stone...and he was compromising with al-Hillaj also. Because al-Hillaj must be looking out for Junnaid, to see whether he had come or not, and it would be very cowardly not to go.

Al-Hillaj was smiling when stones were showering on him, hurting him, and blood was flowing all over the body. But when the roseflower of Junnaid hit him, he started crying. Tears came to his eyes.

Somebody asked, "What happened? So many stones and you continued to smile, and somebody has thrown a roseflower and tears have come to your eyes."

Al-Hillaj said, "Yes, because the people who are throwing stones don't know me. And the person who has thrown the roseflower knows me, knows my truth. But he is a coward, and I am ashamed that I have been a student of this man. Stones don't matter. But this roseflower has hit me hard."

Compromise simply means you are on uncertain ground. Rather than compromising, find grounding, roots, individuality. Find a sincerity of feeling, the support of your heart. Then whatever the consequence, it does not matter. The man who knows, knows perfectly well that no harm is possible. You can kill him, but you cannot harm him. And the man who does not know is always trembling, always worried. In that worrying and trembling, that anguish, he goes on compromising with everybody – just to be safe, not to be harmed.

But what are you trying to save? You don't have anything to save. Those who have something to save don't compromise.

A man like Socrates was given an opportunity by the judges, that if he leaves Athens... He can live outside of Athens and in this way he can avoid the death penalty. Anybody would suggest that "This is a simple compromise, you can just live outside the boundary lines of Athens" – because in those days in Greece there were only city-states; every city was a state. Just outside the boundary you were outside the state. He could have lived almost in the suburbs. But men like Socrates are impossible.

He said, "I would rather die than escape. And anyway, I am old. How long am I going to live? And if the most cultured city of these days cannot tolerate me, who is going to tolerate me? It is better to die in Athens than anywhere else – at least I have the consolation that I am being killed by the most cultured people."

The judges were really trying hard somehow to save him, because he had not committed any crime. It was just that the mob wanted him to be killed – he was corrupting the youth. Now, anybody who brings new thoughts to the world can be blamed because he is corrupting the youth – because he is bound to be against the old ideas, he is bound to fight against the old. You can call it corruption: "He is corrupting our tradition, our religion, our culture."

The judges said, "We have another suggestion: you can live in Athens, but stop talking about truth."

Socrates said, "You are asking me to do the impossible. I will speak about truth and truth alone until my last breath. Do you want me to start speaking lies? Do you want me not to speak at all? – that too is a lie, because I know the truth and I am not speaking it, and the lie is spreading in people's minds. No, I will be here, and I will speak the truth. It is up to you – you can kill me – but no compromise on any ground."

Try to find your individuality, your integrity, and make the effort of not compromising, because the more you compromise, the less you are an individual. You are only a cog in the wheel, just a part in the vast mechanism, just a small part of the mob – not an individual in your own beauty, in your own right.

I am absolutely against compromise. Death is far more beautiful than a life of compromise.

This is a joke for my beloved master:

It has always been one of the most profound questions throughout the ages: was Jesus Christ a Jew or not? Recently, scientists have made substantial progress towards finding the answer. The results of their research were first made public a few months ago.

Jesus was a Jew for three important reasons:

(1) He lived with his mother all his life;

(2) His mother always called him 'the best'; and

(3) Starting out with a gift of just two pieces of wood, he managed to set up an international company.

Jews have never been able to forgive themselves for crucifying

Jesus, for the simple reason that he was their best boy. They could not conceive that he would create the greatest and the richest international company. Almost half of the population of the world is Christian.

And he certainly created this whole big show out of two pieces of wood – that's how the cross is made. I never call Christianity *Christianity* – I call it "crossianity" because it is really based on the cross. The findings seem to be perfectly true. And he created a company that has lasted for two thousand years and is still growing. And the commodity that he produces is invisible. As far as salesmanship is concerned, Jesus is the best salesman ever. His commodity is not great. Christianity is not a great religion; it is very primitive and third class, but he managed to sell the product to almost half of the world. And because the product is invisible, it is very difficult to decide its quality.

I have heard that in a New York shop they were selling invisible hairpins for women, and women were certainly excited. Invisible hairpins! And they were charging a lot for nothing. One woman opened the box – of course you cannot see invisible pins – and she asked the salesman, "Are you sure that there are invisible hairpins in it?"

He said, "Don't be worried. We have been out of stock for almost three months, but they are still selling, so we have stopped purchasing, because there is no point. They are invisible – we cannot see them, you cannot see them, nobody can see them. And people are purchasing them, standing in queues for invisible pins."

God is an invisible commodity which you cannot see. Not for a few months, but for eternity it has been out of stock. Heaven and hell: all invisible things, and Jesus managed to create a bogus religion based on these things like God, heaven and hell. The religion has nothing in it.

One can argue against Gautam Buddha. At least there is something in it – you may agree, you may not agree. But Christianity has nothing in it – you cannot even argue against it, it is simply baseless. It is a great hypocrisy. The pope, the archbishops, the bishops, the cardinals and the priests – none of them have experienced anything; none of them have ever said that they have experienced anything. And they are millions in number, and they are converting others to their religion. They don't know anything of what religion is. Perhaps that's why they have such a great appeal for all the idiots. The mediocre mind does not want to experience or even at least to be intelligently convinced. It simply wants to believe: the cheapest thing in the world. Christianity provides belief. You believe and you are saved. And who are these saviors?

Just the other day, I was brought news from a monastery in Europe. It is an old monastery, and now it is divided into two parts. Half of the monks have declared that they are homosexuals – so they are worshipping separately and they have occupied almost half the grounds and the church. And you should not think that the other half are celibate; most probably they are not courageous enough to say what the other brothers have said.

When I was in America, in Texas the government passed a law against homosexuality. Now, Texas is a backward state in America: homosexuality became illegal, criminal, and one million people protested against the law – if there are one million homosexuals in Texas, then what about California?

In parliament in Holland they discussed why they have not allowed me entry into Holland. And the minister concerned said strange things... But nobody in parliament raised the question: "What nonsense are you talking?"

One can understand... He said it was because I have been speaking against the pope. To speak against the pope is not a crime – in no country's constitution, and in no country's law is it a crime to speak against the pope. But it can be understood. Secondly he said that I have been speaking against Mother Teresa. But is this a crime?

And thirdly – the most important – is that I have been speaking against homosexuality. Has the whole of Holland gone homosexual? Then change the name from Holland to "Homosexual-land" – because in parliament nobody raised the simple question that: "This is nonsense; we are not homosexuals." They may be Catholics, they may believe in the pope...

Christianity teaches celibacy, and celibacy is unnatural. It creates homosexuals, lesbians. And finally it has brought the disease AIDS, which is another name for death – because there is no medicine, no medical cure for it. The pope who served just before this pope was a world-famous homosexual. Before becoming a pope, he was the archbishop of Milan, and all of Milan laughed because he was continually moving around with his boyfriend. When he became the pope, he took his boyfriend to the Vatican; the boyfriend became his secretary. And everybody knew, the whole of Milan knew, the whole Vatican knew, but nobody raised the question. It seems Christianity has created the most unintelligent people in the world.

I have heard...

A man and woman were making love in their bed, and suddenly a car drove into the garage. The woman said to the man, "Wake up, wake up! My husband is coming; it is certainly his car. Just get in the closet."

So the man jumped into the closet.

The husband came in; he had come just for half an hour because he was on his way to some other duty. And the man inside the closet heard a small voice. Somebody said, "It is very dark in here."

He said, "My God, who is there? Keep quiet!"

The voice said, "Give me something." So the man gave him fifteen dollars.

The voice said, "I am going to scream."

He said, "You seem to be a very strange fellow," and he gave him fifteen dollars more.

The voice said, "No! It is so dark!" So the man gave him all he had, fifty dollars. He said, "This is all I have; now do whatever you want to do – whether it is dark or not, screaming or not, I don't have anything more."

The next day, the boy said to his mother, "I want to purchase a bicycle."

The mother said, "Bicycle? But a bicycle costs fifty dollars at least."

He said, "Don't be worried, I have got it."

She said, "Where did you get it from?"

About that he remained silent.

The mother said, "You will have to tell me where you got it from. Have you stolen it?"

He said, "No, I have not stolen it. And I am not going to say where it came from. But it is certain that I have not stolen it, and my source of getting it is absolutely moral."

Mother said, "First go to the church and confess to the priest. If you cannot tell me, tell the priest where you got the money from."

So he went to the confession booth, and the priest came. The boy said, "It is very dark in here."

And the priest said, "You son-of-a-bitch! Don't start it again!"

24 Eastern Psychology: The Science of the Soul

Osho,
Why can modern psychologists not think or write about, or even conceive of enlightenment? Is enlightenment a new phenomenon beyond their conception? Will they ever understand a phenomenon "beyond enlightenment"?

Please comment.

Modern psychology is in its very childhood. It is just one century old. The concept of enlightenment belongs to Eastern psychology, which is almost ten thousand years old. Modern psychology is just beginning from scratch, it is at the *ABC* stage. Enlightenment and beyond enlightenment are the very end of the alphabet of human endeavor: *XYZ*.

Modern psychology is a misnomer because the word *psychology* originates from the word *psyche*. Psyche means the soul. The exact meaning of the word *psychology* would be the science of the soul. But it is a very weird word. Psychology denies the existence of the soul and still goes on calling itself *psychology*. It accepts only the physical body and its byproduct, the mind. As the physical body dies, the mind also dies; there is no rebirth, there is no reincarnation. Life is not an eternal principle, but just a byproduct of certain physical material things put together.

You have to understand the word *byproduct*. Even the idea of a byproduct is not very original. In India, there has been a school of materialists, at least five thousand years old, called *charvakas*. They describe mind as a byproduct of the body. Their example is very fitting. Remember, it is a five thousand year-old example. We can find modern contemporary parallels to it. In India you must have seen people chewing betel leaves, pan. It consists of four or five things – the betel leaf and three or four things more. You can eat them separately and they will not give the color red to your lips; but if you eat them together they will create the color red as a byproduct. That red color has no existence of its own, it is a byproduct.

In a contemporary example, look at a watch working.

I have heard that Mulla Nasruddin when he retired, was presented with a gold pocket watch by his friends. It was automatic, and from the very beginning he was surprised; he thought what a miracle it was that it went on and on. But after three or four days it stopped. He was very much surprised, what had happened?

When it stopped he opened it up and found a small dead ant inside.

He said, "Now I know the secret! This ant is the driver, and now he's dead how can the watch continue? But those idiots should have told me that there is a driver! – it needs food, it needs water. And sometimes you even have to change the driver!"

When a watch is running, and if it is automatic, what makes it tick? Is there some immaterial entity like a soul? Open the watch and take the parts apart, and you will not find any soul. That's what charvakas said five thousand years ago: that if there is a soul, then cut a man open and you should find it. Or when soldiers are cut open in the war – so many souls would be flying upwards. Or when ordinarily a death happens in your house naturally, the soul must leave the body.

Charvakas were very stubborn materialists. In five thousand years, materialism has not gone even a step further than charvakas. They weighed a dying person, and when he was dead they weighed him again and the weight was the same – it proves that nothing left the body. Then what was ticking in the body? It *was* something – a byproduct of the constituents of the body. And the materialists of all ages – Epicurus in Greece, Karl Marx and Engels in Germany and England – continued to repeat the same idea: that consciousness is a byproduct. And modern psychology has accepted it as their basic foundation: there is no soul in man; man is only a body.

Joseph Stalin was able to kill almost one million Russians after the revolution. Anybody who was unwilling to give up his rights to his property was killed mercilessly. The whole family of the czar which had ruled for hundreds of years – one of the oldest empires in the world, and one of the biggest – nineteen persons in that family were killed so mercilessly that they did not even leave a six-month-old baby, they killed that baby too. Killing was easy because of the philosophy, nothing is killed; it is almost like breaking a chair. Otherwise it would be difficult for any man to kill one million people and not feel any prick in his conscience. But the philosophy was supportive of all these murders – because nothing is murdered, only the physical body. There is no consciousness, which is separate from the body.

Modern psychology is still behaving stupidly because it is still clinging to the five thousand year-old primitive idea of charvaka, that consciousness is a byproduct. Hence, all that modern psychology can do is a mechanical job. Your car is broken down. You go to the workshop and a mechanic fixes it. The psychologist is a mechanic, no different from a plumber. He simply fixes nuts and bolts in your mind, which get loose once in a while; he tightens them here and there. Somewhere they are too tight, somewhere they are loose. But it is a question of nuts and bolts.

The question of enlightenment does not arise for the modern psychologist because enlightenment is based on the experience that mind is not your whole reality. Beyond mind there is your consciousness, and going beyond mind is what enlightenment is all about. The moment you cross the borders of the mind, there is enlightenment: a world of tremendous light, awareness, fulfillment, rejoicings.

But there is a possibility to go even beyond that – because that is your individual consciousness. If you can go beyond it, you enter into the cosmic consciousness. We are living in the ocean of cosmic consciousness, just as a fish lives in the ocean and is not aware of the ocean. Because it is born in the ocean, it lives in the ocean, it dies in the ocean; the fish knows only the ocean. If a fisherman pulls it out of the ocean, throws it in the sand on the beach, then for the first time it becomes aware that something had been surrounding it, nursing it, and giving it life, and that without it, it cannot remain alive.

It is easy to give a fish the experience of being out of the ocean. It is very difficult to give man the experience of being out of the cosmic consciousness. Because the cosmic consciousness is everywhere – there is no beach, there are no boundaries to the cosmic consciousness. So wherever you are, you are always in an invisible ocean of consciousness.

Modern psychology stops at the mind. The mind is only an instrument, and it is an instrument of the physical body – so they are not wrong in saying that it is a byproduct. But the mind is not all. The mind is only a bio-computer, and the day is not far away when the function of the mind will be almost taken over by computers.

You will be able to keep just a small computer in your pocket containing the whole *Encyclopedia Britanica*. Any information about any subject will be immediately available – there is no need to remember it, there is no need to read it, there is no need to study it. Your mind is going to lose its job very soon.

But the psychologist is concerned only with the mind. And there are people called behaviorists who say there is no mind either, that man is only a physical organism.

In the Russia they don't accept the mind. The Russian psychology is even more primitive; it accepts only the behavior of your body. There is nothing which you can call mind; hence in Russia there is nothing parallel to psychoanalysis. There is no question – if somebody's mind is behaving in an abnormal way then medicine is needed, not psychoanalysis. Then he has to be hospitalized; he is suffering from a sickness just like any other sickness.

At least in the West they have taken the first step beyond the body – not a very big step, very small, very negligible, but still a step accepting that there is something like the mind, that although it is a byproduct, it functions on its own as long as the body is alive. And now it is a great profession: psychologists, psychoanalysts, psychotherapists; they are all fixing people's minds because everybody's mind is in trouble.

There are only two kinds of people in the world: normally mad, and abnormally mad. Normally mad means you are mad, but not beyond limits. You are mad just like everybody else. You can see these normally mad people watching a football match. Now can a sane person watch a football match? They need some nuts and bolts, because with a few idiots on this side and a few idiots on that side throwing a ball, and millions of idiots so excited in the stadium and at their television sets, glued to their chairs for six hours so they cannot move, as if something immensely valuable is happening because a ball is being thrown from this side to that side... And millions more, who are not so fortunate to be able to see, keep a transistor at their ears, at least listening to the commentary. You call this world sane?

There are boxing matches: people are hitting each other, and millions of people are so excited. In California, the University of California has been researching... Whenever a boxing match happens in California the crime rate immediately rises by thirteen percent; and it remains thirteen percent higher for seven to ten days afterwards – rape, murder, suicide. And now it is confirmed by other studies that boxing is simply our animal heritage. The one who gets excited in you is the animal; it is not you. You *also* want to kill somebody – many times you have thought of killing somebody – but you are not ready to take the consequences. In a boxing match there is a psychological consolation; you get identified. Every boxer has his own fans. Those fans are identified with him. If he hits the opponent and the opponent's nose is dripping blood, they are rejoicing. What they have not been able to do, somebody else is doing on their part, on their behalf. In any world which is sane, boxing would be a crime. It is a game, but all your games seem to be primitive – nothing of intelligence, nothing of humanity.

These normally mad people are always just on the boundary line. At any time they can slip. A small accident – the wife dies or goes away with somebody else – and you forget the normal boundary, you cross it. Then you are declared mad, insane, and immediately you have to be taken to the psychiatrist or the psychoanalyst. And what is his function? His profession is the highest paid profession in the world. Naturally he makes people normal again, he pulls them back, he keeps them from going farther away from the normal line. His whole expertise is how to put you back and make you normally mad.

Naturally the people who are functioning as psychologists, psychoanalysts, psychotherapists are in danger because they are constantly dealing with mad people. Naturally more psychologists go mad than any other profession – the number is twice as many. More psychologists commit suicide than any other profession – the number again is twice as many. And once in a while every psychologist goes to another psychologist to put himself back into the normal world, because he is slipping out. One would expect that at least the psychologist should be a sane person; he is trying to help other insane people. But this is not the case. They behave more insanely than anybody else, for the simple reason that from morning till night they are constantly coming in contact with all kinds of weird, strange people with weird ideas.

One man was brought to a psychoanalyst. The man was convinced that he was dead. Everybody had tried to tell him: "Don't be foolish, you eat perfectly well, you sleep perfectly well, you talk perfectly well, you go for a morning walk – and you say you are dead?"

He said, "Who says that dead people don't go for a morning walk? Every day I meet many dead people going for a morning walk."

The family was very much puzzled – what to do with the man?

When they found it impossible to convince him – because he wouldn't go to the shop. His argument was clear: "Dead people don't run businesses. I have never come across a single dead man. If you can convince me by bringing a dead man who runs a business, I will go to the shop. I will do only things which dead people are supposed to do – nothing else."

They told the psychoanalyst the whole story: "This man is in a poor state."

The psychologist said, "Don't be worried, I will fix him."

He took a needle and asked this madman: "What do you think about the proverb that 'Dead people don't bleed'?"

He said, "It is absolutely right. I heard it when I was alive: 'Dead people don't bleed.'"

The psychologist was very happy. The family was very happy also, listening, thinking that the psychologist is really great; he is catching him on the first point.

The psychologist pushed the needle into the dead man's hand and blood came out. He looked at the dead man and said, "What do you say now?"

The man said, "That means that proverb is wrong – dead people *do* bleed. I had only *heard* it; now it is my own experience."

If you come across such people the whole day long, in the night you will dream of the same people. Naturally, psychologists don't live a very sane life. And they cannot live a sane life until and unless they accept that there is something beyond the mind. The beyond is the rest, the shelter. The mind is a continuous chattering, it is twenty-four hours chattering. Only beyond the mind is peace and silence. In that peace and silence sanity is born.

Enlightenment is the ultimate peak of sanity: when one becomes perfectly sane, has come to a point where silence, serenity, consciousness are twenty-four hours his, waking or sleeping. There runs a current of tranquility, blissfulness, benediction, which is nourishment, food from the beyond.

Eastern psychology accepts the mind as the lowest part of human consciousness – dismal and dark. You have to go beyond it. And enlightenment is not the end, because it is only individual consciousness. Individuality is still like two banks of a river. The moment the river moves into the ocean, all banks disappear, all boundaries are annihilated. You have gone beyond enlightenment.

Modern psychology has to learn much from the Eastern experiment. It knows nothing. All that modern psychology is doing is analyzing dreams, fixing people to somehow carry on their normal business and repressing their abnormalities. But it brings no transformation. Even the founders of modern psychology – Freud or Jung or Adler or Assagioli – are not people who you can put into the category of Gautam Buddha, Lao Tzu, Chuang Tzu. You cannot put these people with the seers of the Upanishads, with Kabir and Nanak and Farid. They are the sanest people humanity has produced, and they have not bothered about dreams, they have not gone through psychoanalysis for years together.

It is such a strange phenomenon: in the whole world there is not a single person who has completed psychoanalysis – because it goes on and on...ten years, twelve years. There are people who have been in psychoanalysis for twenty years, wasting millions of dollars. In fact, just as everywhere ladies talk about diamonds and emeralds and rubies, in America ladies say: "How long have you been in psychoanalysis? I have been in it for thirteen years!" It is a criterion of wealth; it shows you can afford to pay millions of dollars.

The poor man, the psychoanalyst, has to listen to all kinds of garbage. No wonder that they start going mad, they start committing suicide, they jump from the window of a thirty-story building or hundred-story building! Just listen to a woman's dreams for twenty years... It is a great relief for the husband, he is perfectly happy that she throws all her garbage and tantrums and everything on the psychoanalyst; it is not too costly, he can manage to pay – but for the poor psychoanalyst... Twenty years of listening to one woman and her stupid dreams! If one day he suddenly jumps out of the window, you cannot condemn him – he needs everybody's sympathy.

But it is big business. Just the other day I was telling you that Jesus founded a big business: Christianity. Another Jew, Sigmund Freud, founded another business: psychoanalysis. Another Jew, Karl Marx founded another business: communism.

Jews are strange people. Whenever they do something, nobody can compete with them. Now half the world is communist in one

Jew's hands; the other half is Christian in another Jew's hands. And who knows? – maybe both are partners. Jews are always business minded; they don't bother about Christianity, they don't bother about communism. Sigmund Freud is dead; Karl Marx is dead. Wherever they are – in hell or in heaven – they may be enjoying the fact that their businesses are going well; they may have even joined with Jesus. This would be the real trinity: three Jews running the whole world.

Modern psychology will not accept meditation because meditation will destroy its business. A man of meditation needs no psychoanalysis. The deeper his meditation goes, the saner he becomes and the further beyond the mind is his flight.

Meditation is the greatest danger for psychoanalysis, for psychologists. They have to insist that there is nothing beyond the mind because if there is something beyond the mind, then their whole business can flop. The East has to assert itself, show that what they are doing is simply foolish.

In a Zen monastery in Japan the same kind of psychological case is treated within three weeks; in the West he would not be treated in twelve years. And in the Zen monastery in those three weeks there is no psychoanalysis. You will be surprised: nothing is done; the person is put in an isolated place...a beautiful garden, pond. In time food will be provided, in time tea will be sent; but nobody will talk with him, he has to remain silent. You can see the difference.

In psychoanalysis he has to talk about his dreams continually, for years, one hour every day, two hours, two sessions a week, three sessions a week – as much as you can afford. And here in a Zen monastery they simply put the man in a beautiful, comfortable place. There are musical instruments available, painting material is available, or if there is anything special he wants to do that is made available; but it has to be something to *do* – not talking. And for three weeks nobody will to talk to him. During the three weeks, people paint, people play music, people dance, people work in the garden, and after three weeks they are perfectly normal, they are ready to go back home.

What has happened? If you ask the Zen master, he will say,

"Nothing! These people were working too hard, and their mind got wound up too much. They needed unwinding. So just three weeks rest and their mind was unwound. They needed physical work so that the whole energy went into the body, not into the mind." And these people certainly became interested... Without doing anything all the strange and weird things that they had been thinking had disappeared. This is a simple way for sick people to unwind the overloaded mind.

For those who are healthy – not sick people – the way is meditation. There are different methods for different types. And thousands of people have achieved such luminosity, such glory, such godliness, that all the psychologists of the world should be ashamed. They have not been able to produce a single person like that. Even their founders are just very ordinary – worse than ordinary. Sigmund Freud was so afraid of death that even the word *death* was prohibited. Nobody should mention the word *death* in his presence because just hearing the word he would fall into a fit, he would go unconscious. These are the founders of modern psychology; they are going to give humanity sanity!

And on the other hand, a Zen monk, just before dying, said to his disciples, "Listen, I have always lived in my own way. I am an independent person and I want to die in my own way also. When I am dead I will not be here, so I will give you the instructions to be followed."

Just as in India, it happens in exactly the same way in Japan too; before he is taken to the funeral, the person's clothes are changed, he is given a bath and new clothes are put on him.

The Zen monk said, "I have taken the bath myself, I have changed my clothes, you can see. So when I am dead, there is no need for any bath or changing of clothes. And these are the orders from your master, so remember. At least a dying man's wishes should not be denied – and I am not asking much."

His disciples said, "We will do as you say. There is nothing much to it."

He died, and thousands of disciples were there. When his body was put on the funeral pyre, they all started laughing and giggling.

He had hidden firecrackers inside his clothes. He had made it into a *divali*, just to make everybody laugh – because that was his basic teaching, that life should be a dance, a joy; and death should be a celebration. And people said that even after death he managed it so that nobody should stand around him with a long face, so that everybody was laughing. Even the strangers who had come started laughing; they had never seen such a scene.

These are the people who have understood life and death. They can make death a joke. Not Sigmund Freud, for whom the word *death* becomes a fit. And the same is the case with other great psychologists. Jung wanted to go to Egypt to see the old mummies of kings and queens, dead bodies preserved for three thousand years. But he was very much afraid of death and dead bodies. He was a disciple of Freud. He booked the ticket twelve times, and each time he would find some excuse: "I am feeling feverish," or, "Some urgent work has come."

And he knew. He wrote in his diary: "I knew it was all an excuse. I was avoiding going to Egypt, but the more I avoided it, the more I was attracted – as if I had to go, it was a challenge to my manliness. Am I such a coward? So I would book again, and I would gather courage, and I would try to convince myself that there is nothing to be worried about – they are dead bodies, they cannot do anything to you. And so many people go to see them. They are there in the museums. Thousands of people see them every day. Why are you afraid?" – but arguments won't do. Finally, the twelfth time he booked, he managed to get to the airport, but when the plane came on the airstrip all his courage, arguments and everything disappeared. He said, "I am feeling very sick and nauseous. I want to go back home. Cancel the trip." And after that, he never dared book again; twelve times was enough. He never managed to reach Egypt – which was only a few hours' flight.

He came to India, and he went to all the universities of India. He was here for three months. But he would not go to one man, where he needed to go. He would not go to Shri Raman Maharshi. And in every university it was suggested that he was wasting his time: "You have come to understand the Eastern approach, but we are all

Western-educated psychologists in the Indian universities' psychology departments. You are just wasting your time. These people may be educated in the West or in the East but their education is Western; they know nothing of the East. But by chance there is a man... He knows nothing of psychology, he is absolutely uneducated, but he represents the East. This man has experienced the ultimate flights of meditation. Just go and sit by his side." Jung went up to Madras, but he would not go to see him. It was only a two-hour journey from Madras, but he would not go. And he had come to India to understand what the Eastern attitude to psychology was.

Western psychology – which is the contemporary psychology – is very childish. The East has a ten thousand year-old inquiry into human consciousness. It has touched every nook and corner of human beings, within and without, as individual and as universal.

But it is unfortunate that even the Eastern psychologists and professors of psychology have no idea about the Eastern approach. They are just parrots repeating Western psychology secondhand. That too is not their own original contribution. Sometimes even parrots are better and more intelligent.

I have been a professor in the university, and I have been in constant conflict with the professors: "You are parrots and you are agents of the West without your knowing. You are corrupting the Eastern mind because you don't know what you are doing. You are not even aware of what the East has already discovered. You are just carbon copies carrying certificates from Western universities."

I have often told a story in the universities:

A bishop was looking for a parrot. His own parrot had died. He had been a very religious parrot – religious in the sense that he was able to repeat the Sermon on the Mount accurately, word for word. And whoever heard him was simply amazed. And the parrot had died and the bishop was missing his parrot.

So he went to a very big pet shop, and he looked around. There were many parrots there with many qualities. But he said, "No, my parrot was almost a saint, I want a very religious parrot."

The pet shop owner said, "I have a special parrot – but the price may be too much. He is no ordinary saint, he is a very special saint. Come inside with me. I keep my special parrots in my house behind the shop, not in the shop itself. There in a golden cage was a beautiful parrot.

The pet shop owner said, "This is the religious parrot. You have talked so much about your parrot, but this parrot is unique – you will forget all about yours. Come close and see: on its right leg there is a small thread; if you pull that thread, he will repeat the Sermon on the Mount. There is also a small thread on its left leg; if you pull that, it will repeat the Song of Solomon. So if you have a Jew for a guest, you can make the parrot repeat the Song of Solomon from the Old Testament; or if you have a Christian guest, then the Sermon on the Mount from the New Testament."

The bishop said, "Great, this is really great. And what will happen if I pull both threads together?"

Before the owner could say anything, the parrot said, "Never do that, you idiot. I will fall on my ass!"

Even parrots have some intelligence.

Sooner or later psychology has to inquire into the states created by meditation, into spaces which are beyond mind. And unless it dares to penetrate the innermost core of human beings, it will not become a science. Right now its name is wrong; it has to prove that it is psychology – the science of the soul.

Osho,

During deep relaxation I have experienced some strange things. One is that I felt lifted from the earth, and the second that I felt touched by hands trying to help me.

Every time it happened I felt totally scared, didn't dare to open my eyes, and did everything I know to ground myself.

Osho, can I trust and just let go, or is there danger? "I" don't make myself fly. I don't know how far it would go, and whether I would ever be able to come back.

Can you please comment?

First, can't you recognize my hands? Open your eyes, and just take a good look! You see my hands every day. If in meditation you feel two hands appearing, don't close your eyes. And you will be able to recognize my hands. There is nothing to fear.

In fact, the feeling that you are uplifted from the earth is tremendously valuable. You are not *really* lifted up, you are on the earth; it is not that your body is really lifted up. But you have three bodies. Your physical body will remain on the earth. And because of meditation your mental body is silent, relaxing.

Only the astral body is capable of rising upwards; it is beyond gravitation. Gravitation has no power over it.

Light is not under the control of gravitation. That's why the flame of a candle can go upwards. Even if you put the candle upside down, the flame will immediately turn upwards. The flame cannot go downwards because the gravitation has no pull on light.

Your astral body is made only of light, of electrons.

It is very indicative that you feel that your body is uplifted. Naturally in the beginning you will be gripped by fear: what is happening? But open your eyes.

These are the moments when I am *really* with you in case you need me; hence, you feel two hands because it is a very delicate moment. Any accident is possible. Open your eyes and see. You will be surprised, because it will seem as if you are floating above your body and your body is lying down on the floor. But you will see a thin cord as if made of silver, shining, joined with the body lying down on the floor. The point the silver cord is joined to is your navel, and it is very flexible. You can fly higher, and it will stretch without any difficulty. You can come closer. But don't be afraid. Don't start thinking, "How am I going to get into my body again?"

You have not come out of the body with your effort. It is your silence, your peace that has helped your astral body move out. The moment you feel like getting back into the body, you will immediately find yourself back in the body. And those two hands that were close to you will disappear the moment you are back in the body.

And just watch my hands closely because these will be the same hands, and naturally you need not be afraid of my hands. My hands have never done any harm to anybody. In fact, I cannot do anything with my hands – these must be the laziest hands in the whole world.

But your experience is immensely significant, impeccably beautiful. And the fear that if you go on and on, how far and where it will lead... Don't be worried. Wherever it leads you is the right place, the right space.

Relax and remain in a let-go. You have not to control its movements, because you are far smaller than the energy that you are trying to control. The best way is to simply surrender to existence and allow it to take you wherever it takes you; it has never taken anybody into any wrong space. It always takes you back home.

Osho,

Out on the sparkling seas of oneness, a mysterious wind fills my sails, giving direction to my journey and beckoning me onwards into unknown waters.

My beloved captain, when does the unknown become the unknowable?

Your question is very simple. The mind can be divided into two parts: the known and the unknown. The known is your knowledge; the unknown is your ignorance. And all your universities and educational systems are trying to do only one thing: to put your mind completely in the field of the known, to dispel the unknown, to dispel ignorance.

Beyond the known and the unknown is what I call the unknowable. That is beyond mind. That is the world of the mysterious, the world of the miraculous. The moment you pass beyond the mind, the unknown is left behind, the known is left behind, and you enter into the unknowable. And the unknowable is the field of true religion. You experience it, you live it, you feel it, it becomes your heartbeat, but you can never say you *know* it. Knowledge seems to be a much lower category. The unknowable belongs to the category of being, not to the category of knowing.

The mystics of all the ages, of all countries, are making every effort to push you from the known and unknown into the unknowable, to push you from the mind into the ocean of the mysterious. There you will experience much – much that you can imagine, much that you can dream about – but you will not be able to bring anything from it into the world of knowledge, you will not be able to translate it into words, into language, into anything that can become a symbol for it.

I am reminded of a small child – and a mystic is almost like a small child – the child was sitting with a canvas with all his colors and brushes, and his father was reading the newspaper. Again and again the father looked at the child...he's not doing anything, just sitting there. He said, "What are you doing?"

The child said, "I am painting."

After half an hour the father said, "But I don't see any painting on your canvas. Haven't you decided what you are going to paint yet?"

The boy said, "No, that's not the point. I have painted it."

The father came close to see. He said, "Painted it? I never thought that you would befool me. A plain canvas; you have not even touched it!"

He said, "No, father; I have done my painting. A cow is grazing the grass."

The father said, "A cow grazing in the grass. Where is the cow?"

The boy said, "After grazing the grass, she has gone. What would she do here now?"

The father said, "Okay, where is the grass?"

The boy said, "You are strange; the cow has eaten the grass and gone."

The father said, "How did you make this idea up? To befool me?"

The boy said, "No, I am not befooling you. I saw the grass, I saw the cow, I saw the grass disappearing and I saw her go away."

The child is innocent. Perhaps his imagination... And a child's imagination is really powerful – they cannot make any distinction between the dream and the real. He may have seen a cow and the grass, and when the cow was there and the grass was there he did not paint anything. What is the point of painting on a canvas when there is a cow and grass and everything is already there? But then the cow eats the grass and the cow goes...

The father said, "Stop painting from today, and stop all kind of imagination; otherwise you will go mad."

That's what we are doing with every child. We are not allowing the child's imagination to be refined to such a point that it becomes almost real; otherwise, every person would carry a poet in him, a painter in him, a singer in him, a dancer in him. And finally, the culmination of all that is creative is the mystic.

When you have sung the best of your songs, then silence is the song.

When you have danced the best dance, the dancer disappears. And without the dancer, how can the dance remain?

When your poetry is perfect, there is no poet. The poetry has immense significance but no meaning.

In ancient China a Taoist proverb says: "When the archer is perfect, he throws away his bow and his arrows. When the musician is perfect, he forgets all about his instruments."

There is a mysterious world – illogical to the mind – supra-logical to those who understand the world of the mystic. It surrounds us; we just need the right perception, clear eyes unburdened with knowledge – innocent, weightless. We need wings – wings of love, not of logic. Logic pulls you downwards. It is under the rule of gravitation. Love takes you towards the stars.

Allow the mystic in you, and you have found all that is worth finding.

25 You Are What You Are Seeking

Osho,
From time to time a beautiful story you told us more than a year ago comes to my mind.
It is about a young man who set out to look for truth, and after some failures was given the task of looking after some cows. Starting with just a few of them on the mountains, he had not to come back until he had succeeded in raising one thousand of them. Years went by, until one day the man heard the cows talking to him, saying, "We are one thousand!" Eventually he returned to the valley, where people could hardly distinguish the man from the animals.
Often, simply by recalling this story, tears come to my eyes. There is so much beauty and freshness in the end of the story, that for a few moments it brings my being to a standstill.
Osho, I would love to hear you telling this story again and again: "We are one thousand! We are one thousand!"
Osho, what is the meaning this small tale is carrying? Why do these few words fill me with awe and tears? Would you kindly comment?

The story is one of the most ancient stories of the heart, of the world beyond words – of knowing, not of knowledge, of utter innocence as the door to the divine. The story contains the very essence of meditativeness. It has many dimensions, many implications, and it is no wonder that it fills you with tears of joy. Those tears are indicative that the story has touched your heart, your very being, that you have tasted it although you don't understand what it is. You have felt its beauty, its glory, its depth, but you find it hard to explain to yourself what it is that you have found.

You have found a world of magic, mystery and miracles.

I would love to tell you the whole story. It needs to be told thousands and thousands of times because each time you will find some new fragrance, some new sweetness, some new height, some new door opening, some new sky with new stars. And there are skies beyond skies.

I used to live in a place...I lived there for twenty years, in Jabalpur. Its ancient name was *Jabalipur*; it was named after a great mystic and seer of the Upanishads, Satyakam Jabal. And this story is concerned with Satyakam Jabal.

Satyakam was a very inquiring child. He did not believe in anything unless he had experienced it. When he became a young man – he must have been nearabout the age of twelve – he said to his mother, "Now it is time. The prince of the kingdom has gone to the forest to join the family of a seer. He is my age. I also want to go, I also want to learn what this life is all about."

The mother said, "It is very difficult, Satyakam, but I know that you are a born seeker. I was afraid that one day you would ask me to send you to a master. I am a poor woman, but that is not a great difficulty. The difficulty is that when I was young I served in many houses – I was poor, but I was beautiful. I don't know who your father is. And if I send you to a master, you are going to be asked what the name of your father is. And I am afraid they may reject you.

But there is no harm in making an effort. You go and tell the truth in the same way I have told the truth to you. Many men have used my body because I was poor. Just say that you don't know who your father is. Tell the master that your name is Satyakam, your mother's name is Jabala; so they can call you Satyakam Jabal. And as far as the search for truth is concerned, who your father is does not matter."

Satyakam went to an ancient seer in the forest, and sure enough the first question was, "What is your name? Who is your father?"

And he repeated exactly what his mother had said.

There were many disciples – princes, rich people's sons. They all started laughing.

But the old master said, "I will accept you. It does not matter who your father is. What matters is that you are authentic, sincere, unafraid – capable of saying the truth without feeling embarrassed. Your mother has given you the right name, Satyakam. *Satyakam* means one whose only desire is truth. You have a beautiful mother, and you will be known as Satyakam Jabal. And the tradition is that only brahmins can be accepted as disciples. I declare you a brahmin – because only a brahmin can have the courage of such truth."

Those were beautiful days. The old seer's name was Uddalak. Satyakam became his most loved disciple. He deserved it; he was so pure and so innocent.

But Uddalak had his own limitations. Although he was a man of great learning, he was not an enlightened master. So he taught Satyakam all the scriptures, he taught him everything that he was capable of, but he could not deceive Satyakam as he had been deceiving everybody else. Not that Satyakam was raising any doubts; it was just that his innocence had such power that the old man had to confess, "Whatever I have been telling you is knowledge gathered from the scriptures. It is not my own. I have not experienced it; I have not lived it. I suggest that you go deeper into the forest. I know a man who has realized, who has become an embodiment of truth, love, compassion. Go to him."

Uddalak had heard about the man, but did not know the man personally. Uddalak was far more famous; he was a great scholar.

Satyakam went to the other man. This man taught him many new scriptures, and all the Vedas: the most ancient scriptures of the world. And after years he told him, "Now you know everything; there is nothing more to know. You can go back home."

First he went to see Uddalak. From his window, Uddalak saw Satyakam coming on the footpath through the forest. He was shocked. Satyakam's innocence was lost; in place of innocence there was pride – naturally, because now he thought he knew everything in the world that is worth knowing. The very idea was so ego fulfilling.

He came in. As he started to touch the feet of Uddalak, Uddalak said, "Don't touch my feet! First, I want to know where you have lost your innocence. It seems I have sent you to the wrong man."

Satyakam said, "To the wrong man? He has taught me everything that is worth knowing."

Uddalak said, "Before you touch my feet, I would like to ask you: have you experienced anything or it is just information? Has any transformation happened? Can you say that whatever you know is *your* knowledge?"

Satyakam said, "I cannot say that. What I know is written in the scriptures; I have not experienced anything."

Uddalak said, "Then go back, but now go to another person I have come to know about while you were gone. And unless you have experienced, don't come back. You have come here not more than when I sent you but less. You have lost something of immense value. And what you call knowledge – if it is borrowed, it only covers your ignorance; it does not make you a knower. Go to this man and tell him that you have not come for more information about truth, about God, about love. Tell him you have come to *know* truth, to *know* love, to *know* God. Tell him, 'If you can fulfill the promise, only then waste my time; otherwise I will find another master.'"

Satyakam said exactly this.

The master was sitting under a tree with a few of his disciples. After listening to the request, he said, "It is possible, but you are asking something very difficult. There are so many disciples here – they all want more knowledge. They want to know about and about. But if you insist that you are not interested in information, that you are ready to do anything, that your devotion to truth is total, then I will find a way for you."

Satyakam said, "I am ready to sacrifice my life, but I cannot go without knowing the truth. Neither can I go to my teacher nor can I go to my mother, who has given me the name Satyakam. And my teacher accepted me without knowing whether I was a brahmin or not, just on the simple grounds that I was truthful. Tell me what has to be done."

The master said, "Take all these cows that you see here, deep into the forest. Go as deep as possible, so you don't come in contact again with any human being. The purpose is that you forget language, words. Live with the cows, take care of the cows, play on your flute, dance – but forget words. And when the cows have grown to one thousand, come back."

The other disciples could not believe what was happening – because there were just a dozen or two dozen cows. How long is it going to take for them to become one thousand?

But Satyakam took the cows, went as deep as possible into the forest, beyond human contact, beyond human context. For a few days it was difficult but slowly, slowly... The cows were his only company. And they are very silent people. He played on the flute, he danced alone in the forest; he rested under the trees.

For a few years he continued to count the cows. Then by and by he dropped it, because it seemed impossible that they would become one thousand. And moreover he was forgetting how to count; language was disappearing. Words disappeared; counting could not be saved.

And the story is so immensely beautiful: the cows became worried when they became one thousand, because they wanted to go back home, and this man had forgotten how to count. Finally the cows decided, "We have to speak; otherwise this lonely forest is going to become our grave."

So one day the cows caught hold of him and told him, "Listen, Satyakam, we are now one thousand and it is time to go back home."

He said, "I am very grateful to you. If you had not told me... I had even forgotten about home or about returning. Each moment was so tremendously beautiful – so many blessings. In the silence, flowers went on showering. I had forgotten everything. I had no idea why I had come here, who I am. Everything had become an end in itself: playing the flute was enough, resting under the trees was enough, seeing the beautiful cows sitting silently all around was so beautiful. But if you insist, we should return."

The disciples of the great master saw him coming with one thousand cows. They reported to the master, "We had never believed that he would come back. He is coming, and we have counted exactly one thousand cows. He is coming!"

And when he came, he stood there – just in the crowd of cows.

The master said to the other disciples, "You counted wrong. There are one thousand and one cows; you forgot to count Satyakam! He has moved beyond your world, he has entered into the innocent, the silent, the mysterious. He is not saying anything, he is just standing there as the cows are standing there."

The master said, "Satyakam, come out. Now you have to go to your other master who sent you here. He is an old man and he must be waiting. Your mother must be waiting."

And when Satyakam came to Uddalak, his first teacher – who had not allowed him to touch his feet because he had lost his innocence, he was no longer a brahmin, he had fallen, he had become just a knowledgeable parrot – as Uddalak saw him from the window again, he ran out the back door, because now Satyakam cannot be allowed to touch his feet; now Uddalak would have to touch Satyakam's feet. Because Uddalak was still a scholar, and Satyakam was coming not as a scholar but as one who is awakened.

Uddalak escaped from the house: "I cannot face him. I am ashamed of myself. Just tell him," he told his wife, "that Uddalak is dead and he can go now to his mother. Tell him I died remembering him." These were people made of different mettle. Satyakam went back home.

The mother had become very old, but she had waited and waited and waited. And she said, "You have proved, Satyakam, that truth is always victorious. And you have proved that a brahmin is not born, a brahmin is a quality to be achieved. Everybody by his birth is a *sudra,* because everybody's birth is the same. One has to prove by purifying himself, by crystallizing himself, by becoming centered and enlightened, that he is a brahmin. Just to be born into the family of a brahmin does not make you a brahmin."

If you meditate on the story, you will see: the very essence of meditation is to be so silent that there is no stirring of thoughts in you, that words don't come between you and reality, that the whole net of words falls down, that you are left alone.

This aloneness, this purity, this unclouded sky of your being is meditation. And meditation is the golden key to all the mysteries of life.

Osho,

I have the most beautiful master ever – life has given me so much since I have been with you – but still, except for moments of beatitude with you or in my meditation, deep down in myself there is always a deep-rooted sadness and a longing for some space that I hardly can remember.

Can you please comment?

Meditation always opens doors, different doors to different people. Sadness is not necessarily something bad. Don't judge it as a bad or negative quality. When a person who has never been silent, for the first time becomes silent, the very silence feels sad because there is no excitement, no firecrackers.

You can misunderstand your first acquaintance with silence as sadness, but it is not sadness. It is just that you have always been engaged in a thousand and one things and now they have all disappeared. You feel a little lost. Before silence becomes a song, a small period, a transitory period, is absolutely necessary. You know sadness. And sadness has something of silence in it – whenever you are sad, you are a little silent. So there is an association between your sadness and silence. When you become silent for the first time, the only thing you can feel from your past experience is sadness.

Allow it to deepen. Don't judge it as sadness, because that very judgment may become a barrier. The moment you say something negative you are trying to get rid of it. Don't say anything negative about it. Just accept it as a bridge between silence and song. Just wait a little, and you will start feeling that this silence is not dead, it is not the silence of the graveyard. It is a silence which is very much alive, a silence which is not empty but too full, overflowing.

Overflowing with what? Again, a new experience is waiting for you. You have known only songs with words. You have never known a pure song without words, music without sound. Just a little waiting, and the sadness will start turning into a song with no words, into music with no sounds, into a dance with no movements.

Everything is going perfectly well; just a little bit of patience is needed.

When you are sick, in the hospitals you are called *patients*. Have you ever thought about why? It is because healing takes time, and you have to be patient. This is inner healing, and you need a deeper patience.

But if silence is there and meditation is happening, then there is no problem at all. Spring will be coming soon with all its colors and all its flowers and all its beauty. Just wait a little.

Osho,

I was born in the mountains, and throughout my childhood and youth I was pulled to explore, climb, or just sit on the peaks, on the steep walls, or by the side of a glacier stream. I lived in the mountains, and they fed me, like a mother, with something very precious.

Somewhere I read that the mountains, the high, snow-capped peaks are the very essence of Buddha.

Osho, the beauty that surrounds you, the cool breeze that hovers around you, is like the one coming from the highest, the wildest peak in the world.

I've been with you for seven years, and in this last period of time I felt that I was passing through the same pastures, the same plains I remember leaving for the heights seven years ago. I see the starting point as completely different now: it is sweet and beautiful, enough unto itself, no longer awful and disgusting as it used to be.

Osho, I haven't come to know anything; the thousand suns did not shine in my head. All I've got now is myself, contented, at the same point from where I started my journey seven years ago.

Have I been dreaming all these years of traveling far away when my feet did not leave the base camp? Or was all this to realize that where I started from is where I belong?

Osho, please tell me... Sometimes this dream seems to be real, but now my being does not feel as if it is pulled to go anywhere. Have I been cheating myself? Or is this as far as it is allowed for me to go in this life?

Will you tell me the truth? I'm tired now; be merciless, but please say what is really happening to me.

It is not only with you, but with everybody exactly the same. You are what you are seeking. You are standing at exactly the place towards which you have been traveling – for seven years, seventy years or seven hundred years. Your reality is within you; it is not somewhere else. But to understand the point, sometimes it takes years. You knock on many doors before you come to your own door, and then you are puzzled, because this is the house you had left *and* this is the house you have been searching for.

But the search has not been useless; it has given you the eyes to recognize.

I have often told a Sufi story: a man renounces the world, his wife, his home. He is young and he is going in search of a master. Just outside his village under a tree, an old man is sitting. The sun is just setting, and darkness is descending. The young man says to the old man, "You look as if you are a traveler; you certainly don't belong to my village. I am a young man and I am in search of a master. You are old; perhaps you have come across a master in your journeys, and will be kind enough to help me with some directives, some guidelines, because I am feeling at a loss where to go."

The old man said, "I will give you exact details. The master looks like this" – and he described the face of the master, the eyes of the master, the nose of the master, the beard of the master, his robe. "And he sits under a certain tree" – and he described the tree.

And he said, "You will find him; just remember these details. Whenever you find a man who fulfills these criteria, you have found your master."

Thirty years passed. The young man became old, tired. He never came across anybody fitting the description given by the old man.

Finally he gave up the whole idea of finding a master: "Perhaps there is no master anywhere."

He went back to his village. And as he was entering the village, under the same tree... It was sunrise, there was more light. The old man had become very old. The last time they had met he must have been sixty; now he was ninety. And because for thirty years the man had been looking for certain eyes, a certain nose, a certain beard, a certain robe, a certain tree... As he saw the tree and he saw the old man he said, "My God, so you were describing yourself! Why didn't you tell me? Why did you force me to travel unnecessarily around the world for thirty years searching for you, while you were sitting here?"

The old man said, "First throw out all your tantrums and your anger; then I will tell you the truth. Thirty years ago you were too young. The time was not right; it was sunset, darkness was descending. And you were in such a hurry to go in search, that if I had told you that I was the master you would have laughed and said, 'This is strange that you are sitting just outside my village.' And you cannot blame *me* because I explained every detail, but your eyes were looking far away. You were listening to me, but you were not looking to see that I was describing my eyes, my nose, my beard, my robe; that I was describing the tree under which I was sitting. You were not ripe.

"These thirty years have not gone to waste; they have matured you. Now you can recognize me. Just look; it is sunrise, the right time. And it is not the beginning of your journey; you had already given up. I am meeting you at the end of thirty years of long, arduous effort. That which you can get cheap you cannot recognize. You had to pay these thirty years and all the troubles that you went through just to be mature enough to recognize me.

"I could have told you on that day too – but it would have been pointless, and you would have missed me.

"And you think *you* have been in trouble for thirty years? Just think about *me* – for thirty years I have been sitting under the same tree, because I described *this* tree. I have not left it for a single day because I was aware that any moment you might come, and if you didn't find me here I would have been proved to have spoken lies. I have been sitting here for thirty years continuously – day in, day out; summer, winter, rain, but I have been sitting here. And you see I am old. I was worried that if I died before you came back, it would be a tragedy. So I have been trying to somehow cling to life, because as far as I am concerned there is nothing left, I have realized myself. Life has given everything that it can give. I have been sitting just for you."

The story is strange, but significant. It takes time to realize that which you are. Basically there is no need; you can realize just now, this very moment. But to realize it you will need a certain maturity, a certain centering, a certain awareness, a certain silence. Seven years are not long. And don't be worried that you have not seen a thousand suns rising in you; it is not necessary. Everybody experiences his innermost being in his own way. Somebody experiences it as light, but that is his type. There are people who have realized it as immense darkness. You are hearing the firecrackers all around.

Two religions in India, Hindus and Jainas, celebrate a festival, the festival of lights. They have different reasons; it is just a coincidence that something has happened on the same day in the history of both religions.

Hindus celebrate it because Rama, one of the Hindu incarnations of God, was victorious over Ravana. He came back after fourteen years of wandering in the forest and the mountains to his capitol, Ayodhya. And because he was coming back after fourteen years, the capitol celebrated with lights and firecrackers and rejoicings. That is the Hindu reason.

For Jainas this is not the reason. Mahavira became enlightened on the same day, and Mahavira is the most important individual in the history of Jainism. Jainas are celebrating because Mahavira attained liberation. And he attained liberation in a unique way. Mahavira is unique in that he became enlightened on the night of *amawas*, no moon, complete darkness. He is alone; there is nobody else who has become enlightened on the night of amawas.

Gautam Buddha became enlightened on a full-moon night. And except for Mahavira, anybody who has become enlightened has become enlightened either on a full-moon night or close to it. Individual types... Gautam Buddha was born on a full-moon night. He became enlightened on a full-moon night. He died on a full-moon night. This cannot be just coincidence. His type has something to do with a synchronicity with the full-moon night.

There are saints, mystics...when they become enlightened, they smell some perfume which is not of this world. Because of this experience, among Sufi mystics perfume has become very significant, and Sufi mystics of different schools use different kinds of perfume. Because their master experienced a certain perfume, they use something parallel to it. It cannot be exactly the same, but something parallel, on the lowest rung of the same ladder, which the master experienced on the highest rung. They use that perfume as a remembrance of their master. Some have heard unworldly music, *anahat nad*. Because people are of different types, their ultimate experience is also going to be of a different type; it is going to have their signature on it.

So don't be worried if you are not seeing a thousand and one suns rising in you. Kabir has seen them. Gautam Buddha has not seen them. Mahavira has not seen them. But there are a few other mystics who have seen them. Just as you are unique in your ordinary life... You know people who have a sensitivity for music, and there are others who don't have any ear for music.

Mulla Nasruddin's wife bought two tickets for a classical concert. Mulla tried hard, but could not escape; he had to go to the concert. It was classical Indian music. So when the musician started doing his *aalap*, tuning his instrument, Mulla Nasruddin's eyes became full of tears. His wife said, "I never thought you loved classical music so much."

He said, "It is not the classical music. I am crying because this man is going to die!"

The wife said, "What gave you the idea this man is going to die?"

He said, "You wouldn't understand. One night one of my goats started doing exactly what this man is doing. And I said, 'What is the matter?' I tried hard to stop her but she wouldn't listen, and in the morning she was dead. I can guarantee that by morning this man is going to be dead; this is the beginning of the disease. This is not music."

He had never heard classical music. The poor fellow had one similar experience...a natural conclusion.

There are people who are sensitive to certain things, for example paintings, and there are a few who are not at all sensitive to paintings. In the life of Michelangelo there was one incident. Just a few years ago, you may have read in the newspapers, a man, a madman destroyed one of the most beautiful statues in the Vatican. It was of Jesus Christ lying in his mother's lap after he was taken down from the cross. That statue was thought to be the best statue in the whole world. And certainly it was so alive. Michelangelo had put all his art into it; it was his masterpiece. And this man simply destroyed it with a hammer because he wanted to become world famous. He became world famous. This incident in Michelangelo's life concerns the same statue.

Michelangelo went into a shop in the market where there were shops selling marble. Just in front of the shop on the open ground there was a big rock – a huge marble rock that had been lying there for years – and he asked, "What is the price?"

The owner said, "There is no price; it has been lying there for almost ten years, and you are the first person ever to ask about it. If you can take it away, it is yours. It will be enough payment that our grounds are cleared and we can put out other rocks for show. That rock is taking so much space. And every artist comes here; no artist has ever seen any possibility for that rock."

And Michelangelo cut from that same rock this statue that was destroyed a few years ago.

When the statue was ready, he invited the shop owner. The man could not believe it. He said, "Where did you get such a beautiful piece of marble?"

Michelangelo said, "This is the same rock that you gave me at no charge."

The man said, "My God, but you have created the most beautiful statue I have ever seen. How could you manage to think, looking at that ugly rock, that you would be able to do it?"

He said, "I have not done anything. It was just that Jesus cried out to me, 'Michelangelo, I am encaged in this rock. Make me free.'"

This is genius. Jesus was there; Mary was there. But to see the possibility in that ugly rock, you need a certain insight.

Now, if Michelangelo becomes enlightened, his experience will have something to do with his genius. If Yehudi Menuhin becomes enlightened, *his* enlightenment will have something to do with his musical genius.

Each individual is unique in ordinary life. The uniqueness becomes even sharper and clearer, crystal clear, when the person becomes enlightened – because only then his pure genius, his pure individuality, uncontaminated, unpolluted, is revealed.

So never be concerned that what has happened to others should happen to you. Sometimes it can happen because in this big world, millions of people have lived before, and thousands of people have become enlightened; you may have something similar. You may have something which will look strange to others.

Ashok Bharti has recently asked a question which is unique because it happened only once before. Since he has been here he has been singing songs; those who have been here can see that the quality, the joy, the celebration has been growing. But something else has been happening that you cannot see. He has written in his question, "Osho, my breasts are growing like women's breasts. And feminine qualities which I was not aware of before are becoming more and more expressive." If he says this to anybody else, they will think he is mad: "Just go to a doctor, you have some hormonal disturbance."

But it happened in Ramakrishna's life, and something much more. After his enlightenment Ramakrishna tried whatever methods were available. He wanted to see whether he could reach the same experience through other methods, because he wanted there to be only one religion in the world. Every religious person should have that desire. It is ugly to see that there are three hundred religions in the world, continually fighting and continually destroying each other, talking about love and killing each other.

In Bengal, there is a small religious group which believes that Krishna is the only man and everybody else is a woman. It is a strange kind of idea, and everybody else laughs about it, and particularly at the behavior of those people because they sleep with a statue of Krishna close to their bosom at night, just like a woman sleeps with her husband or her lover.

Ramakrishna tried their ideology also, and in six months time his breasts became just like those of women. But what was even stranger was that he started having a menstrual period. The sincerity of the man, the totality of the man: whenever he followed anything, whenever he did anything he did it completely.

So it is possible: singing songs of love... Your mind is the creator of your body, it affects your body. You can see it happening in the West in the women who are concerned with the liberation movement. Their breasts slowly disappear because they don't want to be women; they want to be men. And they want in every possible way to be exactly like men: in their dress, in their behavior, in their language. For example, nowhere in the East will any woman use a four-letter word; that is simply ungraceful. But in the West, that is part of the liberated woman: to smoke cigarettes and to use four-letter words. One is just waiting for the day when they start pissing standing up! They might start – equality is equality! One can go to stupid lengths. But in the West, the breast has suffered immensely. The Eastern woman is still rich as far as breasts are concerned. Your mind has immense power over your body. If your mind takes up a certain idea, sooner or later the body will follow it. The body is slow, but it will follow it.

But even beyond the mind, your individuality is intact. No two individuals' experience is exactly the same. That has been the cause of a great tragedy, because Mohammed experiences something which Mahavira does not experience, and then the followers start making criteria: if they follow Mahavira then Mahavira's experience becomes the criterion; unless somebody experiences the same, his experience is not right. The same is true of the followers of Mohammed or Moses or Zarathustra.

But the truth is – and nobody has been insisting on it – that all are unique people; they all grow different flowers. The similarity is in the blossoming but not in the color of the flowers or in the fragrance of the flowers. The color and the fragrance is going to be unique – and it is good, because it makes spiritual life rich; otherwise it will be very monotonous.

So don't be worried about anybody's experience. And if you are fed up with the journey, perhaps you are coming back to your village and I am sitting there under the tree. Just recognize me! I have been telling you in every possible way who the master is.

Osho,

You described in "The Mustard Seed" how Ramakrishna was addicted to food, and people would never have thought that a liberated man could be addicted to food. Before he died, he said he was clinging to something imperfect in him so he could be here and serve people.

You say many masters have done this. The moment they feel that something is going to become completely perfect in them, they will cling to some imperfection just to stay here.

Now Osho, what are you clinging to, or planning to cling onto?

I am addicted to you!

26 The Alchemy of Enlightenment

Osho,
Since my childhood, I have seen you as a buddha; even before your enlightenment I saw you as a buddha – the same serenity, the same natural glow, the same spontaneity, the same love, the same compassion, the same carefree-ness, the same blissfulness as today.

I have seen many of your phases, and I say again and again that you were a buddha before your enlightenment.

The story of your enlightenment is a device for us, is a beautiful assurance for us.

I am immensely grateful. I feel fortunate that you showered your love and compassion on me from the beginning. You have helped me at each step, at each turning point of my life. You changed my life, you filled my life with love and joy, you gave me immense clarity, you made me free.

I bow down to you. Buddham sharanam gachchhami, buddham sharanam gachchhami, buddham sharanam gachchhami.

Narendra, you are almost right. But remember my emphasis on the word *almost*.

And this is true not only about me, this is true about everybody else too: Everybody is by nature a divine being, an awakened soul, a Gautam Buddha, who has just fallen asleep for a while, has just forgotten himself for a moment and is lost in dreams, beautiful dreams of ambition, desire, success, to be someone special in the world, to leave footprints behind.

The moment your dream is broken, your sleep has gone, suddenly you are in for a great surprise, perhaps the greatest surprise: that the treasure you have been looking for is within you, that the paradise you have been searching for is within you, that there is no God who can drive you out of the Garden of Eden because the Garden of Eden is your very being. At the most you can forget it but you cannot lose it. And once you recognize it, then life becomes really hilarious; you can laugh at your own efforts and endeavors, at your whole past that you have spent in searching for it.

And the goal of your search was not *away* from you, not even *close* to you. *You* were the goal; the seeker was the sought.

And everything that you have done before you became enlightened, everything that you have been before you became aware of your tremendous beauty, of your eternal life, will take a different meaning after your enlightenment. To you and to those who are close to you, the enlightenment will make such a great difference.

Narendra has known me since he was a child. But if I had not become enlightened he would not have asked me this question or raised this question to himself. Even the very idea of buddhahood might not have happened to him; he would have known me as a friend, he would have known me as a loving companion.

It is the enlightenment that changes the meaning of all his experiences, gives them a new color, a new light, a new luminosity. The same incidents start having a totally new meaning. I can understand your question. Now you look backwards, but because now you know my enlightenment you can easily conclude that I was always enlightened, that I was born enlightened; otherwise those incidents of love, care, understanding would not have taken such a colorful and meaningful significance. That's why I say you are almost right.

I myself can look retrospectively, then everything starts taking on a new meaning. It would not have had the same meaning. It is the alchemy of enlightenment that everything has become pure gold, that small and meaningless things have taken wings and have become great.

I will give you a few examples which could not have been understood in the same way they have been understood; there was no possibility, no hope.

One of my teachers was very perfectionist, a great disciplinarian, a very beautiful man. Every year he started his class with the same introduction, because the students were new; he introduced himself by saying, "It is better that I should make clear to you what kind of man I am, so you are not in the dark and you don't do anything without understanding the nature of the teacher. First: I don't believe in headaches, stomach aches, no. Anything that you cannot prove and anything that I cannot check by myself will not be an excuse to take a holiday or to go home. You can have a fever; I can feel your fever. So remember it. I simply don't believe in headaches and stomach aches because there is no proof. Even a physician has to rely upon the patient, that he has a headache – he may be lying, or he may be in illusion. What is the guarantee? How do you know that you are right?"

I thought, "This is strange; this is going to be difficult" – because those were simple excuses to escape from any class, to say, "I have a strong headache and I want to go home."

He used to go every evening for a walk. Just by the side of the school there was a beautiful road, covered from both sides with big trees, mango trees.

I thought, "Things have to be settled from the very beginning."

So I climbed up into a tree, high up, and waited for this teacher – he was a Mohammedan, his name was Rahimuddin. He came exactly on time. He was very precise in everything; at exactly the same time each day he used to pass by that tree.

I dropped a big mango on his head. He said, "Ahhhh!" and looked up. And he saw me there.

I asked, "What is the matter? What has happened?"

For a moment there was silence. He said, "Come down."

I came down.

He said, "You have proved that there is something like a headache, but don't tell anybody. If you have a headache, just raise one finger and I will give you a holiday. If you have a stomach ache, you need not prove it to me – just raise two fingers, because you seem to be dangerous!"

He was a bachelor, an old man; he had never married. He lived a very beautiful life, had a small cottage, a garden.

And he was very famous for one strange thing – because he had enough money, unmarried, no children, no wife... He had three hundred and sixty-five suits of clothes, one for each day; then for the whole year that suit of clothes would not be used again. Naturally every husband was jealous.

He said, "I live alone. I sleep outside in the garden, and I don't want any proof for stomach ache! – so one is enough. You have given me the proof that you are capable, so when you have a stomach ache raise two fingers and I will understand. But this is an agreement between us: that you will not tell anybody else that headaches or stomach aches exist."

I said, "I am not worried about anybody else. My problem is solved because I want things from the very beginning to be clear, just like you do."

He said, "You have made it *very* clear – it is still hurting! I have been a teacher thirty years and nobody ever thought of this idea. I will remember you for my whole life."

It was a small incident, and would have been forgotten – but when people started coming to me many years after this incident he started telling people, "I knew beforehand that this boy was going to be someone extraordinary."

People asked, "How did you come to know? – and you never mentioned it before."

He said, "I had almost forgotten it; just now, as his name is becoming known around the world and people are coming to him from all over the world, I remembered. And now that incident has a totally different meaning. Because for my whole life I was introducing every class in the same way and nobody ever tried anything. And this was the only one – a singular instance – who proved to me that a headache had to be accepted. I knew it that very day."

In 1970 I went to that village for the last time. He had become very old. Hearing that I was there, he came to see me. I said, "I was going to come to you. You are too old, you should not have bothered to walk almost two miles."

He said, "I am feeling so happy. Seeing you it still hurts, but now I feel a certain pride that you were *my* student."

Now the whole thing takes a different color, it becomes a pride. Otherwise, if I had turned out to be a thief or a criminal, then the same incident would have been a proof: "I knew from the very beginning that this boy was going to be a criminal, that sooner or later he would murder somebody."

Retrospectively you always look at things in a way you would not have looked at them if life had moved in a different direction. The same things would not have given you the same indications.

By the way, I would like to remind you that all autobiographies are false because they are all written retrospectively. A man becomes a Mahatma Gandhi and then he writes his autobiography in the light of what he has become. He starts looking at things in the past when he was not Mahatma Gandhi, and everything now has to fit with Mahatma Gandhi. There has to be a logical connection, a coherence. So it is as if you are reading a novel backwards – things will be totally different. All autobiographies are fictions. They should not be categorized separately in any library. The science of librarianship should understand a simple fact: that every autobiography is a fiction.

For example, the day Mahatma Gandhi's father died he was with his father massaging his feet, and the doctors had said that this was going to be the last night; there was no hope that this man would ever see the sunrise, before sunrise he would be gone. In the middle of the night, Mahatma Gandhi was massaging his father's feet, but he was thinking of his wife. The father was dying. It was an absolute certainty that this was his last night, and he had fallen asleep. Seeing that he was asleep, Mahatma Gandhi slipped silently into his wife's room, and while he was making love to his wife, his father died. And suddenly the whole house was awake. He heard the noise. "What is the matter?" And he could not forgive himself, that even for one night he could not remain away from his wife when the death of his father was absolutely certain.

If he had not become a famous man, a world-famous man, this incident would not have carried any importance; perhaps he himself would have forgiven it, forgotten it – just an ordinary incident. But writing his autobiography, he connects it with the great mahatma that he became. And this is all fiction. He says that he became concerned about celibacy because of this incident. He started thinking of *brahmacharya*, celibacy, because of this incident. This is not true, but he has to fit the incident into the life of a mahatma. And it fits perfectly well; anybody reading it will feel that there seems to be a certain connection. But it is not true, because all his four sons were born *after* this incident. So he cannot deceive me. He is deceiving himself, he is deceiving his followers; he is deceiving the historians. But if this was the cause of his becoming a celibate, then he would have remained without any children. All four sons were born after this incident, so this incident has nothing to do with celibacy.

But in his mind – and in anybody's mind who is reading Mahatma Gandhi – it seems relevant, that perhaps the shock was too much, as if: "I am guilty of the death of my father. I could have stayed a few more minutes, but my lust, my sexuality proved to be more powerful than my love and respect for my father. And my wife was going to remain with me for my whole life, but my father was going to disappear that very night into darkness and into the unknown and there would not be another meeting again."

I have read many autobiographies, and I have seen how people when they look backwards look with the eyes that they have now, and with all the experience they have accumulated meanwhile. With all this experience, with these new eyes, the meaning of the incidents starts changing.

Narendra, you have been with me from your very childhood. If

I had not become what I have become, you would have remembered me as loving, as friendly, but you would have never thought I was born as a buddha. That idea arises now. It is my enlightenment that gives you the feeling: "My God, he was always loving." But it was not the same love.

In a sense, the dewdrop and the ocean are both water. But a dewdrop is a dewdrop, and an ocean is an ocean. What you had seen in me was only a dewdrop. Now that dewdrop looks like an ocean because now you are seeing the ocean. It is exactly as if you see the Ganges in the Himalayas at Gangotri – it is just a small stream. You could not even hope that it would ever reach the ocean; it is so small. Hindus have placed a marble face of a cow there, and the Ganges falls from the mouth of the cow, it is such a small stream. You will find millions of streams in the Himalayas which are much bigger.

But if you see the same Ganges near Calcutta, in Gangasagar – *Gangasagar* means the "ocean of Ganges" – it has become so big, so vast, so immense that it is difficult to think of it as a river; it looks oceanic. To connect the two is very difficult. The Ganges in Gangotri could have been one of those millions of streams, which disappear in the forest, in the desert, and nobody would have remembered it. But because this stream became *Gangasagar*, retrospectively, looking backwards, even standing at the source where the stream is so small, you have the feeling of vastness, of potentiality, of all the possibilities that it is going to become. You cannot see it just like a small stream; it is the stream that is going to become *Gangasagar*. Each autobiography is fictitious; small incidents with no meaning in themselves suddenly start having meaning in the context of the person that has come to be.

Essentially it is true: everybody is a buddha, and naturally I am not an exception. Please don't exclude me out. But this buddhahood is only a seed, and out of millions of seeds perhaps one seed comes to blossom. It indicates that every seed can come to blossom. It is a tremendous encouragement to every human being.

In this sense your seeing me as a born buddha is right, but don't forget *your* responsibility. It means you have to prove it too – that you are also a born buddha. Maybe you started growing a little late. And in the eternity of time, what is late? There are only seven days. Choose any day, but start.

I am not interested at all in converting anybody to my ideology – I don't have any. Secondly, I believe that the very effort to convert anybody is violence; it is interfering in his individuality, in his uniqueness, into his freedom. So my function is not that of a teacher, not that of a prophet, not that of a savior, not that of a messenger. My function simply is that of a reminder. I want to be just a mirror to you so that you can see your original face.

And if you can see a buddha in me, there is no difficulty in seeing the buddha in you too – maybe a little lazy, a little sleepy, a little gone off the track. But a buddha is a buddha. It does not matter whether his nuts and bolts are a little loose, we will fix them. One's buddhahood is one's essential nature.

I don't want you to worship buddhas, I want you to become buddhas. That is the only right worship. If you love, become it.

Osho,

Gautam Buddha, Mahavira, J. Krishnamurti were traveling from one place to another for their whole lives. It was reported about J. Krishnamurti that before he left India for California for the last time he told someone that if the doctor in California said, "No more travel, no more talk," then all would be finished; he would be gone in four weeks – and that's exactly what actually happened.

Osho, what is the insight of all the masters who were traveling all the time and didn't stay in one place like Raman Maharshi?

Raman Maharshi is a mystic, but not a master. The mystics have never traveled because the mystics are not making any effort of any kind to transfer their experience to others. They have decided that what they have experienced is non-transferable, that it cannot be communicated. So the mystics all through the ages have remained in one place. What is the point of moving around, going from village to village or country to country – for what? The mystic's experience is expressed in the ancient saying that "The well remains in its own place; it is the thirsty who should go to the well, the well cannot go to the thirsty."

Buddha, Mahavira, Bodhidharma, Shankara, Nagarjuna, Mohammed, Jesus, J. Krishnamurti, they were all traveling, going continuously... Mohammed has countered the proverb about the well and the thirsty, and countered it in such a beautiful way. He says, "If the mountain cannot come to Mohammed, then Mohammed will go to the mountain." These are masters.

Not that they are against the mystics; basically they agree that it is difficult, almost impossible to communicate, to say anything about the truth, about self-realization. It is beyond words, beyond language; they agree on that point. But still the masters say that some indirect ways can be always tried, and there is no harm.

There is no direct way of translating the inner experience into the outer languages, but ways can be found, devices can be created in which something may be said, may not be said, but may be *heard*. The emphasis is not that the truth can be said. On that, the mystics and the masters agree: it cannot be said. But the masters disagree with the mystics on one point: that it may not be said but it can be *heard* – through the eyes of the master, through the presence of the master, through his love, through his compassion, through his silence, just being with him. Nothing is said, but somebody's heart may start dancing, a song may arise.

In the presence of the master, the disciple may become aware that the ordinary human life is not all there is; there is something more. Even to make them aware that there is something more – greater peace, deeper silence, overflowing ecstasy – perhaps they may start searching for it; perhaps they may become seekers. And what is the harm? If nobody listens, then still the effort is worth making. The mystic and the master both have the same experience, but they have different views about its transfer – and both seem to be right.

My own understanding is this: that the mystics are of a more ordinary variety. They come from the categories of human beings who are not articulate, who are not poets, who are not painters, who are not musicians, who are not dancers. They come from the common masses.

And the master is more articulate, more talented. If he cannot say, he will paint; if he cannot say, he will sculpt; if he cannot say, he will dance; if he cannot say, he will sing – and singing, dancing, painting or any other creative art may become a vehicle for that which language is not capable of.

And there are people who are articulate with language too; they can speak in such a way that through the words they can send the wordless message to you. The words will be only the package; the content will be the wordless. The words will be only the container. But for that, a very articulate person is needed, who can use language in such a way that it becomes music, that it becomes poetry, that it becomes silence; that it becomes not only that which it says but also that which remains unsaid. Language can become a vehicle – now the emphasis will be on those who are listening. Much will depend on those who are listening.

So the basic function of the master is first, to create disciples who can understand the wordless through the words, who can sit in silence but can become filled with immense serenity. Just in the presence of the master, something can start opening up in them, as if the sun has risen and the birds start singing; nobody informs the birds that it is sunrise. There are no alarm clocks for poor birds, but just the light – the darkness has gone, the night is over, and there is a celebration all over nature. Flowers suddenly start opening, there is fragrance all over.

The mystic has achieved, is fulfilled, has completed his journey. But he is not a very talented genius. The master is doing overtime. His work is finished but his genius, his talents, demand expression.

J. Krishnamurti said, "If I have to follow the doctor's advice and not speak and not travel then I cannot live more than four weeks." And within exactly four weeks he died. *His* work was complete; now he was living only for others. And if even that cannot be done then what is the point of being here unnecessarily? His boat had arrived long ago. He had been delaying his departure – somebody may listen, somebody may hear, somebody may be touched. But if he cannot speak and cannot travel, then there is no reason at all for him to go on breathing. He is not an idiot.

Why did he say four weeks? – because it is just the old momentum. For breathing and heartbeats to slow down and disappear, it takes nearabout three to four weeks. And the older the man, the longer time it takes. If he had been younger, it might have been just one week. It is a very strange phenomenon – it is because the younger person's heart runs fast, it can exhaust the momentum quickly. The older man is already slow; his heart has become accustomed to a slow pace so it will take three to four weeks.

To be a mystic is rare, but to be a master is very rare. And to be a successful master, you will have to come to me!

Osho,

Whenever I am in a silent space I hear a sound – something like *aum* or humming. I love this rhythmic, sweet, unending sound. In certain activities too, when I am total and silent, this listening happens.

Is it okay to listen and enjoy this sound, or is it a projection or daydreaming?

Please guide me.

First thing to remember: you should not repeat any sound as a mantra, as a chanting, because when you repeat you create – then it is your mental projection. If you are simply silent and you hear a certain humming, then it is the sound of existence. That humming has been heard for centuries by meditators. That humming has been given a special name in the East: *Om*. It is not exactly *Om* but it is something similar.

It has to be remembered that in Sanskrit – which is the oldest language in the world, the mother language of all civilized languages in existence – they don't write *Om* in letters. They have made a special symbol for it, just to create a distinction, to indicate that it is not something to do with language, it is beyond language, and it is not part of the Sanskrit alphabet. The way it is written is only with a symbol, and that symbol can be used by any language. Sanskrit has no monopoly over it because it is not part of the alphabet of Sanskrit; it has been heard.

Jainas, Buddhists, Hindus – they differ in their theology on every single point, but they all have heard the sound *Om*. There is no question of differing; it is not a hypothesis and it is not a theory propounded by somebody. Anybody who becomes utterly silent... It is the silence itself singing, it is the song of silence. Hence about *Om* Hindus, Jainas and Buddhists all agree. They begin their scriptures with *Om*, they end their scriptures with *Om* because that is the universal sound.

This has created a problem – and there are many problems of a similar type – because all the mystics in this country and in the Far East have heard the sound *om*. The people who read the scriptures start thinking, "If *om* is the sound of the nature of existence itself, then if we repeat *om* we will be able to hear it soon." It is logical, but it is not realistic. If you repeat it, you will never hear the real thing; you will go on repeating, and you may start hearing your own repetition.

In Tibet, where the greatest work has been done on this "soundless sound," as they call it, they have made a special instrument. It is a certain kind of metal pot made with special proportions of different metals, and a small rod, again made of different proportions of different metals. You put the rod against the rim of the pot, and you move it fast and it creates a certain humming. That is something closer to the existential sound than *om*. In every lamasery in Tibet you will hear that sound – somebody, some lama is continuously making it. When he leaves, then somebody else... Twenty-four hours a day that sound is created, but that is a man-made sound. It is similar, but it is not the same.

Hindus in India have fallen into the same fallacy. They have made *Om* their most significant mantra: just repeat it continuously inside so your whole being is filled with the sound of *om, om, om*. You are deceiving yourself; this is *your* sound.

So if you are not creating it, then there is no need for any anxiety. If the moment you become silent you hear it, then it is a tremendous blessing. It means you have gone very deep into the existential world of serenity.

But don't try to deceive existence. You can go on chanting *om* your whole life; it is meaningless, it has nothing to do with existence. With existence you have to be a listener, absolutely passive, relaxed, in a let-go. Don't impose yourself. You are the only barrier; your impositions are your only sins. Just remain utterly passive in a non-doing witnessing, listening to whatever is happening, allowing it to happen. It is perfectly good, and of great significance. On the path, if you start hearing *om*, you are accepted, you are welcomed. You need not seek anywhere; you have found the door.

Just relax more, and leave everything in the hands of existence: a total trust and a complete passivity. Your absence is the presence of godliness. The moment you are not, the miracle has happened.

Osho,

The other night you pointed out that Jesus, Marx and Freud were perhaps the world's greatest businessmen.

On occasion I have heard you call yourself an old Jew.

Osho, what is your business?

I am a silent partner.

Osho,

Since sannyas in 1981 people have continually been seeing Jesus Christ in me! What have I to do with this guy?

It is dangerous. Cut off your beard, otherwise, they will cut off your head!

Jesus! – they see Jesus Christ in you? Then crucifixion is not far away. The first thing out of this hall, cut off your beard, And if they recognize you even then, keep a small board hanging on your neck that says, "I am not Jesus Christ."

You have to make it clear; otherwise your life is in danger.

27 Whatsoever Happens in Silence Is Your Friend

Osho,
Thirteen years ago I left the world, deadly wounded, and came to you. You healed me and gave me back even more than life.

Then one year ago I went back to that same world I had escaped from, feeling like a child just out of kindergarten, who barely knows the *ABC*. Naturally there were dark moments. During those moments an inner voice – was it your voice, Osho? – kept hammering at me, "Don't get lost in your emotions – watch!" For months this voice became my constant companion until suddenly a realization happened to me: that the darkness and the conflict were created by my own fears, desires, judgments. This glimpse was surrounded by a calm, relaxed feeling of freedom and acceptance.

Now, experiencing again the overwhelming beauty of sitting at your feet, I can see that no matter how long I watch, this desire to be in your presence will remain with me.

Osho, is it really possible not to long for something so unique and beautiful?

The spiritual path has many crossroads. On each crossroad, one feels as if one has arrived. In a certain way it is true, too. It is a certain blessing which was never known before, a peace that is absolutely new, a silence undreamt of, and a love, the fragrance of which one has desired, longed for, for lives and has never found. Naturally one feels the home has come.

This is one of the most difficult tasks for the master – to push you on, to say to you, "This is only the beginning; there is much more waiting for you." And although it is inconceivable to you that there can be anything more than this, the trust, the love, the devotion towards the master helps you to move.

These moments come again and again. Each time it becomes in a way more difficult, in a way easier. It is difficult in the sense that each new realization, new achievement, new revelation is so vast, so absorbing, that everything you have known before simply fades away, so it becomes more difficult to move on. But on the other hand, it becomes easier to move on because each time the master has said to you, "Move on" you have always gained more; it has never been a loss, it has always been a new door to a new mystery, a new sky beyond the old one. So the trust also has increased. It is easier now to listen to the master and move on.

An ancient story – I have always loved it – an old woodcutter, poor, alone, had only one way to earn his everyday bread and that was by cutting wood and selling it. As he came into the forest, just near the entrance under a beautiful bodhi tree, the same tree under which Gautam Buddha became enlightened; hence the name of the tree has become bodhi tree. *Bodhi* means enlightenment.

By the way, you will be surprised to know, scientists have found that the bodhi tree has a certain chemical which no other tree has, and that chemical is absolutely necessary for the growth of intelligence. Perhaps it is a very intelligent, sensitive tree. It may not have been just a coincidence...

The woodcutter would see this old man sitting silently, always there – summer, winter, rain. He would touch his feet before entering the forest, and every time he would do that the old man would smile and say, "You are such an idiot."

The woodcutter was shocked: "Why? – I touch his feet, but rather than giving me a blessing, he simply smiles and says, 'You are such an idiot.'"

One day he gathered courage and asked, "What do you mean?"

The old man said, "I mean that you have been cutting trees in this forest for your whole life, and if you go just a little deeper into it you will find a copper mine. Only an idiot could miss it! Your whole life you have been in this forest... You can collect the copper and that will be enough for seven days' comfortable living, no need to cut wood every day in your old age."

The man could not believe it because he knew the whole forest. "He must be joking!" But perhaps he was right, and there was no harm in going a little further and being alert and watching to see whether there was a copper mine.

And he went in, and he found a copper mine. He said, "Now I know why he was continually saying, 'You are such an idiot, working every day in your old age.'"

Now went only once every week. But the old tradition continued: he would touch his feet, and the old man would smile and say, "You are such an idiot!'"

"But," the woodcutter said, "now this is not right, because I have found the copper mine."

The old man said, "You don't know. If you go a little further, you will find a silver mine."

He said, "My God, why didn't you tell me before?"

The old man said, "You didn't even believe me about the copper mine – how could you believe about the silver mine? Just go a little further."

This time there was suspicion but not so much; there was a certain trust arising. And he found the silver mine.

He came back and he said, "Now I have found enough silver that I will be coming only once in a month. I will miss you very much. I will miss your blessing very much. I have started loving to hear from you: 'What an idiot you are.'"

But the old man said, "You are *still* an idiot, it makes no difference."

The woodcutter said, "Even though I have found the silver mine?"

He said, "Yes, even then. You are just an idiot and nothing more

– because if you go just a little deeper there is gold. So don't wait for a month, come tomorrow."

Now he thought he *must* be joking. If there is gold, why should he be sitting here under this tree in old rags, with no shelter from the rain, no shelter from the sun, depending on people who bring food to him...sometimes they bring it, sometimes they don't. And if he knows where the gold is, I don't think... This time he is certainly joking. But there is no harm. He has always been right. Who knows? This old guy is a little mysterious."

He went further and found a big gold mine. He could not believe his own eyes – this is the forest he has been working in for his whole life, and this is the forest where that old man is sitting.

He brought much gold, and he said, "I think you will not say anymore that I am an idiot."

He said, "I will continue. Come tomorrow because this is not the end; this is only the beginning."

He said, "What? Gold is just a beginning?"

He said, "Come tomorrow. Just a little deeper in the forest you will find diamonds – but that too is not the end. But I will not tell you too much; otherwise you will not be able to sleep tonight. Just go home. Tomorrow morning, first you find the diamonds, and then come to me."

He really could not sleep the whole night. A poor woodcutter... He could not imagine that he was going to become the owner of all these mines – gold and silver and copper, and now diamonds – and the old man was saying this was only the beginning. He thought and thought... What can be more than diamonds?

In the morning he went very early – the old man was asleep – he touched his feet. The old man opened his eyes and said, "Have you come? I knew you would come; you couldn't sleep. First go and see the diamonds."

The woodcutter said, "Can you tell me what can be more?"

He said, "First find the diamonds – step by step, otherwise you will go crazy."

He found the diamonds and he came dancing to the old man. He said, "Now you cannot say that I am an idiot. I have found the diamonds."

But the old man said, "Still, you are an idiot."

He said, "Now I will not leave you unless you explain it to me."

The old man said, "You can see that I know all about these mines – silver, gold, diamonds – and I don't care about them, because there is something more which is not in the forest but within you, just a little deeper, not outside but inside. And because I have found it, I don't care about all these diamonds. Now it is up to you; you can stop your journey at the diamonds but remember; you will remain an idiot. And I am proof, because I know about all these mines and I have not bothered with them. This can make you understand that there is something more which is never found outside, however far you go; it is found inside you."

The man dropped the diamonds. He said, "I am going to sit by your side. Unless you drop this idea that I am an idiot, I am not going to move from here."

He was a simple, innocent woodcutter. It is difficult for knowledgeable people to go in. It was not difficult for the woodcutter. Soon he was entering into a deep silence, a joy, a blissfulness, a benediction.

And the old man shook him and said, "This is the place. Now you need not go into the forest. And I withdraw my word *idiot* about you; you have become a wise man. You can open your eyes. You will see the same world but not in the same light; the same colors, but now they have become psychedelic; the same people, but they are no longer just skeletons covered with skin, they are luminous spiritual beings; the same cosmos, but for the first time it is an ocean of consciousness."

The woodcutter opened his eyes.

He said, "You are a strange fellow. Why did you wait so long? I have been coming here almost my whole life and I have seen you sitting under this tree. You could have said this any day."

The old man said, "I was waiting for the right moment, for the *ripe* moment, for the time when you would be able not only to hear but to understand it. The journey is short, but you should not stop at every achievement – because every achievement is so fulfilling that your imagination cannot think there can be more than this."

You are asking me what can be more beautiful than to be in the presence of the master. Why not dissolve in the presence? To be in the presence of the master, there is still separation. Why be *in* the presence? Why not *become* the presence itself? And only then you will know that to be in the presence was only the beginning of a journey that ends in becoming the presence.

I know you, and I know your heart. I have not told the story of the woodcutter without remembering the fact that you have such an innocent heart yourself. Just don't stop anywhere. It is possible... Make it your realization. Become the light yourself, and then whatever is experienced is inexpressible.

In your dark moments, while you have been away for one year, you have heard the word *watch*. With your innocent mind, it is very simple for me to speak to you from any distance, a heart-to-heart communion. Those words were mine, and you have recognized them. Because there are things you need not bother about, you simply have to watch and they pass on: anger, greed, jealousy. All the components of darkness have one quality in common: that if you can watch them they start dispersing. Watching is enough; you are not supposed to do anything with them.

In the life of one of the great mystics, Baal Shem, there is an incident. He used to go towards the river in the middle of the night just to be in absolute silence, alone, to enjoy the peace and the beauty of the night. Just on the bank of the river was a rich man's mansion, and a watchman was there who was puzzled about this man, Baal Shem. Every night, exactly as the tower bell was tolling twelve, Baal Shem would appear out of the darkness.

The poor watchman could not contain the temptation to inquire, "Why do you come here every night and sit next to the river in the darkness? What is the purpose of it?"

Rather than answering him, Baal Shem asked, "What is your work?"

He said, "I am a watchman."

Baal Shem said, "Exactly! That is *my* work. I am a watchman."

The watchman said, "That is strange. If you are a watchman,

then what are you doing here? You should be watching the house where you are the watchman."

Baal Shem said, "There is something to be explained to you: you watch somebody else's house; I watch my own house. *This* is my house. Wherever I go, I go with my house – but I am continuously the watchman."

I love the story.

Be continuously a watchman of all dark moments. They will pass away. In fact, that is the definition: anything you watch, if it disappears by watching that means it was something wrong. If by watching it becomes clearer, closer, that means it was something to be absorbed. There is no other definition of good and bad. It is watching that decides – the only criterion. What is sin and what is virtue? That which disappears is sin, and that which comes closer, becomes clearer, wants to become part of you is virtue. Watching is certainly the golden key of spiritual life.

Osho,

The other day you talked so beautifully about the sadness which follows the first experience of our innermost silence.

Is it necessarily so, that when I first experience this silence, I also feel with my whole being that I am absolutely alone on my journey?

Aloneness is also one of the fundamental experiences as you enter silence. In silence there is nobody else; you are simply alone.

The deeper your silence will be, thoughts will have gone, emotions will have gone, sentiments will have gone – just pure being, a flame of light, burning alone... One can get scared because we are so much accustomed to living with people: in the crowd, in the marketplace, in all kinds of relationships. You may not be aware that in all these relationships – with friends, with your husbands, with your wives, with your children, with your parents – you are basically trying to avoid the experience of aloneness. These are strategies so that you are always with somebody.

It is a well-known fact, psychologically established, that if a person is left alone in isolation, after seven days he starts talking – a little like whispering. For seven days he keeps talking inside, keeps himself engaged in the mind, but then it becomes too much – things start coming out of his mind through his mouth and he starts whispering. After fourteen days you can hear him clearly: what he is saying. After twenty-one days he does not bother about anybody, he has gone insane; now he is talking to walls, to pillars: "Hello friend, how are you?" – to a pillar, hugging a pillar! And this is true not about somebody special, it is true about everybody. He is trying to find some relationship. If he cannot find it in reality, he will create a hallucination.

You will see: just stand by the side of the road and watch people going from the office to the house, and you will be surprised. They are alone – although there is a crowd all around – but they are talking to themselves. They are making gestures, they are telling somebody something – because the crowd around them is not related to them. They are alone in the crowd, so they are trying to create their own illusion. Maybe they are talking to their wife, to their boss. There are many things which cannot be said but right now they can say them. In front of the wife they cannot say it, but in this crowd, where everybody is engaged in his own thing, everybody is doing his own thing, they can say things to the wife. Nobody is listening, and at least one thing is certain – the wife is not there. But they need the wife, they need someone to talk to.

And after thirty days of isolation, a dramatic change happens. It is not only one-sided; it is not only that they are talking to the pillar, the pillar also starts talking to them! They do both things: first, "Hello, how are you?" and then, "I am good. I am fine, doing well." They answer from the side of the pillar too – in a different voice. Now they have created a world of their own, they are no longer alone. No madman is alone. Either you are mad or not. If you don't know aloneness, there is something of madness in you.

Only pure aloneness gives you a clean sanity. You don't need the other; the dependence on the other is no longer there, you are enough unto yourself. Language is meaningless because language is a medium to relate with the other. The moment you are no longer dependent on the other, language is meaningless; words are meaningless.

In your silence – when there are no words, no language, nobody else is present – you are getting in tune with existence. This serenity, this silence, this aloneness will bring you immense rewards. It will allow you to grow to your full potential. For the first time you will be an individual, for the first time you will have the touch and the taste of freedom, and for the first time the immensity, the unboundedness of existence will be yours with all its blissfulness.

So whatever happens in silence – either sadness or aloneness – remember, in silence nothing wrong can ever happen. Whatever happens is going to enhance the beauty of it, deepen the charm of it; anything that happens will bring more and more flowers, more and more fragrance to it.

Rejoice! Whatever happens in silence is your friend, it is really your bosom friend. It is going to take you to the ultimate peak of ecstasies.

Osho,

I don't really have a question to ask you – everything is very good. Only one thing is confusing me a little. You have often spoken about the "chosen few." Please, who is doing the choosing?

It is a very difficult question.

In the beginning, God used to do it! But there are many hypotheses about what happened to God: some say he died a natural death, some say he committed suicide, some say he got into an accident. Some say he was murdered by man – because without murdering him, man could not really be free. I will not go into what happened to God. One thing is certain: he is missing.

In the beginning, he had chosen the Jews to be the chosen few, "God's own people." But since then, he has had no opportunity. And Jews have been praying continually in every synagogue all over the world, "Now it is time for you to choose somebody else; we have suffered enough!"

And it is true. If God had not chosen them they would have lived just like everybody else. But because he chose them, he made everybody else their enemies – great jealousy and competition.

I remember that once, India's first prime minister, Pandit Jawaharlal Nehru was asked, "Who are you going to choose as your successor?"

He said, "I am not going to choose anyone, because whoever I choose would have to face immense difficulties. Everybody else who is ambitious and wants to become the prime minister would all be together against one single person, and there would be no possibility for that person I have chosen to succeed me. So I will keep my mouth shut."

And you are asking who is choosing here? Here, it is a very different process. Here, the moment you become a sannyasin you have chosen yourself. Every sannyasin belongs to the chosen few, and nobody is doing the choosing; it is you who are doing it; hence there is freedom. If you feel difficulties, you can drop out of it. Nobody prevents you from becoming a sannyasin, nobody prevents you from dropping sannyas. Your freedom is intact. So remember, here nobody is choosing. Everybody is choosing by becoming a sannyasin. So no need to kill me; I have learned from the lesson of God. I will never choose anybody, because it is dangerous! And to choose anybody is to put him in difficulty.

Now Jews have suffered so much in four thousand years for the single reason that they were the chosen few. All over the earth, nobody else has suffered so much. It gave them a superiority complex, a feeling that they are holier than thou, and naturally nobody likes people who think themselves holier than thou. So in every country, in every place, they have been put down and given evidence that they are not holier or higher.

Just in Germany alone, Adolf Hitler killed six million Jews. The responsibility lies with God, because the reason these Jews were coming into conflict with Adolf Hitler was that he was saying that the Nordic Germans were the highest race. Jews have to be completely eradicated from the earth because as long as the Jews remain, you cannot proclaim that Nordic Germans are the highest. Jews are an old race, with a four-thousand-year history, and they have proved in every way that they are more intelligent. No Jew is a beggar; they are all rich, they know how to produce wealth. They are all cultured and well educated. Forty percent of Nobel Prizes go to Jews, and the other sixty percent to the rest of the world – it is simply unimaginable. It was difficult for Adolf Hitler in the presence of Jews, because they had all the intelligence, all the riches, everything that proved that they were somehow more intelligent than others. To make the Nordic Germans a superior race, Jews had to be completely eradicated from the earth.

The fault lies with God; he should not have chosen the poor Jews. And even if he had chosen them, he should have whispered in the ear of Moses and told him, "Please don't tell anybody. Just keep it in your mind that you are the chosen few, but it should not leak out, it is a secret."

But there is no joy if it is a secret. The joy is when you proclaim it.

Here I am not proclaiming anybody as chosen, but I am giving you an opportunity. If you want to be chosen, there will be difficulties. My sannyasins everywhere are going through all the difficulties. One has to pay for everything. You want to be the chosen few for free? It is not possible; you will have to pay for it.

Osho,

Often, in the past, you have spoken on doubt and the value of doubting everything.

On the level where you are my master and I, through your grace, have become your disciple, there has never been any doubt – forgetfulness on my part, yes; unawareness on my part, yes, but never the torment of doubt.

Beloved Master, could you speak on doubt in the relationship of the disciple with the master?

There is no possibility. A disciple becomes a disciple only when he drops all doubts. So in the very nature of things, a disciple cannot doubt. If he doubts, he is not a disciple.

As a student he can doubt as much as he wants. When all his doubts are finished and a trust beyond doubt has arisen, he enters into the world of disciplehood; now there is no possibility of doubt arising. If it arises, the disciple immediately falls back into the category of student.

So as far as the master and discipleship is concerned, doubt is an impossibility.

Osho,

Why do you always look in your hand before you start answering the first question? Do I see it wrongly, or do you find the answer there?

My hands are empty. I don't have any answer.

You have questions; I don't answer you, I simply destroy your questions. And before destroying your questions I have to look at my hand because it is not only with my language that I destroy your questions, it is also with my hands. So I have to prepare them, to ask, "Are you ready?"

When they say, "Yes, master, go ahead," I start!

Without my hands, I cannot answer you. They almost do most of the work. My words keep you engaged, and my hands go on doing the real work.

So you are not seeing wrongly; you are seeing absolutely right.

I look at them, not for answers, but just to see whether they are ready or not.

Osho,

It is for the first time I have been so close to you. When I am sitting here with you I feel my heart in tune with your heart, I feel a deep love for you. But I also feel my outer seriousness.

Why is laughter so difficult for me?

Laughter is one of the things most repressed by society all over the world, in all the ages. Society wants you to be serious. Parents want their children to be serious, teachers want their students to be serious, the bosses want their servants to be serious, the commanders want their armies to be serious. Seriousness is required of everybody.

Laughter is dangerous and rebellious.

When the teacher is teaching you, and you start laughing, it will be taken as an insult. Your parents are saying something to you and you start laughing – it will be taken as an insult. Seriousness is thought to be honor, respect.

Naturally laughter has been repressed so much that even though life all around is hilarious, nobody is laughing. If your laughter is freed from its chains, from its bondage, you will be surprised – on each step there is something hilarious happening. Life is not serious. Only graveyards are serious, death is serious.

Life is love, life is laughter; life is dance, song.

But we will have to give life a new orientation. The past has crippled life very badly; it has made you almost laughter-blind, just like there are people who are colorblind. There are ten percent of people who are colorblind – it is a big percentage, but they are not aware that they are colorblind.

George Bernard Shaw was colorblind, and he came to know it when he was sixty years old. On his birthday somebody sent a present, a beautiful suit, a coat, but the person forgot to send a tie. So Bernard Shaw went with his secretary to find a matching tie. He liked the suit very much. He looked at ties and he chose one, and the secretary was surprised; she could not believe it – because the suit was yellow and the tie was green. She said, "What are you doing? This will look very strange."

He said, "Why will it look strange? It is the same color."

The manager, the salesman, they all gathered, and they tried in many ways to find out. He could not distinguish between yellow and green; they both appeared the same to him. He was colorblind. But for sixty years he was not aware of it. And there are ten percent of people in the world who are colorblind. Some color they are missing, or maybe they are mixing it up with some other color.

The constant repression of laughter has made you laughter-blind. Situations are happening everywhere, but you cannot see that there is any reason to laugh. If your laughter is freed from its bondage, the whole world will be full of laughter. It needs to be full of laughter; it will change almost everything in human life. You will not be as miserable as you are. In fact, you are not as miserable as you look – it is misery plus seriousness that makes you look so miserable. Just misery plus laughter, and you will not look so miserable.

In one apartment house... And modern apartments have such thin walls that whether you want to or not, you have to hear what is going on, on the other side of the wall. In a way, it is very human. The whole apartment house was puzzled about one thing: every couple was fighting, throwing pillows, throwing things, breaking cups and saucers, shouting at each other, husbands beating wives, wives screaming. They didn't need any loudspeaker systems or anything, and the whole apartment house enjoyed.

The only problem was with one *sardarji*. From his flat they never heard any fight; on the contrary, they always heard laughter. The whole crowd was puzzled: "What is the matter? These people never fight. There is always laughter – and both are laughing so loudly that the whole building can hear it!"

One day they decided that it had to be looked into: "We are missing so much, and they are enjoying so much. What is their secret?"

So they caught hold of the *sardarji* as he was coming from the market, carrying vegetables and other things. They all caught hold of him and they said, "First you have to tell us what the secret is. Why do you laugh when everybody fights?"

The sardar said, "Don't force me, because the secret is very embarrassing."

They said, "Embarrassing? But we thought you are doing great. We always hear laughter, either you laugh or your wife laughs...no fight."

The sardar said, "What happens is, she throws things at me. If she misses, then I laugh; if she hits me then she laughs. The same things are going on, but it is just that we have made a different arrangement – what is the point? So I have learned how to dodge her, and she is learning how to..."

After twenty years the same sardar wanted to divorce his wife. The magistrate had heard about them: that this was the only couple in the whole city who had never been known to fight. They simply laugh – the whole city knows them as the laughing couple.

The magistrate said, "What has gone wrong? You are so famous."

The sardar said, "Forget all about that, just give us permission to divorce."

"But," the magistrate said, "I have to know the reason."

The sardar said, "The reason is very clear: she hits me, and it is too much; I have been getting those hits for years."

The magistrate asked, "How long have you been married?"

He said, "Almost thirty years."

The magistrate said, "If you have been able to cope with the woman for thirty years, then just ten, twenty years more..."

He said, "That is not the point. At first I used to dodge, but now she has become such a good...there is no way that I can dodge. So only she laughs, I have not laughed for ten years. This is unbearable. In the beginning it was perfect; it was almost fifty-fifty, there was no problem. I was laughing, she was also laughing. But now a hundred percent of the time she laughs, and a hundred percent I am just standing there, looking like a fool. No, I cannot tolerate it any more."

Just look around at life and try to see the humorous side of things. Every event that is happening has its own humorous side; you just need a sense of humor. No religion has accepted sense of humor as a quality. I want a sense of humor to be a fundamental quality of a good man, of a moral man, of a religious man. And it does not need much looking for; just try to see it, and everywhere...

Once I was traveling in a bus when I was a student. The bus conductor was in trouble because there were thirty-one passengers and he had taken money only for thirty tickets. So he was asking, "Who is the fellow who has not given his money?"

Nobody would speak.

He said, "This is strange; now how am I going to find out?"

I said to him, "Do one thing: tell the driver to stop the bus, and tell the people that unless the person who has not given the money confesses, the bus will not move."

He said, "That's right."

The bus was stopped. Everybody looked at each other – now what to do? Nobody knew who the person was...

Finally one man stood up and said, "Forgive me, I am the person who has not given the money. Here it is."

The bus conductor asked, "What is your name?"

He said, "My name is Achchelal." *Achchelal* means "a good man."

And I was surprised that out of thirty people, nobody laughed! When he said Achchelal, I could not believe it – a good man doing such a thing, and nobody seemed to see the humor in it.

Seriousness has become almost part of our bones and blood. You will have to make some effort to get rid of seriousness, and you will have to be on the lookout – wherever you can find something humorous happening, don't miss the opportunity.

Everywhere there are people who are slipping on banana peels, just nobody is looking at them. In fact, it is thought to be ungentlemanly. It is not, because only bananas slip on banana peels. Laughter needs a great learning, and laughter is a great medicine. It can cure many of your tensions, anxieties, worries; the whole energy can flow into laughter.

And there is no need that there should be some occasion, some cause. In my meditation camps I used to have a laughing meditation – for no reason, people would sit and just start laughing. At first they would feel a little awkward that there was no reason, but when everybody was doing it, they would also start. Soon, everybody was in such a great laughter, people were rolling on the ground. They were laughing at the very fact that so many people were laughing for no reason at all; there was nothing, not even a joke had been told. And it went on like waves.

So there is no harm. Even just sitting in your room, close the doors and have one hour of simple laughter. Laugh at yourself. But learn to laugh. Seriousness is a sin, and it is a disease. Laughter has tremendous beauty, lightness. It will bring lightness to you, and it will give you wings to fly.

And life is so full of opportunities. You just need the sensitivity. And create chances for other people to laugh. Laughter should be one of the most valued, cherished qualities of human beings, because only man can laugh, no animals are capable of it. Because it is human, it must be of the highest order. To repress it is to destroy a human quality.

28 Unless the Whole Existence...

Osho,
You have recently said that most of humanity is vegetating, not living. Please explain to us the art of living so that death may become also a celebration.

Man is born to achieve life, but it all depends on him. He can miss it. He can go on breathing, he can go on eating, he can go on growing old, he can go on moving towards the grave – but this is not life. This is gradual death from the cradle to the grave, a seventy-year-long gradual death. And because millions of people around you are dying in this gradual, slow death, you also start imitating them. Children learn everything from those who are around them, and we are surrounded by the dead.

So first we have to understand what I mean by *life*. It must not be simply growing old. It has to be growing up. And these are two different things. Growing old, any animal is capable of. Growing up is the prerogative of human beings. Only a few claim the right.

Growing up means moving every moment deeper into the principle of life, it means going farther away from death, not towards death. The deeper you go into life, the more you understand the immortality within you. You are going away from death; a moment comes when you can see that death is nothing but changing clothes, or changing houses, changing forms. Nothing dies, nothing *can* die; death is the greatest illusion there is.

For growing up, just watch a tree. As the tree grows up, its roots are growing down, deeper. There is a balance: the higher the tree goes, the deeper the roots will go. You cannot have a tree one hundred and fifty feet high with small roots; they could not support such a huge tree. In life, growing up means growing deep within yourself – that's where your roots are.

To me, the first principle of life is meditation.

Everything else comes second. And childhood is the best time. As you grow older, it means you are coming closer to death, and it becomes more and more difficult to go into meditation. Meditation means going into your immortality, going into your eternity, going into your godliness. And the child is the most qualified person because he is still unburdened by knowledge, unburdened by religion, unburdened by education, unburdened by all kinds of rubbish. He is innocent.

But unfortunately his innocence is being condemned as ignorance. Ignorance and innocence have a similarity, but they are not the same. Ignorance is also a state of not knowing, just as innocence is. But there is a great difference too, which has been overlooked by the whole of humanity up to now. Innocence is not knowledgeable, but it is not desirous of being knowledgeable either. It is utterly content, fulfilled. A small child has no ambitions; he has no desires. He is so absorbed in the moment: a bird on the wing catches his eye so totally; just a butterfly, its beautiful colors, and he is enchanted; the rainbow in the sky... And he cannot conceive that there can be anything more significant, richer than this rainbow. And the night full of stars, stars beyond stars... Innocence is rich, it is full, it is pure.

Ignorance is poor, it is a beggar – it wants this, it wants that, it wants to be knowledgeable, it wants to be respectable, it wants to be wealthy; it wants to be powerful. Ignorance moves on the path of desire. Innocence is a state of desirelessness.

But because they both are without knowledge, we have

remained confused about their natures. We have taken it for granted that they are both the same. The first step, in the art of living, will be to create a demarcation line between ignorance and innocence. Innocence has to be supported, protected – because the child has brought with him the greatest treasure, the treasure that sages find after arduous effort. Sages have said that they become children again, that they are reborn.

In India the real brahmin, the real knower, has called himself *dwij*, twice born. Why twice born? What happened to the first birth? What is the need of the second birth? And what is he going to gain in the second birth? In the second birth he is going to gain what was available in the first birth but society, parents, the people surrounding him crushed it, destroyed it.

Every child is being stuffed with knowledge. His simplicity has somehow to be removed, because simplicity is not going to help him in this competitive world. His simplicity will look to the world as if he is a simpleton; his innocence will be exploited in every possible way. Afraid of the society, afraid of the world we have created ourselves, we try to make every child be clever, cunning, knowledgeable, to be in the category of the powerful, not in the category of the oppressed and the powerless. And once the child starts growing in the wrong direction, he goes on moving that way, his whole life moves in that direction.

Whenever you understand that you have missed life, the first principle to be brought back is innocence. Drop your knowledge, forget your scriptures, forget your religions, your theologies, your philosophies. Be born again, become innocent – and it is in your hands. Clean your mind of all that is not known by you, of all that is borrowed, all that has come from tradition, convention, all that has been given to you by others: parents, teachers, universities. Just get rid of it. Once again be simple; once again be a child. And this miracle is possible by meditation.

Meditation is simply a strange surgical method which cuts you away from all that is not yours and saves only that which is your authentic being. It burns everything else and leaves you standing naked, alone under the sun, in the wind. It is as if you are the first man who has descended onto earth – who knows nothing, who has to discover everything, who has to be a seeker, who has to go on a pilgrimage.

The second principle is the pilgrimage. Life must be a seeking, not a desire, but a search; not an ambition to become this, to become that, a president of a country or a prime minister of a country, but a search to find out: "Who am I?"

It is very strange that people who don't know who they are are trying to become somebody. They don't even know who they are right now! They are unacquainted with their being, but they have a goal of becoming. Becoming is the disease of the soul.

Being is you. And to discover your being is the beginning of life. Then each moment is a new discovery, each moment brings a new joy; a new mystery opens its doors, a new love starts growing in you, a new compassion that you have never felt before, a new sensitivity about beauty, about goodness. You become so sensitive that even the smallest blade of grass takes on an immense importance for you. Your sensitivity makes it clear to you that this small blade of grass is as important to existence as the biggest star; without this blade of grass, existence would be less than it is. And this small blade of grass is unique, it is irreplaceable, it has its own individuality.

And this sensitivity will create new friendships for you – friendships with trees, with birds, with animals, with mountains, with rivers, with oceans, with stars. Life becomes richer as love grows, as friendliness grows.

In the life of St. Francis, there is a beautiful incident. He is dying, and he has always traveled on a donkey from place to place sharing his experiences. All his disciples are gathered to listen to his last words.

The last words of a man are always the most significant that he has ever uttered because they contain the whole experience of his life.

But what the disciples heard, they could not believe... St. Francis did not address the disciples; he addressed the donkey. He said, "Brother, I am immensely indebted to you. You have been carrying me from one place to another place with never a complaint, never grumbling. Before I leave this world, all that I want is forgiveness from you; I have not been humane to you."

These were the last words of St. Francis – a tremendous sensitivity to say to the donkey, "Brother donkey," and ask to be forgiven.

As you become more sensitive, life becomes bigger. It is not a small pond; it becomes oceanic. It is not confined to you and your wife and your children; it is not confined at all. This whole existence becomes your family, and unless the whole existence is your family, you have not known what life is – because no man is an island, we are all connected. We are a part of a vast continent, joined in millions of ways. And if our hearts are not full of love for the whole, in the same proportion our life is cut short.

Meditation will bring you sensitivity, a great sense of belonging to the world. It is our world – the stars are ours, and we are not foreigners here. We belong intrinsically to existence. We are part of it; we are the *heart* of it.

Secondly, meditation will bring you a great silence, because all rubbish knowledge will have gone. Thoughts that are part of that knowledge have gone too...an immense silence, and you are surprised: this silence is the only music there is.

All music is an effort to bring this silence somehow into manifestation.

The seers of the ancient East have been very emphatic about the point that all the great arts – music, poetry, dance, painting, sculpture – are all born out of meditation. They are an effort to in some way bring the unknowable into the world of the known for those who are not ready for the pilgrimage – just gifts for those who are not ready to go on the pilgrimage. Perhaps a song, perhaps a statue may trigger a desire to go in search of the source.

The next time you enter a temple of Gautam Buddha or Mahavira, just sit silently and watch the statue. The statue has been made in such a way, in such proportions that if you watch it you will fall silent. It is a statue of meditation; it is not concerned with Gautam Buddha or Mahavira. That's why all those statues look alike – Mahavira, Gautam Buddha, Neminatha, Adinatha... In the same temple you will find twenty-four statues, twenty-four *tirthankaras* of the Jainas, all alike, exactly alike.

In my childhood I used to ask my father, "Can you explain to me how it is possible that twenty-four persons are exactly alike? – the same size, the same nose, the same face, the same body."

And he used to say, "I don't know. I am always puzzled myself that there is not a bit of difference. And it is almost unheard of; there are not even two persons in the whole world who are alike, what to say about twenty-four?"

But as my meditation blossomed I found the answer – not from anybody else; I found the answer: that these statues have nothing to do with the people. These statues have something to do with what was happening inside those twenty-four people, and that was exactly the same.

And we have not bothered about the outside; we have insisted that only the inner should be paid attention to. The outer is unimportant. Somebody is young, somebody is old, somebody is black, somebody is white, somebody is man, somebody is woman; it does not matter, what matters is that inside there is an ocean of silence. In that oceanic state, the body takes a certain posture. You have observed it yourself, but you have not been alert. When you are angry, have you observed? – your body takes a certain posture. In anger you cannot keep your hands open, in anger...the fist. In anger you cannot smile – or can you?

With a certain emotion, the body has to follow a certain posture. Just small things are deeply related inside. So those statues are made in such a way that if you simply sit silently and watch, and then close your eyes, a negative shadow image enters into your body, and you start feeling something you have not felt before.

Those statues and temples were not built for worshipping; they were built for experiencing. They are scientific laboratories. They have nothing to do with religion. A certain secret science has been used for centuries so the coming generations could come in contact with the experiences of the older generations – not through books, not through words, but through something which goes deeper – through silence, through meditation, through peace.

As your silence grows, your friendliness, your love grows; your life becomes a moment-to-moment dance, a joy, a celebration.

Do you hear the firecrackers outside? Have you ever thought about why, all over the world, in every culture, in every society, there are a few days in the year for celebration? These few days for celebration are just a compensation – because these societies have taken away all celebration in your life, and if nothing is given to you in compensation, your life can become a danger to the culture. Every culture has to give some compensation to you so that you don't feel completely lost in misery, in sadness. But these compensations are false. These firecrackers outside and these lights outside cannot make you rejoice. They are only for children; for you, they are just a nuisance. But in your inner world there can be a continuity of lights, songs, joys. Always remember that society compensates you when it feels that the repressed may explode into a dangerous situation if it is not compensated. Society finds some way of allowing you to let out the repressed. But this is not true celebration, and it cannot be true.

True celebration should come from your life, *in* your life.

And true celebration cannot be according to the calendar, that on the first of November you will celebrate. Strange, the whole year you are miserable and on the first of November suddenly you come out of misery, dancing. Either, the misery is false, or the first of November is false; both cannot be true. And once the first of November has gone, you are back in your dark hole, everybody in his misery, everybody in his anxiety.

Life should be a continual celebration, a festival of lights the whole year round. Only then can you grow up, can you blossom.

Transform small things into celebration. For example, in Japan they have the tea ceremony. In every Zen monastery and in every person's house, who can afford it, they have a small temple for drinking tea. Now, tea is no longer an ordinary, profane thing; they have transformed it into a celebration. The temple for drinking tea is made in a certain way: in a beautiful garden, with a beautiful pond, swans in the pond, flowers all around. Guests come and they have to leave their shoes outside. It is a temple.

And as you enter the temple, you cannot speak; you have to leave your thinking and thoughts and speech outside with your shoes. You sit down in a meditative posture. And the host, the lady who prepares tea for you, her movements are so graceful, as if she is dancing, moving around preparing tea, putting cups and saucers before you as if you are gods. With such respect, she will bow down, and you will receive it with the same respect.

The tea is prepared in a special samovar, which makes beautiful sounds – music of its own. And it is part of the tea ceremony that everybody should listen first to the music of the tea. So everybody is silent, listening...birds chirping outside in the garden, and the samovar...the tea is creating its own song. A peace surrounds. When the tea is ready and it is poured into everybody's cup, you are not just to drink it the way people are doing everywhere. First you will smell the aroma of the tea. You will sip the tea as if it has come from the beyond, you will take time – there is no hurry. Somebody may start playing on the flute or on the sitar. An ordinary thing – just tea – and they have made it a beautiful religious festival, and everybody comes out of it nourished, fresh, feeling younger, feeling juicier. And what can be done with tea, can be done with everything: with your clothes, with your food.

People are living almost in sleep; otherwise, every fabric, every cloth has its own beauty, its own feel. If you are sensitive, then the clothing is not just to cover your body; then it is something expressing your individuality, something expressing your taste, your culture, your being. Everything that you do should be expressive of you; it should have your signature on it. Then life becomes a continuous celebration.

Even if you fall sick and you are lying in bed, you will make those moments of lying in bed moments of beauty and joy, moments of relaxation and rest, moments of meditation, moments of listening to music or to poetry. There is no need to be sad that you are sick. You should be happy that everybody is in the office and you are in your bed like a king, relaxing – somebody is preparing tea for you, the samovar is singing a song and a friend has offered to come and play the flute for you. These things are more important than any medicine. When you are sick, call a doctor. But more important, call those who love you, because there is no medicine more important than love. Call those who can create beauty, music, poetry around you, because there is nothing that heals like a mood of celebration. Medicine is the lowest kind of treatment.

But it seems we have forgotten everything, so we have to depend on medicine and be grumpy and sad – as if you are missing some great joy that you were having in the office. In the office you were miserable – just one day off, and you cling to misery too; you won't let it go.

Make everything creative; make the best out of the worst – that's what I call "the art." And if a man has lived his whole life making every moment and every phase of it a beauty, a love, a joy, naturally his death is going to be the ultimate peak of his whole life's endeavor. The last touches... His death is not going to be ugly as it ordinarily happens every day to everyone. If death is ugly, that means your whole life has been a wastage. Death should be a peaceful acceptance, a loving entry into the unknown, a joyful good-bye to old friends, to the old world. There should not be any tragedy in it.

One Zen master, Lin Chi, was dying. Thousands of his disciples had gathered to listen to the last sermon, but Lin Chi was simply lying down – joyous, smiling, but not saying a single word.

Seeing that he was going to die and he was not saying a single word, somebody reminded Lin Chi – an old friend, a master in his own right... He was not a disciple of Lin Chi. That's why he could say to him, "Lin Chi, have you forgotten that you have to say your last words? I have always said your memory isn't right. You are dying, have you forgotten?"

Lin Chi said, "Just listen." And on the roof two squirrels were running, screeching. And he said, "How beautiful," and he died.

For a moment, when he said just listen, there was absolute silence. Everybody thought he was going to say something great, but only two squirrels fighting, screeching, running on the roof... And he smiled and he died.

But he *had* given his last message: don't make things small and big, trivial and important. Everything is important. At this moment, Lin Chi's death is as important as the two squirrels running on the roof, there is no difference. In existence it is all the same. That was his whole philosophy, his whole life's teaching: that there is nothing which is great and there is nothing which is small; it all depends on you, what you make out of it.

Start with meditation, and things will go on growing in you – silence, serenity, blissfulness, sensitivity. And whatever comes out of meditation, try to bring it out in life. Share it, because everything shared grows fast. And when you have reached the point of death, you will know there is no death. You can say good-bye, there is no need for any tears of sadness – maybe tears of joy, but not of sadness. But you have to begin from being innocent.

So first, throw out all crap that you are carrying. And everybody is carrying so much crap – and one wonders, for what? Just because people have been telling you that these are great ideas, principles... You have not been intelligent with yourself. Be intelligent with yourself.

Life is very simple; it is a joyful dance. And the whole earth can be full of joy and dance, but there are people who are seriously vested in their interest that nobody should enjoy life, that nobody should smile, that nobody should laugh, that life is a sin, that it is a punishment. How can you enjoy when the climate is such that you have been told continually that it is a punishment, that you are suffering because you have done wrong things, and it is a kind of jail where you have been thrown in order to suffer?

I say to you life is not a jail; it is not a punishment. It is a reward, and it is given only to those who have earned it, who deserve it. Now it is your right to enjoy; it will be a sin if you *don't* enjoy. It will be against existence if you don't beautify it, if you leave it just as you have found it. No, leave it a little happier, a little more beautiful, a little more fragrant.

Osho,

As a disciple of your mystery school, I want to ask you the

following question: when I heard you say that you were beyond enlightenment now, it felt like a relaxation in my heart. That very moment a picture arose in me showing me that you are even closer to us now, and it feels to me as if I can somehow understand "beyond enlightenment" better than enlightenment itself.

Can you please say something about this?

It raises a few fundamental questions. First, if you cannot understand enlightenment, how can you understand that which is beyond it? You are misunderstanding. Your misunderstanding is that perhaps beyond enlightenment means below enlightenment. And you are feeling happy, but I cannot feel happy with your happiness. I feel sorry for it. You are feeling happy that I have come close to you. You should feel happy when you come close to me.

Just think: if I say that I have dropped even "beyond enlightenment," that it was all fiction – enlightenment, beyond enlightenment; I am just one of you who had a few imaginative, fictitious ideas – you will feel even happier. Now there is nothing for you to worry about, nowhere to go, nothing to achieve, you are perfectly okay.

Your question makes me understand why Gautam Buddha remained with enlightenment – although he was seeing it, the stars beyond were calling him. He was the first man to see beyond enlightenment, but he didn't *go* beyond; he remained at the stage of enlightenment. Perhaps it was for people like you, because you will not be able to understand the person who goes beyond enlightenment, in a way he will become almost ordinary, and there is the danger. Your ordinariness and his ordinariness are poles apart – but both are ordinariness, and the danger is that you will misunderstand. He has come back home. You have not even started the journey.

It is almost like meeting someone on a staircase – you are both standing on the same step; one is going, one is coming. Both are on the same step – in a way equal – but one is going up, one is going down. Hence, they are not equal; their equality is illusory.

I thought perhaps that in the twenty-five centuries after Gautam Buddha man might have become a little more intelligent – and someone some day has to try going beyond and see what happens, how people take it. The way you have understood it is absolutely wrong. I have not come closer to you; I have gone farther away. And you cannot avoid enlightenment; if you avoid it, you cannot reach beyond it. It is simple arithmetic. That's what is making you happy, that perhaps enlightenment can be avoided: when one has to go beyond it, what is the need to first go to enlightenment and then go beyond it? We are already beyond it! You are not beyond it. You are behind it. And in any case enlightenment cannot be avoided. One has to pass through that fire, through that great experience.

So drop that idea that I have come closer to you. My being closer to you is not significant. What is significant is your being closer to me. You say, "Now you are a friend to us." I have always been a friend to you. The question is from your side: are you a friend to me? And my friendship will enhance and enrich *my* life, not your life. It is your friendship that is going to enhance and enrich *your* life. And if you can be a friend to one who is enlightened you have taken a long jump, you have extended your hands to a faraway star, you have stretched your being to its fullest. This will give you an evolution.

And only after you have reached the point of enlightenment can you see that there are skies beyond skies, that enlightenment is not the end. Existence is not exhausted yet; there is still much more ahead, the journey continues.

Osho,

Now that I am slowly, slowly turning inward, I find this longing mixed with sadness welling up frequently. It seems connected with the feelings that arise when I see you or dream about you.

Is it the realization that I really don't know much love and bliss in my life, or is it the longing for home?

Would you please speak to me about this?

It is good and fortunate that nothing satisfies you completely and entirely. That means you don't become stagnant, that means you have to keep moving. Slowly, slowly, you will understand that there is no home, that movement itself is the home; that there is no end to the pilgrimage, but the pilgrimage itself is the end.

It is very difficult to understand because we are accustomed to a certain logic: if we want to go somewhere, going is always just a means, reaching somewhere is the end. But as far as the universal life is concerned, there cannot be a place where you can say "I have come and now there is nothing further."

It is inconceivable that you will find a place which will be the end, and there will be a fence and a board saying, "Here ends the world." And even if you can find such a place, I would like you to jump the fence – because there must be something beyond the fence. If the fence cannot just stand by itself, there must be something beyond it. Somebody is playing a joke by putting up a board: "Here ends the world," and fixing a fence there. Don't be deceived.

You will come to many places where you would like to make your home because it is so blissful, so peaceful; you feel so fulfilled you don't see the point... Why should you continue? But I say unless you continue, you will never know that there is much more. But if you stop, nobody is going to prevent you. You need a master to go on goading you, to go on destroying every home you make, so finally you decide not to make any home – it is better to be homeless under the sky and continue the journey.

In the life of al-Hillaj Mansoor, a beautiful incident is related. He was a poor man. He collected money from people because he wanted to go to Kaaba, the sacred place of pilgrimage for the Mohammedans. And everybody contributed because he was going to Kaaba, and whoever contributes also gets a share in the virtue that he will get by reaching there. It is according to how much you give. So people gave him money – those who could give more gave more. People even gave beyond their capacity; they borrowed and gave him the money.

The next day he was back. And they said, "So soon?" – because in those days the journey from his place to Kaaba and back used to take three to six months. "What happened? And where is the money?"

He said, "A strange man met me on the way just as I was going out of town. He said, 'Listen, where are you going?' I said, 'I am going to Kaaba.' He said, 'There is no need.' I said, 'But every scripture says there is a need.' He said, 'I am a living master, and I am saying there is no need. Just go around me seven times and put all the money in front of me. I am Junnaid, the great master. Give the money first.' So I said, 'If you are Junnaid, then...'"

Junnaid's name was known all over the country. So al-Hillaj said, "If Junnaid says something he cannot be wrong. I gave the money to Junnaid, went around him seven times, and he told me to go back home."

Those people said, "You idiot. First, have you inquired whether he is Junnaid or not? It seems some cheat has deceived you. Let us go and find out. If he was really Junnaid, he would be sitting there."

They reached, and Junnaid *was* sitting there. Junnaid said, "So you have all come. Put your money here, whatever money you have. Take seven rounds – I am a living Kaaba – and then go home. And whenever you have money you can come again."

So the poor fellows had to put their money there and take seven rounds, sadly. "This is strange, we never thought that Kaaba would come just outside our village."

But the news spread. People started coming from other villages. They said, "If Junnaid says so, it must be right. That is a dead stone in Kaaba, and this is a living master."

Somebody told him, "We have come. We heard that you were here, so we have come for the pilgrimage."

He said, "Just give the money and do the pilgrimage."

But the man said, "I have a question: after taking seven rounds around you, is the journey finished? Is the pilgrimage over?"

He said, "No, whenever you have money, again you can come. This pilgrimage is never going to end. And if you don't find me here, you will find somebody else. You can do this pilgrimage around anybody; you just have to be sensitive to see the real, the living god within. It is not only within me, it is within you also. If you are alert, you can take seven rounds around yourself – no need to waste the money and no need to go anywhere. Remember, there is no home. Or, the home is everywhere – both are true."

I will not say to you that the home is everywhere – although it is true. I will say there is no home.

If you can continue your pilgrimage with this sincerity – that there is no home and there is no place you are going to, that just the going is in itself the beauty, the joy, the blissfulness, everything...the going itself – then the second will also be true: that wherever you are, it is home. But the second can be deceptive because people are very cunning, even cunning with themselves. They have misused all truths, they have managed to give them meanings which support their own ideas. If I say "Everywhere is home" then they will relax wherever they are, then there is no need...

So I say there is no home, and the journey has to be continued. It has to be a dance. Take your guitars and go on, and never stop anywhere. That does not mean that you cannot rest for a while. There are caravanserais but no homes – stay over for the night, but in the morning we have to go. This ongoing process is what life is. The moment it stops, it is death – and there is no death.

And why do people hanker for the home – security, safety? But in the name of security and safety, they don't make homes, they make prisons, and they are the jailed and they are the jailers, but because they have the keys in their own hands, they think they are free. They are not free...only a constantly moving river sometimes slow, sometimes fast, sometimes falling from the mountains, sometimes moving very slowly on the plains, but moving all the time. Movement is life; change is life.

Stay for a while if you feel tired, but stay only to regain enough energy so that tomorrow morning you can move again. The home *is* everywhere, but that home is just a caravanserai. Never make anything in life stable. That's how things die, that's how things start stinking. Allow movement – it keeps things fresh; it keeps things alive. It keeps the adventure alive, the excitement, the ecstasy of the discovery of the unknown and finally the unknowable.

Osho,

Ever since I have been with you listening, listening, I have never been able to remember anything you said. As so often before, you are speaking from my own heart, but the moment the words are heard, they are forgotten too.

Can you please say something? Am I not really listening?

It is perfectly good. It is as it should be, because this is not a kindergarten school where you have to remember every word spoken by me. Here the emphasis is not on remembering; the emphasis is on listening. If you have listened in silence, then whatever is significant will be absorbed by the heart. You may forget the words. Words are only containers, not the content. The content will be absorbed in the heart, and the containers have to be thrown away. You cannot always carry all the containers.

Listen perfectly. Never bother about remembering, because that is a disturbance. Doing the two things together, then one starts taking notes – if not visibly, then inside in the mind. No, don't create disturbance; just listen. If something is true, your heart will simply absorb it. And the heart has no memory system. The memory system is in the head. But whatever the heart absorbs will be changing your actions, will be changing your behavior, will be changing you. It will bring a transformation.

It will not bring you knowledge; it will bring you transformation. It will make you a new man. So don't be worried about memory at all.

Osho,

Is there any way to transcend being a German?

There is only one way. And you have done it; you have become a sannyasin. A sannyasin is neither German nor Indian, neither Chinese nor Japanese. A sannyasin declares that he is simply a human being. He drops all boundaries, all limitations of nations, of religions, of ideologies. And that you have done; now don't be worried. Now the whole of Germany is afraid of sannyasins.

You need not be worried about being a German. You just be a sannyasin and make more and more sannyasins, and Germany will disappear! We are going to make Germany the first Sannyasland.

29 I Am Crazy, but You Are Crazier!

Osho,
Research over the past few years has suggested that certain states of consciousness brought about by meditation techniques appear to evoke specific brainwave patterns. These states are now being created by feeding electronic and auditory stimulation to the brain, and they can also be learned through biofeedback.

The traditional "meditative state" – sitting silently, or at least quietly alert, is composed of bilateral, synchronous alpha waves. Deeper meditation also has bilateral theta waves. A state called "lucid awareness" has the bilateral synchronous alpha and theta waves of deep meditation, plus the beta waves of normal thought processes. Lucid awareness can be learned through biofeedback, using the most modern equipment.

Are these kinds of stimulation feeding and biofeedback useful tools for the meditator? What is the relationship of these technological techniques to the meditation beyond technique? Is this an example of bringing science together with meditation?

I would like to experiment with these new technologies – both personally in my own meditation, and professionally in my work as a physician. Do I have your blessings?

It is a very complex question. You will have to understand one of the most fundamental things about meditation: that no technique leads to meditation. The old so-called techniques and the new scientific biofeed techniques are the same as far as meditation is concerned. Meditation is not a byproduct of any technique.

Meditation happens beyond mind. No technique can go beyond mind.

But there is going to be a great misunderstanding in scientific circles, and it has a certain basis. The basis of all misunderstanding is: when the being of a person is in a state of meditation, it creates certain waves in the mind. These waves can be created from the outside by technical means. But those waves will not create meditation – this is the misunderstanding.

Meditation creates those waves; it is the mind reflecting the inner world. You cannot see what is happening inside. But you can see what is happening in the mind. Now there are sensitive instruments... We can judge what kinds of waves are there when a person is asleep, what kinds of waves are there when a person is dreaming, what kinds of waves are there when a person is in meditation. But by creating the waves, you cannot create the situation – because those waves are only symptoms, indicators. It is perfectly good; you can study them. But remember that there is no shortcut to meditation, and no mechanical device can be of any help. In fact, meditation needs no technique – scientific or otherwise. Meditation is simply an understanding.

It is not a question of sitting silently, it is not a question of chanting a mantra. It is a question of understanding the subtle workings of the mind. As you understand those workings of the mind a great awareness arises in you, which is not of the mind. That awareness arises in your being, in your soul, in your consciousness.

The mind is only a mechanism, but when awareness arises it is bound to create a certain energy pattern around it. That energy pattern is noted by the mind. The mind is a very subtle mechanism. And you are studying from the outside, so at the most you can study the mind. Seeing that whenever a person is silent, serene, peaceful, a certain wave pattern always, inevitably appears in the mind, the scientific thinking will say: if we can create this wave pattern in the mind through some biofeed technology, then the being inside will reach the heights of awareness.

This is not going to happen. It is not a question of cause and effect. These waves in the mind are not the cause of meditation; they are, on the contrary, the effect. But from the effect you cannot move towards the cause. It is possible that by biofeed you can create certain patterns in the mind and they will give a feeling of peace, silence and serenity to the person. Because the person himself does not know what meditation is and has no way of comparing, he may be misled into believing that this is meditation. But it is not, because the moment the biofeed mechanism stops, the waves disappear, and the silence and the peace and the serenity also disappear.

And you may go on practicing with those scientific instruments for years; it will not change your character, it will not change your morality, it will not change your individuality. You will remain the same.

Meditation transforms. It takes you to higher levels of consciousness and changes your whole lifestyle. It changes your reactions into responses to such an extent that it is unbelievable that the person who would have reacted in the same situation in anger is now acting in deep compassion, with love, in the same situation.

Meditation is a state of being, arrived at through understanding. It needs intelligence; it does not need techniques. There is no technique that can give you intelligence. Otherwise, we would have changed all the idiots into geniuses; all the mediocre people would have become Albert Einsteins, Bertrand Russells, Jean-Paul Sartres. There is no way to change your intelligence from the outside, to sharpen it, to make it more penetrating, to give it more insight. It is simply a question of understanding, and nobody else can do it for you – no machine, no man.

For centuries the so-called gurus have been cheating humanity. Now, in the future instead of gurus, these guru machines will cheat humanity. The gurus were cheating people, saying, "We will give you a mantra. Repeat the mantra." Certainly by repeating a mantra continuously, you create the energy field of a certain wave-length, but the man remains the same, because it is only on the surface. Just as if you throw a pebble into a silent lake, and ripples arise and move all over the lake from one corner to the other corner, but they do not touch the depths of the lake at all. The depths are completely unaware of what is happening on the surface. And what you see on the surface is also illusory. You think that ripples are moving; that's not true, nothing is moving.

When you throw a pebble into the lake, it is not that ripples start moving. You can check it by putting a small flower on the water. You will be surprised: the flower remains in the same place. If the waves were moving and going towards the shore, they would have taken the flower with them. The flower remains there. The waves are not moving; it is just the water going up and down in the same place, creating the illusion of movement. The depths of the lake will not know anything about it. And there is going to be no change in the character, in the beauty of the lake, by creating those waves.

The mind is between the world and you. Whatever happens in the world, the mind is affected by it; and you can understand through the mind what is happening outside. For example, you see me – *you* cannot see me; it is your mind that is affected by certain rays and creates a picture in the mind. You are inside, and from inside you see the picture. You don't see me; you can't see me. The mind is the mediator. Just as when it is affected by the outside, the inner consciousness can read it – what is happening outside – what the scientists are trying to do is just the same: they are studying meditators and reading their wave lengths, the energy fields created by meditation. And naturally, the scientific approach is that if these certain patterns appear without any exception when a person is in meditation, then we have got the key; if we can create these patterns in the mind, then meditation is bound to appear inside. That's where the fallacy is.

You can create the pattern in the mind, and if the person does not know about meditation, he may feel a silence, serenity, for the moment, as long as those waves remain. But you cannot deceive a meditator, because the meditator will see that those patterns are appearing in the mind. The mind is a lower reality, and the lower reality cannot change the higher reality. The mind is the servant; it cannot change the master. But you can experiment. Just remain aware that whether it is a biofeed machine or the chanting of *Om*, it does not matter; it only creates a mental peace, and mental peace is not meditation. Meditation is the flight beyond the mind. It has nothing to do with mental peace.

One of America's great thinkers, Joshua Liebman, has written a very famous book, *Peace of Mind*. I wrote him a letter many years ago when I came across the book, saying, "If you are sincere and honest, you should withdraw the book from the market because there is no such thing as peace of mind. The mind is the problem. When there is no mind then there is peace, so how there can be "peace of mind?" And any peace of mind is only fallacious; it simply means the noise has slowed down to such a point that you think it is silence. And you don't have anything to compare it with."

A man who knows what meditation is cannot be deceived by any techniques, because no technique can give you understanding of the workings of the mind. For example, you feel anger, you feel jealousy, you feel hatred; you feel lust. Is there any technique that can help you to get rid of anger, of jealousy, of hatred, of sexual lust? And if these things continue to remain, your lifestyle is going to remain the same as before.

There is only one way – there has never been a second. There is one and only one way to understand that to be angry is to be stupid: watch anger in all its phases, be alert to it so it does not catch you unawares; remain watchful, seeing every step of the anger. And you will be surprised: that as awareness about the ways of anger grows, the anger starts evaporating. And when the anger disappears, then there is peace. Peace is not a positive achievement. When the hatred disappears, there is love. Love is not a positive achievement. When jealousy disappears, there is a deep friendliness towards all.

Try to understand – but all the religions have corrupted your minds, because they have not taught you how to watch, how to understand; instead they have given you conclusions that anger is bad. And the moment you condemn something, you have already taken a certain position of judgment. You have judged. Now you cannot be aware. Awareness needs a state of no-judgment. And all the religions have been teaching people judgments: this is good, this is bad, this is sin, this is virtue. This is the whole crap that for centuries man's mind has been loaded with. So, with everything – the moment you see it – there is immediately a judgment about it within you. You cannot simply see it; you cannot be just a mirror without saying anything.

Understanding arises by becoming a mirror, a mirror of all that goes on in the mind.

There is a beautiful story – not just a story but an actual historical fact.

One disciple of Gautam Buddha was going on a journey to spread his message. He had come to see Gautam Buddha and to get his blessings, and to ask if there was any last message, any last words to be said to him.

And Gautam Buddha said, "Just remember one thing: while walking, keep your gaze just four feet ahead, looking four feet ahead of you."

Since that day, for twenty-five centuries, Buddhist monks have walked in the same way. That was a strategy to keep you from seeing women in particular. Those disciples were monks. They had taken the vow of celibacy.

Ananda, another of Gautam Buddha's disciples, could not understand what the matter was, why the monk should keep his eyes always focused four feet ahead. He inquired, "I want to know what is the matter?"

Buddha said, "That's how he will avoid looking at a woman, at least a woman's face – at the most he will see her feet."

But Ananda said, "There may be situations when a woman is in a danger. For example, she has fallen into a well and is shouting for help. What is your disciple supposed to do? He will have to see her face, her body."

Buddha said, "In special situations he is allowed to see her, but it is not the rule, it is only the exception."

Ananda said, "What about touching? – because there may be situations when a woman has fallen on the road. What is your disciple supposed to do? Should he help her to get up or not? Or an old woman wants to cross the road – what is your disciple supposed to do?"

Buddha said, "As an exception – but remember it is not a rule – he can touch the woman with one condition, and if he cannot fulfill the condition he is not allowed the exceptions. The condition is that he should remain just a mirror; he should not take any judgment, any attitude. The woman is beautiful – that is a judgment. The woman is fair – that is a judgment. He should remain a mirror, then he is allowed the exceptions. Otherwise, let the woman drown in the well – somebody else will save her. You save yourself!"

What he is saying is this: in every situation where mind starts any kind of desire, greed, lust, ambition, possessiveness, the meditator has to be just a mirror. And what is that going to do? To be just a mirror means you are simply aware. In pure awareness the mind cannot drag you down into the mud, into the gutter. In anger, in hatred, in jealousy, the mind is absolutely impotent in the face of awareness. And because the mind is absolutely impotent, your whole being is in profound silence: the peace that passeth understanding.

Naturally that peace, that silence, that joy, that blissfulness will affect the mind. It will create ripples in the mind, it will change the wave lengths in the mind, and the scientist will be reading those waves, those wave patterns and he will be thinking, "If these wave patterns can be created in someone by mechanical devices, then we will be able to create the profoundness of a Gautam Buddha." Don't be stupid!

All your technical devices can be good, can be helpful. They are not going to do any harm; they will be giving some taste of peace, of silence. Although very superficial, still it is something for those who have never known anything of peace. For the thirsty, even dirty water does not look dirty. For the thirsty, even dirty water is a great blessing.

So you can start your experiments with all my blessings, but remember it is not meditation that you are giving to people – you don't know meditation yourself. You may be giving them a little rest, a little relaxation, and there is nothing wrong in it. But if you give them the idea that this is meditation then you are certainly being harmful, because these people will stop at the technical things, with the superficial silence; thinking that this is all and they have gained it.

You can be helpful to people. Tell them that this is just a mechanical way of putting your mind at peace, and the mind at peace is not the real peace – real peace is when the mind is absent. And that is not possible from the outside, but only from the inside. And inside you have the intelligence, the understanding to do the miracle.

It is good for people who cannot relax, who cannot find a few moments of peace, whose minds are continuously chattering. Your technical devices are good, your biofeedback mechanisms are good. But make it clear to them that this is not meditation; this is just a mechanical device to help you relax, to give you a superficial feeling of silence. If this silence creates an urge in you to find the real, the inner, the authentic source of peace, then those technical devices have been friends, and the technicians who have been using them have not been barriers but have been bridges. Become a bridge!

Give people the little taste that is possible through machines, but don't give them the false idea that this is what meditation is. Tell them that this is only a faraway echo of the real; if you want the real, you will have to go through a deep inner search, a profound understanding of your mind, an awareness of all the cunning ways of the mind, so that the mind can be put aside. Then the mind is no longer between you and existence, and the doors are open.

Meditation is the ultimate experience of blissfulness. It cannot be produced by drugs, it cannot be produced by machines; it cannot be produced from the outside.

Osho,

The communes of Mahavira and Buddha survived even after their lifetimes, but your communes are not surviving in your lifetime although they are self-sufficient.

Does survival of communes depend on social structure, affluence of the society, prevalent religions, or national and international politics? Please comment.

The first thing to understand: Gautam Buddha and Mahavira had no communes. Their disciples were wandering monks; they were not living a commune life in one place, they were always on the move, except for the rainy season. And even in the rainy season they used to stay in different places.

My commune was an alternative society. Gautam Buddha and Mahavira did not provide an alternative society; hence they were not in conflict with the society. On the contrary, they were dependent on the society for food, for clothes, for shelter; their disciples were dependent on the society for everything. They could not be rebellious. How can you be rebellious against a society which gives you food, which gives you clothes, which gives you shelter, which gives you everything that you need? You cannot go against its morality – it may be rotten, but you have to support it. You cannot go against its traditions.

My commune was a totally new experiment. It has never happened before. There is no comparison with the past because my people were not dependent on anybody, and they were against the society, the culture, the civilization, the religion, the politics, the education – everything that constitutes the world. We were fighting an impossible fight – a small group trying to live in a totally different way from the whole of humanity. Mahavira was not against marriage; I am. Mahavira was not respectful towards women; I am. Buddha was as much a male chauvinist as anybody else. For twenty years continually, he refused to initiate any women into Buddhism. He never accepted the idea that they are equal to men. I say they are not only equal but in some respects superior. My commune was a revolt.

Their religions – Gautam Buddha's and Mahavira's religions – were simply offshoots of the same civilization, the same society, the same morality, the same superstitions. Yes, they were arguing about invisible things which nobody bothers about – whether God is seven feet high or six feet high is nobody's business. Whether God has three faces or only one face – it is God's problem, it is nobody else's problem. Maybe if he has three faces then God's tailor might have a problem!

They were disagreeing on many points, but all those points were immaterial, not substantial, not concerned with the life that man is living here and now – about that they were all in absolute agreement.

Hence it was absolutely to be expected that my commune would be destroyed. It was against the church, it was against the state; it was against all that your so-called civilization stands for – because I don't believe man has yet become civilized. If man has become civilized, then there is no need for wars; if man has become civilized, then there is no need for discrimination between blacks and whites, men and women; if man has become civilized then there is no need for people to die because they have nothing to eat – and there are people who are dying because they have too *much* to eat. In America, thirty million people are dying from overeating, and thirty million people are dying because they have nothing to eat.

And you call this world a civilized world? It is not even sane. And it cannot be just coincidence: exactly thirty million people overeating, knowing perfectly well that they are eating themselves to death, knowing perfectly well that thirty million people are on the streets dying without food. Strange: sixty million people can be saved within a second, but these sixty million people will die.

I have heard...

A man was very worried because his wife was getting fatter and fatter and fatter.

And women have greater capacity for becoming fatter than men – it is a biological privilege, because the woman has to be able to become pregnant, to become a mother; then for nine months she cannot eat well, she throws up, she is carrying such a load in her belly. And every day the child needs more and more food. It is a very strange situation: the woman cannot eat, and the child wants more food because he is growing. Hence nature has made woman's body capable of collecting more fat for emergency measures. So even if she does not eat, the child can get as much as he needs from the reserve fat the woman has; and the woman can also go on eating her own fat. And nine months is a long time, so the woman has immense capacity. If she uses her full capacity, then man is no competitor.

And women are thinner while they are not married. Once they are married they start becoming fat, because now there is no problem. They have got hold of a man who cannot escape, so it does not matter what happens to their body proportions; they are no longer interested in any beauty competition.

The man asked his doctor, "What has to be done?"

The doctor said, "Do one thing: take a beautiful picture of a naked woman and paste it inside the fridge, so whenever your wife opens the fridge for more ice cream she will think, 'What a beautiful body.' And she may start thinking about herself, that this is not good."

The man said, "That idea is very good."

After two months the doctor met the man, and he could not believe it. He said, "What happened? I have not seen you for two months, and you have become so fat!"

The man said, "Everything went wrong because of your suggestion, you idiot! Are you my doctor or my enemy? I pasted a beautiful woman, naked, inside the fridge. Since then my wife does not open the fridge, but I cannot remain more than fifteen minutes away before a desire arises to see the photo. But when one opens the fridge, it is not just the photo one sees – the ice cream, the cake... You have destroyed my life. So my wife has become slimmer, beautiful, and I have become ugly. And the whole credit goes to you."

This society, this world is based on insane superstitions. My commune was a revolt. It survived five years – it was a miracle, because the whole fascist and imperialist government of America tried everything to destroy it. Legally they could not do it because we had four hundred legal experts in the commune, the commune had the biggest legal firm in the whole world: four hundred sannyasins – a few of them very well known legal experts; others, new graduates from the universities – four hundred legal experts continually fighting the American government on every legal point. Finally the government decided that legally it was impossible to destroy us, and then they started doing illegal things. And when a world power – the world's greatest power – starts being criminal and illegal, what can four hundred people do? We were ready to fight legally, rationally, logically, in every possible way. But illegally it was impossible to fight.

I was arrested illegally, without any arrest warrant – because they could not find a reason to arrest me, so how to issue an arrest warrant? In the middle of the night at the point of twelve loaded guns, I was arrested. And I asked them, "Where is the arrest warrant?"

They said, "There is no arrest warrant."

I said, "You can at least tell me verbally what the reason is, why I am being arrested."

They said, "We don't know."

I asked them, "Then give me the opportunity to inform my attorney."

And they refused. That is every citizen's right everywhere in the world – to inform his attorney if the government is doing such an illegal act. But they were worried that if the attorney comes, the first thing he is going to ask is, "Where is the arrest warrant?"

They destroyed the commune in such a way that the world would think nothing criminal had been done, but everything criminal... In court they produced one hundred and thirty-six charges against me. I was silent for three and a half years, never going out of my room. And if a man remaining silent – not meeting anybody, not talking to anybody, not going out of his room – can manage to commit one hundred and thirty-six crimes, then I thought there must be miracles, I must be doing miracles! And they had no proof of anything.

They asked for negotiations. The government attorney made it clear to my attorneys that the government could not accept defeat. They themselves had foolishly called the case "The United States of

America versus Osho," they themselves had called the case that; there was no need to give it such a name. Now they were in trouble: if I had won the case that would mean the United States of America would have been defeated in their own courts under their own law, by their own constitution. So they said, "We cannot... The government cannot accept defeat. And you know and we know that we don't have any proof. So the best way will be not to go to trial. We are ready for negotiations. And the negotiating agreement is that Osho should accept any two charges, should admit that he has committed two crimes – just to show the world that we have not done anything wrong by arresting him – and pay a nominal fine. Then on the surface everything looks legal."

But my attorney said, "It will be very difficult to convince him to accept."

They said, "We should make you aware of the fact that if he does not accept and if the case goes to trial, then the trial can be prolonged for ten years, twenty years. It is a case against the government, and you should be aware that the government is not ready to lose the case. So we will go on postponing it, and bail will be canceled and Osho will have to remain in jail. His whole movement will be destroyed, and all his sannyasins all over the world will be in immense torture." And they suggested – whispered into my chief attorney's ear – "You should be aware that he can be killed too. If we see that the case is going to be lost, he can be killed too."

My attorneys came to me crying – and they were the topmost attorneys of America. I asked them, "Why you are crying? What is the matter? – because there is nothing in those hundred and thirty-six charges. We are going to win."

They said, "We are going to win, but your life is at risk and we don't want your life to be at risk."

And my attorneys were right, because a bomb had already been planted under my seat, so if something went wrong then they could finish me on that very day. It was just a coincidence that I reached the jail earlier than they expected – and the bomb was a time bomb, so it did not explode.

After I left America, the attorney general told the press, "Our first priority was to destroy the commune."

Why? – because the commune had done no harm to America in any way. But deep down it had hurt America's ego, its pride – because we have shown them that a dream can be realized, that five thousand people can live without any law enforcement authority, without any court, without any fight, without any drugs, without any murder, without any suicide, nobody going mad. And people were living so joyously and so beautifully that the whole of America was starting to feel jealous.

The very existence of the commune was dangerous to the American politicians because it showed that they don't have any intelligence; otherwise they could have done what we had done very easily – they had all the power, all the money. This small commune of five thousand people had everything that man needs, and all the freedom, all the love. And everybody was working seven days a week, twelve to fourteen hours a day, and still were not tired, because it was not something forced; it was something they wanted to do, they wanted to create. It was such a creative act that after working fourteen hours they were still dancing in the streets; late into the night they were playing on their guitars, singing, dancing.

The commune was destined to be destroyed. It was too good not to be destroyed. It was the alternative society.

Mahavira and Buddha did not create any alternative society. They were part of this society, they remained dependent on this society. Their revolution was intellectual, verbal. My revolt was actual and existential.

And the destruction of the commune in America does not mean that the idea of the commune will disappear. There are still communes around the world flourishing in many countries. More and more communes will be coming up.

America is going to repent; it has missed an opportunity. It could have supported the commune and made it clear to the world that it stands for freedom, that it stands for a new man, that it stands for a future humanity. It missed a great opportunity. By destroying the commune, it has destroyed its own credibility, its own democracy. It has proved itself simply nothing but a hypocritical society.

Osho,

The most powerful experience in my life is the love that I feel for you. It's like a shower that cleanses my soul and fills my heart with gratitude.

But still I keep searching for something else, as if there is a secret you haven't shared with me yet. Is this crazy love affair between us really and truly all that is needed? Why am I not satisfied with this experience?

Love can never be satisfied. If it is satisfied, it is not much of a love. The greater and deeper it is, the more dissatisfaction there will be. That is not against love; it simply shows the vastness, that your heart wants to love in a way, which is infinite, that it will never be satisfied. And it is good that it is not satisfied. The moment it is satisfied, it is dead.

The love between the master and the disciple can never be satisfied. It will always remain a thrill, a new excitement, a new ecstasy. It will always go on opening doors upon doors. Disciplehood will become devotion; one day devotion will become a merger, just as the river merges in the ocean. But that too is not going to satisfy.

Satisfaction is not a great quality. It belongs to the little minds, to the little hearts which are satisfied with small things. There are people who are satisfied with a little money, there are people who are satisfied with a house, there are people who are satisfied with a little name, a little fame – these are pygmies.

Giants are never satisfied. On every new step they find the journey is becoming deeper, more miraculous, more mysterious – and the longing is growing and the heart is full of a sweet ache. To be in a love affair with a master is to be in a love affair with existence itself; the master is only an arrow pointing towards the unknowable, the miraculous, the mysterious. The master is not the end; the master is only the beginning.

The whole function of the master is to push you the same way a mother bird pushes a small bird, a new bird who has never opened his wings into the sky. Naturally he is afraid – a vast sky. He has lived in a small cozy nest, safe and secure, the mother has been taking care, and now she wants him to take a jump and fly. And one day she pushes him. And the moment he is pushed out of the nest, for a moment it feels as if he is going to fall down on the earth, but before he falls on the earth his wings open and the whole sky is his. And there are skies beyond skies.

The function of the master is nothing but to push you into a more divine discontentment, into a discontentment that knows no satisfaction.

Osho,

You are really something – talking about "beyond enlightenment" when most of us are not beyond pettiness, futility and postponement!

Do you believe in miracles or something, perhaps love?

It is true; I am something!

I know you are not beyond pettiness, beyond jealousy, beyond greed, beyond anger. But I don't talk about going beyond them for the simple reason that if you start struggling with your pettiness, you will remain petty; if you start struggling against your jealousy, you will remain jealous.

An ancient proverb is: Always choose the enemy very carefully.

A friend can be chosen without much care, but an enemy has to be chosen very carefully because you will be fighting with him, and in fighting you will become just like the enemy, because you will have to use the same methods, the same means. Enemies are very precious!

I don't want you to fight with small things. Rather than looking down at the earth, and all around is your pettiness and jealousy and anger, my effort is to show you the stars and help you to know that you have wings. And once you start moving towards the stars, those small things will disappear on their own accord. It is better to look at a star and to strive to get to it because the journey is beautiful, the heart is throbbing with excitement, rather than fighting with small things. You will remain small, fighting with small things. All your religions teach you to fight with small things, and that's why the whole of humanity has remained small – fight with small things. I insist: don't fight with small things. Fight for something great, and as you move towards the great the small ones will disappear.

I am crazy, but you are crazier! And that is the only bond between us: I am crazy, you are crazier. That is the only commitment. We will reach to the stars, we will not bother about small things. Leave them here for other people; they will fight with them.

Osho,

What is needed to not miss you?

Only one thing is needed not to miss me, and that is: you have to remember constantly that in every mind, in every person who comes in search of truth, the ego plays a very cunning game.

I will tell you one story:

It is said that one of the great Zen masters, Bokuju, used to ask every newcomer: "Have you realized that the path of disciplehood is very difficult? Before you enter on the path, it is my duty to make you alert to all the difficulties, arduousness, hostilities; it is an uphill task. Are you ready, or you have come here just out of curiosity?"

One man said, "No, I have come here to find the truth, but if it is too difficult to be a disciple then what about making me a master?"

It is a very strange story.

But that is the only thing that can prevent you coming closer to me – the desire in the ego somewhere to become a master. You have to become something bigger, something greater. The master is just a finger pointing to the moon. Don't be bothered to become a master; while you can become the moon, why become the finger?

You are asking what can keep you missing me. Only one thing: the desire to be a master. It is one of the mysteries of life that only those who don't have any desire to be a master become masters, and those who have the desire even fall from the status of being a disciple, because the desire to be a master is nothing but a subtle ego. So just watch your mind.

From disciple become a devotee; from devotee take a quantum leap, a merger with existence. Never think for a moment of becoming a master. Leave it to existence; if existence wants you to become a master – that means if existence wants to use you as a master, you will be used. If existence thinks you have done enough and wants you to relax, disperse into eternity, leave it to existence. You should not be desirous of anything. The moment you come to the state of desirelessness, then existence uses you in whatever way is needed: as a mystic, as a master, as a singer, as a dancer, as a flute player, or just as nobody; but everything is a benediction.

That which comes to you from existence, without your desiring it, is always the greatest ecstasy there is.

30 You Are the Watcher, Not the Actor

Osho,
I have heard you speak for the past month on "beyond enlightenment" – and I don't understand it.
I have heard you speak for the past twelve years on enlightenment – and I don't understand it.
All I know is the moment when I sit before you, you feel like blood to my body, your voice more familiar than my own heartbeat.
Osho, have I let you down?

There are things which are beyond understanding.

Enlightenment is beyond understanding, and of course beyond enlightenment is going to be more miraculous, more mysterious. Understanding itself is not the heart of human beings, it is not their very being. It is useful only as far as the outside world is concerned. The moment you start moving inwards, you have to learn new ways of feeling, of loving, of knowing, and finally of being.

Understanding is perfectly right for the mind, for intelligence, for the objective world; but life does not consist only of those things which you can understand. In fact, the things that you can understand don't make life a celebration, they don't give life a meaning, a significance; they don't allow life to become love.

Understanding is the demarcation line between the mundane and the sacred. The mundane can be understood and should be understood. And the sacred cannot be understood and should not be understood. Its sacredness is basically a secret that you experience, just the way you feel the heartbeat, the way you feel your breathing.

The sacred gives color to existence, gives music to that which is mundane. It transforms all prose into poetry and makes everything a mystery unto itself, so that the whole existence becomes a constant challenge to discover. You go on discovering, but the discovery is never finished, hence you can never say you have understood. On the contrary, the deeper you enter into the sacred dimension of life the more you feel you don't understand, you don't know.

Socrates had become very old, and before he was given poison, the oracle of the temple of Delphi declared him to be the wisest man in the whole world. A few people who knew Socrates were immensely glad, they rushed to Athens to inform Socrates: "It has never happened before, it is unprecedented that the oracle of Delphi should declare anybody as the wisest man in the world. You are the first."

Socrates said, "You will have to go back to the temple of Delphi and tell the oracle that although it has always been right, this time it has missed – because I know nothing."

The people who brought the news were shocked.

They went back and told to the oracle: "Socrates refuses... Not only does he refuse to be the wisest man in the world, he says, 'I know nothing.'"

And here is the beauty of the incident: The oracle said, "That's why he is the wisest man in the world, there is no contradiction."

If you had understood what I was saying for twelve years about enlightenment, you would have missed. If you had understood what I have been saying for one month continually about beyond-enlightenment, you would have missed. Because you are aware that you have not been able to understand anything, you have not missed.

And your feeling that sitting close to me you feel as if I have become your heartbeat, your breathing, your circulation of blood – this is true understanding. This is not knowledge; this is the same understanding as when Socrates says, "I know nothing." This is closer to love, this is closer to music; this is closer to feeling beauty. You don't understand beauty, you don't understand music, you don't understand dance – you enjoy, you rejoice, you feel. It enters into your being. It becomes part of you, but you cannot say it is knowledge.

Listening to the music of the winds as they pass through the pine trees, what can you understand? Or listening to the sound of running water, what can you understand? Or looking at a beautiful sunset and all the colors spread over the horizon, what can you understand? What do you understand? But something happens which is far more precious than understanding. You fall in love, you feel it; you become it. This is how it should be – *aes dhammo sanantano*. This is how religion has always been; this is the eternal mystery I call religion – not the religion of the mind, but the religion of the heart, of the being; not the religion of knowing, but the religion of innocence.

Whatever is happening to you is exactly what should happen to everybody. Those who go from here understanding things, knowing things, becoming more knowledgeable, it would have been better that they had not come, because I have not been a help to them, I have burdened them; I have not been able to unburden them. And my whole effort is to take all the weight of knowing, knowledge, wisdom, from you and to make you innocent children again – again collecting flowers in the garden, running after butterflies, collecting seashells, making houses of sand on the beach utterly absorbed in whatsoever you are doing, utterly blissful – so the whole existence around you is a fairyland because everything is mysterious. If I can take away your knowledge and give you back the sense of mystery, then I have done my job, I have fulfilled my function.

Osho,

Reading a scientific report about brain manipulation, questions arose in me.

For instance, if every feeling – like happiness, sadness, sexuality, aggression, and so on – can be stimulated by electrodes, or indirectly by chemistry, can be manipulated from the outside, then these feelings are not my own; they are just puppets in someone's hands. They are either manipulated from the outside or from the inside as automatic reactions to situations; they are not me. This is about feelings.

Maybe some day thoughts can be manipulated equally easily. Then what is really mine? Then what is left? Then who am I?

Questioning and thinking in these directions, I came to recognize that I often think about myself, about life, about truth in these ways. And then the question arose: is this way of questioning and thinking the way the mind tries to know something? Is it able to reach any truth at all? If not, is this thinking or questioning just a futile effort, just a waste of time? Or is it not the mind, not the intellect, but a deeper intelligence, a deeper instrument that is able to come to some truth?

Would you please comment?

It is absolutely true: your emotions, your sentiments, your thoughts – the whole paraphernalia of the mind – are from the outside, are manipulated by the outside.

Scientifically it has become clearer. But even without scientific investigation, the mystics, for thousands of years, have been saying exactly the same thing: that all these things that your mind is filled with are not yours; you are beyond them. You get identified with them, and that's the only sin. For example, somebody insults you and you become angry. You think *you* are becoming angry – but seen scientifically, his insult is only a remote controller. The man who has insulted you is managing your behavior. Your anger is in his hands, you are behaving like a puppet.

Now scientists are able to put electrodes in the brain at certain centers – there are seven hundred centers. And it is almost unbelievable – the mystics have been talking about these seven hundred centers in the brain for almost seven, eight thousand years. Science has just now discovered that there are exactly seven hundred centers controlling all your behavior. An electrode can be put at a particular center – for example, anger – with a remote control so you cannot see that anybody is doing anything to you. Nobody insults you, nobody humiliates you, nobody says anything to you; you are sitting silently, happily, and somebody pushes the button of the remote control and you become angry. It is a very strange feeling because you cannot see the reason anywhere, why you are becoming angry. Perhaps you will rationalize somehow – you see a man passing down the street and you remember that he insulted you – you will find some rationalization just to console yourself that you are not going mad. Sitting silently...and suddenly feeling so angry without any provocation?

And the same remote controller can work to make you happy: sitting in your chair you start giggling, and you look all around in case somebody sees you – he will think you are going crazy. Nobody has said anything, nothing has happened, nobody has slipped on a banana peel, so why are you giggling? But you will rationalize it; you will give some apparently rational grounds for giggling. And the strangest thing is that when the next time the same button is pushed and you giggle, you will again have the same rationale, the same consolation, the same explanation – that too is not yours. It is almost like a gramophone record.

And the scientists have come to discover a tremendously meaningful thing: the moment the remote controller releases the center it rewinds itself immediately. For example, your speech center, the remote control can force you to speak. There is no audience, you will feel awkward, but you cannot do anything, you have to speak. It is just like a recording. When the remote controller releases the button, the pressure on the electrode, you become silent. Press the button again...and the strange thing is, you start your speech again from the very beginning!

When I was reading about the scientific investigations into these centers, I was reminded of my student days. I was a competitor in an inter-university debate; all the universities of the country were participating. The Sanskrit University of Varanasi was also participating, but naturally the students from the Sanskrit University were feeling a little inferior compared with competitors from other universities. They knew ancient scriptures, they knew Sanskrit poetry, drama, but they were not familiar with the contemporary world of art, literature, philosophy or logic. And the inferiority complex works in very strange ways.

Just after I had spoken, the next person was the representative from the Sanskrit University. And just to impress the audience and to hide his inferiority complex he started his speech with a quotation from Bertrand Russell – he had crammed it, and Sanskrit students are more capable of cramming things than anybody else. But his stage fright... He knew nothing about Bertrand Russell, he knew nothing about what he was quoting. It would have been better to have quoted something from Sanskrit, because he would have been more at ease. In the middle he stopped – just in the middle of a sentence. And I was sitting by his side, because I had just finished. There was silence, and he was perspiring. And just to help him, I said, "Start again" – because what else to do? He was simply stuck. "And if you cannot go ahead, you start again; perhaps it may come back to you."

So he started again: "Brothers and sisters..." And at exactly the same point he got stuck again. Now it became a joke. The whole hall was shouting, "Again!" And he was in such a difficult situation: neither could he go ahead nor could he keep standing there, silent; it looked very idiotic. So he had to start again. But he would start again, "Brothers and sisters..." For a whole fifteen minutes we heard only that portion: "Brothers and sisters" up to the point where he got stuck, again and again.

When his time was finished he came and sat next to me. He said, "You destroyed my whole thing."

I said, "I was trying to help you."

He said, "This is help?"

I said, "You were going to be in difficulty anyway. This way at least everybody enjoyed it except you – that I can understand, but you should rejoice that you made so many people happy. And why did you choose that quotation? When I was saying to you, 'Start again' there was no need to start over – you could have dropped that quotation, there was no need to begin again from the very beginning."

But I came to know through reading the scientific research that the speech center is exactly like a gramophone record, but with one thing very strange and special: the moment the needle is taken away from the record you cannot put the needle back where you took it from. Once it is taken away, it will have to begin again exactly at the beginning. The center instantly goes back to the beginning.

And if this happens, can you say you are the master of what you are saying? Are you the master of what you are feeling? Certainly there are no electrodes scientifically put into you, but biologically exactly the same work is going on. You see a certain woman, and immediately your mind reacts: "How beautiful!" This is nothing but remote control. That woman functioned like a remote control and your speech center simply went into a recorded speech: "How beautiful!" The mind is a mechanism. It is not you.

It records things from outside, and then reacts to outside situations according to the recordings. That's the only difference between a Hindu and a Mohammedan and a Christian and a Jew: they have just got different gramophone records; inside they are one humanity. And do you think when you play a gramophone record – it may be in Hebrew, it may be in Sanskrit, it may be in Persian, it may be in Arabic, but it is the same machine that plays the record... To the machine it does not matter whether it plays Hebrew or Sanskrit. All your religions, all your political ideas, all your cultural attitudes are nothing but recordings. And in certain situations certain recordings are provoked.

There is a beautiful incident in the life of one of the very wisest kings of India, Raja Bhoj. He was very interested in wise people. His whole treasury was open only for one purpose: to collect all the wise people of the country, whatsoever the cost. His capital was Ujjain, and he had thirty of the country's most famous people in his court. It was the most precious court in the whole country. One of the greatest poets of the world, Kalidas, was one of the members of the court of Raja Bhoj.

One day a man appeared at the court saying that he spoke thirty languages with the same fluency, the same accuracy and accent as any native person could, and he had come to make a challenge: "Hearing that you have in your court the wisest people of the country, here are one thousand gold pieces..."

The rupee used to be golden. We should stop calling it the rupee now, because the word *rupee* comes from the word *rupya*. *Rupya* means gold. It went on falling from gold to silver, from silver to something else. Now it is just paper and you go on calling it rupee. The very word means gold.

And he said, "Anybody who can recognize my mother tongue, these one thousand gold pieces are his. And if he cannot recognize it, then he will have to give me one thousand gold pieces."

There were great scholars there, and everybody knows that whatever you do, you can never speak any language the way you can speak your own mother tongue, because every other language has to be learned by effort. Only the mother tongue is spontaneous, you don't even learn it, just...the very situation and you start speaking it. It has spontaneity.

That's why even Germans who call their country *fatherland*... It is the only country which calls itself *fatherland*. All other countries call their land *motherland*. But even the Germans don't call their language *father tongue*. Every language is called a mother tongue because the child starts learning from the mother, and anyway the father never has the chance to speak in the house. It is always the mother who is speaking; father is listening.

Many took the challenge. He spoke in thirty languages – a few pieces in one language, a few pieces in another language – and it was really hard; he was certainly a master artist. He was speaking each language the way only a native can speak his own mother language. All of the thirty great scholars lost. The competition continued for thirty days, and every day one person took the challenge and lost it. The man would say, "This is not my mother tongue."

On the thirty-first day... King Bhoj had been continually saying to Kalidas, "Why don't *you* accept the challenge? – because a poet knows language in a more delicate way, with all its nuances, more than anybody else."

But Kalidas remained silent. He had been watching for thirty days, trying to find out which language the man spoke with more ease, with more spontaneity, with more joy. But he could not manage to find any difference, the man spoke all the languages in exactly the same way.

On the thirty-first day, Kalidas asked King Bhoj and all the wise people to stand outside in front of the court. There was a long row of steps and the man was coming up; as he came up to the last step, Kalidas pushed him down. And as he fell rolling down the steps, anger came up – he shouted.

And Kalidas said, "This is your mother tongue!" Because in anger you cannot remember, and the man had not been expecting this to be a challenge.

And that actually was his mother tongue. Deepest in his mind, the recording was of the mother tongue.

One of my professors used to say – he lived all over the world, teaching in different universities – that only in two situations in life have I been in difficulty in different countries, fighting or falling in love. In those times one remembers one's mother tongue. However beautifully you express your love, it is not the same; it seems superficial. And when you are angry and fighting in somebody else's language, you cannot have that joy.

He said, "Those are two very significant situations – fighting and loving – and mostly they are together with the same person. With the same person you are in love, with that same person you have to fight."

And he was right, that everything remains superficial – you can neither sing a beautiful song nor can you use real four-letter words of your language. In both cases, it remains lukewarm. The mind certainly is a mechanism for recording experiences from the outside, and reacting and responding accordingly. It is not you. But unfortunately the psychologists think the mind is all, beyond mind there is nothing. That means you are nothing but impressions from the outside. You don't have any soul of your own. The very idea of the soul is also given by the outside.

This is where the mystics are different; they will agree absolutely that about the mind, the contemporary scientific research is right. But it is not right about man's total personality. Beyond the mind, there is an awareness which is not given by the outside and which is not an idea, and there is no experiment up to now which has found any center in the brain which corresponds to awareness.

The whole work of religion, of meditation, is to make you aware of all that is the mind and dis-identify yourself with it. When the mind is angry, you should think it is simply a gramophone record. When the mind is sad, you should simply remember it is only a gramophone record. A certain situation is pressing the remote controller, and you feel sad, you feel angry, you feel frustrated, you feel worried, you feel tense – all these things are coming from the outside, and the mind is responding to them.

But you are the watcher. You are not the actor. It is not *your* reaction. Hence the whole art of meditation is to learn awareness, alertness, consciousness.

While you are feeling angry, don't repress it; let it be there. Just become aware. See it as if it is some object outside you. Slowly, slowly, go on cutting your identifications with the mind. Then you have found your real individuality, your being, your soul. Finding this awareness is enlightenment – you have become luminous. You are no longer in darkness, and you are no longer just a puppet in the hands of the mind. You are a master, not a servant. Now the mind cannot react automatically, autonomously, the way it used to do before. It needs your permission.

Somebody insults you, and you don't want to be angry... Gautam Buddha used to say to his disciples that to be angry is so stupid that it is inconceivable that intelligent human beings go on doing it. Somebody else is doing something and you are getting angry. He may be doing something wrong, he may be saying something wrong, he may be making some effort to humiliate you, to insult you, but that is his freedom. If you react, you are a slave. And if you say to the person, "It is your joy to insult me, it is my joy not to be angry," you are behaving like a master. And unless this master becomes crystal clear in you, crystallized, you don't have any soul. You are just a phonograph record. As you grow older, your recording goes on becoming longer and longer. You become more knowledgeable. People think you are becoming wiser – you are simply becoming a donkey loaded with scriptures.

Wisdom consists only of one thing, not of knowing many things but of knowing only one thing: that is your awareness and its separation from the mind. Just try watching small things, and you will be surprised. People go on doing the same things every day. They go on deciding to do something, and they go on repenting because they have not done it; it becomes a routine.

Everything you do is not new. The things which have been giving you misery, sadness, worries, wounds, and you don't want, somehow mechanically you go on doing these things again and again as if you are helpless. And you will remain helpless unless you create a separation between mind and awareness. That very separation is the greatest revolution that can happen to man. And from that very moment your life is a life of continuous celebration – because you need not do anything that harms you, you need not do anything that makes you miserable. Now you can do and act on only that which makes you more joyous, fulfills you, gives you contentment, makes your life a piece of art, a beauty. But this is possible only if the master in you is awake. Right now the master is fast asleep, and the servant is playing the role of master. And the servant is not *your* servant; the servant is created by the outside world, it belongs to the outside world, it follows the outside world and its laws.

This is the whole tragedy of human life: you are asleep, and the outside world is dominating you, creating your mind according to its own needs – and the mind is a puppet. Once your awareness becomes a flame, it burns up the whole slavery that the mind has created. And there is no blissfulness more precious than freedom, than being a master of your own destiny.

The mind is not your friend. Either the mind is pretending to be the master or it has to be put into its right place as a servant, but the mind is not your friend. And the struggle for freedom, for bliss, for truth is not with the world; it is a fight with this puppet mind. It is very simple.

Kahlil Gibran has a beautiful story. The farmers in the villages, to protect their cultivated farms, create a false man: just a stick, another stick... It looks almost like a cross. And then they put a *kurta* on it, and a mud pot in place of the head. That's enough to make poor animals afraid that somebody may be standing there. The white *kurta* and two hands, in the night...somebody is watching. For the animals it is enough, they keep away from the farm.

Gibran says, "Once I asked such a false man, 'I can understand the farmer who made you, he needs you. I can understand the poor animals; they don't have great intelligence to see that you are bogus. But in rain, in sun, in hot summer, in cold winter you remain standing here – for what?'

"And the false, bogus man said, 'You don't know my joy. Just to make those animals afraid is such a joy that it is worth suffering rain, suffering sun, suffering heat, winter – everything. I am making thousands of animals afraid! I know I am bogus, there is nothing inside me – but I don't care about that. My joy is in making others afraid.'"

I want to ask you: would you like to be just like this bogus man, nothing inside, making somebody afraid, making somebody happy, making somebody humiliated, making somebody respectful? Is your life only for others? Will you ever look inside? Is there anybody in the house or not?

The people who are with me, their search is to find the master of the house. I say to you the master is there – perhaps asleep, but he can be awakened. And once the master is awakened within you, your whole life takes new colors, new rainbows, new flowers, new music, new dances. For the first time you become alive. Before, you were only vegetating.

Osho,

I love being here. I wanted and felt to be with you even if it were just for two days.

At your birthday in 1981 we met for the first time. The reason was that I had just read a book about Gurdjieff and the phenomenon of *baraka*. This gave me such a hit that I came to the ranch.

These days I am working with managers and teaching them meditation techniques. I'm also preparing a worldwide meditation project. Again I feel I need *baraka*.

Please can you say something about *baraka*?

Baraka is a Sufi word meaning grace. George Gurdjieff was trained in Sufi schools. He has carried many ideas of the Sufis into the West.

The Sufi master – just like any other master in the world – is full of grace. If you are receptive, if you are open, just coming close to the master something invisible, some vibe of the divine, some rays of the unknowable start penetrating you. It also has the meaning of blessing. People come to the masters and ask for blessing.

In English there is no exact word to translate *baraka*, but in Sanskrit, in Hindi, we have the word *prasad*. Blessings carry a faraway echo of it. If you are receptive... And unless one is receptive one never goes to a master. That has been the Eastern tradition. Why waste your time and why waste the master's time? You go only when you see that your heart is opening; it needs a ray of light, as if your being is just like thirsty earth which needs a raincloud to shower on you. Only in such moments people go to a master, they touch the feet of the master; they sit with the master. Nothing is said and everything is heard; nothing is asked and everything is given.

Baraka is a mystical principle that happens between the receiving disciple and the overflowing master. It is possible to pass a master without even noticing him, if you are not open. Sufis are very careful. It is not easy to find a Sufi master; he may take months or sometimes years to find – and perhaps the master is just living in front of your house. The Sufis wait for the right moment.

They have their disciples who come to know that a certain man is asking if this village has a Sufi master. And the disciples go on telling him, "Yes, the Sufi master is here, and you will be called only when you are ready – because the real thing is your openness. The master is ready, but what will you be doing? Even if we take you to the master, you will not be able to recognize him." So the disciples will keep the person hanging around, giving him hope, giving him time – "Next month we will try" – making him more and more thirsty. And when they see that he has become a longing, that now it is no longer an ordinary inquiry, it is not just a curiosity to see a Sufi master, but a deep longing, a question of life and death: that if this man does not get in contact with a master he may die, only then will he be introduced into the company of the master. And he will be surprised: the master is a man he has passed in the village many times, he sells vegetables – because Sufis keep themselves hiding in very ordinary life. Somebody is a shoemaker, somebody is a weaver, somebody sells vegetables – ordinary things, nothing special about it. And they meet in the middle of the night.

Then the same man sits with the dignity of an emperor. It is called "the court of the master." The same man who was selling vegetables the whole day long in the marketplace – now even the emperor comes to touch his feet. But nobody can come to the Sufi master unless somebody from his company introduces him, unless somebody takes the responsibility that the person is ready, somebody brings him, introduces him: "He is ready. He needs your grace."

When Gurdjieff entered into a Sufi circle for the first time – it took him three years to enter the circle – when he entered, almost a dozen people were sitting there silently with their eyes closed. He was brought close to the master.

The friend who brought him told him, "Just sit down. Nothing is needed on your part except a silent opening, and the rain will come. And then don't close yourself. Drink of the master as much as you can – this is his blessing; this will keep you on the path, on the right track. It will keep you courageous enough to pass all the dark nights; it will keep you trusting that the morning is going to happen. The face of the master, the eyes of the master, the gestures of the master, the silence of the master – everything has to be soaked up so it becomes part of you." When the master is no longer outside you only, but inside you too, that is real blessing. Then the disciple is pregnant, the master has come into his womb, and it will help him in times of danger, in times of discouragement, in times of darkness. It will always keep him together, remembering that if truth can happen to one man, if godliness can happen to one man, then it is everybody's birthright.

Remembering: "It may take a little time for me, I have joined the path a little late. But the dawn is not far away."

Osho,

Rajneeshpuram was a rare experiment in the history of human consciousness, where for the first time seekers of truth from the whole world gathered around a master. It was an international commune for the most intense and the fastest growth of human consciousness.

The Rajneeshpuram commune could not survive because of orthodox religions and international politics.

Is there any hope of such a rare experiment happening again around you? Or is there any alternative experiment possible on an individual scale in the present situation? Or is it destined that such a rare opportunity for human consciousness to flower to its optimum should be missed?

Please comment.

The commune in America was only a beginning; a beginning of many communes around the world. They will go on spreading, because it is not only a question of orthodox religions and dirty politics, it is also a question of the future of humanity. And the future is always more important than the past. The past is heavy and long. The future is light, unknown. But the past is dead, and life belongs to the future; and death cannot win over life. One commune can be destroyed. Thousands of other communes will arise.

Of course my way of functioning will be different, because the experiment in Rajneeshpuram needed me to be there, it was the first commune. Every step had to be taken carefully. And within five years, so much was done that is not possible to do even in fifty years. But now the basic rules are clear. And my being in any commune is going to be dangerous for the commune.

It was absolutely necessary for the first commune that I should be present. I took the risk, and the commune has succeeded. Now there are communes all around the world. More communes will be arising. I am just waiting for the right moment to trigger a new kind of process. I will not be part of any commune because my presence will be dangerous for the commune. So now I will be just wandering from one commune to another. Before my presence becomes dangerous in one commune, I will move to another so the commune is saved, and whatever I can give and my presence can give, can be given on a much bigger scale around the globe. There is no need for people to come to me. I can move from commune to commune. This way, many more communes can flourish.

I am just waiting for the right moment. Preparations are being made, and soon I will start working on a series of communes – because the movement has to become worldwide, it is already worldwide. The commune is the lifestyle of the future. The family has gone and the commune is going to take its place. Much depends on the success of commune life, and we have to make the commune life such a celebration that it starts spreading like wildfire, that others start communes of their own.

Each village can become a commune, there is no need to establish different villages. We just have to prove that life in a commune is much richer, much more lovely, much more meditative, that there is a possibility of living in a different way, different from the way humanity has lived up to now. We have proved it in Rajneeshpuram.

It was our success that forced America to destroy the commune. If we were not successful, nobody would have bothered about us. Remember this: it was not a failure that we were destroyed; it was our success which could not be tolerated.

And if we have been successful in one place... We are successful in Germany, in Italy, in Holland, in Japan, in Australia, in other different countries. Because I am not there, the politicians are not worried, the theologians are not afraid. So I want the communes to become more consolidated before I start my world tours, because now it will not be *a* world tour, it will be just the beginning of world tours. I will be continually rotating like a satellite around the earth, creating as much trouble as possible. Only then these traditional vested interests can be destroyed.

But if the truth is with us, the victory is also with us.

Osho,

Do those cells needed for a lively and growing intelligence have only a limited life span, so that there is a point beyond which one either becomes senile or simply stagnates?

Or, given the necessary stimulus, is it possible for intelligence to continue to grow right up to the moment of one's death?

The ordinary human being stops his growth of intelligence at age fourteen because the biological purpose is complete. At the age of fourteen, the person is mature enough to give birth, to reproduce. Biology is no longer interested beyond this point. This is the reason why the average human being is stuck at the age of fourteen as far as his mental age is concerned. People go on growing physically up to seventy, eighty, ninety, a hundred years – in some places like Caucasia, up to one hundred and fifty, even one hundred and eighty. But their mental age remains stuck at fourteen. This has been the routine up to now.

This can be changed. And this should be changed because there is infinite potential for growth, but the change will come only if you have some goals beyond biology. If your life remains concerned only with sex, children, family, food, house, then there is no need; that much intelligence is enough. But if your interest is that of an Albert Einstein then your intelligence starts moving sometimes even ahead of your physical body.

Emerson is reported to have said – and rightly so when asked how old he was – "Three hundred and sixty years."

The journalist who was asking asked, "Three hundred and sixty? You don't look more than sixty."

Emerson said, "That's right. From one point of view, I am sixty years old. But I have done so much work as far as my intelligence is concerned that either six people would be needed to do it or I would need three hundred and sixty years. My intelligence is so far ahead of my physical body."

Intelligence depends on what you are doing with it. The person who is meditating has the greatest possibility of reaching the highest peaks of intelligence, because in meditation he is doing the greatest possible work that a man is capable of, and that is realizing oneself, knowing: "Who am I." Entering into the deepest interiority of one's subjectivity is the greatest work for intelligence. Then you cannot even count; you cannot count Gautam Buddha's intelligence, it is beyond calculations, beyond measurements.

And if you are a meditator, as your meditation goes on becoming more and more luminous, your intelligence will be growing to the last breath of your life. Not only that, even after the last breath your intelligence will continue to grow – because *you* are not going to die, only your body will be dying. And the body has nothing to do with intelligence; the mind has nothing to do with intelligence.

Intelligence is the quality of your awareness – more aware, more intelligent. And if you are totally aware, you are as intelligent as this whole existence is.

31 Discarding the Container, Discovering the Content

Osho,
I am afraid to jump from a three-meter tower into a swimming pool.
Will I still be able to jump into enlightenment?

The first basic thing to understand is that you are not expected to jump into enlightenment. You have to climb for it; it is higher than you, not lower than you. So at least, one fear you can drop!

And climbing to enlightenment is a simple process. It is not something tortuous, arduous. It is something like peeling an onion: after one layer there is another layer, fresher, younger, juicier, after that layer there are still more juicier layers. And if you go on peeling, finally nothing is left in your hands, because the onion was nothing but layers upon layers. Enlightenment is a kind of peeling of the ego.

It is parallel to the onion because it has no inner substance, only layers. And those layers sometimes slip by themselves; they become old sometimes by accident. If you watch your life, you can see it happening. It is not a theorization. Sometimes you can see that you are not wearing the right mask for the right occasion. When you are expected to smile, you are not smiling; when you are expected to weep, you are not weeping.

I used to live with a distant uncle's family. His wife died. In fact it is very difficult to find a husband who never thinks that if his wife died it would be good, a good riddance. And my uncle's wife was certainly a nightmare. In fact everybody was happy that she died, and everybody knew that the husband was happy that she had died, but still the convention, the tradition...

I used to sit in the garden. He told me, "I cannot remain in a miserable posture the whole day long because really I am not miserable. You know it. I cannot hide it from you – twenty-four hours a day you are in the house – but when relatives come, I have to show that I am very miserable." Not to be caught being happy and at ease, he told me, "You mostly sit in the garden reading, so you can just give me a signal from there that somebody is coming." So I had to give him signals.

And the miracle was that the moment I would give him the signal, *immediately* he would become miserable. Sometimes I would play a joke; I would give the signal and nobody would turn up. And he would be very angry: "This you should not do, because this is a dangerous joke. Sometimes I may think you are joking and somebody may turn up. You have to understand that I should not be caught enjoying myself. In fact I have never enjoyed myself because of this woman! She was such a pain in the neck. And even today, although she is dead, she is torturing me through these relatives – relatives I have not seen for years, relatives I don't even recognize as relatives. They come and I have to be miserable; whether the relative is real or false, I have to bring tears to my eyes.

"I am surprised myself that I am capable of it: being miserable, tears flowing. And I pray to you that when I am acting this way, please don't stand so close. Just be out in the garden; you don't have to be present to watch the whole scene, because then it becomes more difficult for me to do the performance."

One day a man came. He was known to me, he was a bookseller. And I asked him, "Can you pretend just for two minutes to be a far-off relative of a dead wife?"

He said, "What?"

I said, "I will explain it to you later on when I come to your shop. But remember, it has to be done in a certain way. First, I will introduce you as the best shopkeeper in town, who is not only a shopkeeper but who loves books and has a collection of rare books: 'It is not just a business for him, it is his love affair.' I will introduce you first in this way. And then in the middle I will tell him, 'He's also a relative of your dead wife.' I just want to see how he changes his mask."

I introduced the man. My uncle was perfectly happy. He said, "Very good, I will come some time. I don't have much time to read, but if you can suggest some rare books I will try to find the time."

And then I said, "But I forgot one thing. He has not come here to sell books; he is a relative of your dead wife." And immediately my uncle started crying, tears came to his eyes and he was so miserable.

The bookseller was also amazed at how quickly he changed. He had just been laughing and there had been no question of misery or anything.

And then I said, "Just don't harass yourself. He is not related to your wife, it is just a misunderstanding."

He said, "What kind of misunderstanding?"

I said, "Another woman in the neighborhood has also died; he is related to that woman."

And immediately, all the tears had gone and he started laughing. He said, "This is a great joke! Why didn't you tell me?"

The bookseller said, "I am very new to this locality, I have never been here, and he misled me. He told me that my relative used to live here, and she has died. I came because of my relative who has died, but I am not acquainted with this locality, and I have never seen the husband of my relative, so just forgive me. But it has been a great experience! You could have been a great actor – within minutes, from laughter to misery, from misery back to laughter."

I said, "This is nothing. If I tell him the reality, he will be back again to tears and misery."

He said, "What reality?"

I said, "No other woman has died. He *is* a relative of your wife."

He said, "Listen, I have told you this is a serious affair" – and again misery and tears.

And that man felt so sad for this miserable creature...he told me, "Don't torture him this way."

I said, "I am not torturing him; he is torturing himself. What is the need? The wife is dead; she cannot come back. He need not be afraid of her, at least not now. While she was alive, it was difficult to say. I knew his wife, and he was perfectly right to be afraid of her. But now he need not be afraid, she cannot come."

I said to my uncle, "Just be your natural self. If you are feeling pleasant, why change personalities? Why make your life a drama instead of a reality?"

But we are all doing that in different measures. Your personality consists only of cultivated layers. Many masks are hanging around you – whichever one you need, you put it on. In fact, humanity has developed, by and by, almost an automatic system – you need not do anything, it happens by itself. The moment you see your boss, your face changes – not that you change it; it is so unconscious that you start smiling, just like a dog wagging his tail.

Even dogs are very clever. If they are not certain about a stranger who is coming towards their house – he may be a friend, he may not be a friend – they do both things: they go on barking, and they go on wagging their tail also. They are just waiting to see which direction the camel turns; if the man is received by the family as a friend, the barking stops and the tail continues. And if the family rejects the man, then the tail stops and barking continues. Poor dogs are being corrupted because of the company they keep with human beings; they have learned your tricks.

A person meeting the boss has one face. The same person meeting his servant has a different face. He behaves with the servant as if he does not matter at all; he is not human. You can pass him without taking any note of him; he is only a servant. But as far as the boss is concerned, you have to take a joyous attitude, an ear-to-ear smile, a Jimmy Carter smile. And you are not doing it deliberately; now it is your autonomous, unconscious functioning.

Enlightenment is simply the process of becoming aware of your unconscious layers of personality and dropping those layers. They are not you; they are false faces. And because of those false faces, you cannot discover your original face.

Enlightenment is nothing but the discovery of the original face: the essential reality you brought with you, and the essential reality you will have to take with you when you die. All these layers gathered between birth and death will be left here behind you.

The man of enlightenment does exactly what death does to everybody, but he does it himself. He dies in a way and is reborn, dies in a way and is resurrected. And his originality is luminous because it is part of eternal life. It is a simple process of discovering yourself.

You are not the container but the content. Discarding the container and discovering the content is the whole process of enlightenment.

Osho,

I feel your presence all around me – your love and your compassion – but I myself feel unworthy of it. Who am I that I should deserve you? Just because of this, I have closed a door in front of you. My heart is suffering, but I have forgotten where the door is.

Please comment.

It is one of the crimes that has been committed against everybody everywhere in human society: you have been continually conditioned and told that you are unworthy. Because of this conditioning, the major part of humanity has given up even desiring any adventure, any pilgrimage to the stars; they are so convinced of their unworthiness. Their parents were telling them, "You are unworthy." Their teachers were telling them, "You are unworthy." Their priests were telling them, "You are unworthy." Everybody was forcing the idea on them that they were unworthy. Naturally they accepted the idea.

And once you accept the idea of unworthiness, you naturally close. You cannot believe that you have wings, that the whole sky is yours, that you have just to open your wings and the sky is going to be yours, with all its stars.

And it is not a question that somewhere you have forgotten to open one door. You don't have any doors; you don't have any walls. This unworthiness is simply a concept, an idea. You have become hypnotized by the idea. Since the very beginning, all cultures, all societies have been using hypnotism to destroy individuals – their freedom, their uniqueness, their genius – because the vested interests are not in need of geniuses, not in need of unique individuals, not in need of people who love freedom. They are in need of slaves. And the only psychological way to create slaves is to condition your mind that you are unworthy, that you don't deserve, that you don't even deserve whatever you have, you should not go for anything more. Already you owe too much for things which you are not worthy of.

And hypnotism is a simple process of continuous repetition. Just go on repeating a certain idea and it starts settling inside you, and it becomes a thick wall, invisible; there are no doors, no windows. There is no wall either.

George Gurdjieff has remembered his childhood. He was born in the Caucasus, one of the most primitive parts of the world. It is still at the stage where humanity was when it lived by hunting; even cultivation has not started. The people of the Caucasus are great hunters. And any society that lives by hunting is bound to be a nomadic society. It cannot make houses, it cannot make cities, because it cannot depend on animals – today they are available there, tomorrow they are not available there. And certainly you will kill them, and because of your presence they will escape – either they will be killed or they will escape.

Cities are possible only with cultivation because trees cannot escape, and you have to be there to protect them, to water them, to take care of them – so you have to live in villages near your fields. The Caucasus is still nomadic. The people are on their horses, moving from one place to another place, hunting.

Gurdjieff was brought up by a nomadic society, so he was coming from almost another planet. He knew a few things which we have forgotten. He remembered that in his childhood the nomads hypnotized their children – because they could not carry them continuously while they were hunting; they had to leave them somewhere under a tree, in a safe place, but what was the guarantee that those children would remain there? They had to be hypnot zed. So they used a small strategy – and they have used it for centuries. From the very beginning when the child was very small, they would make him sit under a tree. They would draw a circle around the child with a stick and tell him, "You cannot go out of this circle; if you go out of it, you will be dead."

Now those small children believed, just like you. Why are you Christian? – because your parents told you. Why are you Hindus? Why are you Jainas? Why are you Mohammedans? – because your parents told you. Those children believed that if they went out of the circle they would die. They grew up with this conditioning. And you might try to persuade them: "Come out, I will give you a sweet." They could not, because death... Even sometimes if they tried, they felt as if an invisible wall prevented them, pushed them back nto the circle. And that wall existed only in their minds – there is no wall, there is nothing. Unless the person who had put them in the circle came and withdrew the circle, took the child out, the child remained inside.

And the child goes on growing, but the idea remains in the unconscious. So even an old man, if his father draws a circle around him, cannot get out of it. So it is not only a question of the child; the old man also still carries his childhood in his unconscious. And it is not a question of one child. The whole group of nomads have put their children under trees nearby, and all the children are sitting there the whole day long. By the time their parents come back, it has become such a conditioning that no matter what happens, the child will not leave the circle.

Exactly the same kind of circles are drawn around you by your society. Of course they are more sophisticated. Your religion is nothing but a circle, but very sophisticated; your church, your temple, your holy book is nothing but a hypnotic circle. One has to understand that one is living surrounded by many circles which are only in your mind. They don't have a real existence, but they function almost as if they are real.

One night it happened, it must have been nearabout twelve, a young man knocked on my door. I was still awake, writing a few letters. He fell on the ground, took hold of my feet, and said, "Just give me one glass of water with your hand."

I said, "What is the purpose?"

He said, "I have been sent by a Dr. S.C. Barat. I am his patient. I have been suffering from a stomachache for years. He has tried all kinds of medicines, nothing helps. And today he said, 'Now medical science cannot help you, only a miracle can help you.' So I asked where I had to go for the miracle and he sent me to you. And he said, 'Whatever happens, go on holding his feet unless he gives you a glass of water – just that water will be the cure.'"

Dr. Barat was my friend. He had told me that he was going to send this young man. He said, "He is a hypochondriac. He has no stomachache, nothing, he is just rich – too much money and nothing to do. So he is doing stomachache, headache... He gets any kind of disease. I have not found any disease in him; he is perfectly healthy. But every day he tortures me for hours. I know that no medicine is going to help because he is not sick. In fact, to give him any medicine is dangerous.

"So I have been giving him just colored water, especially prepared for him. I have a whole cabinet full of colored water in bottles; I make a mixture from these bottles and give it to him. He says, 'Yes, a little relief but the pain remains.' And if it disappears from one place, it starts appearing in another place. I am tired. And because of him, I am losing many patients. So you have to save me from this rich young man. His father has died and he has a big inheritance, enough money to throw away on anything. But he is destroying my business."

I said, "I don't understand – how is he destroying your business?"

He said, "It is very simple – because my other patients see him, and see that he has been coming for ten years and I have not been able to cure him. It creates a bad impression. So I am sending him to you, and you have to do the miracle."

I said, "I don't do miracles, and miracles don't happen. But if you want, I will try."

So when the young man came, I went on denying him: "Just water touched by me is not going to help. You should go to another doctor – why are you after this Dr. Barat? If one doctor has failed, go to another doctor. If one "pathy" fails... Change from allopathy, try ayurveda; if ayurveda fails, try homeopathy; if homeopathy fails, try naturopathy. And by that time you will be dead, don't be worried. Whether the disease goes or not, you will have gone!"

He said, "But I want to live! I am too young to die right now." And he was not more than twenty-six. He said, "I am not even married. Because my father died, I have enough money – many people are after me. They want me to marry their daughters, and I don't want to be encaged. And first I want to take care of my health. Getting married means bringing more sicknesses, more diseases into the house. You *have* to give me a glass of water!"

I said, "It is very difficult, because miracles don't happen."

I was staying in a friend's house. His wife was listening as this whole conversation was going on and on, and he was crying. Finally the woman came out and said, "I never thought that you are so hard. Whether it helps or not, just give him a glass of water. Half of the night has passed; neither are you going to sleep, nor are you allowing anybody else in the house to sleep – because we are all excited, waiting to see what happens, whether the miracle happens or not."

I said, "Because you say so, and because I don't want to torture your family, bring a glass of water."

And I told the young man, "Remember, you are not to talk about it to anybody, because I don't want it to happen that from tomorrow the whole day long a queue of patients is here. I don't have time for all this, so promise me that you will not talk."

He said, "I promise that I will not talk, but you also have to promise me one thing."

I said, "What is it?"

He said, "You will have to promise me that once in a while I can come with a bottle of water and you will touch it."

I said, "What you are going to do with it?"

He said, "I will not say anything to anybody about you. But if the miracle happens and my stomachache disappears, there are many people who are suffering. I can distribute the water. But I promise I will not talk."

So I said, "Okay, it is a promise. But don't bring anybody here."

I gave him a glass of water, and as he drank the water – just drinking it – you could see his face changing. And he said, "My God! the pain has gone."

My friend's wife was standing behind me. She said, "You did it!"

I said, "I have *not* done it – and remember that you are not to talk about it to anybody."

She said, "I may not talk, but everybody in the house knows – everybody is hiding, all the children are there. Now," she said, "if this was going to happen, why did you waste one hour?"

I said, "Without wasting that hour, the water wouldn't have helped. It was not the water; it was my insistence that I wouldn't give it to him. He became more and more convinced that the water was going to work. And when I told him that he had to promise not to talk to anybody, he was absolutely convinced that the miracle was going to happen."

He started distributing the water.

And people told me, even Dr. Barat told me, "It is strange. You cured my patient and now he is curing my patients. I was thinking I was finished with him – now he comes with a bottle into my dispensary. He sits there and says, 'Don't bother about this medicine, it won't help. Take the miraculous water.' That young man seems to be my enemy from a past life. And he has cured a few of my patients."

Seventy percent of sick people are only sick in their minds; they don't have a real sickness. Hence it has been found that all "pathies" – allopathy, ayurveda, yunani, naturopathy, homeopathy – they all succeed in seventy percent of cases. In seventy percent of cases *anybody* can do miracles, one just has to make the right arrangement so that the mind is convinced that the miracle is going to happen. It is simply a conditioning that you are unworthy. Nobody is unworthy. Existence does not produce people who are unworthy.

Existence is not unintelligent. If existence produces so many unworthy people, then the whole responsibility goes to existence. Then it can be definitely concluded that existence is not intelligent, that there is no intelligence behind it; that it is an unintelligent, accidental materialist phenomenon and there is no consciousness in it.

And this is our whole fight, our whole struggle: to prove that existence is intelligent, that existence is immensely conscious. It is the same existence which creates Gautam Buddhas. It cannot create unworthy people. You are not unworthy.

So there is no question of finding a door; there is only an understanding that unworthiness is a false idea imposed on you by those who want you to be a slave for your whole life. You can drop it right now.

Existence gives the same sun to you as to Gautam Buddha, the same moon as to Zarathustra, the same wind as to Mahavira, the same rain as to Jesus – it makes no difference, it has no idea of discrimination. For existence, Gautam Buddha, Zarathustra, Lao Tzu, Bodhidharma, Kabir, Nanak or you, are just the same. The only difference is that Gautam Buddha did not accept the idea of being unworthy; he rejected the idea. It was easy for him to reject it – he was the prince of a great kingdom, the only son of the king, and the king was thought to be almost a god. So he had no idea of unworthiness.

But what about Kabir? What about Raidas the shoemaker? What about Gora the potter? These poor people were burdened by society with the idea that they were unworthy, but they rejected it. In Kabir's life there were clearcut examples. Kabir lived his whole life in Kashi. For centuries Hindus have believed that to die in Kashi is the greatest thing you can do in life, because for one who dies in Kashi, his paradise is guaranteed. It does not matter what kind of man he is, whether he is a murderer, a thief, a saint or a sinner – these things are all irrelevant. His dying in Kashi erases everything and he becomes qualified for paradise. So in Kashi you will find old people, old women who have come there just to die. They have not done anything in their life, but they don't want to miss paradise.

And Kabir lived his whole life in Kashi, and when he was going to die he said, "Take me out of Kashi to the other side, to the small village." Just on the other side of the Ganges was a small village.

His disciples said, "Are you mad or something? People come to Kashi, the whole of Kashi is full of people who have come here to die. You have lived your whole life in Kashi, what kind of nonsense is this? And the village you are pointing to is a condemned village; people say whoever dies there is born again as a donkey."

But Kabir said, "I will go to that village, and I will die in that village. I want to enter paradise on my own worth, not because of Kashi. And I know my worth."

They had to take him. Against their will they had to take him to the other side, and he died there.

This man was so certain of his worth. He was a weaver. It is not certain whether he was Hindu or Mohammedan because his name, Kabir, is Mohammedan; it is one of the names of God. He was found on the Ganges – a small child, just a few days old, abandoned by his parents.

One great Hindu scholar, Ramananda, had gone for his early bath and he found the child. And he could not be so hard as to leave him there, so he brought him into his ashram – he had an ashram and hundreds of disciples. So the child was brought up by a brahmin.

But on his hand was written the name Kabir. He didn't change his name. It is still uncertain whether he was Mohammedan or Hindu. He never cared. Once there was a great conference in Kashi. It used to convene only after each twelve years to decide about certain spiritual matters, problems which may have arisen over scriptures. Naturally Kabir was not invited because it was not even certain that he was a Hindu, and only brahmins could be allowed.

But about a certain point in the scriptures they could not come to a conclusion. One man said, "You have to forget about whether Kabir is Hindu or Mohammedan, it doesn't matter. He is the only man alive in Kashi who can immediately decide the meaning, the insight of this scriptural passage."

I am telling you about this incident for a particular reason. At that very time Meera was also in Kashi, she had just come. She was traveling around India.

Reluctantly, the scholars told Kabir, "You are invited to the conference because we are stuck at a certain point, and nobody has the experience. And there are many people in the conference who say, 'Kabir has the experience.' This passage needs to be interpreted only by one who has known himself; so although we are not certain whether you are Hindu or Mohammedan or brahmin, still we are inviting you, against all precedents."

Kabir said, "There is a condition: I will come only if Meera is also invited."

Now that was even more difficult for the male chauvinist mind – a woman! What does a woman have to do with it? When wise scholars are deciding things, a woman's function is in the house.

Kabir said, "Then Kabir is not coming. Kabir can come only if Meera is allowed to come. When you are ready to allow Kabir, whose caste is not certain, whose religion is not certain, what is the problem about Meera? – because she can also decide. Even if I don't come, she also has the same experience as I have." And the scholars had to agree.

This has happened only once, that a woman and a non-brahmin joined with the highest hierarchy of Hinduism to interpret their scriptures. And their interpretation was accepted.

Kabir's disciples asked, "From where did you get such authority?"

He said, "If existence accepts me, if existence gives me life, that is enough to prove that I am needed, that existence cannot do without me."

So drop the idea of unworthiness, it is simply an idea. And with the dropping of it, you are under the sky; there is no question of doors, everything is open, all directions are open. That you *are* is enough to prove that existence needs you, loves you, nourishes you, respects you. The idea of unworthiness is created by the social parasites. Drop that idea. And be grateful to existence, because it only creates people who are worthy, it never creates anything which is worthless. It only creates people who are needed.

My emphasis is that every sannyasin should respect himself and feel grateful to existence that he has been required to be here at this juncture of time and space.

Osho,

There is a Sufi saying that no human being can avoid his fate. This is a world of limitations – blessed are those who gain a taste of the limitless, despite this fact.

A famous astrologer and composer, Dane Rudhyar, who was a friend of George Gurdjieff, said, "The old idea of astrology that experience happens to human beings is not true. On the contrary, human beings happen to their experience."

My observation is that every astrologer who is courageous enough will find out that Gurdjieff is true when he says, "Man is a machine."

On the other hand, my experience with you, Christ, and Buddhist teachers has revealed the existence of the limitless in the midst of limitations. While religiousness opens the doors to the limitless, astrology studies the world of forms and limitations. And without the first, the second could have become intolerable to me. Now, slowly, slowly, the formless and the form seem to meet and marry inside of me.

Would you please comment?

George Gurdjieff is right when he says that man is a machine, but by *man* he means all those who are living unconsciously, who are not aware, who are not awake, who do not respond to reality but only react. Ninety-nine point nine percent of human beings are in the category of machines. With these machines, astrology is possible. In fact, predictions can be made, guarantees can be issued only about machines. A watch can be guaranteed for five years, a car can be guaranteed for a certain time, because we know the capacity of the machine, how much it can work, how long it can go. Its scope is limited. And it cannot do anything on its own accord, it can only react to situations, which are almost predictable.

For example, at a certain stage a boy and a girl will become sexually mature, and their hormones and their biology will start forcing them towards each other. They will call it love because nobody wants to be categorized as a machine. But two machines cannot love, two machines can only be together, can struggle, can stumble against each other.

And it is not coincidence that in every language, love is called *falling* in love. It is an unconscious process; it *is* a fall. You cannot answer why you love a certain person. And now the science of human biology, genetics, has grown much more mature. It is possible to inject hormones into you, which can make all your love disappear, or which can make you a great lover. But these are hormones; it is chemical. You are not consciously involved in it.

It happened in Mumbai nearabout twenty years ago, an astrologer came to see me. I told him, "You will be disappointed. Astrology won't work with me."

He said, "It is not a question of you or anybody else, there are no exceptions in astrology."

I said, "Then do one thing: write down twelve things that I am going to do in one year. You keep one copy and I will keep one copy, I will write on both copies that these are the twelve things that I will *not* do. That's the only way to decide whether your astrology works or not."

He got a little afraid because he had not thought of this possibility.

I said, "Even to the extent...if you say that I will live, I will die – just to make the point clear that astrology won't work with me."

He said, "Now I have to study more in depth. And after three days I will be coming back."

Twenty years have passed; he has not come.

And whenever I have been in Mumbai, I have inquired, "Phone the astrologer and ask when that in-depth study is going to be complete, because twenty years have passed. Has he dropped the idea?"

If you are enlightened, then astrology cannot function for you. Then you can love, then you can do, then you can act, then you have a certain mastery over your own being.

But unconscious, you are just moving hither and thither as the wind blows. And anybody who has studied human nature deeply... There are many astrological schools which have studied for centuries how the mechanical man works. They have come to certain conclusions, and their conclusions are almost always correct. If they are incorrect, that means the astrologer is not well prepared, his studies in human nature and unconscious behavior are not complete. But the moment you start becoming conscious, you start becoming really a man – not a machine.

When Gurdjieff said for the first time that man is a machine, it shocked many people. But he was saying the truth. Only the truth is applicable just to 99.9 percent of people – 0.1 percent of people have to be left out of it.

Gautam Buddha was born... And in the East those were the days of the highest possibilities for human genius. In all directions in which the East was working, it reached the very peak, the climax, to such an extent that you cannot find a new yoga posture; Patanjali exhausted all the possibilities of postures, the science is complete. Five thousand years have passed, and in five thousand years thousands of people have tried but there is no way to find a new posture.

You cannot find a new sex posture; Vatsyayana has completed all the postures possible – and a few which may even look impossible!

Shiva completed all the techniques – one hundred and twelve. You can play with new combinations, but nothing new is possible. Astrology was at its peak.

And as Gautam Buddha was born, the son of a great king, the king immediately called the best astrologers. They all studied the birth chart and they all remained silent. Only one, a young astrologer, said to the king, "These people are silent because this is a strange boy, and we cannot be decisive about him. There are two possibilities..." And astrology never speaks in that way. Astrology means you have to predict what is going to be; you are not there to predict all the possibilities, that will not be prediction.

But the young astrologer said, "These are old wise people, they will not even say this. I am young and I can stick my neck out, I can risk, because I don't have any reputation. There are two possibilities: either this boy will become an emperor of the world, a *chakravartin*, or he will become an enlightened, awakened liberated soul – but then he will be a beggar. Either he will be the emperor of the whole world or he will be just a beggar with a begging bowl in his hands. And it is not in our power to say what the outcome will be."

And all the old astrologers agreed. "The young man is right. We were silent because this is not the way astrology functions. We say, 'this is definitely going to happen.' But about this boy we cannot say. And the possibilities are so diametrically opposite: either the emperor or the beggar." And that's what happened. The king asked all those wise astrologers, "Then tell me how to protect him so that he does not move towards becoming a beggar but becomes the world emperor. That has been my lifelong desire. I could not achieve it, but *he* has the possibility. So just tell me how to prevent him from becoming a beggar." They gave all their advice, and their advice turned out to create just the opposite to what they intended. They suggested, "Give him all the luxuries. Don't let him know about death, old age. Don't let him know about sannyas. He should not be given time to think, 'What is the meaning of life?' Keep him engaged continually in singing, in dancing, wine and women; drown him completely."

And that's what created the trouble – because for twenty-nine years he was kept so isolated from the world, so ignorant about the ordinary reality of the world where people become sick, people become old, people die, there are sannyasins, there are seekers of truth... If he had been allowed from the very beginning, he would have become immune; from the very beginning he would have seen that people become old, people become sick, a few people become sannyasins. But for twenty-nine years he was kept completely aloof. And after twenty-nine years when he came into contact with the world – one day, one *has to* come into contact with the world – then it was a great shock. He could not believe his eyes that people become old; he could not believe that life is going to end in death. He could not believe that he had been kept in darkness while there were people searching to find the meaning of life, trying to find out whether there was something immortal in man or not. The shock would not have been so much. It is not such a shock for anybody else – from the very childhood, everything... One becomes, slowly, slowly, accustomed. But for him the shock was tremendous. That very night he left the palace as a sannyasin in search of truth. The father was trying to save him from the begging bowl, and that's what he adopted that night.

It was possible he might have become Alexander the Great if he had not been kept in darkness. But in a way it was good, because Alexander the Great and his kind have not helped human consciousness. This man alone, with his begging bowl raised humanity more than anybody else – towards the stars, towards immortality, towards truth. With such a man, astrology is not possible.

It is good to accept that you are functioning like a machine. Don't feel offended – because if you feel offended, you will defend yourself and you will remain what you are. Try to understand your behavior – is it mechanical or not? Somebody insults you – how do you react? Is that reaction mechanical or conscious? Do you think before you become angry? Do you meditate for a moment before you respond? Perhaps what the man has said is right, and if you had not got angry immediately, instantly, without giving a small gap for meditation, you might have been grateful to the man rather than being angry: "You are right."

In fact, things which are right hurt you much more. Lies don't hurt you at all.

Just the other day, Nirvano brought a newspaper cutting. A Western traveler coming from Tibet gave his first press conference, and in the press conference he said, "My greatest experience was meeting with Osho in Tibet."

Now people can lie like anything, and whoever reads it will believe it. The printed word has a certain impact on people.

Just a few days before, there was another news item – no ifs and no buts, a certainty – that Osho is going to appear in Israel very soon. He has decided to become converted to Judaism, and after converting to Judaism, he will declare himself to be the reincarnation of Moses.

Now what can you do with these people? You can laugh, but you cannot be angry. You can enjoy, you can thank them for their imagination. These are the people who keep the world going!

Just watch your actions, and try not to be mechanical. Try to do something that you have never done before in the same situation. That's what the meaning is when Jesus says, "When somebody slaps your face, give him the other cheek too." The real meaning is, simply act non-mechanically – because the mechanical thing would be, when somebody slaps you, you slap him. Or if you are not capable of slapping him right now, then wait for the right moment. But to give him the other cheek is behaving non-mechanically, is behaving very consciously. But people can make anything mechanical.

I have heard about a Christian saint who was continually quoting the same thing: "Love your enemy, and if somebody slaps you on one cheek give him the other too."

One day a man who was against Christianity found the saint alone, hit him hard on one of his cheeks, looked into the eyes of the saint... For a moment the saint wanted to hit him back – but being a saint, remembering all his teachings and remembering that this man sits in his congregation in the front, he gave him the other cheek, thinking that he would not hit it. The man hit him harder on the other cheek! And that very moment the saint jumped on the man, hitting him hard on the nose. The man said, "What are you doing? You are a Christian, you have to love your enemy."

He said, "Forget all about it. Jesus only talked about two cheeks – about the third, I am free. Now there is no third cheek to give you. And he has not said that when he hits you on the second, give him your nose too!"

Because Jesus has not said, why...

Gautam Buddha in one of his sermons said, "Try to be non-mechanical as much as possible. If somebody hits you, insults you, humiliates you, forgive him seven times. Be conscious."

Jesus was saying only one time – because you have only two cheeks, and one he has hit already. Only one is left, so there is not much... Buddha is saying seven times.

One of the disciples stood up and said, "What about the eighth? Seven times we will keep patience, but what about the eighth?"

Even Buddha was silent for a moment. So deep is man's mechanicalness... He said, "Then change it, make it seventy-seven times."

The man said, "You can make it any number, but the question will remain the same – what about the seventy-eighth time? We can wait seventy-seven times..."

You can behave in a saintly way, but if it is mechanical it doesn't change anything. Be alert and see that yesterday you have done the same thing. Today make a little difference – you are not a machine.

You said the same thing to your wife, make a little difference – you are not a machine. And if in twenty-four hours time you continually go on changing, slowly, slowly you will slip out of the mechanical behavior and a consciousness will arise in you. That consciousness makes you really human. Before, you only appear human; in reality you are not.

32 Truth Has to Wait...but Not to Wait Forever

Osho,
Many things have happened in your world during the past fourteen months that were very controversial and looked strange for a spiritual group.

Just reading the facts and figures set forth in the 156-page, two-part article in recent issues of The New Yorker *could make most people angry.*
Though some sannyasins left, I notice that many of us, including myself, were undisturbed in our inner beings. With no regrets, many of us jumped into the new way, the new adventure.
Family, friends, strangers, are either curious about this or suspect we're brainwashed dummies, or irresponsible. Is there any way to explain this inner trust that happens to a disciple with a master? Is it possible for any of us to explain anything beyond these facts and figures – the love, the fun, the mystery of spiritual transformation that we are so fortunate to participate in with you? Should I even bother, or just concentrate on you and the inner journey and ignore the curious and the skeptics?

It would have been very easy if life were only facts and figures – easy but boring; easy but flat; easy but not worth living. And the mind is concerned only with facts and figures. It is a great blessing of existence that the mind is not all, that there is much more to life, which cannot be confined to facts, explanations, theories. Something mysterious remains always unexplained, and that is the most valuable, the most significant part of life. It is impossible to explain love, trust, beauty, grace, gratitude, silence. All that is meaningful seems to be beyond the mind, and all that is meaningless seems to be the boundary of the mind.

I am reminded of a great Sufi master, Junnaid. One day one of his disciples who had managed somehow to trust in Junnaid, who had with effort remained non-skeptical, had gone hunting in the forest. And he saw Junnaid sitting by the side of a beautiful lake with a beautiful woman. He saw from far away, and from far away everything is beautiful, and particularly a Mohammedan woman. No Mohammedan woman is ugly; her face is veiled. It is a great strategy of ugly women against the beautiful; in this way the beautiful are lost.

All his repressed suspicions and doubts arose, surfaced – and it was not only that Junnaid was sitting with the woman; the woman was pouring wine from a flask into a cup for Junnaid. All his trust was shattered, all his love was finished: "There is a limit to everything. This is going too far. This man is a fraud!"

And if he had returned without going to Junnaid to say something, he would have remained with the idea that the man was a fraud. He had all the facts, he had seen with his own eyes, he was a witness. He needed no other evidence, no other proof. No argument would have convinced him that he could have been wrong.

But Junnaid shouted loudly, "Don't go back! Come close, because when you come close many facts prove to be fictions. The closer you come, the more fictitious they are. Just come close."

A little bit afraid, but he came.

Junnaid lifted the veil from the woman's face. She was Junnaid's mother, an old woman. And he said, "What about the beautiful woman you had seen? – and you had seen her with your own eyes.

Could you have imagined an old woman, my own mother? It was beyond your imagination. And take this flask and look closely, taste it; it is pure water, not wine. Just the flask is of the wine. But you were thinking with absolute certainty that this man is a fraud: women and wine in privacy, in the forest; and in public he has another face, of a great master."

The disciple fell at his feet and said, "Please forgive me."

Junnaid said, "It is not a question of forgiveness; it is a question of understanding. You have a trust which is forced, and a forced trust is bound to sooner or later go through a breakdown. Your love is an effort, and love cannot be an effort – either you love or you don't, the question of effort does not arise. You were trying to imitate other disciples, and the path of the truth is not for imitators.

"I had come to this place only for you, knowing that you were going hunting and you were bound to come to this lake. You have to start from the beginning, and this time your love has not to be an effort and your trust has not to be something forced."

These things are beautiful when they grow naturally, and when they grow naturally then no facts, no figures can destroy them. They have such tremendous energy of their own that all facts and figures simply evaporate. Facts are not truths, but just like soap bubbles. Yes, a soap bubble is...but its existence or non-existence is almost equal.

Truth has is eternal: it was true, it is true, it will remain true. There is no way for the truth to be otherwise.

Facts go on changing. Facts depend on interpretations. The same fact can be interpreted in a thousand and one ways. And that's what we are all doing; otherwise, there would be no need of so many religions, so many philosophies, so many ideologies.

Truth is one.

The mystic has no philosophy; the mystic has no ideology, because he has the truth itself.

Just look at a few facts and how they can be interpreted not only differently but in a diametrically opposite way. The most important Jaina master, Mahavira, lived naked all his life. He renounced the world, his kingdom, he renounced everything –

clothes, shoes. He lived just as a child is born, naked, with nothing in his hands. He did not even carry a begging bowl. He used to make a begging bowl with his own hands. He would not use anything on which one becomes dependent. His ultimate goal was total freedom. And he was so logically consistent that he was not ready even to use a small blade, a razor blade, to cut his hair or to shave his beard. To use scissors or a blade would be a dependency, so he used to pull his hair out with his own hand. It was painful, but he managed.

He lived eighty-two years. And he had to pull out the hairs because he was not taking baths. According to his approach, to take a bath is to decorate the body, is to believe in the body – and the body is nothing but bones, blood, flesh, everything rotten, just covered with skin. What is the point of taking a bath? – you are not the body. And consciousness needs no cleanliness because it cannot become unclean.

In India he has been worshipped by the Jainas for twenty-five centuries as one of the most important mystics of the whole world. And even those who are not of his fold have immense respect for the man.

But I bring Sigmund Freud to analyze Mahavira's attitude and character – the same facts.

It is strange that there are thousands of madmen in the insane asylums around the world, and there is a certain kind of madness in which nakedness and pulling out the hair happens together. Those mad people live naked and they pull out their hair – they don't allow anybody to cut their hair or shave their beards. And the same mad people don't allow themselves to be given showers or baths. Strange! Is Mahavira a madman of the same category? Or are these mad people Mahaviras, great masters misunderstood by an insane world? Somewhere something has to be decided.

Strangely enough, these mad people who live naked, pull out their hair, don't take any baths, are absolutely non-violent. They are not dangerous; they never hurt anybody, they never kill anybody. They are very harmless people. And that is the whole philosophy of Mahavira: non-violence. Perhaps he was a madman with a genius, with such talented intelligence that he made a philosophical standpoint out of his madness. Now, who is going to decide?

The fact in itself is without any judgment; in itself it says nothing, it is simply a fact. The moment you start thinking about it, you start creating interpretations, and those interpretations will depend on your attitude. They have nothing to do with the fact.

Because I have brought Sigmund Freud in, I cannot allow him to go out so easily. He was the founder of psychoanalysis, and yet he remained a practicing Jew for his whole life, subscribing to all the superstitions of the Jews. For example, circumcision.: Every Jewish male child, as he is born, is immediately circumcised. Mohammedans are also circumcised but after two or three years, not immediately.

And Jews believe that they are the most intelligent people in the world because of circumcision. It is true that they are perhaps the most intelligent group of people in the world. The whole contemporary world is dominated by Jews: Sigmund Freud, Karl Marx, Albert Einstein. These three figures stand out amongst billions of people. Their contribution to human wellbeing is immense. I have told you that forty percent of Nobel Prizes go to Jews. That is simply out of all proportion – forty percent to the small group of Jews, and sixty percent to the rest of the world. Naturally they have more intelligence, you cannot doubt it; it is a fact. And they have this idea that they are so intelligent because of circumcision, and they provide philosophical, logical, scientific proofs for it.

And one never knows, they may be right – because now many governments of the world are getting ready to pass resolutions that every child born in hospitals should be circumcised. It doesn't matter whether he is Jew or Hindu or Christian or Mohammedan, that is not a question; it is a question of hygiene. It is certainly hygienic.

But Jews have a very far-fetched philosophical idea behind it: they say when the child is born...and the genitals are the most sensitive parts. This is recognized by science, by physiology, that the genitals are connected with a certain center in the mind. Strangely enough, the center in the mind that is connected with the genitals is absolutely close to the center for intelligence, they are neighbors. And they have to be very close because there are seven hundred centers in your brain, so they are very close knit. Jews say that when you cut the skin of the small child, the shock goes to the sex center. But the shock is so much and the child is so delicate that the shock does not remain confined to the sex center; the shock goes to the nearby center, which is the center of intelligence. And intelligence gets a great impetus, which other children are missing, so they are far ahead of anybody else.

Now the rest of the world has looked upon circumcision as a superstition. The fact is the same, but now they are providing scientific fragments to support it. They also are not absolute proofs; that is why I say far-fetched. But Sigmund Freud also believed in them, and he didn't have all these facts that I have, because at that time it was not known that the centers of sex and intelligence are very close. Neither was it known that sex is really in the mind and the genitals are only extensions, they are not really the sex organs. They can be bypassed, and you can enjoy a sexual experience without your genitals even knowing about it.

Sigmund Freud never inquired, never raised the question about the Jewish idea of circumcision – which he should have, because he was a Jew, and his whole work was with sexuality. His whole life was devoted to finding out everything about sexuality, but he bypassed circumcision, he did not talk about it. Others have laughed for centuries.

I have heard that one bishop and one rabbi lived opposite each other, and naturally there was great competition in everything. One day the bishop purchased a beautiful Chevrolet. The rabbi came out and he said, "A beautiful car, whose car is this?"

And the bishop came out with a bucket of water and poured the water on the car. He said, "I have purchased it."

The rabbi said, "But what are you doing?"

He said, "Baptism." He was a Christian Baptist. "Now the car is a Christian Baptist car – baptized."

This was too much for the rabbi.

Next day, as the bishop woke up, he saw a beautiful Cadillac sitting in the garage of the rabbi. He was shocked, because the Chevrolet is a poor man's car in America. The poor peoples' neighborhoods are called "Chevrolet neighborhoods." It is a rich man's car in other countries, but in America the Chevrolet is a poor man's car. But the Cadillac is especially Jewish.

The bishop came out and he said, "How could you manage it?"

The rabbi said, "God looks after his chosen few." And he said, "Come on, because there is going to be a ceremony."

The bishop said, "What kind of ceremony?"

He said, "Come inside."

The bishop came into the garage, and the rabbi went into his house and brought out a big pair of garden scissors. The bishop could not believe what was happening? What kind of ceremony...? The rabbi started chanting some mantras in Hebrew, and then finally he cut the exhaust pipe.

The bishop asked, "What are you doing?"

He said, "Circumcision – now the car is absolutely Jewish. If you can baptize, what do you think, can't we do something to make the car a Jew?"

Everybody has been laughing about circumcision. But Sigmund Freud never even raised a question about it. He never raised a single question that goes against Jewish tradition. All his logic, all his reason was used to criticize everybody else.

I have asked a Jaina saint: "Sigmund Freud would say these things about Mahavira, although he has not said them, because he knew nothing about Mahavira. But I am absolutely certain he would say these things. Have you something to say about Sigmund Freud, about Jews?"

And the first thing he said was: "If the skin on the male genitals was not needed, then existence would not have given it to the child. Existence gives only that which is needed. To remove that skin is egoistic, it is an effort to prove that you are wiser than existence itself. And the very idea that man is wiser than existence is stupid."

I asked him about Jesus – because I had taken with me a Christian missionary, Stanley Jones, to meet the Jaina saint. And I said, "Stanley Jones is here, and his criticism against Jaina saints, Buddhist saints, Hindu saints, is that they don't do any service to humanity. On the contrary, they demand that they should be served, worshipped, that it is their birthright.

"People may be dying from starvation – that is not their concern. Mahavira and Buddha have not opened a single hospital, not a single school for poor children, not a single orphanage, like Mother Teresa. But these people are thought to be great compassionate people. What compassion is there? What do you think about Jesus?"

He said, "About Jesus? According to us, everything in life is a connected link of cause and effect, the theory of action."

There are stories that if Mahavira is passing on the road and a thorn is there, the thorn will jump out of the road – because Mahavira has finished all evil actions. Now no pain can be given to him by existence. It looks logical. If existence is deciding rewards and punishments, certainly the thorn must jump out of the road.

Mohammedans say – because Mohammed was in Arabia: hot sun, no clouds, no shade, no trees... But a beautiful cloud always moved over Mohammed, wherever he went, because he had finished with all evil acts. That's why he was chosen by God as his best messenger; he had become so pure that he could be a vehicle. Now it is God's duty to protect him. In the hot burning sun, a cool breeze surrounds him, and a big cloud goes on keeping him in shadow.

The Jaina saint said, "Jesus being crucified proves that he must have done some very evil acts in his past life. Crucifixion was the punishment."

It has nothing to do with Jews crucifying him or the Romans crucifying him. Those are the visible facts, but the invisible truth is that he must have committed something really heinous – murder, rape – and the result is crucifixion. So crucifixion is not something to be worshipped; it is a condemnation.

Now for the Christian the same fact, the crucifixion of Jesus, makes him the greatest man on the earth because he suffered for humanity, he was crucified for you; to save you he gave his own life. That is their interpretation.

But the Jainas, Hindus and Buddhists will all explain that he is suffering from many past lives of crimes. "He is not giving his life to save anybody – because we don't see anybody saved. Who is saved? He could not even save himself."

One thing should always be remembered: don't be bothered about facts. They can be interpreted this way or that way very convincingly, but facts belong to the mundane world. Truth is the thing you should concentrate on.

You have mentioned *The New Yorker* article about me and the commune. Perhaps they may not have ever written such a big article before – one hundred and fifty-six pages. And what they call facts are only the facts that the government has supplied to them. They have not asked me; otherwise for every fact there is a counter-fact. But it is easy not to ask both parties.

I have heard that Mulla Nasruddin in his old age became an honorary magistrate. His first case came up. He heard one side, and started writing the judgment.

The court clerk could not believe what was happening. He whispered in his ear, "Honorable magistrate, what are you doing? You have not heard the other side yet. They are waiting."

Mulla Nasruddin said, "I am not going to hear anybody, because right now I am absolutely clear what the situation is, and if I hear the other side also I will become confused. And out of confusion, judgment will be very difficult."

The New Yorker is simply presenting one side. I will give you a few facts on the other side so you can see how facts should not be decisive.

The land that we purchased for the commune had been for sale for almost half a century, and nobody had purchased it, because it was a desert. Not a single flower ever blossomed there, no cultivation was ever done; it was just a useless wasteland. And it was big – one hundred and twenty-six square miles, eighty-four thousand acres.

We purchased the land. The man was very happy because he had lost hope that the land could ever be sold. And the government was asking him to give it to them for three million dollars. It was almost a small country – one hundred and twenty-six square miles, three times bigger than Manhattan. And the man was just going to say yes to the government as we entered the scene. We immediately offered him six million dollars. He could not believe it – from three million to six million! Immediately everything was settled. And this was the beginning of conflict with the government. But if the government had really been interested, they could have offered more. They should not have felt offended, it was a simple business matter. And it is not their land either.

The whole world has forgotten completely that the real Americans are the red Americans who are living in reservations in the forests. They have been forced to live almost in concentration camps, an American version of the German concentration camps – far better, because the German concentration camp was barbed wire, guns all around, very crude. The American concentration camp is very sophisticated – no barbed wire, no guards – you cannot say that this is a concentration camp. But this is a concentration camp of a higher order, of a more subtle and delicate quality. What they have done is to give every red Indian a pension – because America belongs to them, it is their country. They don't have any work, but they get enough pension. All they do is to go on producing more children, because the more children they have, the more pension they will get. Each individual gets a pension.

But you should understand that when you have no work and enough money, what are you going to do? They gamble, they are all drunkards...all kinds of drugs, prostitution, and no worries about anything – every month the salary is there. Salary for nothing, salary for remaining silent about the fact that America belongs to them, that the people who are known as Americans are not Americans. Somebody is from England, somebody is from Italy, somebody is from France, somebody is from Holland, somebody is from Germany, somebody is from Switzerland – from all the European countries, but nobody is an American. They are all foreigners.

And my first conflict with the government was that I told it exactly the same way I am telling you: that the American president is as much a foreigner as I am a foreigner. The only difference is that he has been here perhaps for two generations, three generations – he is a two hundred year-old foreigner. I am fresh. And the fresh is always better than the old and rotten.

I told them: Neither does the land belong to you nor does the land belong to us. And we purchased the land, we paid money, you invaded the land, you killed people, innocent people. You are criminals. If anybody needs permission to live in America, it is you – from the American president to the last American beggar. And if you really mean what you say in your constitution – that you are for democracy, for freedom – if you are sincere and honest, then give the country back to the red Indians. It belongs to them. And apply for your green cards. If they want you here, you can be here; otherwise go home.

And you have killed, you have invaded, you are criminals. We have simply purchased. Sometimes you have also purchased, but your purchase was simply a facade. For example, New York – the whole New York area was purchased for thirty silver pieces. Is this business? Do you think it was done by people willingly, or was it just because at the point of the bayonet, at gunpoint they had to sign: "We sell the land for thirty silver pieces."

The conflict started because I said: "Not one of you is any different from the people in my commune. We are newcomers; you came a little earlier. And you have committed all kinds of crimes; we have simply purchased the land. And you were there, you could have purchased it by offering more money – it was a simple business matter." But the American government will not say this. And America must remain the only country in the world where people like the poor red Americans cannot revolt. It is such a cunning strategy that you are giving them money. They think, "Revolt for what? We are getting money, enough money, no work, enjoy, dance, sing, take all kinds of drugs. No problems of worrying about poverty or anything – why bother about revolution?" The very idea is not possible. And they are all drunkards, opium addicted, lotus eaters. They are not in a position to fight a revolution. Their revolution has been killed, their spirit has been killed by money.

Because I said it clearly, and because the land we purchased had belonged to an ancient red Indian tribe which lived just nearby in a forest... And they had a prophecy from the old days: that a man from the East, with his followers wearing red clothes, would come to this land and free them from the slavery imposed on them by the invaders. By coincidence, my people were wearing red clothes; by coincidence, I was coming from the East. And red Indians started coming, saying, "We have been waiting, because we have heard this prophecy for generations."

These were the fears the government would never talk about. I could have provoked the red Indians against the whole American government, I could have created a revolution – this was their fear. They wanted to destroy me and the commune as quickly as possible.

The land had never produced anything, but they said that it was farmland; hence, we could not make more than twenty houses, twenty farmhouses. And we fought and we said, "You have to come and prove: in fifty years what has been produced? If it is farmland, then something must have been cultivated. Just because you have written in your papers... And we don't know when you have written it. You may have written it just now, just to harass us. You have to prove what kind of cultivation has been happening here. If this is farmland, we will cultivate it; but such a big land area cannot be cultivated by a small group living in twenty houses. This much land needs at least five thousand people to make it lush green, to make lakes, reservoirs – because everything has to depend on the rainwater. And tremendous effort is needed to make roads, houses."

But they would not change the zoning – which was simply stupid, because we were not going to destroy their farmland. We were creating farmland from a desert, we were changing the desert into an oasis. So they went on creating legal problems, and for five years we went on fighting – and we were winning in every court, because the facts were so clear. When they saw that they could not win legally, then they started behaving illegally. And when a government itself starts behaving illegally, then it becomes very difficult to fight – a small minority of five thousand people. The government was fighting, the Christian church was fighting, and nobody could say what harm we were doing to them, what harm we *had* done.

The nearest American town was twenty miles away from us. We were living and doing our own thing. But they became so much afraid... The fear had unconscious reasons. America does not belong to them, and they are talking about democracy, they are talking about liberty, they are talking about freedom, they are talking about the rights of man. And they have taken all of the land from the poor natives, and they have destroyed them in such a sophisticated way as has not been done anywhere else.

There is no hope for the red Indians for two reasons: one, they are not in their senses, they are continuously drunk, continuously unconscious – fighting, murdering each other. Secondly, slavery is paying well; without working you are getting a salary. To fight against this government means you will lose your salary and you will have all kinds of problems, so why bother?

And because I said things exactly... And I invited the president, the governor, the attorney general of America to come and see, to show us what cultivation they had done on this land. And we had transformed the whole land. Rather than praising us, they wanted us to destroy the commune and leave America. It seems they loved the desert so much that now they have made it desert again. Perhaps they need a third world war to make the whole of America a desert. If they love the desert so much, their wishes should be fulfilled.

But these facts that they have produced after one year... Where was this *New Yorker* when I was there to reply? Now they are writing facts and figures. And they have not consulted the other party at all, to ask, "What are your facts and what are your figures? How has the government misbehaved with you? How has the government proved to be fascist, violent, crude, primitive, undemocratic?" They should have asked us, because we have suffered. But the press is either in the hands of the church or in the hands of a political party, or in the hands of the government, or in the hands of rich people.

The man who came first into the conflict was the ex-vice-president Rockefeller – because he was planning that the whole of Oregon should become a federal state. The federal government owns half of the land of Oregon, and their desire was to have all of the land in Oregon to create shelters in case of a nuclear war. And Oregon is perfectly the right place – not very populated, could easily be converted into a vast shelter in case of nuclear war. When we entered the state, the first person who became annoyed was

Rockefeller – because now that one hundred and twenty-six square miles could in no way become federal land. It was he who said in a press conference that this commune is an independent country within a country, and this cannot be tolerated.

If they had asked us... It was a simple thing. They could have given us land somewhere else, we would have moved the commune. Or from the very beginning they could have told us, "We are ready to give you another piece of land." There was no problem; to us it was the same. But these people have faces of one kind, they say one thing, and they do something else. And they are thinking still something else – you never know exactly what is in their minds, what they are doing, what their purpose is.

They accepted our right to be a city, and it was accepted by the court – three judges. One judge was against us, was a fanatic Christian. But seeing that two of the judges were ready, and his being against us would be useless, he also signed, and we became a city. Now that was the most difficult thing for them to swallow: that against the president, against the whole government, we won the case and we became a city.

You will be surprised, in the twentieth century... The one judge who was in our favor was a Mormon. They are very good people, a sect of Christians, but very honest and sincere. And they have suffered very much in America at the hands of other Christians because of certain of their ideologies. One idea they have is that the head of the Mormons is in direct contact with God, with no pope, no mediator in between. The Mormon head has a direct communication line with God. This is not acceptable to catholic Christians – you are bypassing the pope. They killed the first Mormon founder, and because they killed him they consolidated the Mormons, and they had to give them a city. The same story was being repeated again, so they became afraid. Now Mormons have a city – one of the most beautiful in America – Salt Lake City.

This one judge was a Mormon. And a trick was played: the head of the Mormons informed him that he had been chosen by God to resign from his post and go to Nigeria to serve humanity. I informed that judge, "This is simple politics. They want to remove you from the post because when you are removed... One person is against us, one person is half-half – he will be on the side of whoever is in power. It was because of you and your sincerity, your fairness that we got the city. Now you are leaving us in the dumps!"

And what a stupid idea: billions of people in the world, and God has chosen this poor man to resign from his post and go to Nigeria for one year. But they are such simple people that they believed that it was God's order and they could not go against it. So he resigned, and immediately they appointed a fanatic Christian. The same court that had given us the sanction to be a city, after six months denied that we were a city. And the simple trick was that they removed the man who would not do anything wrong, and replaced him with a man who was an absolutely fanatical Christian. They completely forgot their own laws, their own constitution, and they did everything against their constitution.

For two years continually there was a rumor that they were going to arrest me, but they would not dare to enter the campus of the commune for the simple reason that they knew that unless they killed five thousand sannyasins they would not be able to arrest me. And they were not ready to take that risk – killing five thousand people, most of them Americans, would condemn their democracy forever.

They wanted me in some way to be out of the commune so they could find me alone. That's why they waited for two years. And we were hearing the rumor continually, so by and by it became accepted that this was just a rumor, they didn't have the courage. They had their National Guard just twenty miles away in the American town, every day collecting more and more army forces, so that if there was a need they could be ready to kill five thousand people.

But once they could get me out of the commune, things became easy for them. Without any arrest warrant, they arrested me and five sannyasins who were with me. That is absolutely illegal. They could not even show the cause; not even for three days in court could they prove anything to show why they had arrested me. Still they would not set bail. These are the facts and figures. The government was pressuring the magistrate: "If you want to be promoted to federal judge, don't give this man bail." So all five sannyasins were given bail; only I was retained.

And the government attorney said in the court, "We have not been able to prove any charge; still, the government asks that bail should not be granted for this man because he is very intelligent" – I heard for the first time that to be intelligent is criminal – "and he has thousands of friends." I had never thought that these things were enough to be a criminal, if that is enough to be a criminal, then Jesus Christ must be the greatest criminal in the world – because half of the world is Christian. And thirdly, that I had resources enough that I could jump bail. Even if it were ten million dollars' bail, I could jump it.

And this shows the poverty and the weakness... The greatest power of the world – you have all your armies and all your nuclear weapons and all your police forces, and you cannot manage to prevent a man from crossing the country. Then all your power is impotent.

But the reality was that the woman magistrate was not interested in anything else, she was interested in becoming a federal judge. Even the jailer did not think that I would go back to jail, he thought that there would be no reason: "They don't have an arrest warrant, they don't have any cause, so you will be released." So he brought my clothes and everything in his car so that: "I can free you direct from court; there is no need to come back to the jail." When he had to take me back, he was annoyed. He said, "In my whole life I have not seen such unfairness. The attorney could not prove – and he accepts that he has not been able to prove in three days of continuous arguing – anything against this man. Still the government wants..." Who is the government? The government was only a part in the case. And against an individual, the government forces the magistrate, bribes, blackmails...

The jailer told me, "The reality is that woman has been told that if she gives you bail – which is your right – she will not be promoted to federal judge. And she wants to become a federal judge." And within just three days she was a federal judge.

These journalists should think not only of those who have power, but also of those who don't have power, and they should be guards against injustice.

They had produced one hundred and thirty-six crimes against me – a man who never leaves the house. I have not gone out of this house for three months, not even into the garden; how can I manage one hundred and thirty-six crimes?

But the government attorneys told my attorneys, "If you don't accept at least two crimes, then Osho's life will be in danger." That was the last blackmail. "If you want to put his life in danger, you can go for trial." This was just when the court case was going to start, five minutes before. "It is better you accept and convince Osho to accept any two counts." Just to save the government's face, so that they can be right: I must have committed a crime, because I have accepted. And the threat was, "If you don't accept, then bail will be canceled and the case can go on for ten to twenty years. It is in the hands of the government. And there is every risk for the life of Osho. So if you want to save him, try some way to convince him to accept."

My attorneys came with tears in their eyes, and they said, "We have never seen such blackmail, and the blackmail is being done by the government – a clearcut threat. So accept two counts. And they don't want you to be in America more than fifteen minutes longer. Accept two of the charges and your plane is ready at the airport, you immediately move out of America, and for five years you cannot re-enter."

My whole idea was to refuse. But I looked at my attorneys and I looked at my sannyasins all over the world. And I had heard that a few sannyasins were not even eating. For the twelve days I had been in jail, a few sannyasins had not been eating at all; they were fasting. And I am not a rigid man. And I am not a serious man either.

So I said, "There is no problem. Don't be worried – I accept. And outside the court, just in front of the courthouse, I will announce to the world press that this is blackmail." And it was true that they were ready to kill me, because as I reached the jail to pick up my things, they had planted a bomb under my chair. It did not explode because it was a time bomb.

And I reached there early – because I had accepted immediately. I said, "There is no point." I said, "Whatever crimes they want, I have committed. I don't even need to know what those crimes are." So within five minutes the case was over. They were thinking I would reach there nearabout five, and I reached there just nearabout one o'clock. So the timing was not right. And as I left the jail, they had to remove the bomb. And they have to accept it – now, in jail nobody can put a bomb except for the government, nobody else can reach there.

The American jail... First you have to pass three big gates, which are all automatic, electric gates. You cannot open them, they open only with remote control buttons. When one gate opens, the other two remain closed. And the second opens only when the first is closed. After three gates, then there are offices. And the room where my clothes were to be given to me was in the most interior part of the building. It would be impossible for anybody from the outside to reach there and plant a bomb. The bomb was planted by the government. They must have thought that if I refused to accept the crimes, then it would be better to finish me rather than carry on for years with a case which they were going to lose – because they don't have any evidence, they don't have any proof.

All those one hundred and thirty-six crimes are their imagination, and nothing else – and this has been accepted by the attorney general just now, a few days ago. In a press conference, he was asked, "Why has Osho not been put into jail?"

And he said, "Because he has not committed any crime, and we don't have any proof of any crime."

This same man was standing in court with the list of one hundred and thirty-six crimes. And this man is the right-hand man of president Ronald Reagan; they are boyhood friends, they were both actors in Hollywood. And when Reagan became president he called him and made him the attorney general of America; now he is the highest legal authority in America. So it is not possible that whatever he is doing is not known to Ronald Reagan. It is a conspiracy in the White House.

Journalists should gather a little courage, and when they start writing stories about facts and figures they should look at the other side also. Just put both sides; don't give your judgment. Let the people decide. And truth has a quality of its own. If both sides are placed before you without any prejudice, you will be able to figure out what is true and what is false.

And it has helped the whole movement around the world. Those whose trust was forced, whose love was managed, naturally have to fall out of my world, from my people. But it has been a fire test for those who really love and trust me. Their trust has become stronger, their love has become deeper. And thousands of new people have come into the movement. Seeing that against a single man, the whole world and the whole worlds' governments are against him – it is not possible that the man can be wrong.

Otherwise, there is no need for so many governments to be against me. They can simply refute me, their theologians can refute me; their legal systems can prove me wrong. Because they cannot do anything, now they have come down to the lowest. Ronald Reagan and the people who are cooperating with him have sunk to the status of terrorists. Now, putting a bomb against a man who is under your protection in the jail – this is pure inhumanity.

And existence will not tolerate it, existence will not forgive it, existence will not forget it. And you will see every day these people disappearing from the scene.

Truth has to wait, but not to wait forever. It is patient; it is patient because it knows its victory is certain.

About Osho

Osho defies categorization. His thousands of talks cover everything from the individual quest for meaning to the most urgent social and political issues facing society today. Osho's books are not written but are transcribed from audio and video recordings of his extemporaneous talks to international audiences. As he puts it, "So remember: whatever I am saying is not just for you... I am talking also for the future generations."

Osho has been described by *The Sunday Times* in London as one of the "1000 Makers of the 20th Century" and by American author Tom Robbins as "the most dangerous man since Jesus Christ." *Sunday Mid-Day* (India) has selected Osho as one of ten people – along with Gandhi, Nehru and Buddha – who have changed the destiny of India.

About his own work Osho has said that he is helping to create the conditions for the birth of a new kind of human being. He often characterizes this new human being as "Zorba the Buddha" – capable both of enjoying the earthy pleasures of a Zorba the Greek and the silent serenity of a Gautama the Buddha.

Running like a thread through all aspects of Osho's talks and meditations is a vision that encompasses both the timeless wisdom of all ages past and the highest potential of today's (and tomorrow's) science and technology.

Osho is known for his revolutionary contribution to the science of inner transformation, with an approach to meditation that acknowledges the accelerated pace of contemporary life. His unique OSHO Active Meditations™ are designed to first release the accumulated stresses of body and mind, so that it is then easier to take an experience of stillness and thought-free relaxation into daily life.

Two autobiographical works by the author are available:

Autobiography of a Spiritually Incorrect Mystic, St Martins Press, New York (book and eBook)

Glimpses of a Golden Childhood, OSHO Media International, Pune, India

OSHO International Meditation Resort

Each year the Meditation Resort welcomes thousands of people from more than 100 countries. The unique campus provides an opportunity for a direct personal experience of a new way of living – with more awareness, relaxation, celebration and creativity. A great variety of around-the-clock and around-the-year program options are available. Doing nothing and just relaxing is one of them!

All the programs are based on Osho's vision of "Zorba the Buddha" – a qualitatively new kind of human being who is able *both* to participate creatively in everyday life *and* to relax into silence and meditation.

Location

Located 100 miles southeast of Mumbai in the thriving modern city of Pune, India, the OSHO International Meditation Resort is a holiday destination with a difference. The Meditation Resort is spread over 28 acres of spectacular gardens in a beautiful tree-lined residential area.

OSHO Meditations

A full daily schedule of meditations for every type of person includes both traditional and revolutionary methods, and particularly the OSHO Active Meditations™. The meditations take place in what may be the world's largest meditation hall, the OSHO Auditorium.

OSHO Multiversity

Individual sessions, courses and workshops cover everything from creative arts to holistic health, personal transformation, relationship and life transition, transforming meditation into a lifestyle for life and work, esoteric sciences, and the "Zen" approach to sports and recreation. The secret of the OSHO Multiversity's success lies in the fact that all its programs are combined with meditation, supporting the understanding that as human beings we are far more than the sum of our parts.

OSHO Basho Spa

The luxurious Basho Spa provides for leisurely open-air swimming surrounded by trees and tropical green. The uniquely styled, spacious Jacuzzi, the saunas, gym, tennis courts...all these are enhanced by their stunningly beautiful setting.

Cuisine

A variety of different eating areas serve delicious Western, Asian and Indian vegetarian food – most of it organically grown especially for the Meditation Resort. Breads and cakes are baked in the resort's own bakery.

Night life

There are many evening events to choose from – dancing being at the top of the list! Other activities include full-moon meditations beneath the stars, variety shows, music performances and meditations for daily life.

Or you can just enjoy meeting people at the Plaza Café, or walking in the nighttime serenity of the gardens of this fairytale environment.

Facilities

You can buy all of your basic necessities and toiletries in the Galleria. The OSHO Multimedia Gallery sells a large range of OSHO media products. There is also a bank, a travel agency and a Cyber Café on-campus. For those who enjoy shopping, Pune provides all the options, ranging from traditional and ethnic Indian products to all of the global brand-name stores.

Accommodation

You can choose to stay in the elegant rooms of the OSHO Guesthouse, or for longer stays on campus you can select one of the OSHO Living-In program packages. Additionally there is a plentiful variety of nearby hotels and serviced apartments.

www.osho.com/meditationresort
www.osho.com/guesthouse
www.osho.com/livingin

Books by Osho in English Language

Early Discourses and Writings
A Cup of Tea
Compassion and Revolution
Dimensions beyond the Known
Earthen Lamps
From Sex to Superconsciousness
The Great Challenge
Hidden Mysteries
I Am the Gate
Life Is a Soap Bubble
Nine Sutras
The Art of Living
The Path of Meditation
The Psychology of the Esoteric
Seeds of Wisdom
Work Is Love Made Visible

Meditation
And Now and Here (Vols 1 & 2)
In Search of the Miraculous (Vols 1 &.2)
Meditation: The Art of Ecstasy
Meditation: The First and Last Freedom
The Inner Journey
The Perfect Way

Buddha and Buddhist Masters
The Book of Wisdom
The Dhammapada: The Way of the Buddha (Vols 1-12)
The Diamond Sutra
The Discipline of Transcendence (Vols 1-4)
The Heart Sutra

Indian Mystics
Enlightenment: The Only Revolution (Ashtavakra)
Showering without Clouds (Sahajo)
The Last Morning Star (Daya)
The Song of Ecstasy (Adi Shankara)

Baul Mystics
The Beloved (Vols 1 & 2)

Kabir
The Divine Melody
Ecstasy: The Forgotten Language
The Fabric of Life
The Fish in the Sea is Not Thirsty
The Great Secret
The Guest
The Path of Love
The Revolution

Jesus and Christian Mystics
Come Follow to You (Vols 1-4)
I Say Unto You (Vols 1 & 2)
The Mustard Seed
Theologia Mystica

Jewish Mystics
The Art of Dying
The True Sage

Western Mystics
Guida Spirituale (*Desiderata*)
The Hidden Harmony (Heraclitus)
Reflections on Kahlil Gibran's *The Prophet*)
The New Alchemy: To Turn You On (Talks on Mabel Collins' *Light on the Path*)

Philosophia Perennis (Vol. 1 & 2) (*The Golden Verses of Pythagoras*)

Zarathustra: A God That Can Dance

Zarathustra: The Laughing Prophet (Talks on Nietzsche's *Thus Spake Zarathustra*)

The Voice of Silence

Sufism

Just Like That

Journey to the Heart

The Perfect Master (Vols 1 & 2)

The Secret

Sufis: The People of the Path (Vols 1 & 2)

Unio Mystica (Vols 1 & 2)

The Wisdom of the Sands (Vols 1 & 2)

Tantra

Tantra: The Supreme Understanding

The Tantra Experience: The Royal Song of Saraha (same as Tantra Vision, Vol. 1)

Tantric Transformation: The Royal Song of Saraha (same as Tantra Vision, Vol. 2)

The Book of Secrets: Vigyan Bhairav Tantra

The Upanishads

Behind a Thousand Names (Nirvana Upanishad)

Finger Pointing to the Moon (Adhyatma Upanishad)

Flight of the Alone to the Alone (Kaivalya Upanishad)

Heartbeat of the Absolute (Ishavasya Upanishad)

I Am That (Isa Upanishad)

The Message beyond Words (Kathopanishad)

Philosophia Ultima (Mandukya Upanishad)

The Supreme Doctrine (Kenopanishad)

That Art Thou (Sarvasar Upanishad, Kaivalya Upanishad, Adhyatma Upanishad)

The Ultimate Alchemy Vols 1 & 2 (Atma Pooja Upanishad)
Vedanta: Seven Steps to Samadhi (Akshaya Upanishad)
The Way beyond Any Way (Sarvasar Upanishad)

Tao
The Empty Boat
The Secret of Secrets
Tao:The Golden Gate (Vols 1 & 2)
Tao:The Pathless Path (Vols 1 & 2)
Tao: The Three Treasures (Vols 1-4)
When the Shoe Fits

Yoga
Yoga: The Alpha and the Omega (Vols 1-10)
The Path of Yoga (Vol.1)
Yoga: The Science of the Soul (Vol.2)
Yoga: The Mystery beyond Mind (Vol.3)
The Alchemy of Yoga (Vol.4)
Yoga: A New Direction (Vol.5)
Essence of Yoga (Vol.6)
Yoga: The Science of Living (Vol.7)
Secrets of Yoga (Vol.8)
Yoga: The Path to Liberation (Vol.9)
Yoga: The Supreme Science (Vol.10)

Zen and Zen Masters
Ah, This!
Ancient Music in the Pines
And the Flowers Showered
A Bird on the Wing
Bodhidharma: The Greatest Zen Master
The Buddha: The Emptiness of the Heart
Communism and Zen Fire, Zen Wind
Dang Dang Doko Dang
The First Principle

God Is Dead: Now Zen Is the Only Living Truth
The Grass Grows By Itself
The Great Zen Master Ta Hui
Hsin Hsin Ming: The Book of Nothing
I Celebrate Myself: God Is No Where, Life Is Now Here
Kyozan: A True Man of Zen
The Language of Existence
Live Zen
The Miracle
Nirvana: The Last Nightmare
No Mind: The Flowers of Eternity
No Water, No Moon
One Seed Makes the Whole Earth Green
The Original Man
Returning to the Source
The Search: Talks on the 10 Bulls of Zen
A Sudden Clash of Thunder
The Sun Rises in the Evening
Take it Easy
This. This. A Thousand Times This
This Very Body the Buddha
Turning In
Walking in Zen, Sitting in Zen
The White Lotus
Yakusan: Straight to the Point of Enlightenment
The Zen Manifesto: Freedom from Oneself
Zen: The Diamond Thunderbolt
Zen: The Mystery and the Poetry of the Beyond
Zen: The Path of Paradox (Vols 1-3)
Zen: The Quantum Leap from Mind to No-Mind
Zen: The Solitary Bird, Cuckoo of the Forest
Zen: The Special Transmission

Osho: On the Ancient Masters of Zen (7 volumes)*
Dogen: The Zen Master
Hyakujo: The Everest of Zen – With Basho's haikus

Isan: No Footprints in the Blue Sky
Joshu: The Lion's Roar
Ma Tzu: The Empty Mirror
Nansen: The Point Of Departure
Rinzai: Master of the Irrational

Responses to Questions
Be Still and Know
Beyond Enlightenment (Talks in Bombay)
Beyond Psychology (Talks in Uruguay)
Come, Come, Yet Again Come
From Bondage to Freedom
From Darkness to Light
From Death to Deathlessness
From the False to the Truth
From Unconsciousness to Consciousness
The Goose Is Out
The Great Pilgrimage: From Here to Here
The Invitation
Light on the Path (Talks in the Himalayas)
My Way: The Way of the White Clouds
Nowhere to Go but In
The Path of the Mystic (Talks in Uruguay)
The Razor's Edge
Sermons in Stones (Talks in Bombay)
Socrates Poisoned Again After 25 Centuries (Talks in Greece)
The Sword and the Lotus (Talks in the Himalayas)
Transmission of the Lamp (Talks in Uruguay)
Walk without Feet, Fly without Wings and Think without Mind
The Wild Geese and the Water
Yaa-Hoo! The Mystic Rose
Zen: Zest, Zip, Zap and Zing

Osho's Vision for the World
The Golden Future
The Hidden Splendor

The New Dawn
The Rebel
The Rebellious Spirit

The Mantra Series
Hari Om Tat Sat
Om Mani Padme Hum
Om Shantih Shantih Shantih
Sat Chit Anand
Satyam Shivam Sundaram

Personal Glimpses
Books I Have Loved
Glimpses of a Golden Childhood
Notes of a Madman

Interviews with the World Press
The Man of Truth: A Majority of One

For any information about OSHO Books, please contact:

OSHO Media International
17 Koregaon Park, Pune – 411001, MS, India
Phone: +91-20-66019999 Fax: +91-20-66019990
E-mail: distribution@osho.net
Website: http://www.osho.com